1993  1994  1995

1996  1997  1998

1999  2000  2001

2002  *Tenth*  2003

BENTLEY
GUIDE

anniversary

a
j.phillip
INCORPORATED
publication

# *Acknowledgments*

This Tenth Edition of The Bentley Collection Guide® is dedicated to all who love and enjoy collecting Longaberger Baskets® and Products®. We are so thankful to all who have helped contribute basket information, market values, and baskets for photography purposes. It is because of all of you that this Guide continues to be the most comprehensive and accurate listing of Longaberger Products® available.

Our goal is to provide you with an accurate representation of the history of Longaberger Products® and to encourage the collectibility of these beautiful items. We continue to work hard to offer you the highest quality of information and hope that through "The Bentley", you will find great joy in your collection.

## *Please understand . . .*

This Guide is published by J. Phillip Inc. and is in no way affiliated with, authorized, endorsed or licensed by The Longaberger Company®. The Longaberger Company in no way sets, reviews, approves or determines the secondary market prices published in this Guide. Longaberger Baskets®, Longaberger Pottery®, J.W. Collection® and other basket names are trademarks registered and owned by The Longaberger Company and J. Phillip, Inc. has no interest therein.

**Photographs by:**
Terry Thurston, *Morning Light Photography*
Andrew Korcok, *Lighthouse Photo Services*

Copyright© 2002 by J. Phillip, Incorporated
• 5870 Zarley Street, Suite C • New Albany, Ohio  43054 •
• (800) 837-4394  •  (614) 855-8507 •
• **Email**:  info@bentleyguide.com •
• **Website**: www.bentleyguide.com •

ISBN 0-9646280-7-4
ISSN 1082-4790

# *Bentley*

# *Table of Contents*

There are many small **Fun Facts** throughout the Guide.
Listed below is a directory listed by topic.

## *Letter from the Editor*

elcome to our

TENTH EDITION
# *Bentley Guide*®

We are so very excited to be sharing this special anniversary with all of you!

Who would have believed ten years ago that a book about the Longaberger secondary market would be here a decade later . . . but we are and it is all due to all of the Consultants and Collectors out there who have valued their Longaberger Basket collections as much as we have!

We have changed a lot over the past years and we would like to thank all of you for your countless number of transactions and market input, which has made us what we are today. ***Thank you for the first ten years of The Bentley Collection Guide!*** We hope that you will stay with us as we move into another decade of bringing you the most accurate and reliable information available for the Longaberger secondary market!

In this special edition, we visit the past, while looking forward to the future of Longaberger Baskets®. The *Fun Facts* throughout will remind you of *why* you are so crazy about these baskets . . . the rich history that started as one man's large vision in a very small garage. The new items listed – over 130 of them – will excite you for the future of The Longaberger Company® and fill you with wonder as you dream of what they could possibly do next!

As always, the objective of this Guide is to provide a comprehensive and accurate listing of all baskets and products that have been produced by The Longaberger Company® of Dresden, Ohio. Although we are not affiliated with the company, our goal is to promote and further the collectibility of Longaberger Products®. Therefore, with each new Edition, we make improvements and additions to the Guide to provide more information and detail of the products.

Please keep in mind that the current market values listed throughout this book should be used *only as a guide*. They are not intended to set prices, which vary from one section of the country to another. Secondary market prices vary greatly and are affected by many things, such as condition and demand. To better represent your specific market, we encourage you to report your results to us regularly.

We hope that you enjoy this special Tenth Edition. The Fun Facts, the photos of personal collections, and the improvements in information are all for you, the Collector. Through the Bentley Collection Guide, we hope to bring you many hours of happy collecting!

2

# History of The Longaberger Company®

In the early 1900's, in the small Ohio town of Dresden, John Wendell "J.W." Longaberger developed a love for hand-woven baskets. As a teenager, J.W. joined his father, Daddy John, at the Dresden Basket Company as a full-time basket weaver to help support the family. In 1927, J.W. married Bonnie Jean Gist and together they had 12 children. In order to support his large family, J.W. worked at the Dresden Paper Mill during the day, but continued to make baskets at night. In 1973, J.W. and his fifth child, Dave, began to teach others how to weave baskets. Although J.W. died that year, the quality and attention to detail that he wove into his baskets were kept alive, by Dave, through The Longaberger Company®. On March 17, 1999, Dave Longaberger passed away after a battle with cancer. His vision for The Longaberger Company continues through his daughters, Tami and Rachel.

Each basket is hand-woven, using hardwood maple splints. Since 1978, once a basket is completed, it is dated and signed by the weaver. In 1982, the practice of burning The Longaberger® name and logo into the bottom of each basket began, guaranteeing its authenticity.

The company started selling through home parties in 1979. In 1981, the company had 100 consultants and delivery of baskets took approximately 8-12 weeks. Back then, the consultants delivered the orders to each hostess *personally*. Many changes have taken place since this humble beginning. They now employ more than 7,000 people and have approximately 70,000 independent Sales Consultants throughout all 50 states. From 1977 – 1991, the Company generated a total of $14 Million in sales, compared to their 2001 performance, reporting close to $1 Billion.

Along with its growing popularity among collectors, The Longaberger Company® has also been recognized nationally for its dedication to quality and commitment to excellence by many major sources. They have been recognized as one of the Top Ten Most Generous Companies in America by *George Magazine* and *Newman's Own, Inc*. They have also been listed on the Top 500 Largest Privately Held Companies by *Forbes Magazine*.

The Longaberger Company® has come a long way from the garage that once housed Dave's dream over 25 years ago. We encourage you to visit Dresden, Ohio to fully catch the history and commitment behind his entrepreneurial vision. If you are interested in touring the Dresden area, call the Dresden Village Association at 1-800-315-1809 or The Longaberger Company® directly at 740-322-5000.

# *Purpose of this Guide*

Interest in collecting Longaberger Baskets® and Pottery® has increased in recent years due to their increasing value, both inherently and monetarily. It no longer is surprising to see a collector basket double in value in only one year. Due to this interest, there is a need for reliable and accurate information about the value and identification of Longaberger Baskets® and Pottery®. As more Longaberger® products are produced, keeping this information updated is essential.

## THE PURPOSE OF THE BENTLEY COLLECTION GUIDE:

- **To provide a reference tool to Secondary Market Dealers, Consultants, Collectors, Investors and Enthusiasts.**

## THIS IS ACCOMPLISHED BY:

- **Providing *actual* selling (market) prices – not just "asking" prices.**

- **Lending credibility to Longaberger Products® as true collectibles.**

- **Providing a complete, up-to-date compilation of Longaberger Products®, including individual pictures of products for identification purposes.**

- **Providing a "Quick Find" Index that acts as a cross-reference of baskets made from the same form.**

- **Providing valuable information on how to identify and appraise Longaberger Products®.**

## APPLICATIONS FOR THIS GUIDE:

- **An essential educational manual for new, as well as experienced Consultants.**

- **A great training tool for Consultants on the history of Longaberger® products.**

- **A sales tool for Consultants to show customers that Longaberger® products have indeed increased in value.**

- **A price guide for those wanting to buy, sell, or trade baskets on the Secondary Market.**

- **An inventory checklist to record and price all of one's baskets.**

- **A reference tool for valuing one's baskets for insurance purposes.**

- **Identifying one's baskets and evaluating their condition.**

Ｂｅｎｔ

**N**ew Longaberger Baskets® can be obtained only through Sales Consultants, usually at a basket home show. The baskets are ordered from a *Wish List*™ containing products currently available directly from The Longaberger Company®. If you are interested in ordering a current line basket, but do not know a Consultant, contact The Longaberger Company® at (800) 966-0374 to be directed to a Consultant in your area.

**C**ollector and specialty baskets are available only for a limited time throughout the year. For example, the 1992 Christmas Collection Season's Greeting™ Basket was offered only from September through December of 1992. After this, the basket was no longer available from Longaberger®.

**O**lder Longaberger Products® can be obtained only on the Secondary Market, which is made up of people wanting to buy and sell these older products. These items are available from a number of sources. The directory on the next page is a listing of the various services we have found to be available for collectors to buy and sell their products.

**P**lease understand . . .

The Directory of Secondary Market Resources on the next couple of pages is for informational purposes only and constitutes neither an endorsement nor a recommendation. The publisher does not assume any responsibility with regard to the selection, performance, or use of these services. All understandings, agreements, or warranties, if any, take place directly between the services and the prospective users. This listing of secondary market resources is based on information available at the time of publication and J. Phillip, Inc. makes no warranties as to the completeness or accuracy.

**T**o help our customers better evaluate the services that are listed on the next pages, we have devised a system to inform our customers of the length of our relationship with each service. The number of 'βs' listed to the right of each name stands for the number of years that we have been in contact with the service.

## It is not a rating system

We do not charge these services to be listed in this publication. The only requirement is that they have been in business for at least a year and consistently report their market results every month to us for at least a year. When dealing with any of these services, we do encourage you to let us know of your experience as we do wish to continue providing you with quality information about the secondary market.

# Market directory

*Secondary Market Resourc*

**Auctioneers** Baskets can be purchased through the bidding process or can be put up for auction on a consignment basis. Each auctioneer has different commission rates.

## The Rebel Yell Auction Company, Inc. [ β β β ]

Brent Witt, Auctioneer
(540) 966-4656
brentwitt@rbnet.com

84 School Drive
Troutville, VA 24175
www.rebelyellauctions.com

## Williams Auction Company [ β β ]

Ron and Karen Williams
(217) 636-8415
rlwcw4@aol.com

PO Box 149
Athens, IL 62613

**Dealers** There are many dealers in the market that specialize in buying, selling or trading Longaberger Products®. This type of source is often preferred for collectors who have a need to acquire or liquidate items very quickly.

## Baskets Galore & More [ β β β β β β β β β β ]

Ask for Emily
(740) 754-1143 or (740) 453-9154
emily@y-city.net

#3 Lacy Alley
Dresden, OH 43821
www.basketsgaloreandmore.com

## Bay-Side Baskets [ β β β ]

Greg & Cathy Burr
(740) 754-1193, fax:(740) 754-2377
bayside@bright.net

315 Main Street
Dresden, OH 43821

## Greg Michael, Auctioneer [ β β β β β β β β β β ]

(574) 686-2615 or (574) 967-4442
fax: (574) 686-9100
bbaskets@pammichael.com

P.O. Box 7
Camden, IN 46917

## Lighthouse Antiques [ β β β ]

Bette & John Emry
(317) 738-3344, fax:(317) 736-6070
lightantiq@att.net
bettemry@att.net

62 West Jefferson Street
Franklin, IN 46131-2311

**Newsletters** Most newsletters are designed to bring basket lovers together through articles of interest. Many have the primary focus of providing a place for collectors to advertise items to buy, sell or trade. Often information regarding events for collectors is also included.

## The Basket Collector's Gazette [ β β β β β β β β β β ]

Ask for Suzy
(970) 641-5838, fax: (970) 641-2624
bsklover@aol.com

PO Box 100
Pitkin, CO 81241-0100
www.basketlover.com

**Newspapers** The following source has sections dedicated to advertising baskets to buy, sell, or trade. Most also have feature articles concerning The Longaberger Company® and other subjects of interest. It is not necessary to subscribe in order to advertise; however, some offer free space with a subscription.

## Dresden Transcript                          [ β β β β β β β β β β ]
(740) 754-1608,  fax: (740) 754-1609                    PO Box 105
                                              Dresden, OH  43821-0105

dresdentranscript@columbus.rr.com

**Internet** Here are some areas on the information super-highway that you may also find helpful.

## American Online (AOL) Posting Board:
Keyword:  Collecting -> Other Collectibles -> Longaberger

## The Bentley Collection
1-800-837-4394

info@bentleyguide.com                        www.bentleyguide.com

## Basket City USA®                                    [ β β β ]
Christine Hendershot                            2285 June Drive
(419) 229-1285                                  Lima, OH  45805

christine@basketcityusa.com                  www.basketcityusa.com

## The Basket House                                   [ β β β β ]
Ask for Wendy
(540) 438-1977,  fax: (540) 438-8187
info@baskethouse.com                         www.baskethouse.com

## The Basket Market                                    [ β β ]
Bill & Joann Wright                      4345 W.Darr-Hopfinger Rd
(419) 734-4161                            Port Clinton, OH  43452
                                              1 Loch Ness Estates
bwright@1awsm.com                        www.thebasketmarket.com

## The Longaberger Company
(informational purposes only)                www.Longaberger.com

For other internet sites, use your *search engines* and type in the word *Longaberger*.  This will connect you to a variety of different locations.

T he prices provided in this Guide are Secondary Market values obtained from various sources, such as Dealers, Auctioneers, Collectors and Consultants.  For this Tenth Edition, we have collected and confirmed almost 26,000 transactions from all different markets.

The values shown are the *average* and the *highest* reported "selling price" for that particular basket, not the "asking" price. By providing the "selling" price of the baskets, the most accurate and reliable value is given for each basket.  However, several points must be understood in relation to this pricing Guide:

### TIME-SENSITIVE INFORMATION

It is the intent of this Guide to gather all pricing data up to the last possible moment before the Guide is published.  However, some prices may have changed due to the time it takes to publish and send this Guide.  This is one reason for offering an update to this annual collector's guide; to keep the value of Longaberger® products continually up-to-date.

### LIMITED INFORMATION

The market values shown are not absolute.  Increased demand in some areas may result in higher prices for particular baskets.  It is also impossible to be aware of every sales transaction; therefore the market values listed may not be the absolute highest selling price during that particular period of time.  We encourage you to help us represent your market even more accurately by reporting to us all transactions that you participate in throughout the year.

### SHIPPING COSTS CONSIDERED

Although some transactions reported to us may include shipping costs from seller to buyer, the prices reported in this Guide **do not include shipping and handling costs.**  Even though shipping is often a part of a transaction, it is a cost of participating in the market and should not be considered part of a basket's value.  However, you may need to consider this additional cost when insuring your collection because most insurance agencies will only cover up to the insured value listed, regardless if there are additional costs incurred to replace the item.

## RANGE OF VALUES DEFINED

The range of values that are listed throughout the Guide reflect the range of activity that is occurring in the Secondary Market.

*Average Value* is determined by taking a straight average of the values reported for an item during a specific period.

*High Value* is the highest value within the range of values reported. If a transaction is reported which we consider to be much higher than other results, we do not consider this to be a true reflection of the market and therefore will not report on it until more transactions in this area are reported. It is important to note that this definition of High is different from the one used in the Fourth Edition Guide, but is the same definition used in all other editions.

## SOURCE OF THE VALUES

We try to collect a large variety of information from a large variety of markets: internet, person-to-person, dealers, stores, or auctions. Please remember that your market could, and mostly like is, very different from other markets. What is selling "hot" in the West coast may be "dead" in Dresden, or vice versa.

**If you have reported a value to us, but do not think that it has been reflected, it could be for the following reasons.**

- It may have been out of range of the other values reported. For example, if we receive 100, 120, 115, 140, and then 500, we will not show 500 as the *High* until we have more values to support that activity.

- It is possible that we did not receive your information. Please feel free to call for clarification.

## REPRESENT YOUR MARKET — REPORT TO US!

- *Call Us*: 1-800-837-4394

- *Report Online*: www.bentleyguide.com

- See page 106 for more information

**Although this Guide and Collector's Checklist reflect what J. Phillip, Inc. considers to be current market values, J. Phillip, Inc. in no way warrants the prices listed therein. The publisher assumes no responsibility for any losses that might be incurred as a result of consulting this Guide.**

**The Bentley Collection Guide® is the most accurate and most reliable reference tool available for valuing Longaberger Products®.**

## Finding your way through the Guide . . .

All collector series and specialty baskets are listed categorically in the first part of this publication. The order of the categories is alphabetical and can be found in the Table of Contents in the front of this book. *Regular Line* baskets are not listed in the Guide, but are listed in the *Collector's Checklist* for inventory purposes. We do not include pictures of Regular Line baskets because we do not consider them a part of the secondary market since they are still available directly from the company. It is a good idea to keep a copy of a current *Wish List*™ with your Guide to have pictures of these baskets on hand.

The dimensions, form number(s) and quantities produced are now listed directly under the picture. If it is not photographed, most of this information can be found in the *Quick Find*.

## Reading the notations in the Guide . . .

Each basket in the Guide is listed by its year and name(s). Special characteristics may also be listed, such as "swinging handles" (sw/h), "stationary handles" (st/h), "no handles" (no/h), "inverted bottom", etc. If the basket was originally sold with accessories, the following notations will distinguish which accessories were available: Protector: **(P)**; Liner: **(L)**; Lid: **(Lid)**; Divider: **(Div)**.

If a basket was available as a Combo, the parenthesis that follows this notation will distinguish which items were originally a part of the Combo price. When many accessories were offered with a basket, the term "Full Set" has been created to reflect this combination selling in the market. The initials in parenthesis that follow will identify what we are considering a Full Set to include.

## Applying the values to your collection . . .

After the description of the item, an original price, if available, is listed. The next two columns list the range of values from the current market. Before applying these values to your collection, it is important to fully understand how we are determining the Average and the High values throughout the Guide. These definitions can be found on page 9. We consider the *High Value* to represent a basket in excellent condition while the *Average Value* better represents a more average product; however, without having seen each individual product, it is inappropriate for us to judge the condition of items reported to us. We encourage each collector to evaluate the condition of their individual collection before determining its market value. Refer to page 13 to assess the condition of your collection.

When insuring your collection, the best option is to individually determine the unique value for each piece of your collection based on its demand, condition and other characteristics. If time is an issue, the *High Value* represents the potential of the collectible, thus should be used as the potential replacement cost.

# Quick Find Index . . .

Starting on page 243, there is a cross-reference index of baskets listed alphabetically by name, not collection. For example, *J.W. Corn®* is listed under *Corn* and then lists J.W. Collection® as a collection in which the basket was offered. It will also list the other collections that have featured the Corn basket. This tool is great when identifying in which collections a particular basket was available or if the collector knows what the shape or form is, but is unsure of which collection it belongs. This index was specifically designed to be more helpful during auctions where a lot of information is needed quickly and when very little details of the item are made available to the collector. Values listed here are for Basket Only, unless otherwise noted. See page 243 for more information on how to use this section effectively.

# Dimensional Search . . .

This next section is a reference tool that will help when trying to identify a basket by its dimensions. The baskets are divided into four size categories (square, rectangular, round, oval) and the dimensions are then listed in numerical order under each appropriate heading. Page 346 lists specific steps to take when using this great tool to help identify items in your collection.

# Collector's Checklist . . .

The supplemental booklet that came with your Guide is an inventory checklist. The collector edition and specialty baskets are listed in the same manner as in the Guide. Retired and Regular Line baskets are listed at the back in two categories: DARK STAIN (1976-1986) and CLASSIC STAIN (1987-P).

This checklist enables you to indicate the quantity of baskets you may have, as well as your original cost. If any accessories were purchased with the baskets, such as liners or protectors, they can be noted in the description column. Any unique characteristics of the baskets should also be listed, such as special order color weave found in many earlier baskets.

When using the Checklist for insurance purposes, we do give permission to make <u>one</u> copy for your Insurance agent or to place in a safety deposit box. Additional copies are not permitted unless expressed written permission is given by J.Phillip, Inc.

# *Bentley* Word about Insurance

As your basket collection grows, you need to consider how best to cover it with insurance. A relatively small collection is usually not a problem under the normal homeowner's policy; however, any collection can be viewed as more than just a hobby if it reaches a size or falls into a category where the insurance company views it as more than "items normal and incidental to a normal household." A hobby can be viewed as a business, even though you have never sold one basket, simply because the potential to "some day" make money from it exists.

The best person to consult with on this is your insurance agent. He may initially recommend "scheduling" your individual baskets onto your policy, which simply means they are insured separately under a floater from the items listed as "unscheduled personal property" in your policy. If you don't schedule your baskets, at least make sure you have a "replacement cost endorsement" so that you will not have depreciation taken that you cannot recoup after a loss.

If you are an associate, you will need to have a separate business policy since your homeowner's has a limit on the amount they pay for business property. Your agent will be able to advise on the best package for covering your business risk. He also can explain some liability coverages. In today's "lawsuit happy world", even casual statements about "potential resale possibilities" or product durability can come back to haunt salespeople at some future date. Many have secured "professional liability" coverage to provide for defending themselves in court.

If you ever would suffer a smoke or fire loss, do not clean the baskets with normal household cleaners. Smoke has toxic chemicals that not only soil a basket, but interact with it chemically. It needs to be cleaned professionally, the sooner the better. After 24 hours, the damage begins to get substantially worse. Your insurance adjuster will not be upset if you have accrued some "reasonable expenses" to protect your baskets from further damage before he is able to inspect the loss. You will have saved him the cost of replacing them or at least improved their salvage value somewhat, even if they will not clean completely. Again, your agent can advise on who to call since he knows cleaning contractors who specialize in fire and smoke damage restoration.

Finally, as you should do with all your valuables, take photographs/videos in duplicate of each basket; identify it by noting type, age, unique characteristics, condition, original cost and current market value. Then keep a set of the photos/video at a location other than your house. Give the duplicates to your agent to keep in your file. Like any object, baskets get damaged and destroyed so you need to protect yourself from that potential loss, and insurance is a good start.

Richard Gordon, Jr.
Insurance Adjustor

The first step in identifying a Longaberger Basket® is to look on the bottom of the basket for the Longaberger® logo, which is burned into the basket. There have been five different logos used by the company since 1982:

## LONGABERGER STAMP PROGRESSION:

Original stamp. First used in 1982 on the Grandad's Sleigh, but broke in 1983. Prior to 1982, no stamp was used.

This stamp was a temporary replacement in 1983 and was used on several hundred baskets until it was replaced by a permanent one.

This was the third stamp, which started to be used in 1983. The company wanted the baskets to have Dresden, Ohio on them, so it was replaced in 1989.

This stamp was only used for approximately one year, from 1989 to 1990. It was replaced with the fifth stamp.

This stamp was used from 1990 and is still being used currently.

However, if a basket does not have a logo, that does not mean it is not a Longaberger Basket®. In this case, the basket was probably made before 1982. In addition, the weaver of the basket will usually initial the basket and date it. This practice began in 1978, when the company began selling the baskets through the home-party plan.

These are the three markings that help identify the authenticity of a Longaberger Basket®:
- **Longaberger Stamp – starting in 1982**
- **Date – starting in 1978**
- **Weaver's initials – also starting in 1978**

However, there are baskets produced by the company that may be missing any number of these markings, including all three. If your basket is missing any of these markings, we suggest having the basket authenticated directly by The Longaberger Company®. If you

CONTINUED ON NEXT PAGE

13

are not able to take it to Dresden yourself, contact your Consultant and they may be able to help you make arrangements or give you instructions on how to ship it to the company for authentication.

In addition, baskets woven by J.W. himself, most likely will not have any markings on them. If you believe that a basket is an original J.W. basket (a basket hand-woven by J.W. himself), you will need to have it verified by one of the Longaberger family members. These baskets would have been made during the 1930s through the 1970s (before The Longaberger Company® began operations) and do have some identifying "trademarks" on them that were commonly found on J.W.'s work. This year, we have created a collection especially for these baskets. See page 159 for more information about J.W. Originals.

# The value of a basket will depend on several things:

### • IS THE BASKET PART OF A COLLECTION SERIES OR RETIRED FROM THE REGULAR LINE?

Baskets which were part of a series, or were featured only for a short time, will generally increase in value faster than baskets still found in the Regular Line. A *collection series* is a series of baskets produced either on a yearly basis or for a limited time. There are different trends occurring in the market all the time that will make different collections more "sought after". In the past year, some of the more popular series have been:

- Feature Baskets – page 81
- Collectors Club® – page 43
- May Series™ – page 163
- Pottery® – page 177

### • WHAT YEAR WAS THE BASKET WOVEN? IS THE STAIN DARK OR IS IT LIGHT?

Baskets that were a part of the Regular Line, but later retired, tend to have higher values then those still in the Regular Line. However, older (darker stained) Regular Line baskets are beginning to become more popular. We continue to see that collectors are starting to recognize the added value that these older baskets have due to their age as well as to the fact that they have a stain that is no longer available. If the older baskets have been maintained in good condition, they generally should be worth more than newer baskets for the following reasons: (1) There were fewer made each year, (2) older baskets have a

arker stain, which was discontinued in 1986, and (3) these baskets
ould be customized stained or unstained, with colored weaving
nd a variety of handles. These options are rarely offered anymore
rough the company.

## WHAT IS THE CONDITION OF THE BASKET?

e condition of a basket will significantly affect its value. A basket
"excellent" condition is worth much more than the same basket in
oor" condition. Determining the condition can be difficult to do
nd ultimately will need to be agreed upon by the buyer and seller.
eep in mind that these baskets are all handmade; thus some in-
nsistencies in weave or staining are natural to the process and
dd to the uniqueness of the product.

ere are some characteristics, however, that should be considered
t "natural" and may affect the value. Anything within the owner's
ontrol, such as, obvious heavy wear, broken handles, missing or
acked splints, or ink stained liners are just a few conditions that
ould lower the value of the basket.

## IS THE BASKET SIGNED BY A FAMILY MEMBER?

enerally, baskets signed by members of the Longaberger® family
an increase a basket's value, especially if the signature is either
ave's or Grandma Bonnie's. A collector can have their basket
gned by taking it to The Longaberger Homestead® or meeting up
th the family at a Collectors Club™ event. In either case, it is get-
ng more and more difficult to get signatures. The family has really
een cutting back due to many infringements of privacy that have
ccurred in the past year or two.

few of the Longaberger family members can be located at the
ngaberger Homestead. Wendy (#2), Jerry (#3), Larry (#4), Mary
7), Judy (#8), Carmen (#11) and Jeff (#12) can be found at the
W. Workshop, Monday through Saturday. See page 52 later in the
uide for more information on the family members as well as pic-
res of actual signatures.

e value that a signature adds also depends on the circumstance
rrounding the signature. For example, signatures on Bee™ baskets,
ur® baskets, Employee or Incentive baskets are more common
ecause family members are more attainable during the Bee, in
resden or to an employee. This does not mean that signatures on
ese baskets have no additional value, it just means that these sig-
atures were theoretically easier to obtain.

# *Why we do what we do ...*

## WHO IS BENTLEY?

The people at Bentley are a small family of eight employees. Our publishing name is J.Phillip, Inc. and we are located in New Albany, Ohio. We have been publishing the *Bentley Collection Guide®* since 1993 and added *The Collectibles Database®* to our family of products in 1996. We are a privately-owned company, not affiliated with The Longaberger Company® in any way.

## OUR GOAL

*As fellow collectors of Longaberger Baskets®, our goal is to further the collectibility of these beautiful items by educating collectors about the secondary market.*

## OUR COMMITMENT TO YOU

We are dedicated to provide you, our customers, the highest quality product with the highest integrity of service.

We want you to be 100% satisfied with your *"Bentley Experience"*. Not because it's good business practice, but because it is what we would want as a customer. We want you to feel a part of our family and to look forward to getting your *Bentley* year after year!

## OUR INFORMATION

If you have any questions about the Longaberger Secondary Market, our products, or would just like to talk about your collection, please do not hesitate to contact us! We would love to hear from you!

| | |
|---|---|
| **phone**: | 1.800.837.4394 |
| **fax**: | 614.855.7893 |
| **email:** | info@bentleyguide.com |
| **web site**: | www.bentleyguide.com |

*May the God of hope fill you with all joy and peace as you trust in him, so that you may overflow with hope by the power of the Holy Spirit. —— Romans 15: 13*

## Priscilla Patrick
### Morehead, Kentucky

Priscilla has been a Consultant for 5 years. Her very first basket was the Tea Basket™. Her favorite is the Large Picnic™, which she loves having for family reunions. Priscilla believes the baskets make great gifts and always asks for them herself. Her collection now numbers over 270 baskets - that's a lot of gifts!

# All-American®
## Red & Blue Weave and Trim.

### MARKET VALUES

A.        1987
Medium Berry
$7.5^L$ x $7.5^W$ x $3.5^H$

Form No:    1400-ABRS
No. Sold:

| Photo | Description | Original | Avg. | High |
|---|---|---|---|---|
| A. | 1987 Medium Berry™ | 19.95 | **95** | **145** |
| B. | 1987 Large Picnic™ | 64.95 | **255** | **365** |
| C. | 1988 Cake™ | 39.95 | **119** | **165** |
| D. | 1988 Small Picnic™ | 65.95 | **186** | **300** |
| E. | 1989 Stitching™ | 25.95 | **79** | **130** |
| F. | 1989 Quilting™ | 46.95 | **150** | **210** |
| G. | 1990 Small Spoon™ | 23.95 | **93** | **135** |
| H. | 1990 Medium Spoon™ | 27.95 | **74** | **115** |
| I. | 1990 Mini Waste™ | 35.95 | **111** | **140** |
| J. | 1990 Small Waste™ | 45.95 | **138** | **210** |
| K. | 1991 Two-Quart™ | 36.95 | **93** | **135** |
| | Combo (L) | 39.95 | **122** | **160** |
| L. | 1992 Small Market™ | 39.95 | **97** | **100** |
| | with **P**rotector | 48.90 | **103** | **115** |
| | with **L**iner | 56.90 | **103** | **115** |
| | Combo (**P/L**) | 54.95 | **106** | **145** |

E.        1989 Stitching
$7^{RD}$ x $3^H$

Form No:    5400-ABRS
No. Sold:

### collection **note**

The first year for the All-American Series® was 1988, not 1987. The 1987 Medium Berry and Large Picnic were actually called the "Baskets and Stripes Forever" baskets. In 1988, the All-American Collection® was introduced and these baskets were then considered a part of this series.

I.        1990 Mini Waste
$7.5^L$ x $7.5^W$ x $10^H$

Form No:    12000-OBRS
No. Sold:

*Third in All-Around Basket Series*

**B.** 1987 Large Picnic

17^L x 14^W x 11^H

Form No: 300-HBRS
No. Sold:

*Hostess only*

**C.** 1988 Cake

12^L x 12^W x 6^H

Form No: 100-GBRS
No. Sold:

*Divider shelf also came
with the basket.*

**D.** 1988 Small Picnic

12^L x 12^W x 6^H

Form No: 100-HBRS
No. Sold:

*Hostess only*

**F.** 1989 Quilting

12^RD x 5.75^H

Form No: 54000-ABRS
No. Sold:

*Hostess only*

**G.** 1990
Small Spoon

5.5^L x 5.5^W x 6^H

Form No: 10000-OBRS
No. Sold:

*First in All-Around
Basket Series*

**H.** 1990
Medium Spoon

6.5^L x 6.5^W x 8^H

Form No: 11000-OBRS
No. Sold:

*Second in All-Around
Basket Series*

**J.** 1990
Small Waste

9.5^L x 9.5^W x 12^H

Form No: 1800-OBRS
No. Sold:

*Hostess only.
Fourth in All-Around
Basket Series.*

**K.** 1991 Two-Quart

9.5^L x 5^W x 9.5^H

Form No: 1000-CBRS
No. Sold:

*First year for
accessories.*

**L.** 1992 Small Market

15^L x 9.5^W x 5.5^H

Form No: 10707
No. Sold:

## All-American®
### Red & Blue Weave and Trim.

**M.** 1993 Liberty
$11.5^L$ x $5^W$ x $3^H$
Form No: 14541
No. Sold:

## MARKET VALUES

| Photo | Year | Description | Original | Avg. | High |
|---|---|---|---|---|---|
| M. | 1993 | Liberty™ | 29.95 | 60 | 75 |
| | | with Protector | 33.90 | 63 | 77 |
| | | with Liner | 37.90 | 65 | 83 |
| | | Combo (P/L) | 36.95 | 70 | 85 |
| N. | 1994 | Candle™ | 34.95 | 56 | 85 |
| | | with Protector | 39.90 | 60 | 85 |
| | | with Liner | 47.90 | 60 | 91 |
| | | Combo (P/L) | 42.95 | 70 | 115 |
| O. | 1995 | Carry-Along™ | 34.95 | 55 | 85 |
| | | with Protector | 39.90 | 60 | 89 |
| | | with Liner | 48.90 | 63 | 89 |
| | | Combo (P/L) | 44.95 | 65 | 96 |
| O. | 1995 | Flag Tie-On | 6.95 | 17 | 25 |
| P. | 1996 | Summertime™ | 34.95 | 40 | 69 |
| | | with Protector | 39.90 | 50 | 65 |
| | | with Liner | 47.90 | 50 | 70 |
| | | Combo (P/L) | 44.95 | 55 | 95 |
| P. | 1996 | Small Flag Tie-On | 5.95 | 13 | 19 |
| Q. | 1997 | Patriot™ | 32.95 | 55 | 70 |
| | | with Protector | 36.90 | 56 | 80 |
| | | with Liner | 44.90 | 56 | 80 |
| | | Combo (P/L) | 44.95 | 60 | 89 |
| | | Full Set (C/Lid) | 59.90 | 62 | 90 |
| R. | 1998 | Pie™ | 55.00 | 75 | 105 |
| | | with Protector | 64.00 | 80 | 110 |
| | | with Liner | 77.00 | 83 | 110 |
| | | Combo (P/L) | 72.00 | 83 | 135 |
| | | Full Set (C/Lid) | 115.00 | 100 | 140 |
| R. | 1998 | Pie Tie-On | 8.00 | 11 | 15 |
| S. | 1999 | Blue Ribbon Bread™ | 39.00 | 56 | 80 |
| | | with Protector | 44.00 | 57 | 80 |
| | | with Liner | 55.00 | 57 | 80 |
| | | Combo (P/L) | 49.00 | 61 | 89 |
| S. | 1999 | Oval Tie-On[np] | 8.00 | 12 | 16 |
| T. | 2000 | Sparkler™ | 48.00 | 60 | 75 |
| | | with Protector | 58.00 | 70 | 95 |
| | | with Liner | 66.00 | 70 | 95 |
| | | Combo (P/L) | 67.00 | 72 | 100 |
| T. | 2000 | Century Tie-On | 8.00 | 11 | 15 |
| U. | 2000 | Hostess Star-Spangled Serving Tray™ | 98.00 | 104 | 120 |
| | | with Protector | 119.00 | 123 | 130 |
| | | with Liner | 126.00 | 130 | 140 |
| | | Combo (P/L) | 139.00 | 142 | 165 |
| V. | 2001 | Strawberry™ | 34.00 | 41 | 55 |
| | | with Protector | 38.00 | 45 | 60 |
| | | with Liner | 46.00 | 45 | 65 |
| | | Combo (P/L) | 39.00 | 50 | 85 |
| V. | 2001 | Strawberry Tie-On | 8.00 | 12 | 18 |

**Q.** 1997 Patriot
$7^L$ x $5^W$ x $3.5^H$
Form No: 10651
No. Sold:

**U.** 2000 Star-Spangled Serving Tray
$20^L$ x $14^W$ x $3.75^H$
Form No: 18091
No. Sold:

*Hostess only.*

[np] = Not Pictured

**N.** 1994 Candle

$9^L$ x $5^W$ x $5^H$

| | |
|---|---|
| Form No: | 11134 |
| No. Sold: | |

**O.** 1995 Carry-Along

$5.5^L$ x $5.5^W$ x $6^H$

| | |
|---|---|
| Form No: | 14656 |
| Tie-On: | 31551 |
| No. Sold: | |

*Tie-On sold separately.*

**P.** 1996 Summertime

$7.75^L$x $4.5^W$x $2.25^{FH}$x $4.5^{BH}$

| | |
|---|---|
| Form No: | 18911 |
| Tie-On: | 32891 |
| No. Sold: | 146,951 |

*Both regular and divided protector offered. Tie-On sold separately.*

**R.** 1998 Pie

$12^L$ x $12^W$ x $4^H$

| | |
|---|---|
| Form No: | 12289 |
| Tie-On: | 31950 |
| No. Sold: | |

*Pie Plate was retired after April 2000. See Pottery on page 178 for details.*

**S.** 1999 Blue Ribbon Bread

$10.5^L$ x $8.75^W$ x $4^H$

| | |
|---|---|
| Form No: | 14346 |
| Tie-On: | 36218 |
| No. Sold: | |

*Tie-On sold separately.*

**T.** 2000 Sparkler

$11^L$ x $8^W$ x $5.5^H$

| | |
|---|---|
| Form No: | 18694 |
| Tie-On: | 35483 |
| No. Sold: | |

*Tie-On sold separately.*

**V.** 2001 Strawberry

$6.25^L$ x $6.25^W$ x $3.5^H$

| | |
|---|---|
| Form No: | 10141 |
| Tie-On: | 74918 |
| No. Sold: | 150,197 |

## KAYLEE GRACE BALLOU
### already keen on baskets at 5 months!

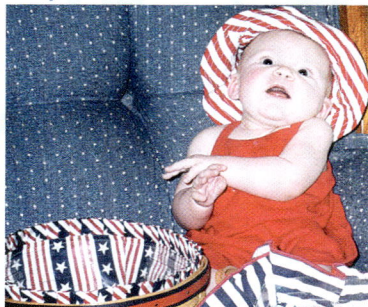

### JUDY FRAZER Mt.Vernon, Ohio

## All-American®
### Red & Blue Weave and Trim.

## MARKET VALUES

| Photo | Description | Original | Avg. | High |
|---|---|---|---|---|
| W. 2002 | Casserole™ | 59.00 | — | — |
| | with **P**rotector | 67.00 | — | — |
| | with **L**iner | 81.00 | — | — |
| | Combo **(P/L)** | 79.00 | — | — |
| W. 2002 | Shield Tie-On | 10.00 | — | — |
| W. 2002 | Hostess Block Party™ | 178.00 | — | — |
| | with **P**rotector | 213.00 | — | — |
| | with **L**iner | 215.00 | — | — |
| | Combo **(P/L)** | 250.00 | — | — |

**W.** 2002

Sm: 10.25$^{RD}$ x 3.5$^H$
Lg: 20.5$^L$ x 12.5$^W$ x 11.5$^H$

| | |
|---|---|
| Casserole: | 12144 |
| Hostess: | 12421 |

*See Pottery Section on pg.182 for details on the American Eagle dish.*

## f u n **f a c t**
# I spy Longaberger. . .

In March this year, all Longaberger fans wished they were sitting in the audience of *The Rosie O'Donnell Show*.

After a cooking segment with special guest JoAnn Cross, mother of Consultant Laura Sheppard, who shared a recipe using her Longaberger Pottery®, every guest in the audience received a free Medium Berry Basket™ with the Spring Floral™ liner, and a Small Cornflower Mixing Bowl™ placed inside!

What a wonderful way to be introduced to Longaberger!

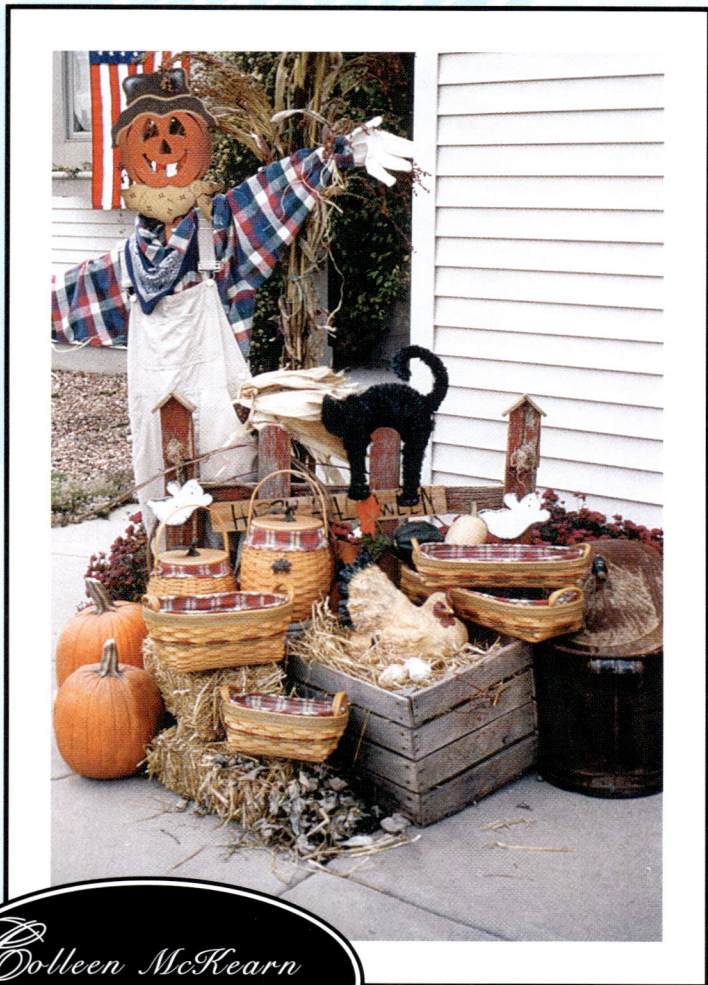

**Colleen McKearn**
**Janesville, Wisconsin**

Colleen's favorite collection is the Heartland®. However, her most prized basket is the '96 Bee with Dave's signature. She has been a consultant for 3 years, and has made 6 trips to the Homestead. On one of her bus trips, she won a prize for spending the most money. The prize was a mug that read "A TRUE BASKET CASE"!

## Autumn Reflections®

Color weaving accents of sage, brown, and burgundy with stitched leather handles. This collection replaced Shades of Autumn®.

### MARKET VALUES

| Photo Description | Original | Avg. | High |
|---|---|---|---|
| A. 2000 Sm Harvest Blessings™ | 42.00 | **56** | **64** |
| with Protector | 50.00 | — | — |
| with Liner | 58.00 | — | — |
| Combo (P/L) | 54.00 | **60** | **75** |
| A. 2000 Lg Harvest Blessings™ | 54.00 | **60** | **86** |
| with Protector | 65.00 | **67** | **90** |
| with Liner | 72.00 | **67** | **100** |
| Combo (P/L) | 69.00 | **70** | **108** |
| B. 2001 Sm Daily Blessings™ | 39.00 | **52** | **60** |
| with Protector | 45.00 | — | — |
| with Liner | 54.00 | — | — |
| Combo (P/L) | 49.00 | **63** | **75** |
| B. 2001 Lg Daily Blessings™ | 49.00 | **69** | **89** |
| with Protector | 63.00 | — | — |
| with Liner | 66.00 | — | — |
| Combo (P/L) | 69.00 | **79** | **96** |

**2000**
**A.** Harvest Blessings

Sm: 15.25$^L$ x 5.75$^W$ x 2.5$^H$
Lg: 19.5$^L$ x 8$^W$ x 3.25$^H$

| Small: | 18058 |
| Large: | 14397 |

*First baskets in the series. Each features the "20th Century" logo on the bottom.*

**2001**
**B.** Daily Blessings

Sm: 10$^L$ x 7.25$^W$ x 3.75$^H$
Lg: 12.75$^L$ x 9.75$^W$ x 5.25$^H$

| Small: | 11404 |
| Large: | 10656 |

*Liner available in three choices: Falling Leaves™, Orchard Park Plaid™, & Botanical Fields™.*

need help?

# How do we get our values?

see page 8

# Bee Baskets™

## Jackie Cusack
### Elkhart, Indiana

Jackie first began collecting baskets 10 years ago. However, in the past year her collection has grown by leaps & bounds. Her favorite collection is the Traditions™. The beautiful old Pennisular stove in the photo was a gift from her husband who lovingly restored it for her.

## Bee™ Baskets

**Only available to those who attend the Basket Bee. Starting in 1990, tagged with Bee Theme. Basket form and accent colors vary each year.**

## MARKET VALUES

| | | Description | Original | Avg. | High |
|---|---|---|---|---|---|
| A. | 1988 | Bee Decorated Basket Contest | | | |
| | | Small Peg | N/C | — | — |
| | | Medium Peg[np] | N/C | — | — |
| | | Large Peg[np] | N/C | — | — |
| B. | 1988 | Large Bee Basket™ | | 145 | 165 |
| | 1988 | Medium Bee Basket™ | | 100 | 100 |
| C. | 1989 | Bee Basket™ | | 145 | 180 |
| D. | 1990 | Bee Basket™ | 19.90 | 44 | 70 |
| E. | 1991 | Bee Basket™ | 19.91 | 56 | 80 |
| F. | 1992 | Bee Basket™ | 20.00 | 69 | 90 |
| G. | 1993 | Bee Basket™ | 25.00 | 100 | 125 |
| | | with **Protector** | | 106 | 130 |
| | | with **Liner** | | 106 | 130 |
| | | Combo **(P/L)** | | 115 | 150 |
| G. | 1993 | Tote | N/C | 13 | 15 |
| H. | 1994 | Bee Basket™ | 25.00 | 155 | 200 |
| | | with **Protector** | | 167 | 215 |
| | | with **Liner** | | 167 | 225 |
| | | Combo **(P/L)** | | 170 | 250 |
| H. | 1994 | Tote | N/C | 24 | 28 |
| H. | 1994 | Bee Tie-On™ | | — | — |

[np] = Not Pictured          ✍ = With Signatures

The Basket Bee™ is the annual convention, usually in August, hosted by the company in Columbus, Ohio for their Consultants. The first year for "The Bee" was 1981. Now, "The Bee" has grown to three conventions, each consisting of three days of speakers and seminars and one day to visit Dresden.

**B.**                    1988

$14^L$ x $7.75^W$ x $5.25^H$

Form No:          3600-AO
No. Sold:

*No Tag. Stained over Medium AND Large Easter baskets. Available with Blue, Green, Lilac, or Pink weaving.*

**E.**                    1991

$8.5^L$ x $8.5^W$ x $5^H$

Form No:          1500-
No. Sold:

*Teal and burgundy weave. Theme: "Imagine the Possibilities".*

## collection **n o t e**
### *About The Bee™*

This celebration of baskets is not for the faint of heart. "Longaberger Homestead Days" are usually held the last day of each Bee™. On these days, vendors from all over the country set up tables throughout Dresden and the town is flooded with enthusiasts from all states. The 2002 Bee™ will be held on 7/24–7/27, 7/28–7/31, 7/31–8/3.

**s e e   y o u   t h e r e**

"Proud To Be Me"

1985 (Potpourri)

$5^L$ x $5^W$ x $2.5^H$

"Our Country Feeling"

1986 (Forget-Me-Not)

$5^{RD}$ x $4.5^H$

*The 1985 and 1986 Bee Baskets shown above were not officially given out by The Longaberger Company®. These baskets were Booking Baskets tagged by a Director for her consultants. The first Bee Basket sponsored by the company was in 1988, in which Large and Medium Easter baskets were stained over.*

**A.** Decorated
1988 Small Peg

$5^L$ x $5^W$ x $4.5^H$

Form No: 14000-AO
No. Sold:

*Med.Peg: $5.5^L$ x $5.5^W$ x $6^H$
Lg. Peg: $6.5^L$ x $6.5^W$ x $8^H$*

**C.** 1989

$8.75^L$ x $4.75^W$ x $6.5^H$

Form No: 5600-BRST
No. Sold:

*Christmas Memory, including Christmas tag. Only difference is wooden bottom.*

**C.** 1989
wooden bottom

*Bee Theme burned into bottom. Theme: "Weave Your American Dream".*

**D.** 1990

$7^{RD}$ x $6.5^H$

Form No: 3900-AO
No. Sold:

*Dusty rose and blue weave. Theme: "Together We're on the Move".*

**F.** 1992

$14^L$ x $9^W$ x $4.5^H$

Form No: 12335
No. Sold:

*Burgundy, teal and golden rod weave. Theme: "Discover the Vision".*

**G.** 1993

Totes:

$13^L$ x $8^W$ x $5^H$

Form No: 13501
No. Sold:

*Pink and teal weave. Theme: "Making it Happen Together" First year for accessories.*

**H.** 1994

Totes:

$6.5^L$ x $6.5^W$ x $8^H$

Form No: unknown
No. Sold:

*Rose pink and purple weave. Theme: "Celebrate Your Success".* **27**

## *Bee™ Baskets*

**The Bee™ is usually held during the first week of August. The 2002 Bee is 7/24–7/27, 7/28–7/31, 7/31–8/3.**

### MARKET VALUES

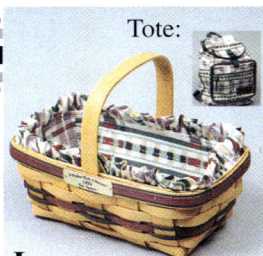

Tote:

**I.** 1995

$10^L$ x $6^W$ x $4^H$

Form No:      unknown
No. Sold:

*Purple and green weave. Theme: "It Begins with a Dream". Accessories sold separately.*

**M.** 1999

$7^L$ x $3.5^W$ x $4.75^H$

Form No:      unknown
No. Sold:

*Theme: "Building Tomorrow Together". Accessories sold separately.*

| Photo | | Description | Original | Avg. | High |
|---|---|---|---|---|---|
| I. | 1995 | Bee Basket™ | 25.00 | 55 | 75 |
| | | with **P**rotector | 29.95 | 62 | 83 |
| | | with **L**iner | 37.95 | 62 | 83 |
| | | Combo (**P/L**) | 42.90 | 67 | 95 |
| I. | 1995 | Tote | N/C | 32 | 40 |
| I. | 1995 | Bee Tie-On™ | | — | — |
| J. | 1996 | Bee Basket™ | 25.00 | 53 | 75 |
| | | with **P**rotector | 29.95 | 61 | 80 |
| | | with **L**iner | 37.95 | 61 | 85 |
| | | Combo (**P/L**) | 42.90 | 78 | 100 |
| | 1996 | Tote | N/C | 17 | 25 |
| J. | 1996 | Bee Tie-On™[np] | | 16 | 20 |
| K. | 1997 | Bee Basket™ | 27.95 | 57 | 100 |
| | | with **P**rotector | 32.90 | 60 | 100 |
| | | with **L**iner | 40.90 | 65 | 100 |
| | | Combo (**P/L**) | 45.85 | 76 | 110 |
| K. | 1997 | Tote | N/C | 26 | 40 |
| K. | 1997 | Bee Tie-On™ | 7.00 | 10 | 19 |
| L. | 1998 | Bee Basket™ | 25.00 | 75 | 80 |
| | | with **P**rotector | 29.00 | 83 | 90 |
| | | with **L**iner | 37.00 | 85 | 99 |
| | | Combo (**P/L**) | 41.00 | 85 | 130 |
| L. | 1998 | Tote | N/C | 27 | 40 |
| L. | 1998 | Bee Tie-On™ | 7.00 | — | — |
| M. | 1999 | Bee Basket™ | 29.00 | 81 | 100 |
| | | with **P**rotector | 33.00 | 81 | 100 |
| | | with **L**iner | 41.00 | 81 | 100 |
| | | Combo (**P/L**) | 45.00 | 85 | 110 |
| M. | 1999 | Tote | N/C | 34 | 52 |
| M. | 1999 | Bee Tie-On™ | 7.00 | — | — |
| N. | 2000 | Bee Basket™ | 0.00 | 72 | 100 |
| | | with **P**rotector | 0.00 | 75 | 110 |
| | | with **L**iner | 0.00 | 75 | 110 |
| | | Combo (**P/L**) | 49.00 | 80 | 120 |
| N. | 2000 | Tote | N/C | 45 | 49 |
| N. | 2000 | Bee Tie-On™ | 7.00 | 10 | 12 |
| O. | 2001 | Bee Basket™ | | 53 | 85 |
| | | Combo (**P/L**) | 49.00 | 83 | 105 |
| O. | 2001 | Tote | N/C | 52 | 60 |
| O. | 2001 | Bee Tie-On™ | 8.00 | — | — |

[np] = Not Pictured

**J.** 1996

$8.5^L$ x $8.5^W$ x $5^H$

Form No: unknown
No. Sold:

*Theme: "Light the Fire Within". Accessories sold separately.*

**K.** 1997

$5.5^L$ x $5.5^W$ x $6^H$

Form No: unknown
No. Sold: ≈ 24,000

*Red, blue and green weave. Theme: "Bringing America Home". Accessories sold separately.*

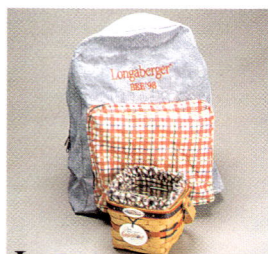

**L.** 1998

$5.25^L$ x $5.25^W$ x $4^H$

Form No: unknown
No. Sold:

*Red and blue weave. Theme: "Join Our Celebration". Accessories sold separately.*

**N.** 2000

$5.5^{RD}$ x $4^H$

Form No: unknown
No. Sold:

*Only offered as Combo with protector and liner. Theme: "Unbeelievable".*

**O.** 2001

$7.5^L$ x $4.75^H$ x $2.5^H$

Form No: 10643
No. Sold:

*Only offered as Combo with protector and liner. Theme: "Imagine – Believe – Achieve".*

## f  u  n  **f a c t**

2000

2001

The "Bea Beary" family added another member in 2001. *Honey Bee Beary* made her debut decked out in full Bee garb ... including her very own Bee Tote and badge ribbons.

This joint venture between The Longaberger Company® and Boyds Bears® is becoming a pretty common sight. Throughout the year, many different basket-toting-bears and friends can be purchased at the Homestead.

Wonderful news for those who collect both!

# ongratulations!

|  |  |  |
| --- | --- | --- |
| Deloris Alexander | Friendsville, TN | page 217 |
| Cathy Burr | Deerfield, OH | page 231 |
| Gail Cada | Hanover, PA | page 31 |
| Jackie Cusack | Elkhart, IN | page 25 |
| Cindy Derflinger | Front Royal, VA | page 163 |
| Lesley DeTitta | Park Ridge, NJ | page 211 |
| Peggy Elkins | Toney, AL | page 155 |
| Deborah Hanyka | Perry, OK | page 173 |
| Yvonne Harris | Auburn, WA | page 113 |
| Diane Jay | Arcanum, OH | page 229 |
| Denise Rae Johnson | Santa Ynez,CA | page 77 |
| Sharon Johnson | Mt. Sterling, KY | page 103 |
| Julie Kokoszka | Issaquah, WA | page 177 |
| Susie Lacy | Chesterfield, IN | page 159 |
| Regina Lemanowicz | Vista, CA | page 53 |
| Candace Madura | Freedom, PA | page 97 |
| Pat McCafferty | Magalia, CA | page 59 |
| Valerie McCuskey | Union, MO | page 37 |
| Colleen McKearn | Janesville, WI | page 23 |
| Cindy Mentzer | Carlisle, PA | page 69 |
| Drena Moll | Lenhartsville, PA | page 43 |
| Lisa Moodie | Dayton, OH | page 223 |
| Jill Neff | Anderson, IN | page 167 |
| Ann Newman | Farmington, AR | page 123 |
| Priscilla Patrick | Morehead, KY | page 17 |
| Millie Pearson | Greentown, IN | page 119 |
| Debbie Puckett | Spotsylvania, VA | page 81 |
| Ruth Reese | Rochester, IN | page 191 |
| Andrea Leigh Shields | Hebron, KY | page 61 |
| Valerie Smith | Blandon, PA | page 193 |
| Kelly Stamm | Washington, KS | page 207 |
| Connie Uhle | Massillon, OH | page 239 |
| Sharon Watson | Kansas City, MO | page 129 |
| Carroll Weinbroer | Valley City, OH | page 107 |

See page 118 for information on how to be a part of our
Nationwide Search for our special Eleventh Edition Guide.

Booking/
Promo

**Gail Cada**
*Hanover, Pennsylvania*

*At the urging of her friend,
Gail began collecting in
1999. Three years later her
collection of over 200 baskets
is still going strong. Gail says she
does not have a favorite basket - she simply LOVES them ALL!*

**A.** 1992-96 Ambrosia
5.5$^L$ x 4$^W$ x 4$^H$
Form No: 10120
No. Sold:

*3/8" Weave. Free to Hostesses with 2+ Bookings.*

**E.** 1990-92 Ivy
5.5$^L$ x 5.5$^W$ x 2.5$^H$
Form No: 13100-JOS
No. Sold:

*3/8" Weave. Free to Hostesses with 2+ Bookings.*

**I.** 1998-01 Oregano
5$^L$ x 3$^W$ x 3.5$^H$
Form No: 13145
No. Sold:

# Booking Baskets

**Available free to Hostesses for achieving certain goals. No color. Items listed here in alphabetical order.**

## MARKET VALUES

| Photo | Description | Original | Avg. | High |
|---|---|---|---|---|
| A. | 1992-96 Ambrosia™ | 22.95* | **32** | **58** |
| | with **P**rotector | 25.90 | **40** | **60** |
| | with **L**iner | 31.90 | **40** | **60** |
| | Combo (**P/L**) | 34.85 | **46** | **65** |
| | 19xx-84 Button [np] | 6.43 | **58** | **65** |
| B. | 1984-90 Candle™ | — | **41** | **65** |
| C. | 1996-00 Chives™ | 25.95 | **30** | **35** |
| | with **P**rotector | 28.90 | **30** | **39** |
| | with **L**iner | 35.90 | **30** | **39** |
| | Combo (**P/L**) | 38.85 | **33** | **50** |
| D. | 1986-87 Forget-Me-Not™ | — | **52** | **74** |
| E. | 1990-92 Ivy™ | ** | **50** | **72** |
| | with **P**rotector | 2.95 | **53** | **75** |
| F. | 1988-90 Keepsake™ | 16.95* | **55** | **77** |
| G. | 1990-92 Laurel™ | ** | **39** | **50** |
| | with **P**rotector | 2.95 | **49** | **78** |
| H. | 1992-99 Lavender™ | 22.95* | **30** | **58** |
| | with **P**rotector | 25.90 | **33** | **60** |
| | with **L**iner | 31.90 | **37** | **62** |
| | Combo (**P/L**) | 34.85 | **41** | **75** |
| | 19xx-84 Measuring, 5" [np] | — | **30** | **35** |
| I. | 1998-01 Oregano™ | 27.00* | **27** | **40** |
| | with **P**rotector | 30.00 | **33** | **40** |
| | with **L**iner | 37.00 | **33** | **40** |
| | Combo (**P/L**) | 40.00 | **36** | **55** |
| J. | 1999-02 Parsley™ | 27.00 | **27** | **35** |
| | with **P**rotector | 30.00 | **30** | **35** |
| | with **L**iner | 37.00 | **37** | **48** |
| | Combo (**P/L**) | 40.00 | **40** | **51** |
| K. | 1985-90 Potpourri™ | 3.00 | **46** | **80** |
| L. | 1992-95 Potpourri Sachet | 11.95* | **13** | **20** |

*Basket Value, not cost.

**Free, with 2+ bookings

[np] = not pictured

**BOOKING/PROMO BASKETS**

Booking/
Promo

**B.** 1984-90 Candle

$9^L$ x $5^W$ x $5^H$

Form No: 1100-AO
No. Sold:

**C.** 1996-00 Chives

$4^L$ x $4^W$ x $4^H$

Form No: 15211
No. Sold:

**D.** 1986-87 Forget-Me-Not

$5^{RD}$ x $4.5^H$

Form No: 3800-AO
No. Sold:

*Free to Hostesses with show sales greater than $150.*

**F.** 1988-90 Keepsake

$5.75^L$ x $3.75^W$ x $3^H$

Form No: 45000-IO
No. Sold:

**G.** 1990-92 Laurel

$5.5^{RD}$ x $3.75^H$

Form No: 17000-JOS
No. Sold:

*3/8" Weave. Free to Hostesses with 2+ Bookings.*

**H.** 1992-99 Lavender

$8^L$ x $4^W$ x $2^H$

Form No: 10138
No. Sold:

**J.** 1999-02 Parsley

$6^L$ x $4.5^W$ x $2.5^H$

Form No: 12882
No. Sold:

**K.** 1985-90 Potpourri

$5^L$ x $5^W$ x $2.5^H$

Form No: 13000-AO
No. Sold:

*Free to Hostesses with show sales greater than $150.*

**L.** 1992-95 Sachet

N/A

Form No: 209581
No. Sold:

*Free with 1 Booking. Available in both Herbal Garden & Garden Splendor fabrics* **33**

## Booking Baskets

**Prior to 1990: 1/2" weave**
**After 1990: 3/8" weave**

### MARKET VALUES

| Photo | Description | Original | Avg. | High |
|---|---|---|---|---|
| M. | 1990-92 Rosemary™ | ** | 52 | 65 |
| | with **P**rotector | 2.95 | 60 | 79 |
| | Spoon Rests: | | | |
| N. | 1996-00 Regular Line | 18.95* | 27 | 49 |
| N. | 1998-00 Holly | 20.00* | 29 | 40 |
| | 19xx-84 Small Spoon[np] | — | 60 | 65 |
| O. | 1988 Sugar and Spice™ | — | 61 | 87 |
| P. | 1980 Sunburst | 3.95 | 181 | 185 |
| Q. | 1992-94 Sweet Basil™ | 22.95* | 32 | 60 |
| | with **P**rotector | 25.90 | 34 | 65 |
| | with **L**iner | 31.90 | 43 | 70 |
| | Combo (**P/L**) | 34.85 | 44 | 78 |
| R. | 1995-98 Thyme™ | 25.95* | 31 | 48 |
| | with **P**rotector | 28.90 | 35 | 60 |
| | with **L**iner | 35.90 | 40 | 60 |
| | Combo (**P/L**) | 38.85 | 40 | 65 |
| | Votives: | | | |
| S. | 1999-01 All-American™ | 20.00* | 23 | 40 |
| S. | 1999-00 Candy Corn™ | 20.00 | 26 | 45 |

*Basket Value, not cost.

[np] = not pictured

1990-92
**M.** Rosemary
5.75^L x 3.75^W x 3^H
Form No:     45000-JOS
No. Sold:

1992-94
**Q.** Sweet Basil
5^L x 5^W x 2.5^H
Form No:     10146
No. Sold:

*3/8" Weave. Free to Hostesses with 2+ Bookings.*

n e e d  help?

Where are the
Booking Baskets that
are still available?

see page 10

**N.** Spoon Rest

9.25$^L$ x 3.25$^W$

Form No: Blue: 32778
Green: 32786
Red: 32794
Ivory: 33651
Holly: 33472

**O.** 1988 Sugar and Spice

5.75$^L$ x 3.75$^W$ x 3$^H$

Form No: 45000-AO
No. Sold:

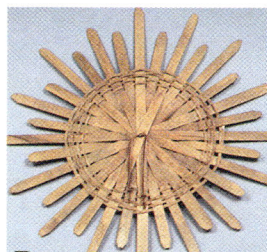

**P.** 1980 Sunburst

22" diameter

Form No: 7000-O
No. Sold:

**R.** 1995-98 Thyme

4.5$^{RD}$ x 3$^H$

Form No: 19003
No. Sold:

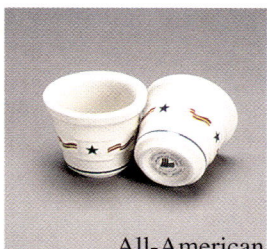

**S.** All-American Votives

3$^{RD}$ x 2$^H$

Form No: 35980

*Set of 2. Not available for purchase.*

**T.** Candy Corn Votives

3$^{RD}$ x 2$^H$

Form No: 37508

*Set of 2. Not available for purchase.*

f u n **f a c t**

# Did you know ...

When Dave started the "basket business", it was his brothers, Larry and Jerry, who trained the weavers on the craft. As a matter-of-fact, Dave hardly ever wove the baskets.

His true calling was obviously as the *Visionary*!

# Director Christmas Baskets

A Longaberger Sales Director holds huge responsibilities within the company. Not only is she personally responsible for motivating hundreds of Sales Consultants within her directorship, but she must also maintain her own level of sales while meeting a mountain of other goals.  Without a question, a Director is an essential part of the well-oiled Longaberger sales force.

Throughout the year, The Company shows their appreciation to their valued Directors in many different ways, and Christmas time is no exception.

Here is a rare look into the very limited *Director Christmas Basket* collection. Starting in Christmas 1993, these Sweetheart–inspired baskets have been given to each Director as a thank you. While they do resemble members of the Sweetheart Collection®, none of the basket forms in this collection have ever been made available to the public with this red accent weaving.

Quite a special collection indeed!

1993

1994

1995

1996

1997

1999

2000

## *Valerie McCuskey*
## *Union, Missouri*

*A May Series*™ *basket given as a housewarming gift 3 years ago began Valerie's love affair with baskets. Now May Series*™ *is her favorite collection. Each year she receives a Christmas*™ *basket from her mom. Valerie loves to change her decor with baskets to match the seasons.*

## Christmas Collection™

**Red or Green Weave and Trim.
Commemorative Brass Tag.**

### MARKET VALUES

| Photo | | Description | Original | Avg. | High |
|---|---|---|---|---|---|
| A. | 1981 | Candle™ | 14.95 | **895** | **1100** |
| B. | 1982 | Grandad's Sleigh™ | 19.95 | **818** | **1000** |
| C. | 1983 | Bell™ | 22.95 | **598** | **850** |
| D. | 1984 | Holly™ | 24.95 | **272** | **355** |
| E. | 1985 | Cookie™ | 24.95 | **151** | **300** |
| | | with Liner | 33.95 | **248** | **285** |
| F. | 1986 | Candy Cane™ | 26.95 | **159** | **245** |
| G. | 1987 | Mistletoe™ | 19.95 | **87** | **155** |
| H. | 1988 | Poinsettia™ | 26.95 | **70** | **155** |
| I. | 1989 | Memory™ | 34.95 | **61** | **110** |
| J. | 1990 | Gingerbread™ | 32.95 | **69** | **125** |
| | | with Protector | 37.90 | **70** | **130** |
| | | with Liner | 45.90 | **73** | **130** |
| | | Combo (P/L) | 50.85 | **79** | **140** |
| K. | 1991 | Yuletide Traditions™ | 38.95 | **50** | **85** |
| | | with Protector | 45.90 | **63** | **105** |
| | | with Liner | 52.90 | **79** | **125** |
| | | Combo (P/L) | 59.85 | **83** | **125** |
| L. | 1992 | Season's Greetings™ | 44.95 | **63** | **95** |
| | | with Protector | 49.90 | **69** | **100** |
| | | with Liner | 57.90 | **69** | **125** |
| | | Combo (P/L) | 53.95 | **75** | **130** |

**A.** 1981 Candle
$9^L$ x $5^W$ x $5^H$
Form No: 1100-
No. Sold: 2,000

**E.** 1985 Cookie
$7^{RD}$ x $3^H$
Form No: 5400-A*
No. Sold:

*First Christmas basket offered with an accessory. Liners were not offered again until 1990.*

**I.** 1989 Memory
$8.75^L$ x $4.75^W$ x $6.5^H$
Form No: 5600-B*ST
No. Sold: 129,651

*need help?*

## How do we get our values?

see page 8

38

**B.** 1982 Grandad's Sleigh

$9.25^L$ x $5.5^W$ x $2^{FH}$ x $5.5^{BH}$

| | |
|---|---|
| Form No: | 4900-Z |
| No. Sold: | 3,200 |

*Available with red tag only. Grandad with one 'd' was an intentional misspelling.*

**C.** 1983 Bell

$6.5^{RD}$ x $7^H$

| | |
|---|---|
| Form No: | 4901-OO |
| No. Sold: | 3,700 |

*Available with red or green tag.*

**D.** 1984 Holly

$15^L$ x $8^W$ x $2.25^H$

| | |
|---|---|
| Form No: | 4600-AZ |
| No. Sold: | 16,494 |

*Only available in red.*

**F.** 1986 Candy Cane

$5^L$ x $5^W$ x $4.5^H$

| | |
|---|---|
| Form No: | 14000-A*T |
| No. Sold: | |

**G.** 1987 Mistletoe

$7^L$ x $5^W$ x $3.5^H$

| | |
|---|---|
| Form No: | 700-A*T |
| No. Sold: | |

**H.** 1988 Poinsettia

$7^{RD}$ x $6.5^H$

| | |
|---|---|
| Form No: | 3900-B*ST |
| No. Sold: | |

**J.** 1990 Gingerbread

$10^L$ x $6^W$ x $4^H$

| | |
|---|---|
| Form No: | 3400-A*ST |
| No. Sold: | 165,117 |

*First year both liner and protector offered with basket.*

**K.** 1991 Yuletide Traditions

$13^L$ x $7.5^W$ x $3^{FH}$ x $8^{BH}$

| | |
|---|---|
| Form No: | 5100-C*ST |
| No. Sold: | 147,247 |

**L.** 1992 Season's Greetings

$9.5^L$ x $6^W$ x $6^H$

| | |
|---|---|
| Form No: | 10316/10219† |
| No. Sold: | |

\* = Substitute R for Red or G for Green.
† = Product numbers are stated Red weave / Green weave **39**

## Christmas Collection™

**This collection is usually promoted from September through the end of December.**

**M.** 1993 Bayberry
$9^L$ x $9^W$ x $4.5^H$

Form No: 11584/11592†
No. Sold:

**Q.** 1997 Snowflake
$10^L$ x $9.25^W$ x $6.5^H$

Form No: 12645/12637†
Tie-On: 34738
No. Sold: 507,000

*Tie-On and Lid not included in Combo.*

| Photo | | Description | Original | MARKET VALUES Avg. | High |
|---|---|---|---|---|---|
| M. | 1993 | Bayberry™ | 42.95 | 65 | 90 |
| | | with Protector | 48.90 | 72 | 90 |
| | | with Liner | 55.90 | 75 | 110 |
| | | Combo (P/L) | 49.95 | 63 | 99 |
| N. | 1994 | Jingle Bell™ | 47.95 | 58 | 95 |
| | | with Protector | 54.90 | 63 | 100 |
| | | with Liner | 62.90 | 67 | 100 |
| | | Combo (P/L) | 59.95 | 70 | 125 |
| | | Full Set (Combo/Lid) | 79.90 | 90 | 135 |
| N. | 1994 | Jingle Bell Tie-On | 6.95 | 16 | 28 |
| O. | 1995 | Cranberry™ | 47.95 | 56 | 90 |
| | | with Protector | 54.90 | 62 | 100 |
| | | with Liner | 64.90 | 62 | 100 |
| | | Combo (P/L) | 59.95 | 70 | 130 |
| | | Full Set (Combo/Lid) | 79.90 | 90 | 140 |
| O. | 1995 | Christmas Tie-On | 6.95 | 14 | 20 |
| O. | 1995 | Hanukkah Tie-On | 6.95 | 9 | 10 |
| P. | 1996 | Holiday Cheer™ | 47.95 | 68 | 90 |
| | | with Protector | 53.90 | 72 | 100 |
| | | with Liner | 64.90 | 72 | 100 |
| | | Combo (P/L) | 59.95 | 77 | 125 |
| | | Full Set (Combo/Lid) | 81.90 | 94 | 148 |
| P. | 1996 | Christmas Tie-On | 6.95 | 13 | 22 |
| | 1996 | Hanukkah Tie-On[np] | 6.95 | — | — |
| Q. | 1997 | Snowflake™ | 49.95 | 70 | 90 |
| | | with Protector | 58.90 | 73 | 95 |
| | | with Liner | 71.90 | 73 | 100 |
| | | Combo (P/L) | 69.95 | 73 | 120 |
| | | Full Set (Combo/Lid) | 93.90 | 77 | 135 |
| Q. | 1997 | Christmas Tie-On | 6.95 | 12 | 20 |
| Q. | 1997 | Hanukkah Tie-On | 6.95 | — | — |
| R. | 1998 | Glad Tidings™ | 49.00 | 66 | 88 |
| | | with Protector | 57.00 | 67 | 90 |
| | | with Liner | 70.00 | 70 | 90 |
| | | Combo (P/L) | 69.00 | 80 | 115 |
| | | Full Set (Combo/Lid) | 91.00 | 93 | 127 |
| R. | 1998 | Christmas Tie-On | 8.00 | 10 | 16 |
| | 1998 | Hanukkah Tie-On[np] | 8.00 | — | — |
| | 1998-99 | Kwanzaa Tie-On[np] | 8.00 | — | — |
| S. | 1999 | Popcorn™ | 59.00 | 68 | 90 |
| | | with Protector | 68.00 | 70 | 93 |
| | | with Liner | 76.00 | 77 | 93 |
| | | Combo (P/L) | 69.00 | 73 | 125 |
| | | Full Set (Combo/Lid) | 101.00 | 109 | 130 |
| S. | 1999 | Christmas Tie-On | 8.00 | 10 | 12 |
| S. | 1999-P | Hanukkah Tie-On | 8.00 | — | — |

[np] = Not Pictured.

**N.** 1994 Jingle Bell

$8^{RD} \times 6^{H}$

Form No: 17906/17914†
Tie-On: 31437
No. Sold:

*Tie-On and Lid not included in Combo.*

**O.** 1995 Cranberry

$8.5^{L} \times 8.5^{W} \times 7^{H}$

Form No: 19500/19518†
Tie-On: 32441
No. Sold:

*Tie-On and Lid not included in Combo.*

**P.** 1996 Holiday Cheer

$12^{L} \times 8^{W} \times 4.25^{H}$

Form No: 18511/18520†
Tie-On: 31704
No. Sold: 403,248

*Tie-On and Lid not included in Combo.*

**R.** 1998 Glad Tidings

$8.75^{L} \times 6^{W} \times 9^{BH} \times 7.5^{FH}$

Form No: 12386/12394†
Tie-On: 33511
No. Sold:

*Tie-On and Lid not included in Combo. Last year for Imperial Stripe fabric.*

**S.** 1999 Popcorn

$10.5^{RD} \times 5^{H}$

Form No: 15156/15351†
Christmas Tie-On: 36935
Hanukkah Tie-On: 36943

*Tie-Ons sold separately. Regular and divided protectors were offered.*

f  u  n  f a c t

Many family Christmas traditions include sitting around a family piano and singing for hours on end.

It's a tradition in the Longaberger household, as well. Grandma Bonnie is a wonderful pianist and they all *still* gather around the piano to sing and share the Holidays.

† = Product numbers are stated: Red weave / Green weave.

## Christmas Collection™

**Since 1994, a lid has been offered with either a red or green knob.**

**T.** 2000 Deck the Halls

8.5ᴸ x 8.5ᵂ x 6ᴴ

| | | Form No: | 17639/17736† |
| | | Tie-On: | 36641 |
| | | No. Sold: | 269,523 |

*Tie-Ons sold separately.*

### MARKET VALUES

| Photo | | Description | Original | Avg. | High |
|---|---|---|---|---|---|
| T. | 2000 | Deck the Halls™ | 64.00 | **67** | **80** |
| | | with **P**rotector | 75.00 | — | — |
| | | with **L**iner | 84.00 | — | — |
| | | Combo (**P/L**) | 79.00 | **76** | **100** |
| | | Full Set (**Combo/Lid**) | 106.00 | **90** | **144** |
| T. | 2000 | Christmas Tie-On | 8.00 | **9** | **14** |
| T. | 2000 | Pear Tie-On | 8.00 | **11** | **15** |
| | 2000-P | Kwanzaa Tie-On[np] | 8.00 | — | — |
| U. | 2001 | Shining Star™ | 59.00 | **75** | **87** |
| | | with **P**rotector | 68.00 | — | — |
| | | with **L**iner | 77.00 | — | — |
| | | Combo (**P/L**) | 75.00 | **81** | **105** |
| | | Full Set (**Combo/Lid**) | 109.00 | **110** | **125** |
| U. | 2001 | Christmas Tie-On | 8.00 | **10** | **13** |
| U. | 2001 | American Holly™ | | | |
| | | Tie-On | 8.00 | **10** | **12** |
| | | Napkin Rings (4)[np] | 29.00 | — | — |

**U.** 2001 Shining Star

10.25ᴸ x 11ᵂ x 3.75ᴴ

| | | Form No: | 10734/10745† |
| | | Christmas TO: | 39438 |
| | | Holly TO: | 30602 |

*Tie-Ons sold separately.*

[np] = Not Pictured.

f u n **f a c t**

After September 11th, Longaberger started the "Longaberger Cares" fund to help assist members of the extended Longaberger family as well as other victims, who lost family members. Eleven Consultants and one employee had family killed in the tragedy.

<u>All</u> profits from this *American Pride* liner, made to fit the Shining Star Basket™, went to this "Longaberger Cares" fund. More than 187,000 liners were sold, raising over $700,000.

## Drena Moll
### Lenhartsville, Pa.

Since 1987, Drena has been hooked on baskets and along the way has hooked her entire family as well. Her collection of 400+ baskets is proof positive of her "habit"! Drena loves the Magazine™ basket, which she uses to hold her mail & TV remote. Her love for baskets is matched only by her love for pottery. She has a service for 16 in an assortment of Blue, Green, Red & Traditional Holly.

# Collectors Club ™

**J.W.® Blue and Traditions™ Green Trim and Weave. Brass tags and boxes are common.**

## MARKET VALUES

| | Description | Original | Avg. | High |
|---|---|---|---|---|
| | ***Membership Items:*** | | | |
| A. | 1995-96 Charter Membership | 75.00 | **105** | **178** |
| | with **P**rotector | 83.95 | **120** | **180** |
| | with **L**iner | 94.95 | **127** | **180** |
| | Combo (**P/L**) | 103.90 | **127** | **265** ✑ |
| A. | 1997-P Membership | 75.00 | **—** | **—** |
| | with **P**rotector | 83.95 | **—** | **—** |
| | with **L**iner | 94.95 | **—** | **—** |
| | Combo (**P/L**) | 103.90 | **—** | **—** |
| B. | 2002-P 5-Year Anniversary | 99.00 | **—** | **—** |
| | with **P**rotector | 107.00 | **—** | **—** |
| | with **L**iner | 123.00 | **—** | **—** |
| | Combo (**P/L**) | 131.00 | **—** | **—** |
| | ***1996 Items:*** | | | |
| C. | 1996 Miniature | | | |
| | J.W. Market® | 125.00 | **233** | **465** |
| | with **P**rotector | 127.95 | **250** | **575** |
| | with **L**iner | 138.95 | **300** | **575** |
| | Combo (**P/L**) | 141.90 | **332** | **600** |
| D. | 1996 Membership Tie-On | N/C | **41** | **75** |
| E. | 1996 Small Serving Tray™ | 69.95 | **110** | **125** |
| | with **P**rotector | 79.90 | **110** | **150** |
| | with **L**iner | 92.90 | **110** | **160** |
| | Combo (**P/L**) | 102.85 | **123** | **180** |
| F. | 1996 Longaberger University Ornament™ | 29.95 | **36** | **75** |
| | ***1997 Items:*** | | | |
| G. | 1997 Renewal Basket™ | 39.95 | **77** | **105** |
| | with **P**rotector | 44.90 | **80** | **110** |
| | with **L**iner | 54.90 | **82** | **115** |
| | Combo (**P/L**) | 59.85 | **65** | **110** |
| H. | 1997 Miniature | | | |
| | J.W. Waste® | 99.95 | **150** | **206** |
| | with **P**rotector | 102.90 | **—** | **—** |
| | with **L**iner | 113.90 | **—** | **—** |
| | Combo (**P/L**) | 116.85 | **177** | **350** |
| I. | 1997 Handle Gripper | N/C | **19** | **25** |
| J. | 1997 Welcome Home™ | 69.95 | **87** | **125** |
| | with **P**rotector | 79.90 | **87** | **145** |
| | with **L**iner | 92.90 | **91** | **145** |
| | Combo (**P/L**) | 102.85 | **91** | **150** |
| K. | 1997 Caroling in Dresden Ornament™ | 29.95 | **35** | **70** |
| | ***1998 Items:*** | | | |
| L. | 1998 Renewal Basket™ | 44.95 | **68** | **95** |
| | with **P**rotector | 50.90 | **80** | **95** |
| | with **L**iner | 62.90 | **80** | **95** |
| | Combo (**P/L**) | 68.85 | **85** | **110** |

✑ = With Signatures

**A.** Membership
9.5$^L$ x 5$^W$ x 9.5$^H$

Form No: 62839
No. Sold: 105,304

*Charter Member version has the notation "Charter Member" on the brass tag.*

**E.** 1996 Serving Tray
11.5$^L$ x 15.5$^W$ x 3.75$^H$

Form No: 12629
No. Given:

**I.** 1997 Membership Handle Gripper

N/A

Form No: unknown
No. Sold:

*Sent FREE to all Members. "CHARTER MEMBER" was embroidered for those who held that status.*

**B.** 5-Year Anniversay 2002-P

6$^L$ x 5$^W$ x 8.25$^H$

Form No: 12020

*This is the same basket as the Charter Member 5-year Anniversary (2001), except this lid is not engraved.*

**C.** Miniature Market 1996

5.75$^L$ x 4$^W$ x 3$^H$

Form No: 150240
Signed: 15024
No. Sold:

*Accessories sold separately. Seal on the box designates the basket was signed by a family member.*

**D.** 1996 Membership Tie-On

2.5$^W$ x 1.75$^H$

Form No: 83089
No. Given: ≈ 95,000

**F.** 1996 Ornament

3.5$^{RD}$

Form No: 33758
No. Sold:

*"Longaberger University – Edition 1996"*

**G.** 1997 Renewal

9$^L$ x 5$^W$ x 5$^H$

Form No: 105702
No. Sold:

**H.** Miniature Waste 1997

3.75$^L$ x 3.75$^W$ x 4.75$^H$

Form No: 17797
No. Sold:

**J.** Welcome Home 1997

15$^L$ x 9.5$^W$ x 5.5$^H$

Form No: 10464
No. Sold:

*Available to Members between Aug. 1, 1997 through Sept. 30, 1997.*

**K.** 1997 Ornament

3.5$^{RD}$

Form No: 34207
No. Sold:

*"Caroling in Dresden – Edition 1997"*

**L.** 1998 Renewal

8.5$^{RD}$ x 4$^H$

Form No: 13340
No. Sold:

## Collectors Club™

**1998
M.  Miniature Apple**

### MARKET VALUES

| Description | Original | Avg. | High |
|---|---|---|---|
| **1998 Items (con't)** | | | |
| M. 1998 Miniature | | | |
| J.W. Apple® | 139.95 | **148** | 210 |
| with **P**rotector | 142.90 | **150** | 210 |
| with **L**iner | 153.90 | **155** | 215 |
| Combo (**P/L**) | 156.85 | **169** | 255 |
| N. 1998 25th Anniversary™ | 115.00 | **157** | 250 |
| with **P**rotector | 128.00 | **162** | 269 |
| with **L**iner | 160.00 | **190** | 269 |
| Combo (**P/L**) | 173.00 | **198** | 300 |
| N. 1998 25th Anniversary | | | |
| Tie-On | N/C | **19** | 30 |
| O. 1998 Thyme™ | N/C | **51** | 71 |
| with **P**rotector | 3.00 | **55** | 75 |
| with **L**iner | 12.00 | **55** | 75 |
| Combo (**P/L**) | 15.00 | **64** | 100 |
| P. 1998 Harbor™ | 85.00 | **98** | 110 |
| with **P**rotector | 95.00 | **100** | 122 |
| with **L**iner | 110.00 | **120** | 130 |
| Combo (**P/L**) | 120.00 | **114** | 200 |
| Full Set (**C/Lid**) | 148.00 | **138** | 225 |
| Q. 1998 "25 Years in Pictures" | N/C | **5** | 10 |
| R. 1998 Shopping on Main Street Ornament™ | 30.00 | **22** | 45 |
| **1999 Items:** | | | |
| S. 1999 Renewal Basket™ | 42.00 | **50** | 57 |
| with **P**rotector | 46.00 | — | — |
| with **L**iner | 58.00 | — | — |
| Combo (**P/L**) | 62.00 | **65** | 85 |
| T. 1999 Miniature | | | |
| J.W. Two-Pie® | 130.00 | **136** | 150 |
| with **P**rotector | 133.00 | **150** | 180 |
| with **L**iner | 144.00 | **155** | 180 |
| Combo (**P/L**) | 147.00 | **163** | 270 |
| U. 1999 Miniature Pie Plate 25th Anniversary | N/C | **46** | 60 |
| V. 1999 Mini Two-Pie Server | 35.00 | **74** | 96 |
| Combo (**w/plates**) | 80.00 | **145** | 195 |
| V. 1999 Miniature Pie Plate Set of 2, Blue design | 45.00 | **68** | 95 |
| W. 1999 Serving Tray™ | 99.00 | **130** | 225 |
| with **P**rotector | 120.00 | — | — |
| with **L**iner | 127.00 | — | — |
| Combo (**P/L**) | 148.00 | **160** | 235 |
| X. 1999 Riding Through the Snow Ornament™ | 30.00 | **32** | 40 |
| Y. 1999 Family Picnic™ | 225.00 | **288** | 300 |

5.25$^{RD}$ x 3.25$^H$

Form No:              13749
No.Sold:

**1998
Q:** "25 Years in Pictures"

11$^L$ x 11$^W$

Form No:              85804
No.Sold:

*Sent FREE to Club Members.*

**1999 Miniature
U.   25th Pie Plate**

3.25$^{RD}$

Form No:              33537
No. Sold:

*Offered FREE to Members who purchased the Mini Two-Pie™ Basket between Nov. 21 – Dec. 31, 1998.*

**N.** 1998 25th Anniversary

$16^L \times 8^W \times 11^H$

| Form No: | 12297 |
|---|---|
| Tie-On: | 32492 |
| No.Sold: | |

*Available to Members from April 1 – 30, 1998.*

**O.** 1998 Thyme

$4.5^{RD} \times 3^H$

| Form No: | 19224 |
|---|---|
| No.Sold: | |

*Free to Members who hosted a show in June 98 and received 2 bookings.*

**P.** 1998 Harbor

$10^L \times 8.25^W \times 8.25^H$

| Form No: | 10677 |
|---|---|
| No. Sold: | |

**R.** 1998 Ornament

$3.5^{RD}$

| Form No: | 32506 |
|---|---|
| No.Sold: | |

*"Shopping on Main Street – Edition 1998"*

**S.** 1999 Renewal

$6.75^L \times 5.75^W \times 4.75^H$

| Form No: | 12998 |
|---|---|
| No.Sold: | |

*Available only within 90 days after membership renewal.*

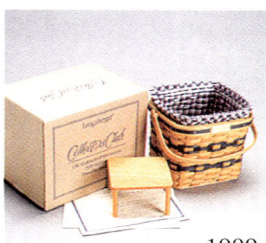

**T.** 1999 Miniature Two-Pie

$4.75^L \times 5^W \times 4^H$

| Form No: | 19356 |
|---|---|
| No. Sold: | |

*Available to Members from Nov. 21, 1998 through Dec. 31, 1999.*

**V.** 1999 Mini Server and Pie Plates

$4^{RD} \times 6^H$

| Form No: | 76902 |
|---|---|
| Pie Plates: | 35581 |

*First piece of Miniature Wrought Iron offered.*

**W.** 1999 Serving Tray

$20^L \times 14^W \times 3.75^H$

| Form No: | 15849 |
|---|---|
| No. Sold: | |

*Unlike other Club items, this item **could** be purchased with Hostess half-price benefits.*

**X.** 1999 Ornament

$3.5^{RD}$

| Form No: | 35599 |
|---|---|
| No. Sold: | |

*This is the final ornament in the series of four.*

**COLLECTORS CLUB™**

| Photo | Description | Original | Avg. | High |
|---|---|---|---|---|
| | **MARKET VALUES** | | | |
| | with **P**rotector | 260.00 | — | — |
| | with **L**iner | 270.00 | — | — |
| | Combo (**P/L**) | 305.00 | 315 | 350 |
| | Full Set (**C/Lid**) | 364.00 | 342 | 500 |
| Y. | 1999 Napkins - Set of 2 | 10.00 | 13 | 23 |
| Y. | 1999 Place Mats - Set of 2 | 20.00 | — | — |
| | 1999 Handle Tie[np] | 7.00 | 8 | 10 |
| Z. | 1999 Tapestry Throw | 60.00 | 77 | 180 |
| A¹ | 1999 Homestead™ | | | |
| | Combo (**P/L**) | 79.00 | 101 | 149 |
| | Full Set (**C/Lid**) | 106.00 | 107 | 165 |
| A¹ | 1999 Homestead Tie-On | 8.00 | 14 | 16 |
| | ***2000 Items:*** | | | |
| B¹ | 2000 Renewal Basket™ | 44.00 | 62 | 70 |
| | with **P**rotector | 48.00 | — | — |
| | with **L**iner | 61.00 | — | — |
| | Combo (**P/L**) | 65.00 | 72 | 95 |
| | Miniatures | | | |
| C¹ | 00  J.W. Bread & Milk® | 130.00 | 140 | 175 |
| | with **P**rotector | 134.00 | — | — |
| | with **L**iner | 145.00 | — | — |
| | Combo (**P/L**) | 149.00 | 158 | 200 |
| D¹ | 00-01 J.W. Banker's Waste® | 150.00 | — | — |
| | with **P**rotector | 154.00 | — | — |
| | with **L**iner | 165.00 | — | — |
| | Combo (**P/L**) | 169.00 | 182 | 190 |
| | with **L**id | 165.00 | — | — |
| | Full Set (**C/Lid**) | 184.00 | — | — |
| E¹ | 00-01 J.W. Gathering® | 130.00 | 137 | 164 |
| | with **P**rotector | 134.00 | — | — |
| | with **L**iner | 145.00 | — | — |
| | Combo (**P/L**) | 149.00 | 150 | 200 |
| | Miniature Pottery | | | |
| E¹ | 2000 Baking Dish | 0.00 | 62 | 82 |
| F¹ | 2000 Milk Pitcher | 30.00 | 54 | 90 |
| G¹ | 2000 Century Celebration™ | 59.00 | 75 | 80 |
| | with **P**rotector | 66.00 | — | — |
| | with **L**iner | 78.00 | — | — |
| | Combo (**P/L**) | 85.00 | 95 | 140 |
| | Full Set (**Combo/Lid**) | 117.00 | 130 | 160 |
| H¹ | 2000 Spring Meadow™ | 95.00 | 111 | 150 |
| | with **P**rotector | 104.00 | — | — |
| | with **L**iner | 121.00 | — | — |
| | Combo (**P/L**) | 130.00 | 116 | 190 |
| H¹ | 2000 Cottage Gate™ Tie-On | 0.00 | 10 | 18 |
| I¹ | 2000 Small Saddlebrook™ | 79.00 | 85 | 95 |
| | with **P**rotector | 83.00 | 115 | 110 |
| I¹ | 2000 Large Saddlebrook™ | 139.00 | 140 | 150 |
| | with **P**rotector | 148.00 | 155 | 200 |
| J¹ | 2000 Shaker Harmony No.1™ | 95.00 | 126 | 175 |
| | Combo (**P/Lid**) | 107.00 | 141 | 180 |
| K¹ | 2000 Snow Days Ornament™ | 32.00 | 35 | 40 |

**Y.** 1999 Family Picnic

$20^L$ x $14^W$ x $9.5^H$

Form No: 13561
Napkins: 2363941
Place Mats: 2353141

*Fabric items sold separately.*

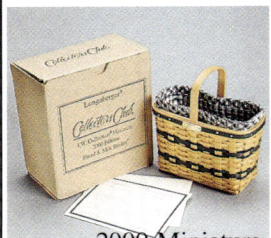

**C¹** 2000 Miniature Bread & Milk

$6.25^L$ x $3.25^W$ x $4.25^H$

Form No: 13391
No. Sold:

*Offered to Members from Jan – Dec 2000.*

**G¹** 2000 Century Celebration

$10.5^L$ x $6.25^W$ x $4.75^H$

Form No: 15385
Tie-On: 36196

*Special pewter tag. Lid and Tie-On were not exclusive to Members. Century Celebration logo on bottom.*

**Z.** 1999 Tapestry Throw

$67^L$ x $46^W$

Form No: 71587
No. Sold:

*Special feature offered from Aug. – Nov. 1999.*

**A¹** 1999 Homestead

$10^{RD}$ x $6.25^H$

Form No: 6609596
Tie-On: 37541

*Sold only as a Combo. Club version has a tag. Lid and Tie-On were not exclusive to Members.*

**B¹** 2000 Renewal

$6.75^L$ x $5.25^W$ x $3.25^H$

Form No: 18783
No. Sold:

*New form. Renewing Members had to purchase it within 30 days of renewal.*

**D¹** 2000-01 Miniature Banker's Waste

$5.25^{RD}$ x $5.25^H$

Form No: 16578
No. Sold:

*Offered to Members from Nov 2000 – Dec 2001.*

**E¹** 2000-01 Miniature Gathering

$7^L$ x $4.5^W$ x $2^H$

Mini Gathering: 18941
Mini Baking Dish: 37974

*Dish was available only as a FREE item when purchasing the Mini Gathering® from 7/00 – 8/00.*

**F¹** 2000 Miniature Milk Pitcher

$1.75^{RD}$ x $2.25^H$

Form No: 36242
No. Sold:

*Offered to Members from Apr – Aug 2000. Promoted along with the Miniature Bread & Milk®.*

**H¹** 2000 Spring Meadow

$16.25^L$ x $10.75^W$ x $4^H$

Form No: 17655
Tie-On: 73326

*The Cottage Gate Tie-on was the first pewter tie-on for club members. It was given free to members.*

**I¹** 2000 Saddlebrook

Sm: $5.5^L$ x $3.5^W$ x $4^H$
Lg: $9.5^L$ x $5.5^W$ x $9.25^H$
Form No: Small: 15679
Large: 15776

*Offered from Sept 2000 – Feb 2001.*

**J¹** 2000 Shaker No.1

$10.75^L$ x $9.75^W$ x $4.5^H$

Form No: 19089
No. Sold:

*First in this series of five Shaker baskets. Basket came with a lid. Protector sold separately. No liner.*

## MARKET VALUES

| Photo | Description | Original | Avg. | High |
|---|---|---|---|---|
| | **2001 Items:** | | | |
| L[1] | 2001 Renewal Basket™ | 45.00 | — | — |
| | with Protector | 52.00 | — | — |
| | with Liner | 62.00 | — | — |
| | Combo (P/L) | 69.00 | — | — |
| M[1] | 2001 Charter Member | | | |
| | 5-Yr Anniversary | 99.00 | **126** | **150** |
| | with Protector | 107.00 | — | — |
| | with Liner | 123.00 | — | — |
| | Combo (P/L) | 131.00 | **150** | **154** |
| | Miniatures | | | |
| N[1] | 01-02 J.W. Berry® | 85.00 | **85** | **100** |
| | with Protector | 87.00 | — | — |
| | with Liner | 97.00 | — | — |
| | Combo (P/L) | 99.00 | **101** | **128** |
| O[1] | 01-02 J.W. Corn® | 185.00 | — | — |
| | with Protector | 189.00 | — | — |
| | with Liner | 200.00 | — | — |
| | Combo (P/L) | 204.00 | — | — |
| | Full Set (C/Lid) | 221.00 | — | — |
| | Miniature Pottery | | | |
| P[1] | 2001 Set of 3 Mini Bowls | 59.00 | **64** | **100** |
| P[1] | 2001 Mini Bowl Stand | 39.00 | **50** | **65** |
| | Combo (w/bowls) | 98.00 | **103** | **135** |
| Q[1] | 2001 Whistle Stop™ | 89.00 | **100** | **130** |
| | with Protector | 98.00 | — | — |
| | with Liner | 109.00 | — | — |
| | Combo (P/L) | 118.00 | **130** | **175** |
| | Full Set (C/Lid) | 141.00 | **146** | **198** |
| Q[1] | 2001 Large Star Tie-On™ | 10.00 | **14** | **18** |
| R[1] | 2001 Gathering Event™ | 55.00 | — | — |
| | with Protector | 64.00 | — | — |
| | with Liner | 79.00 | — | — |
| | Combo (P/L) [np] | 88.00 | — | — |
| | 2001 Gathering Tie-On™ | 5.00 | — | — |
| | Shaker Harmony Baskets | | | |
| S[1] | 2001 Shaker Harmony No.2 | 89.00 | **111** | **129** |
| | Combo (P/Lid) | 99.00 | **114** | **135** |
| S[1] | 2001 Shaker Harmony No.3™ | 79.00 | **88** | **105** |
| | Combo (P/Lid) | 85.00 | **93** | **119** |
| S[1] | 2001 Shaker Harmony No.5™ | 40.00 | — | — |
| | with Protector | 44.00 | — | — |
| | with Lid | 55.00 | **57** | **75** |
| | Combo (P/Lid) | 59.00 | **72** | **90** |
| T[1] | 2001 Sewing Circle™ | 75.00 | **124** | **132** |
| | with Protector | 83.00 | — | — |
| | with Liner | 104.00 | — | — |
| | Combo (P/L) | 112.00 | **135** | **145** |
| | with Lid | 100.00 | — | — |
| | Full Set (C/Lid) | 145.00 | **153** | **185** |
| U[1] | 2001 Dustin Snowflake | | | |
| | Snow Day Ornament™ | 32.00 | — | — |
| | **2002 Items:** | | | |
| V[1] | 2002 Renewal Basket™ | 39.00 | — | — |
| | with Protector | 43.00 | — | — |
| | with Liner | 54.00 | — | — |
| | Combo (P/L) | 58.00 | — | — |

**K[1]** Kaitlin Snowflake

3.75RD

Form No: 36269
No. Sold:

*First in a series of five ornaments featuring snowflakes designed by Tami & Rachel's children.*

2001-02
**O[1]** Miniature Corn

7.75RD x 4.25H

Form No: 11466
No. Sold:

2001 Shaker
**S[1]** Harmony Baskets

<u>No.5</u>: 6.75L x 4.75W x 2H
<u>No.3</u>: 8.75L x 6.75W x 3.25H
<u>No.2</u>: 9.75L x 7.75W x 4H

Form No:
No.5: 18881
No.3: 16870
No.2: 18988

**L¹** 2001 Renewal

$5^{RD}$ x $6^H$

Form No: 10813
Charter: 10273

*Charter Members were noted on the tag. Frame was given free with each renewal.*

**M¹** 2001 Five-Year Anniversary

$6^L$ x $5^W$ x $8.25^H$

Form No: 17345
No. Sold:

*Pin was given Free with each renewal.*

**N¹** 2001-02 Miniature Berry

$3.5^L$ x $3.5^W$ x $3^H$

Form No: 10842
No. Sold:

**P¹** 2001 Mini Bowls with Stand

$4^L$ x $3^W$ x $9^H$

Form No: 75825
Bowls: 31944

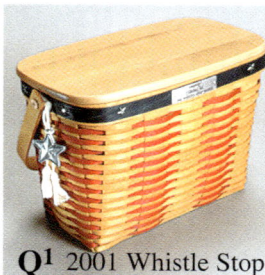

**Q¹** 2001 Whistle Stop

$10.75^L$ x $6.25^W$ x $7.75^H$

Form No: 10303
Tie-On: 73954
No. Sold:

*Woven from a new form. First time for the company to use shaped tacks.*

**R¹** 2001 Gathering Event

$12^L$ x $6.75^W$ x $3.5^H$

Form No: 11222
No. Sold:

*Members who attended Gathering Events were able to purchase these baskets.*

**T¹** 2001 Sewing Circle

$8.5^{RD}$ x $5.5^H$

Form No: 10575
No. Sold:

**U¹** 2001 Dustin Snowflake

$3.5^L$ x $3.75^H$

Form No: 39365
No. Sold:

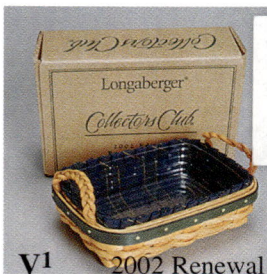

**V¹** 2002 Renewal

$6.25^L$ x $5^W$ x $1.75^H$

Form No: 12081
No. Sold:

**51**

# Family Signatures

J.W. Longaberger was born in 1902.  He left high school at age 17 to help his father make baskets full-time.  He married Bonnie Jean Gist (Grandma Bonnie) in 1927.  They had twelve children between 1928 and 1945.  J.W. continued making baskets while he worked during the day at the Dresden Paper Mill.  He sold each basket for about $1.50.  Dave Longaberger joined his father making baskets in 1972.  J.W. had since stopped making baskets for sale, but agreed to make a few for Dave to sell.  J.W. passed away at age 71 before The Longaberger Company® was established.

**Bonnie Jean**
"Grandma Bonnie"
Born:
            July 16, 1908

## The Longaberger Children:

**Genevieve**          **#1**
Born:          Mar. 25, 1928
Spouse:          Piercy Hard

**Wendy Jean**          **#2**
Born:     Dec. 16, 1929
Spouse:          Bob Little

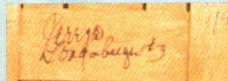

**Jerry Dean**          **#3**
Born:  Nov. 23, 1931
Spouse:          Donna

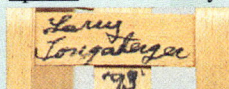

**Dale "Larry"**     **#4**
Born:          June 3, 1933

**David Wendell #5**
Born:     Dec. 7, 1934
Died:     Mar. 17, 1999

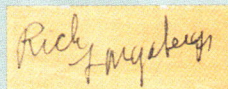

**Richard Lee**          **#6**
Born:  Dec. 18, 1936
Spouse:          Joanne

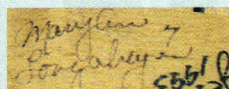

**Maryann**          **#7**
Born:  Nov. 29, 1937
Spouse:
  Wendell McCafferty

**Judy Kay**          **#8**
Born:  Sept. 19, 1939

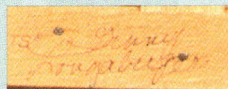

**"Ginny" Lou**          **#9**
Born:          Oct. 8, 1940
Spouse: Dick Wilcox

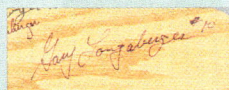

**Gary Conway #10**
Born:          Jan. 6, 1943

**Carmen Lynn**          **#11**
Born:          Nov. 23, 1943
Spouse:     Ronald Fortney

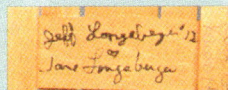

**Jeff Carl**          **#12**
Born:  Mar. 11, 1945
Spouse:          Jane

## Dave's Children:

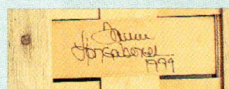

**Tami Lynne**          **#1**

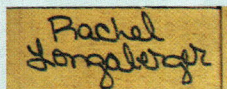

**Rachel Lynne**     **#2**

**Regina Lemanowicz**
**Vista, California**

*While still living in Indiana, Regina became enamoured with Longaberger Baskets®. Her first basket was the 1993 Bayberry™, however, her favorite collection is the May Series™. Regina uses her baskets for storage, because according to her, in California they believe in "tall ceilings, but small closets".*

## Cookie Molds

The stands being used to display the Cookie Molds and books throughout this section were not originally sold with the items. They are being used for photography purposes only.

**A.** 1990 Father Christmas 8.5^H

Form No:          30066
No. Sold:

### MARKET VALUES

| Photo | Description | Original | Avg. | High |
|---|---|---|---|---|
| | **Santa Series™** | | | |
| A. | 1990  Father Christmas™ | 18.95 | **40** | **60** |
| B. | 1990  1st Casting™ | 18.95 | **92** | **106** |
| C. | 1991  Kriss Kringle™ | 18.95 | **19** | **40** |
| D. | 1992  Santa Claus™ | 18.95 | **12** | **29** |
| E. | 1993  St.Nick™ | 18.95 | **11** | **35** |
| | Santa Series Full Set of 4 | | **165** | **200** |
| | **Angel Series™** | | | |
| F. | 1993  Peace™ | 18.95 | **12** | **25** |
| G. | 1994  Hope™ | 19.95 | **11** | **20** |
| H. | 1995  Love™ | 19.95 | **13** | **26** |
| I. | 1996  Joy™ | 19.95 | **13** | **22** |
| | **Easter Series™** | | | |
| J. | 1994  Mama & Baby Bunny™ | 18.95 | **9** | **18** |
| K. | 1994  Bunnies Book™ | 5.95 | **9** | **18** |
| L. | 1995  Grandpa Bunny & Herbie™ | 19.95 | **10** | **27** |

**E.** 1993 St. Nick 10.25^H

Form No:          31062
No. Sold:

f   u   n   **f a c t**

An excerpt from The Longaberger Company's *Vision Statement*

"Our vision is to be the leading designer and provider of natural, handcrafted, American-made baskets and other goods for the home. We are so passionate about our craft as we are about our relationships with our family of collectors, sales associates, employees, suppliers and the communities in which we live... "

**I.** 1996 Joy 9^H

Form No:          31721
No. Sold:

**B.** 1990 1st Casting
### 8.5$^H$
| | |
|---|---|
| Form No: | 30066 |
| No. Sold: | 3,200 |

*Inscription reads:
"Longaberger Pottery – First
Casting– Christmas 1990".*

**C.** 1991 Kriss Kringle
### 8.5$^H$
| | |
|---|---|
| Form No: | 30180 |
| No. Sold: | |

**D.** 1992 Santa Claus
### 7.25$^H$
| | |
|---|---|
| Form No: | 30457 |
| No. Sold: | |

**F.** 1993 Peace
### 7.5$^H$
| | |
|---|---|
| Form No: | 31071 |
| No. Sold: | |

*First year for
this Series.*

**G.** 1994 Hope
### 9$^H$
| | |
|---|---|
| Form No: | 31356 |
| No. Sold: | |

**H.** 1995 Love
### 7.5$^H$
| | |
|---|---|
| Form No: | 32468 |
| No. Sold: | |

**J.** 1994 Mama &
Baby Bunny
### 6.25$^H$
| | |
|---|---|
| Form No: | 31151 |
| No. Sold: | |

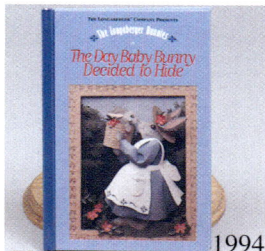

**K.** 1994 Bunnies Book
| | |
|---|---|
| Form No: | 72079 |
| No. Sold: | |

**L.** 1995 Grandpa &Herbie
### 6.25$^L$ x 4.75$^H$
| | |
|---|---|
| Form No: | 31500 |
| No. Sold: | |

*The 1994 Book was available only with a purchase.
Only Hostesses were able to buy it for $5.95 and no
additional purchase necessary.*

# Cookie Molds

**All Angel and Easter Series Cookie Molds are made from Ivory Bisque Pottery and come with a gift box.**

## MARKET VALUES

| Photo | | Description | Original | Avg. | High |
|---|---|---|---|---|---|

### Easter Series™ (con't)

| | | | Original | Avg. | High |
|---|---|---|---|---|---|
| M. | 1995 | Bunnies™ Book | 14.95 | **10** | **15** |
| N. | 1996 | Rosemary Bunny™ | 19.95 | **11** | **26** |
| O. | 1997 | Grandma Bunny & Lavender™ | 19.95 | **10** | **23** |

### Gingerbread Series™

| | | | | | |
|---|---|---|---|---|---|
| P. | 1995 | Country Cottage™ | 29.95 | **10** | **22** |
| Q. | 1996 | Country Cabin™ | 29.95 | **14** | **33** |
| R. | 1997 | Holiday Home™ | 29.95 | **14** | **30** |

### Snow Friends Series™

| | | | | | |
|---|---|---|---|---|---|
| S. | 1997 | Chilly™ | 19.95 | **12** | **29** |
| T. | 1998 | Sleigh Belle™ | 20.00 | **10** | **13** |
| U. | 1999 | Set of 2 Flurry™ Snowball™ | 20.00 | **12** | **20** |
| V. | 2000 | Roger & Ginger™ | 20.00 | **12** | **20** |

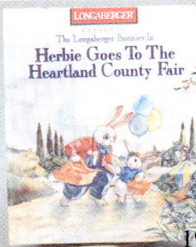

**M.** 1995 Bunnies Book

Form No: 72796
No. Sold:

*Last year that a book was offered.*

**Q.** 1996 Country Cabin

$9^L$ x $13.25^W$

Form No: 33090
No. Sold:

**U.** 1999 Flurry & Snowball

$2.75^L$ x $4.75^W$

Form No: 36994
No. Sold:

*Sold only as a set.*

**N.** 1996 Rosemary Bunny
6.5<sup>L</sup> x 4.25<sup>H</sup>

Form No: 32182
No. Sold:

**O.** 1997 Grandma & Lavender
4.5<sup>L</sup> x 6.5<sup>W</sup>

Form No: 32191
No. Sold:

**P.** 1995 Country Cottage
9<sup>L</sup> x 13.25<sup>W</sup>

Form No: 32476
No. Sold:

*First year for this Series.*

**R.** 1997 Holiday Home
9<sup>L</sup> x 13.25<sup>H</sup>

Form No: 34720
No.Sold:

*Last year for this series.*

**S.** 1997 Chilly
7.5<sup>L</sup> x 4.25<sup>H</sup>

Form No: 34827
No.Sold:

*First year for this Series.*

**T.** 1998 Sleigh Belle
6<sup>L</sup> x 7.5<sup>H</sup>

Form No: 32484
No.Sold:

**V.** 2000 Roger & Gonger
4<sup>W</sup> x 5<sup>H</sup>

Form No: 36536
No. Sold:

*Sold only as a set.*

**SMILE!** we can't help but smile with all those gorgeous baskets around!

**TINA WYATT** Geneva, Ohio

# Heisey Tour Plates

The Heisey Glass Company has become a household name in the homes of many Longaberger Collectors. The special edition Heisey Horse(pg.214) that was commissioned by Longaberger in 1998 to celebrate the Crawford Barn Raising is now selling in the market for more than <u>any</u> baskets from the J.W. Collection®.

Surprisingly, the successful Heisey Horses were not their first project with The Longaberger Company. In 1995, the Heisey Tour Plates, pictured above, debuted in the Longaberger stores throughout Dresden. Because they were an item produced for stores only, they have not been featured in the Bentley. However, there is enough activity in the secondary market to bring it to your attention as an *Item to Watch*.

The 1995 Pink plate originally sold for $21 and was limited to 2,200 pieces. In the next years, production was increased to 5,500 for both the 1996 Blue Plates and the 1997 Green Plates. The series ended in 1998 when the final Yellow Plate incurred production problems with its unique yellow color. There were only 618 pieces made of this final plate.

There have been reports of some counterfeit Yellow plates that resulted in production errors not being destroyed at the factory. The faux pieces are more vibrant yellow and do not come with a product card and box, as the others did.

## Pat McCafferty
### Magalia, California

*Pat travels the world in her RV and takes a lot of her baskets with her. Guess you can say her baskets are "world travelers". Her first basket was the Shamrock™ but her favorite is the Peony™. In her many travels she tries to detour to Dresden to get some of her baskets signed and has been fortunate enough to have a Tour Basket signed by Grandma Bonnie.*

## Crisco® American™

**Red and Blue Weave and Trim.**
**Burned in Crisco® Logo.**
**Series completed in 1993.**

### MARKET VALUES

| Photo | Description | | Original | Avg. | High |
|---|---|---|---|---|---|
| A. | 1991 | Pie™ | 79.95 | **303** | 400 |
| | | with Protector | 89.90 | **318** | 480 |
| B. | 1992 | Cookie™ | 29.95 | **93** | 175 |
| | | with Protector | 35.90 | **128** | 195 |
| | | with Liner | 40.90 | **130** | 175 |
| | | Combo (P/L) | 39.95 | **143** | 195 |
| C. | 1992 | Crisco Apron | 13.95 | **33** | 50 |
| D. | 1993 | Baking™ | 39.95 | **105** | 120 |
| | | with Protector | 44.90 | **107** | 130 |
| | | with Liner | 48.90 | **107** | 140 |
| | | Combo (P/L) | 45.95 | **109** | 175 |
| | Full Crisco® Collection Set | | | **636** | 800 |

Crisco® is a registered trademark of
The Procter & Gamble Company.

### collection **note**

The Crisco® American Series started in 1991 when The Longaberger Company® was invited to create the official Pie Basket for the Crisco American Pie Celebration Bake-Off in New Orleans. Each of the 50 participants received the basket and then the company made it available to their customers to purchase. Although these baskets were sold during the All-American promotional season, they <u>are</u> <u>not</u> part of the All-American Series™. They were, however, designed to compliment that collection.

**A.** 1991 Pie

$12^L$ x $12^W$ x $6^H$

Form No: 100-DBRS
No. Sold:

*Sold with a divider.*

**B.** 1992 Cookie

$10^{RD}$ x $4^H$

Form No: 10081
No. Sold: 153,447

**C.** 1992 Apron

Form No: 20028
No. Sold:

*Not included in the Combo. Sold separately.*

**D.** 1993 Baking

$14.5^L$ x $7.5^W$ x $3.75^H$

Form No: 14745
No. Sold:

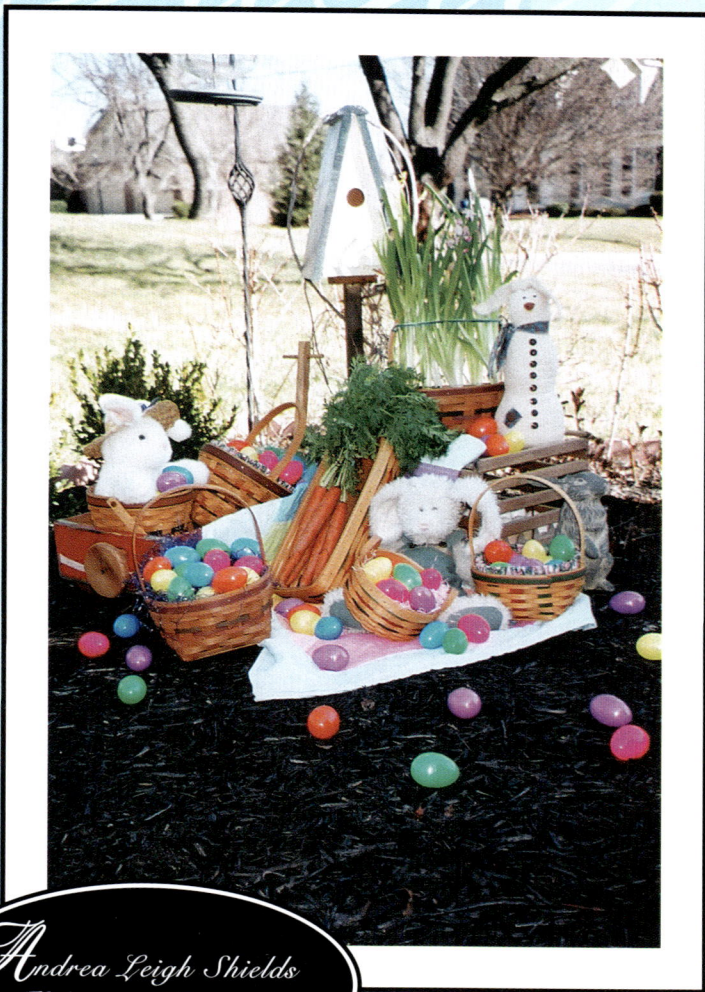

*Andrea Leigh Shields*
*Hebron, Kentucky*

*Andrea's favorite basket is the 2001 Horizon of Hope*®*, which was given to her by her grandmother who has breast cancer. Her biggest find was a 2000 8" Generations with protector & liner for which she paid only $2! Her other big find was a Traditions Family*™ *basket with 13 signatures, including Dave, Bonnie & Tami's! Not bad for a day of shopping!*

EASTER SERIES

# Easter Series™

**One stationary handle, except 1987 Medium Chore.**

## MARKET VALUES

| Photo | Description | Original | Avg. | High |
|---|---|---|---|---|
| | **1987** Easter Signature Series | | | |
| A. | Medium Chore™ | 28.95 | **198** | **300** |
| B. | Single Pie™ | 28.95 | **193** | **300** |
| C. | Small Gathering™ | 28.95 | **172** | **225** |
| D. | Spring™ | 25.95 | **228** | **300** |
| E. | **1988** Baby Easter™ | 18.95 | **74** | **117** |
| F. | Small Easter™ | 22.95 | **68** | **90** |
| G. | Medium Easter™ | 28.95 | **84** | **105** |
| H. | Large Easter™ | 32.95 | **87** | **110** |
| | **1989** Stained Easter™ [np] | 29.95 | **86** | **110** |
| I. | Blue Easter™ | 29.95 | **76** | **105** |
| J. | Pink Easter™ | 29.95 | **70** | **90** |
| K. | **1990** Medium™ | 38.95 | **55** | **100** |
| L. | Large™ | 43.95 | **63** | **110** |

[np] = Not Pictured

## collection **note**

Each of the *Easter Signature Baskets* from 1987 were delivered with Dave Longaberger's signature on it. In addition, only 100 total baskets also have Grandma Bonnie's signature.

**A.** 1987 Medium Chore
$13^L$ x $8^W$ x $5^H$

Form No: 3500-CX
No. Sold:

*Easter Signature Series: Blue, red and green weave. Signed by Dave.*

**E.** 1988 Baby Easter
$7^L$ x $5^W$ x $3.5^H$

Form No: 700-AN
No. Sold:

*Available in natural only; blue, green, lilac, or pink weave.*

**I.** 1989 Blue Easter
$10^{RD}$ x $4^H$

Form No: 5500-ABS
No. Sold:

*Available stained only; pink or blue weave, or no color.*

**B.** 1987 Single Pie

$12^L$ x $12^W$ x $4^H$

Form No: 2200-AX
No. Sold:

*Easter Signature Series:
Blue, red and green
weave. Signed by Dave.*

**C.** 1987 Small Gathering

$14^L$ x $9^W$ x $4.5^H$

Form No: 2300-AX
No. Sold:

*Easter Signature Series:
Blue, red and green
weave. Signed by Dave.*

**D.** 1987 Spring

$11^L$ x $8^W$ x $5.5^H$

Form No: 900-AX
No. Sold:

*Easter Signature Series:
Blue, red and green
weave. Signed by Dave.*

**F.** 1988 Small Easter

$10^L$ x $6^W$ x $4^H$

Form No: 3400-AN
No. Sold:

*Available in natural
only; blue, green, lilac,
or pink weave.*

**G.** 1988 Medium Easter

$13^L$ x $8^W$ x $5^H$

Form No: 3500-AN
No. Sold:

*Available in natural
only; blue, green, lilac,
or pink weave.*

**H.** 1988 Large Easter

$14^L$ x $7.75^W$ x $5.25^H$

Form No: 3600-AN
No. Sold:

*Available in natural
only; blue, green, lilac,
or pink weave.*

**J.** 1989 Pink Easter

$10^{RD}$ x $4^H$

Form No: 5500-APS
No. Sold:

*Available stained only;
pink or blue weave, or
no color.*

**K.** 1990 Medium Easter

$8^{RD}$ x $4.5^H$

Form No: 40000-APVBS
No. Sold:

*Available stained only;
Dresden blue, violet
and pink weave.*

**L.** 1990 Large Easter

$9.5^{RD}$ x $5^H$

Form No: 41000-APVBS
No. Sold:

*Available stained only;
Dresden blue, violet and
pink weave.*

## Easter Series™

**This series is usually promoted during the months of January and February.**

| Photo | | Description | Original | Avg. | High |
|---|---|---|---|---|---|
| M | 1991 | Customer™ | 26.95 | **36** | **60** |
| N. | | Hostess™ | 21.95 | **35** | **70** |
| O. | 1992 | Easter™ | 27.95 | **50** | **75** |
| | | with **P**rotector | 32.90 | **60** | **75** |
| | | with **L**iner | 40.90 | **60** | **75** |
| | | Combo (**P/L**) | 39.95 | **62** | **80** |
| P. | 1993 | Small Easter™ | 24.95 | **44** | **60** |
| | | with **P**rotector | 28.90 | **58** | **60** |
| | | with **L**iner | 34.90 | **58** | **60** |
| | | Combo (**P/L**) | 35.95 | **60** | **75** |
| Q. | 1993 | Large Easter™ | 27.95 | **60** | **80** |
| | | with **P**rotector | 32.90 | **60** | **85** |
| | | with **L**iner | 38.90 | **62** | **85** |
| | | Combo (**P/L**) | 38.95 | **67** | **93** |
| R. | 1994 | Easter™ | 49.95 | **51** | **75** |
| | | with **P**rotector | 55.90 | **52** | **75** |
| | | with **L**iner | 65.90 | **52** | **75** |
| | | Combo (**P/L**) | 59.95 | **55** | **80** |
| S. | 1995 | Easter™ | 49.95 | **55** | **80** |
| | | with **P**rotector | 55.90 | **55** | **80** |
| | | with **L**iner | 65.90 | **55** | **80** |
| | | Combo (**P/L**) | 59.95 | **60** | **86** |
| S. | 1995 | Happy Easter Tie-On | 6.95 | **9** | **15** |
| T. | 1996 | Easter™ | 39.95 | **60** | **83** |
| | | with **P**rotector | 44.90 | **63** | **85** |
| | | with **L**iner | 54.90 | **63** | **85** |
| | | Combo (**P/L**) | 49.95 | **53** | **85** |
| | 1996 | Easter Egg Tie-On | 6.95 | **12** | **15** |
| U. | 1997 | Small Easter™ | | | |
| | | Combo (**P/L**) | 29.95 | **41** | **65** |
| U | 1997 | Large Easter™ | 42.95 | **55** | **60** |
| | | with **P**rotector | 48.90 | **55** | **60** |
| | | with **L**iner | 57.90 | **60** | **80** |
| | | Combo (**P/L**) | 52.95 | **61** | **80** |
| U. | 1997 | Easter Tie-On | 6.95 | **13** | **18** |
| V. | 1998 | Small Easter™ | 32.95 | **45** | **55** |
| | | with **P**rotector | 36.90 | **45** | **55** |
| | | with **L**iner | 43.90 | **45** | **60** |
| | | Combo (**P/L**) | 29.95 | **34** | **50** |
| V. | 1998 | Large Easter™ | 43.95 | **—** | **—** |
| | | with **P**rotector | 48.90 | **—** | **—** |
| | | with **L**iner | 58.90 | **—** | **—** |
| | | Combo (**P/L**) | 52.95 | **60** | **75** |
| V. | 1998 | Easter Tie-On | 6.95 | **10** | **12** |

**M.** 1991 Customer

$11^L$ x $8^W$ x $5.5^H$

Form No: 900-ATM*
No. Sold:

*Available stained or natural; teal and mauve 3/8" weave.*

**Q.** 1993 Large Easter

$10^L$ x $6^W$ x $4^H$

Form No: 13439/13412†
No. Sold:

*Available stained or natural; teal shoestring weave.*

**U.** 1997 Easter

Sm: $8.5^L$ x $5^W$ x $3.5^H$
Lg: $12^L$ x $7^W$ x $4.5^H$

Small: 63541/63550†
Large: 13447/13455†
Tie-On: 30007

*Available stained or natural. Small only available as Combo and with a $42.95 purchase.*

**N.** 1991 Hostess

$7^L$ x $5^W$ x $3.5^H$

Form No: 700-ATM•
No. Sold:

*Available stained or natural; teal and mauve 3/8" weave.*

**O.** 1992 Easter

$10.5^L$ x $7.5^W$ x $4.5^H$

Form No:34000-APVCNK
No. Sold:

*Available stained or natural; Dresden blue, violet and pink weave.*

**P.** 1993 Small Easter

$7^L$ x $5^W$ x $3.5^H$

Form No: 10774/10766†
No. Sold:

*Available stained or natural; teal shoestring weave.*

**R.** 1994 Easter

$13.5^L$ x $8.25^W$ x $5.25^H$

Form No: 16926/16934
          16900/16918†
No. Sold:

*Available stained, natural, stained with color or natural with color; Heartland® blue with pink accent weave.*

**S.** 1995 Easter

$10.75^L$ x $8.75^W$ x $5.25^H$

Form No:        18708
Tie-On:         31518
No. Sold:       109,970

*Available stained only; rose pink and purple weave. Tie-On sold separately.*

**T.** 1996 Easter

$7.5^L$ x $5^W$ x $6^H$

Form No: 12912/12939†
Tie-On:         32271
No. Sold:       220,416

*Available stained or natural; pink, green and purple double shoestring weave with purple and green.*

**V.** 1998 Easter

Sm: $6^L$ x $6^W$ x $3^H$

Lg: $9^L$ x $9^W$ x $4.5^H$

Small:  11959/11967†
Large:  11851/11860†
Tie-On:         34100

*Both baskets available in stained or natural.*

f   u   n   **f a c t**

The new *Tiny Tote Basket*™ just introduced into the *Classic Line,* was inspired by the 1950's circa "plastic purse".

† = Product numbers are stated:  Stained/ Natural weave.

## Easter Series ™

**Since 1991, Easter Baskets have been offered in both the stained and unstained finishes, with the exception of 1995.**

**W.** 1999 Easter

Sm: $5.75^L$ x $5.75^W$ x $3^H$
Lg: $7.5^L$ x $7.5^W$ x $3.75^H$
Small:    14052 / 14168†
Large:    14061 / 14265†
Tie-On:              35637

*†Both baskets available in stained or unstained finishes.*

### MARKET VALUES

| | Description | Original | Avg. | High |
|---|---|---|---|---|
| W. | 1999 Small Easter™ | 33.00 | **50** | **60** |
| | with Protector | 37.00 | **53** | **60** |
| | with Liner | 45.00 | **53** | **60** |
| | with Divider | 42.00 | **53** | **60** |
| | Combo (P/L/Div) | 49.00 | **55** | **90** |
| W. | 1999 Large Easter™ | 39.00 | **50** | **60** |
| | with Protector | 44.00 | **53** | **60** |
| | with Liner | 54.00 | **53** | **60** |
| | with Divider | 50.00 | **53** | **60** |
| | Combo (P/L/Div) | 59.00 | **74** | **110** |
| W. | 1999 Easter Tie-On | 8.00 | **14** | **16** |
| X. | 2000 Jelly Bean™ | 34.00 | **45** | **52** |
| | with Protector | 37.00 | **49** | **53** |
| | with Liner | 46.00 | — | — |
| | Combo (P/L) | 42.00 | **54** | **100** |
| X. | 2000 Jelly Bean Tie-On | 8.00 | **11** | **15** |
| X. | 2000 Large Easter™ | 65.00 | **70** | **85** |
| | with Protector | 72.00 | — | — |
| | with Liner | 86.00 | — | — |
| | Combo (P/L) | 79.00 | **97** | **150** |
| | Full Set (C/Riser) | 85.00 | **115** | **145** |
| X. | 2000 Happy Easter Tie-On | 8.00 | **11** | **15** |
| Y. | 2001 Small Easter™ | 35.00 | **47** | **66** |
| | with Protector | 39.00 | — | — |
| | with Liner | 47.00 | — | — |
| | with Divider | 44.00 | — | — |
| | Combo (P/L/Div) | 49.00 | **50** | **80** |
| Y. | 2001 Small Bunny Tie-On | 7.00 | **10** | **14** |
| Y. | 2001 Bunny Divider | 9.00 | — | — |
| Y. | 2001 Large Easter™ | 65.00 | **84** | **95** |
| | with Protector | 74.00 | — | — |
| | with Liner | 87.00 | — | — |
| | Combo (P/L) | 79.00 | **92** | **115** |
| Y. | 2001 Large Bunny Tie-On | 9.00 | **12** | **18** |
| Y. | 2001-02 Glass Egg Plate | 29.00 | **31** | **60** |
| Z. | 2002 Small Easter™ | 44.00 | — | — |
| | with Protector | 49.00 | — | — |
| | with Liner | 60.00 | — | — |
| | Combo (P/L) | 59.00 | **59** | **70** |
| Z. | 2002 Baby Chick Tie-On | 8.00 | **9** | **10** |
| Z. | 2002 Large Easter™ | 69.00 | — | — |
| | with Protector | 77.00 | — | — |
| | with Liner | 90.00 | — | — |
| | Combo (P/L) | 98.00 | — | — |
| Z. | 2002 Glass Hen Dish | 39.00 | **39** | **51** |

† = Product numbers are stated: Stained/ Natural weave.

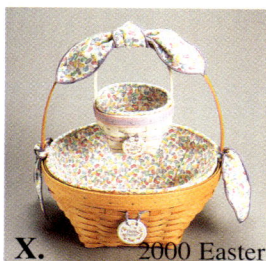

| **X.** | 2000 Easter |
| --- | --- |
| Sm: 5.5$^{RD}$ x 3.75$^H$ | |
| Lg: 12.5$^{RD}$ x 6$^H$ | |

| Small: | 19488$^W$ |
| --- | --- |
| Large: 19186$^C$ | 19283$^W$ |
| Jelly Bean TO: | 38661 |
| Easter TO: | 38644 |

*Small was offered white-washed with color accents only, while the Large was available in Classic or Whitewashed with color accents.*

| **Y.** | 2001 Easter |
| --- | --- |
| Sm: 6$^{RD}$ x 2.75$^H$ | |
| Lg: 12.75$^{RD}$ x 4$^H$ | |

| Small: | 10023$^C$ | 10125$^W$ |
| --- | --- | --- |
| Large: | 10915$^C$ | 11016$^W$ |
| Small TO: | | 39519 |
| Large TO: | | 38644 |
| Egg Plate: | | 35670 |

*Both baskets were offered in Classic stain or Whitewashed.*

| **Z** | |
| --- | --- |
| Sm: 7.75$^L$ x 6.25$^W$ x 2.75$^H$ | |
| Lg: 12.5$^L$ x 10.25$^H$ x 4.25$^H$ | |

| Small: | 12093$^C$ | 12111$^{WP}$ |
| --- | --- | --- |
| | 12101$^{WG}$ | 12123$^{WY}$ |
| Large: | 12233$^C$ | 12411$^W$ |
| Chick TO: | | 30108 |
| Hen Dish: | | 30098 |

*Small was offered 4 ways: Classic or Whitewashed with choice of pink, green or yellow. Large was offered in Classic or Whitewashed only.*

f  u  n  **f a c t**

## A Longaberger Heirloom

This basket was made by J.W. Longaberger for his granddaughter, Becky. She received this as her first Easter Basket in 1960, when she was just 1 year old.

It is natural with green accent weave and trim. The stationary handle has a high arch and was stapled in place instead of tacked. Inside, on the bottom, is the stamp "Made in Dresden Ohio", which J.W. used during the 1950's and 60's.

# White House Easter Egg Roll

this picture found on ebay®

This year, The Longaberger Company® was invited back to the White House for an encore appearance.

Last year, the Virginia Egg Council commissioned the Company to make two giant Easter baskets for the celebration.

This year, a 2002 Small Easter™ basket – whitewash with green accent weave – was given to each Congressmen and special guest of the President attending a special Easter reception.

Along with the basket, a very special hand-painted large Easter egg was tucked into each basket. The smaller eggs are the actual White House Egg Roll eggs that were also used during the event.

No word as to how many are in circulation. Without a question, a very special collectible!

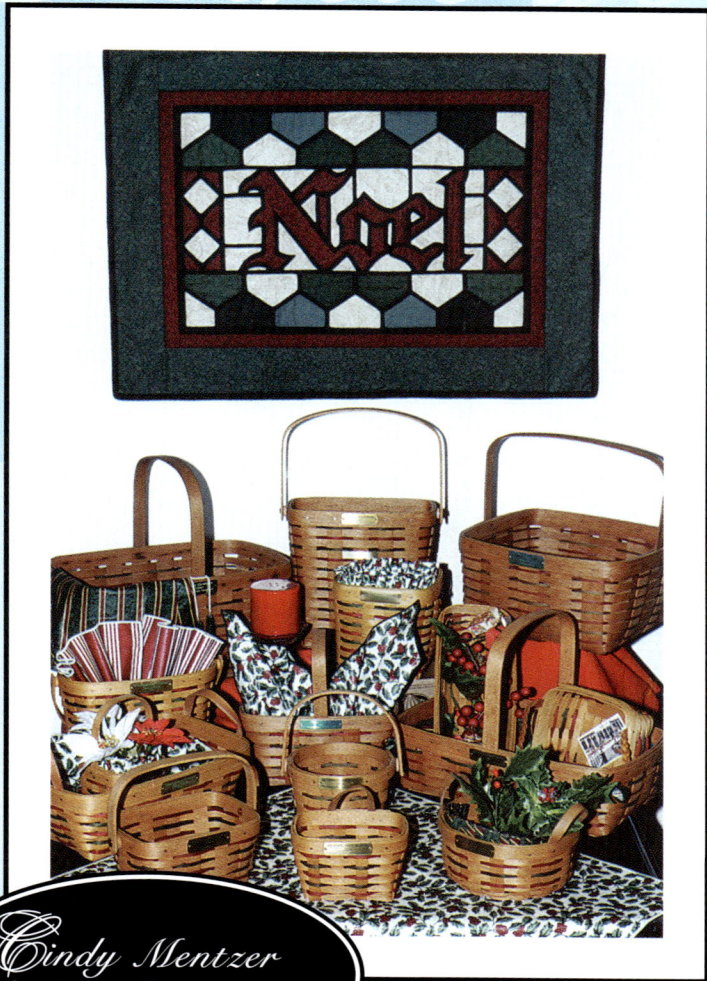

**Cindy Mentzer**
**Carlisle, Pennsylvania**

*Cindy began collecting in 1997. With frequent trips to Zanesville & Dresden, she has collected about 190 baskets. She has all of the Employee Christmas baskets from '87 to '01.*

# *Employee Baskets*

**Given to Employees for different occasions. No original costs are associated with these baskets.**

## MARKET VALUES

| Photo | Description | Avg. | High |
|---|---|---|---|

**A.** 1988 5" Measuring

$5^{RD}$ x $4.5^{H}$

Form No: 3800-
No. Given:

*Birthday – Red shoestring weave and trim. Tags read "Longaberger Company Birthday Basket", Year of basket, and Employee's name (except 1990 did not have Employee's name).*

| | | | Avg. | High |
|---|---|---|---|---|
| A. | 1988 | 5" Measuring™ | 77 | 105 |
| B. | 1989 | Sweetheart™ | 76 | 95 |
| C. | 1990 | Potpourri™ | 87 | 112 |
| D. | 1991 | Ivy™ | 90 | 130 |
| E. | 1992 | Tour™ | 62 | 85 |

**E.** 1992 Tour

$8.75^{L}$ x $4.75^{W}$ x $6.5^{H}$

Form No: 10022
No. Given:

*Last year for a Birthday Basket.*

*Recognition – Given to Employees for years of service. Tag reads "Longaberger" or "Longaberger Company", the Year of award, and Achievement.*

| | | | Avg. | High |
|---|---|---|---|---|
| | (xx–97) | Sophomore[np] (1 yr.) | 67 | 75 |
| F. | (xx–97) | Junior (2 yrs.) | 79 | 85 |
| | (xx–97) | Senior[np] (5 yrs.) | 85 | 125 |
| G. | (xx–97) | Senior Employee | 320 | 425 |
| H. | (97–P) | Senior Employee II | — | 90 |
| I. | (xx–97) | Master (10 yrs.) | 232 | 275 |
| J. | (97–P) | Master II (10 yrs.) | — | 175 |

*Hartville Conversion Baskets*

| | | | | |
|---|---|---|---|---|
| K. | 1992 | Magazine | — | — |
| K. | 1992 | Cake | — | 150 |

**[continued next page]**

[np] = Not Pictured.

**I.** 19xx-97 Master Employee

$12.5^{RD}$ x $13.5^{H}$

Form No: 1900-
No. Given:

*Given to Employees with 10 years of service with the company.*

**B.** 1989 Sweetheart

$5.75^L$ x $3.75^W$ x $3^H$

Form No: 45000-
No. Given:

**C.** 1990 Potpourri

$5^L$ x $5^W$ x $2.5^H$

Form No: 13000-
No. Given:

*Tag did not include Employee's name in this year.*

**D.** 1991 Ivy

$5.5^L$ x $5.5^W$ x $2.5^H$

Form No: 13100-
No. Given:

**F.** Junior Recognition

$8.75^L$ x $4.75^W$ x $6.5^H$

Form No: unknown
No. Given:

*Sophomore — same, except no color weaving Senior — same, except with blue trim and weave.*

**G.** 19xx-97 Senior Employee

$16^L$ x $9^W$ x $6^H$

Form No: unknown
No. Given:

**H.** 1997-P Senior Employee

$6.5^{RD}$ x $5^H$

Form No: unknown
No. Given:

*Lilac weave and double trim.*

**J.** 1997-P Master Employee

$8^{RD}$ x $6.5^H$

Form No: unknown
No. Given:

*Lilac weave and double trim.*

**K.** 1992 Conversion Baskets

Magazine: $16^L$ x $8^W$ x $11^H$
Cake: $12^L$ x $12^W$ x $6^H$

Form No: unknown
No. Given: ≈ 160 total

### Conversion Baskets

In 1992, Longaberger converted the weaving process at their Hartville facility. They moved to a piece rate method of payment. To compensate the weavers and the runners for the change, The Company allowed each one to make their own Magazine or Cake basket. They were tagged and personally signed by Dave.

*Special brass tag. Dave's signature is on the front of the basket, just below the tag. This Magazine pictured still has the tag on it used to return it to Hartville after it was stained.*

## Employee Baskets

**Given to Employees for different occasions. No original costs are associated with these baskets.**

### MARKET VALUES

| Photo | Description | Avg. | High |
|---|---|---|---|

*Perfect Attendance – Given out once a year to Employees who have maintained Perfect Attendance. All have lilac trim and weave.*

| | | Description | Avg. | High |
|---|---|---|---|---|
| L. | 1994 | Small Fruit™ | **433** | **475** |
| M. | 1995 | Pansy™ | **425** | **475** |
| N. | 1996 | Candle™ | **400** | **425** |
| O. | 1997 | 7" Measuring™ | **388** | **425** |
| P. | 1998 | Large Peg™ | **405** | **425** |
| Q. | 1999 | Spring™ | **—** | **425** |

*Christmas – Red and green alternating shoestring weave. No color on trim. Tags read "Merry Christmas" or "Happy Holidays", Year, and "Longaberger Company".*

| | | Description | Avg. | High |
|---|---|---|---|---|
| R. | 1987 | Medium Market™ | **248** | **310** |
| S. | 1988 | Cake™ | **143** | **180** |
| T. | 1989 | Candle™ | **132** | **150** |
| U. | 1990 | Small Gathering™ | **110** | **140** |
| V. | 1991 | Tall Key™ | **98** | **125** |
| W. | 1992 | 5" Measuring™ | **94** | **120** |

**[continued next page]**

1994
**L.** Perfect Attendance
$6.5^{RD}$ x $5^H$

Form No:      unknown
No. Given:      ≈ 200

*Lilac trim and shoestring weave around bottom. First Employee Basket to include accessories.*

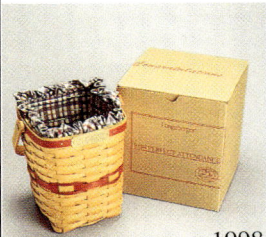

1998
**P.** Perfect Attendance
$6.5^L$ x $6.5^W$ x $8^H$

Form No:      unknown
No. Given:

*First year award was delivered to the employee's home in a box.*

**T.**      1989 Candle
$9^L$ x $5^W$ x $5^H$

Form No:      1100-
No. Given:

**M.** Perfect Attendance — 1995
$7^{RD} \times 4.5^H$
Form No: unknown
No. Given:

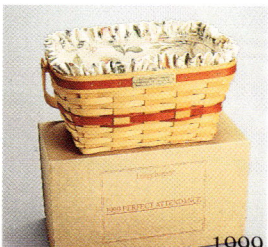

**N.** Perfect Attendance — 1996
$9^L \times 5^W \times 5^H$
Form No: unknown
No. Given: $\approx 309$

**O.** Perfect Attendance — 1997
$7^{RD} \times 6.5^H$
Form No: unknown
No. Given:

**Q.** Perfect Attendance — 1999
$11^L \times 8^W \times 5.5^H$
Form No: unknown
No. Given:

**R.** Medium Market — 1987
$15^L \times 10^W \times 7.5^H$
Form No: 500-
No. Given:

**S.** 1988 Cake
$12^L \times 12^W \times 6^H$
Form No: 100-
No. Given:

**U.** Small Gathering — 1990
$14^L \times 9^W \times 4.5^H$
Form No: 2300-
No. Given:

**V.** 1991 Tall Key
$9.5^L \times 5^W \times 9.5^H$
Form No: 1000-
No. Given:

**W.** 5" Measuring — 1992
$5^{RD} \times 4.5^H$
Form No: 3800-
No. Given:

73

## Employee Baskets

**All Christmas Employee Baskets have alternating red and green shoestring weave.**

**X.** 1993 Button
$7^{RD} \times 3^{H}$

Form No:                 5400-
No. Given:

| Photo Description | MARKET VALUES | |
|---|---|---|
| | Avg. | High |
| X. 1993 Button™ | 99 | 125 |
| Y. 1994 Tea™ | 102 | 125 |
| Z. 1995 Ambrosia™ | 75 | 95 |
| A¹ 1996 Cracker™ | 65 | 95 |
| B¹ 1997 Chives™ | 115 | 130 |
| C¹ 1998 Small Berry™ | 73 | 85 |
| D¹ 1999 Tissue™ | 100 | 115 |
| E¹ 2000 Holiday Cheer™ | 93 | 100 |
| F¹ 2001 Small Boardwalk™ | 98 | 100 |

**B¹** 1997 Chives
$4^{L} \times 4^{W} \times 4^{H}$

Form No:           unknown
No. Given:

## f u n f a c t

### First Weaver

The first weaver, trained by Dave himself, was Ken Birkhimer. He and his wife live in Dresden, where he still works for The Longaberger Company. While he is no longer weaving, he does take care of the first shift maintenance. He says that he would eventually like to get back into weaving, just to keep his skills up.

Many collectors have started looking for his initials as a weaver (above). Or, you might be lucky enough to find his whole signature on a few baskets in the market.

**Y.**  1994 Tea

$7^L$ x $5^W$ x $3.5^H$

Form No: 700-
No. Given:

**Z.**  1995 Ambrosia

$5.5^L$ x $4^W$ x $4^H$

Form No: 10120
No. Given:

*First year for the tag to read "Happy Holidays".*

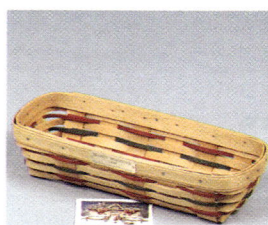

**A$^1$**  1996 Cracker

$11.5^L$ x $5^W$ x $3^H$

Form No: 4500-
No. Given:

**C$^1$**  1998 Small Berry

$6.5^L$ x $6.5^W$ x $3^H$

Form No: unknown
No. Given:

**D$^1$**  1999 Tissue

$6.5^L$ x $6.5^W$ x $6.25^H$

Form No: unknown
No. Given:

*Did not come with the Tissue lid, but one could be purchased.*

**E$^1$**  2000 Holiday Cheer

$12^L$ x $8^W$ x $4.25^H$

Form No: unknown
No. Given:

*Liner was given along with the basket to some employees.*

**F$^1$**  2001 Small Boardwalk

$9.25^L$ x $5^W$ x $6.25^H$

Form No: unknown
No. Given:

f  u  n  **f a c t**

Hours of weaving can take a toll on a weaver's fingers. Moisture from the wood can cause blisters and applying pressure to the wood can develop carpal tunnel syndrome. Many workers tape their fingertips to protect their hands.

# Make-A-Basket

Did you ever wonder what it was like to be a Longaberger Weaver?  Did you know that you <u>can</u> find out on your next trip to Dresden?

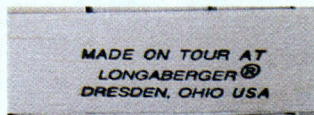

Starting in 1996, The Longaberger opened the Make-A-Basket Shop™.

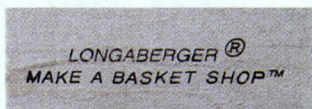

First located in Dresden, but now at The Homestead®, this experience is a once-in-a-lifetime experience for many.  For $54.95, you can choose between a couple different baskets to weave from the bottom up, literally.

The experience takes about an hour of your time, depending on skill level, and is limited to those who are 12 years of age or older.  Due to its popularity, it is necessary to set a "weave time" before-hand.  In 1999, there were over 14,000 visitors who made their own basket souvenir.

Your choice of basket changes from year to year so that you can create your very own "Make-A-Basket" collection.

Spring: 96-98, 01-P

Berry: 98-99

1996:  Spring Basket™ only
1997:  Spring Basket™ only
1998:  Spring™ / Berry™
1999:  Berry™ / Med.Key™
2000:  Med.Key™ /Lg.Peg™
2001-P: Lg.Peg™ /Spring™

Lg Peg: 00-P

(Berry and Lg.Peg baskets were available with or without handles)

## Denise Rae Johnson
### Santa Ynez, California

Denise is known all over town as the "Basket Lady". Her love of baskets is carried over into her catering business, where she delivers and serves in baskets! Although her favorite collection is Christmas™, her favorite basket is the Traditions Family™. She comes from a close knit family, and this basket just cries out FAMILY to her. Not surprisingly the entire family loves baskets too!

# Father's Day™

**Dresden Blue and Burgundy Trim and Weave. Series suspended in 1999, but returned in 2001.**

## MARKET VALUES

| Photo | Description | | Original | Avg. | High |
|---|---|---|---|---|---|
| A. | 1991 | Spare Change™ | 21.95 | **58** | 70 |
| | | with **P**rotector | 25.90 | **60** | 80 |
| | | with **L**iner | 32.90 | **65** | 100 |
| | | with Combo (**P/L**) | 32.95 | **76** | 125 |
| B. | 1992 | Paper™ | 23.95 | **70** | 95 |
| | | with **P**rotector | 27.90 | **73** | 100 |
| | | with **L**iner | 33.90 | **80** | 135 |
| | | Combo (**P/L**) | 33.95 | **92** | 145 |
| C. | 1992 | Pencil™ | 20.95 | **70** | 95 |
| | | with **P**rotector | 23.90 | **76** | 110 |
| | | with **L**iner | 30.90 | **80** | 120 |
| | | Combo (**P/L**) | 29.95 | **83** | 145 |
| D. | 1994 | Tissue™ | 29.95 | **84** | 100 |
| | | with **P**rotector | 35.90 | **85** | 105 |
| | | with **Lid** | 42.90 | **85** | 110 |
| | | Combo (**P/Lid**) | 39.95 | **90** | 115 |
| E. | 1994 | Business Card™ | 22.95 | **49** | 70 |
| | | Combo (**P**) | 25.90 | **50** | 75 |
| | | with **L**iner (1995) | 31.90 | **50** | 75 |
| | | Full Set (**Combo/L**) | 34.85 | **55** | 78 |
| F. | 1995 | Mini Waste™ | 46.95 | **57** | 81 |
| | | Combo (**P**) | 49.95 | **62** | 85 |
| | | with **L**iner | 63.95 | **65** | 90 |
| | | with **Lid** | 63.95 | **78** | 92 |
| | | Full Set (**P/L/Lid**) | 83.85 | **90** | 100 |
| G. | 1996 | Address™ | 29.95 | **42** | 80 |
| | | with **P**rotector | 33.90 | **51** | 85 |
| | | Combo (**P/Card Holder**) | 34.95 | **56** | 90 |
| | | with **L**iner | 42.90 | **51** | 85 |
| | | Full Set (**Combo/L/Lid**) | 61.85 | **65** | 95 |
| H. | 1997 | Personal Organizer™ | 39.95 | **66** | 80 |
| | | with **P**rotector | 46.90 | **66** | 80 |
| | | with **L**iner | 57.90 | **66** | 80 |
| | | Combo (**P/L**) | 54.95 | **74** | 110 |
| | | Full Set (**Combo/L/Lid**) | 77.90 | **93** | 110 |
| I. | 1998 | Finder's Keepers™ | 34.00 | **48** | 65 |
| | | Combo (**P**) | 37.00 | **60** | 80 |
| | | with **L**iner | 48.00 | **60** | 80 |
| | | Full Set (**Combo/L/Lid**) | 67.00 | **68** | 100 |
| J. | 1999 | Tee™ | 29.00 | **38** | 45 |
| | | with **P**rotector | 33.00 | **40** | 49 |
| | | with **L**iner | 40.00 | **40** | 49 |
| | | Combo (**P/L**) | 39.00 | **46** | 70 |

**A.** 1991 Spare Change
$6.5^L$ x $6.5^W$ x $3^H$

Form No: 1300-JCWS
No. Sold:

*Liner also available in new design starting 1995.*

**E.** 1994 Business Card
$4.75^L$ x $3.75^W$ x $2.25^H$

Form No: 17477
No. Sold:

*Hostess only. Liner was not originally offered – available for the first time in 1995, in new fabric design only.*

**I.** 1998 Finder's Keepers
$6^L$ x $6^W$ x $4.25^{FH}$ x $5.25^{BH}$

Form No: 12777
No. Sold:

**B.** 1992 Paper

$7.5^L$ x $5.5^W$ x $2^{FH}$ x $3.5^{BH}$

Form No: 16000
No. Sold:

*Included note paper.
Liner also available in
new design starting 1995.*

**C.** 1992 Pencil

$4^{RD}$ x $4.25^H$

Form No: 15000
No. Sold:

*Liner also available in
new design starting 1995.*

**D.** 1994 Tissue

$6.5^L$ x $6.5^W$ x $6.25^H$

Form No: 18490
No. Sold:

*No Liner available.*

**F.** 1995 Mini Waste

$7.5^L$ x $7.5^W$ x $10^H$

Form No: 11266
No. Sold:

*Lid and Liner sold sep-
arately. First year
for the newly
designed fabric.*

**G.** 1996 Address Basket

$8.25^L$ x $6.25^W$ x $3.75^H$

Form No: 12611
No. Sold: 173,381

*Combo included
Protector, Address Cards
and Card Holder. Lid and
Liner sold separately.*

**H.** 1997 Personal Organizer

$14^L$ x $6^W$ x $3^H$

Form No: 13137
No. Sold:

*Combo came with divid-
ed protector. Regular
protector was also
available for $5.95.*

**J.** 1999 Tee

$5.25^L$ x $5^W$ x $3^H$

Form No: 14940
No. Sold:

*Each Combo included a
set of 50 Longaberger
Golf Tees and a chance
to win an outing on the
Longaberger Course.*

f u n **f a c t**

## Basket tip . . .

The Tissue Basket™ lid can also
be used on the Small Berry™
basket to dispense napkins.

79

## Father's Day™

There was not a Father's Day basket in 2000. Instead, a "Dads & Grads" campaign was featured, but not considered to be a part of this series.

### MARKET VALUES

| Photo | Description | Original | Avg. | High |
|---|---|---|---|---|
| K. | 2001 Tic-Tac-Toe™ | 44.00 | **51** | **58** |
| | with Protector | 50.00 | **63** | **70** |
| | with Liner | 59.00 | — | — |
| | Combo (P/L) | 59.00 | **70** | **78** |
| | Full Set (Combo/L/Lid) | 82.00 | **78** | **100** |
| L. | 2001 Pewter Dad Tie-On | 8.00 | **10** | **12** |
| L. | 2001 Checkerboard™ | 139.00 | **160** | **175** |
| | with Protector | 158.00 | **175** | **200** |
| | with Liner | 163.00 | **180** | **200** |
| | Combo (P/L) | 182.00 | **206** | **225** |
| | Full Set (Combo/L/Lid) | 198.00 | **213** | **400** |
| | 2001 Pewter Games Tie-On[np] | 10.00 | **13** | **16** |
| L. | 2001 Pewter Chess Set | 198.00 | **198** | **249** |
| M. | 2002 Daddy's Caddy™ | 49.00 | — | — |
| | with Protector | 65.00 | — | — |
| | with Liner | 66.00 | — | — |
| | Combo (P/L) | 69.00 | — | — |
| | 2002 Dad Tie-On | 8.00 | — | — |

[np] = Not Pictured

**need help?**

## How do we get our values?
see page 8

**K.** 2001 Tic-Tac-Toe
7.5$^L$ x 7.5$^W$ x 2.75$^H$
Form No: 10346

*First for the new design.*

**L.** 2001 Checkerboard
15$^L$ x 15$^W$ x 6$^H$
Form No: 10036
Chess Set 74748

*Chess Set sold separately.*

**M.** 2002 Daddy's Caddy
8$^L$ x 7.75$^W$ x 7$^H$
Form No: 11854
Tie-On: 77267

# You **MUST** send us this form...

## WHO NEEDS TO **REGISTER FOR THE SIX MONTH UPDATE?**

**Everyone!** If you would like to receive the *free update* for your Tenth Edition Bentley, mail us this card. It doesn't matter if you bought the Guide directly from J. Phillip, or through a Retail Store, from your Advisor, or if you are on a 3-Yr subscription. It is necessary for **everyone** to send in this registration to receive the Six-Month Update automatically and at no additional cost.

## WHEN DO I NEED TO SEND IN THIS REGISTRATION?

Right away! You can send it as soon as you open your Guide, just be sure to send us your winter address. In order to get your Update *without delay*, you must **send it in by December 31, 2002**.

## WHAT IF I MISS THE DEADLINE?

If you have purchased the Guide after this deadline, the Six Month Update should be packaged with the other shrink wrapped items that came with it. **Please still send in this card so that you will be notified of any changes or new editions to the Guide.** If you are missing this update, first contact the store or person from whom you purchased it. If they purchased your Guide before this deadline, it will not have the Update. Call us at **1. 800. 837. 4394** with proof of your purchase: receipt or cancelled check. If you register after the deadline, there will be a cost of **$2.95** for your Update and postage.

## WHEN CAN I EXPECT THE SIX MONTH UPDATE?

For those who register before the deadline, the Updates will be mailed out in late January 2003.

## HOW TO FILL OUT THE REGISTRATION . . .

1. Fill-in <u>all</u> of the requested information
2. Tear this page out of your Guide
3. Fold the page in half, address inside
4. Tape closed
5. Put a first class stamp on the front
6. Put into the mail

### PLEASE PRINT

When did you purchase/receive this Guide?   (mo/yr.) _____ / _____

Did you receive an Update with your Guide?   ❐ **Yes**   ❐ **No**

❐ **New Address** (as of: _____ )   ❐ **Do not exchange my name**

❐ **Collector**      ❐ **Consultant** (circle: MBA / Branch / Reg / Dir)

**Bentley Customer No** (optional): _____

**Name**: _____

**Address**: _____

_____

**City**: _____   **State**: _____   **Zip**: _____

**Day Phone**: ( ____ ) _____   **Evening**: _____

**Email address**: _____

**Which Edition(s) of the Bentley Guide have you owned?**   ❐ All 10

❐ 1st[93]   ❐ 2nd[94]   ❐ 3rd[95]   ❐ 4th[96]   ❐ 5th[97]

❐ 6th[98]   ❐ 7th[99]   ❐ 8th[00]   ❐ 9th[01]   ❐ 10th[02]

### Where did you purchase this year's Edition of the Guide?

❐ From Bentley directly  ❐ From a Consultant  ❐ Through an Advisor

❐ From a Retail Store  ❐ At an Auction  ❐ Other: _____

fold in half

place
stamp
here

# The Bentley Collection Guide®

J. PHILLIP, INCORPORATED
5870 ZARLEY STREET SUITE C
NEW ALBANY, OH 43054

tape closed

# Feature Baskets

**Debbie Puckett**
*Spotsylvania, Virginia*

After years of wondering how one of her neighbors could have such love for baskets, her neighbor gave her a Classic Candle™ basket as a birthday gift. One year and 200 baskets later, Debbie admits she has "caught the FEVER!" Her favorite basket is the Medium Bin™ with lid.

## *Feature Baskets*

**Baskets featured for a limited time.
This section is divided in two sections:
with and without color weaving.**

**A.** 1987 Resolution
$5^{RD}$ x $4.5^{H}$

Form No: 3800-ABS
No. Sold:

*Offered in the month of December 1987.*

### MARKET VALUES

| Photo | Description | Original | Avg. | High |
|---|---|---|---|---|
| | **Baskets featured WITH Color Weaving:** | | | |
| A. | 1987 Resolution™ | 16.95 | **118** | 160 |
| B. | 1988 Memory™ | | **112** | 165 |
| | & 89 with Longaberger Book | 39.95 | **147** | 200 |
| C. | 1990 Basket O'Luck™ | | **89** | 150 |
| D. | 1990 Shamrock™ | 19.95 | **99** | 165 |
| E. | 1993 All-Star Trio™ | 29.95 | **48** | 80 |
| F. | 1993 Red Pottery Thank-You Basket™ | N/A | **123** | 155 |
| G. | 1994 Boo™ | 34.95 | **93** | 135 |
| | with **P**rotector | 39.90 | **93** | 150 |
| | with **L**iner | 48.90 | **93** | 150 |
| | Combo (**P/L**) | 44.95 | **80** | 125 |
| H. | 1994 <u>Three Key Baskets</u> | 98.85 | **146** | 203 |
| | Small Key™ | 27.95 | **36** | 46 |
| | Medium Key™ | 29.95 | **38** | 50 |
| | Tall Key™ | 40.95 | **52** | 75 |
| | *1996-97 Six Baskets / Three Colors Promotion* | | | |
| I. | 1996-97 Medium Berry™ | 29.95 | **41** | 50 |
| | Combo (**P/L**) | 36.43 | **53** | 65 |
| J. | 1996-97 Medium Spoon™ | 36.95 | **53** | 63 |
| | Combo (**P/L**) | 44.93 | **62** | 75 |
| K. | 1996-97 Pantry™ | 46.95 | **59** | 80 |
| | Combo (**P/L**) | 55.93 | **86** | 90 |
| L. | 1996-97 Large Vegetable™ | 61.95 | **79** | 95 |
| | Combo (**P/L**) | 72.43 | **85** | 95 |
| | **continued next page** | | | |

**E.** 1993 All-Star Trio
$5.75^{L}$ x $3.75^{W}$ x $3^{H}$

Form No: 64408
No. Sold:

*Sold only as a three-piece combo. Form number for the basket can be found on the product card: 14494.*

**continued next page**

*n e e d help?*

## Can't find something?

**Try the Quick Find**

**I.** 1996-97 Med. Berry
$7.5^{L}$ x $7.5^{W}$ x $3.5^{H}$

Form No: 16241/25/33†
No. Sold:

*Liner was only available in stand-up.*

**B.** 1988 & 89 Memory

Form No:          5600-BBS
No. Sold:

*Only sold as a combo of book and basket. Continued to be available through 1991.*

**C.**            1990
            Basket O'Luck
5.5$^{RD}$ x 3.75$^{H}$

Form No:          17000-AGS
No. Sold:

*Hostess only*

**D.**            1990
            Shamrock
5$^{L}$ x 5$^{W}$ x 2.5$^{H}$

Form No:          13000-HGS
No. Sold:

**F.**            1993
            Thank-You
11$^{L}$ x 8$^{W}$ x 5.5$^{H}$

Form No:          190xx
No. Sold:          7,478

*This basket was sent as a Thank-You from Dave to the customers who had ordered the Red Pottery and waited for it through its production problems.*

**G.**            1994 Boo
11$^{L}$ x 8$^{W}$ x 5.5$^{H}$

Form No:          10987
No. Sold:

**H.**            1994
            Key Basket Set

Form No:
Sm: **R**17078 /**B** -51 /**G** -60
Md: **R**15172 /**B** -99 /**G** -81
Tall: **R**14672 /**B** -99 /**G** -81

*Available in Red, Blue, or Green weave.*

**J.**            1996-97
            Medium Spoon
6.5$^{L}$ x 6.5$^{W}$ x 8$^{H}$

Form No:   16349/22/31$^{†}$
No. Sold:

**K.**     1996-97 Pantry
14$^{L}$ x 9$^{W}$ x 4.5$^{H}$

Form No:   16446/20/38$^{†}$
No. Sold:

**L.**            1996-97
            Large Vegetable
16$^{L}$ x 19$^{W}$ x 3.5$^{H}$ x 9$^{H}$

Form No:   16543/27/35$^{†}$
No. Sold:

† = Product numbers are stated: Blue weave / Red weave / Green weave.          **83**

## Feature Baskets

### MARKET VALUES

| | Description | Original | Avg. | High |
|---|---|---|---|---|
| | *1996 -97 Six Baskets / Three Colors (con't)* | | | |
| M. | 1996-97 Large Market™ | 77.95 | **94** | **135** |
| | Combo (**P/L**) | 92.43 | **115** | **190** |
| N. | 1996-97 Remembrance™ | 99.95 | **115** | **118** |
| | Combo (**P/L**) | 112.93 | **121** | **185** |
| | *1997-99 Sleigh Baskets* | | | |
| O. | Large | Holiday Sleigh™ | 47.95 | **58** | **97** |
| | with **P**rotector | 55.90 | **72** | **105** |
| | with **L**iner | 65.90 | **72** | **105** |
| | Combo (**P/L**) | 59.95 | **74** | **110** |
| | Full Set (**C/Runners**) | 85.85 | **86** | **120** |
| O. | Med | Dash Away Sleigh™ | 36.00 | **50** | **84** |
| | with **P**rotector | 41.00 | **50** | **87** |
| | with **L**iner | 50.00 | **50** | **87** |
| | Combo (**Runners**) | 50.00 | **51** | **89** |
| | Full Set (**P/L/Runners**) | 69.00 | **69** | **100** |
| O. | Small | Santa's Little Helper™ | 30.00 | **55** | **60** |
| | with **P**rotector | 33.00 | — | — |
| | with **L**iner | 40.00 | **65** | **71** |
| | Combo (**P/L**) | 42.00 | **50** | **75** |
| | Full Set (**C/Runners**) | 55.00 | **69** | **85** |
| P. | 1999 | Little Joy™ | 38.00 | **53** | **69** |
| | with **P**rotector | 41.00 | **55** | **80** |
| | with **L**iner | 50.00 | **60** | **82** |
| | Combo (**P/L**) | 53.00 | **65** | **93** |
| Q. | 1999 | Lots of Luck™ | 29.00 | **90** | **130** |
| | with **P**rotector | 32.00 | **90** | **130** |
| | with **L**iner | 41.00 | **90** | **130** |
| | Combo (**P/L**) | 39.00 | **104** | **175** |
| | Full Set (**Combo/Lid/HT**) | 58.00 | **129** | **180** |
| Q. | 1999 | Shamrock Tie-On | 6.00 | **32** | **45** |
| R. | 1999 | Homestead™ | 59.00 | **84** | **95** |
| | with **P**rotector | 67.00 | — | — |
| | with **L**iner | 83.00 | — | — |
| | Combo (**P/L**) | 79.00 | **95** | **125** |
| | Full Set (**C/Lid**) | 113.00 | **120** | **165** |
| R. | 1999 | Homestead Tie-On | 8.00 | **14** | **16** |
| S. | 1999 | Candy Corn™ | 29.00 | **46** | **53** |
| | with **P**rotector | 33.00 | **50** | **55** |
| | with **L**iner | 41.00 | **51** | **55** |
| | Combo (**P/L**) | 39.00 | **56** | **89** |
| S. | 1999 | Candy Corn Tie-On | 8.00 | **10** | **15** |

**continued next page**

**M.** 1996-97 Lg. Market
16$^L$ x 11$^W$ x 9$^H$

Form No: 16641/24/32$^†$
No. Sold:

*Liner was only available in over-the-edge.*

**Q.** 1999 Lots of Luck
4.25$^L$ x 4.25$^W$ x 3$^H$

Form No: 18465
Tie-On: 36056
No. Sold:

*Basket features a unique burned in shamrock logo and date on its bottom.*

### In this Section

Baskets are listed in chronological order by the year they were featured.

**N.** Remembrance

$10.5^L \times 9^W \times 8^H$

Form No: 16748/21/30†
No. Sold:

*Hostess Only.
Liner was only available in over-the-edge.*

**O.** 1997-99 Sleigh Basket

$13^L \times 7.5^W \times 3^{FH} \times 8^{BH}$
$7.75^L \times 4.5^W \times 2.25^{FH} \times 4.5^{BH}$
$5.75^L \times 3.75^W \times 1.5^{FH} \times 3.5^{BH}$

*This unofficial collection was started in 1997 and then added to each year until 1999.*

**P.** 1999 Little Joy

$5^L \times 3.75^W \times 4.5^H$

Form No: 19445
No. Sold:

*Hostess Appreciation Basket. Available FREE to Hostesses sponsoring a $250 show in both Oct.98 and Jan.99.*

**R.** 1999 Homestead

$10^{RD} \times 6.25^H$

Form No: 13871
Tie-On: 37541
No. Sold:

*There are 2 versions of this basket: this one for all customers, and another for Collectors Club Members.*

**S.** 1999 Candy Corn

$7.75^L \times 4^W \times 3.75^H$

Form No: 14354
Tie-On: 36676
No. Sold:

*Unique form is shaped like a candy corn.*

f  u  n  **f a c t**

## Did you know?

The Longaberger Home Office is a replica of the Medium Market™ Basket. The award-winning design is 160 times larger than its inspiration.

† = Product numbers are stated: Blue weave / Red weave / Green weave.

## MARKET VALUES

| Description | Original | Avg. | High |
|---|---|---|---|
| T. 2000 Hostess Appreciation | | | |
| Century Celebration | 44.00 | **42** | **60** |
| with **P**rotector | 48.00 | **45** | **60** |
| with **L**iner | 59.00 | **50** | **60** |
| Combo (**P/L**) | 63.00 | **62** | **85** |
| Full Set (**C/Lid**) | 80.00 | **75** | **105** |
| T. 2000 Century Star Tie-On | 8.00 | **12** | **16** |
| T. 2000 Cheers™ | 39.00 | **61** | **71** |
| with **P**rotector | 43.00 | — | — |
| with **L**iner | 54.00 | — | — |
| Combo (**P/L**) | 49.00 | **68** | **95** |
| Full Set (**C/Lid**) | 72.00 | **98** | **100** |
| U. 2000 Frosty™ | 43.00 | **47** | **54** |
| with **P**rotector | 52.00 | — | — |
| with **L**iner | 60.00 | — | — |
| Combo (**P/L**) | 69.00 | — | — |
| U. 2000 Frosty Jr.™ | 33.00 | **35** | **52** |
| with **P**rotector | 40.00 | — | — |
| with **L**iner | 47.00 | — | — |
| Combo (**P/L**) | 53.00 | **53** | **70** |
| V. 2000 Noel Bell™ | 43.00 | **46** | **80** |
| Combo (**tassel/hanger**) | 59.00 | **65** | **90** |
| W. 2001 Hostess Appreciation | | | |
| Inaugural™ | 39.00 | **44** | **50** |
| with **P**rotector | 41.00 | — | — |
| with **L**iner | 53.00 | — | — |
| Combo (**P/L**) | 56.00 | **63** | **100** |
| Full Set (**C/Lid**) | 70.00 | — | — |
| X. 2001 Little Star™ | 49.00 | **51** | **60** |
| with **P**rotector | 54.00 | — | — |
| with **L**iner | 64.00 | — | — |
| Combo (**P/L**) | 69.00 | **69** | **75** |
| Full Set (**C/Lid**) | 88.00 | **88** | **95** |
| Y. 2001 Lucky You™ | 34.00 | **40** | **50** |
| with **P**rotector | 38.00 | — | — |
| with **L**iner | 48.00 | — | — |
| Combo (**P/L**) | 44.00 | **51** | **75** |
| Full Set (**C/Lid**) | 59.00 | **78** | **106** |
| Y. 2001 Lucky You Tie-On™ | 8.00 | **9** | **13** |

| **Baskets featured WITHOUT Color** | | | |
|---|---|---|---|
| A. 1981 Grandma Bonnie's Bread & Milk™ | | **675** | **850** |
| B. 1982 Old Oak Lid Picnic™ | | **600** | **650** |
| 1983-84 Cake (2 sw/h)[WL] | 20.95 | — | — |
| C. 1984 Patio Planter™ | 21.95 | **90** | **135** |
| D. 1984 Shaker Peg Basket™ | 14.95 | **45** | **60** |
| E. 1985 Single Pie™ | 19.95 | — | **50** |
| F. 1985 Pantry™ | 21.95 | **62** | **70** |

**T.** 2000 Celebration Baskets

7.5$^L$ x 4.5$^W$ x 3.5$^H$

Hostess: 13498
Cheers: 18945
Tie-On: 36196

*Hostess Appreciation is the natural with color version.*

**X.** 2001 Little Star

7.5$^L$ x 8$^W$ x 3$^H$

Form No: 12202$^R$/12214$^G$
No. Sold:

*Offered with Red or Green accents.*

**C.** 1984 Patio Planter

10$^{RD}$ x 5.5$^H$

Form No: 6000-R
No. Sold:

**U.** 2000 Frosty Baskets

Sm: 7$^{RD}$ x 3$^H$
Lg: 10$^{RD}$ x 4$^H$

Small: 10230
Large: 10242

*Promoted along with the Small Snowman Stand. See Foundry Collection.*

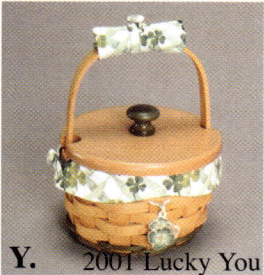

**V.** 2000 Noel Bell

5.5$^{RD}$ x 5.5$^H$

Form No: 16845

*Sold by itself, or in the tassel tie and hanger combination.*

**W.** 2001 Hostess Appreciation

5.5$^L$ x 4$^W$ x 4$^H$

Form No: 15873
No. Sold:

*Resembles the 2001 Inaugural basket, without stain.*

**Y.** 2001 Lucky You

4.75$^{RD}$ x 3$^H$

Form No: 11911
Tie-On 30542
No. Sold:

*4th basket to feature the St.Patrick's Day theme.*

**Baskets WITHOUT Color**

**A.** 1981 Bread & Milk

16$^L$ x 8$^W$ x 11$^H$

Form No: 2100-
No. Sold:

*First Tagged Basket*

**B.** 1982 Oak Lid Picnic

12$^L$ x 12$^W$ x 6$^H$

Form No: unknown
No. Sold: < 2,500

*2,500 were to be made, but far less were actually produced. Included riser.*

**D.** 1984 Shaker Peg

5.5$^L$ x 5.5$^W$ x 6$^H$

Form No: 10000-AO
No. Sold:

**E.** 1985 Single Pie

12$^L$ x 12$^W$ x 4$^H$

Form No: 2200-AO
No. Sold:

**F.** 1985 Pantry

14$^L$ x 9$^W$ x 4.5$^H$

Form No: 2300-JO
No. Sold:

## MARKET VALUES

| Photo | Description | Original | Avg. | High |
|---|---|---|---|---|
| G. | 1985, 87 Two-Quart™ | 28.95 | **74** | **85** |
| H. | 1985, 87 Round Sewing™ (no stand) | 37.95 | **207** | **218** |
| | *1985 & 88 Berry Baskets™ (1 st/h)* | | | |
| I. | Small Berry™ | 16.95 | **50** | **55** |
| J. | Medium Berry™ | 17.95 | **53** | **58** |
| K. | Large Berry™ | 18.95 | **58** | **60** |
| L. | *1985-86 Chore Baskets™ (2 sw/h)* | | | |
| L. | 1986 Small Chore™ | 17.95 | **55** | **60** |
| L. | 1985-86 Medium Chore™ | 18.95 | **53** | **69** |
| L. | 1986 Large Chore™ | 23.95 | **68** | **85** |
| | 1986 Daisy™, Natural[np] | 27.95 | **63** | **70** |
| M. | 1986 Daisy™, Stained & 87 | 25.95 | **62** | **85** |
| N. | 1986 Large Hamper™ | 79.95 | **223** | **295** |
| O. | 1986 Herb™ | | **59** | **75** |
| P. | Garden™ | | **78** | **85** |
| | Sold <u>only</u> as a Set | 32.90 | — | — |
| Q. | 1987 Bakery™ | 19.95 | **48** | **50** |
| R. | 1987 Lg.Inverted Waste™ | 59.95 | **124** | **150** |
| | **continued next page** | | | |

[np] = Not Pictured

How do we
get our values?

see page 8

need help?

**G.** 1985,1987
Two-Quart

9.5$^L$ x 5$^W$ x 9.5$^H$

Form No:     1000-CO
No. Sold:

**K.** 1985, 1988
Large Berry

8.5$^L$ x 8.5$^W$ x 5$^H$

Form No:     1500-AO
No. Sold:

*See note under pictures
I. and J. regarding these
Berry Baskets.*

**O.** 1986 Herb

11.5$^L$ x 5$^W$ x 3$^H$

Form No:     4500-AO
No. Sold:

FEATURE BASKETS

**H.** 1985, 1987 Round Sewing

13<sup>RD</sup> x 8.5<sup>H</sup>

Form No: 3200-EO
No. Sold:

**I.** 1985, 1988 Small Berry

6.5<sup>L</sup> x 6.5<sup>W</sup> x 3<sup>H</sup>

Form No: 1300-AO
No. Sold:

**J.** 1985, 1988 Medium Berry

7.5<sup>L</sup> x 7.5<sup>W</sup> x 3.5<sup>H</sup>

Form No: 1400-AO
No. Sold:

*These 1985 and 1988 features were the only times that the Berry Baskets™ were offered with 1 stationary handle.*

**L.** 1985-86 Chore Baskets

13<sup>L</sup> x 8<sup>W</sup> x 5<sup>H</sup>

Form No: 3500-CO
No. Sold:

Small: 10<sup>L</sup> x 6<sup>W</sup> x 4<sup>H</sup>
Large: 14<sup>L</sup> x 7.75<sup>W</sup> x 5.25<sup>H</sup>

**M.** 1986, 87 Daisy, Stained

10<sup>RD</sup> x 4<sup>H</sup>

Form No: 5500-AO
No. Sold:

*In '86, this basket was available in both Natural and Stained. In '87, it was only offered Stained.*

**N.** 1986 Large Hamper

16.5<sup>L</sup> x 16.5<sup>W</sup> x 21.5<sup>H</sup>

Form No: 1600-OO
No. Sold:

*Only available to Hostesses with their half-price benefit. No lid. First time for hand slots.*

**P.** 1986 Garden

15<sup>L</sup> x 8<sup>W</sup> x 2.25<sup>H</sup>

Form No: 4600-AO
No. Sold:

**Q.** 1987 Bakery

14.5<sup>L</sup> x 7.5<sup>W</sup> x 3.75<sup>H</sup>

Form No: 4700-JO
No. Sold:

**R.** 1987 Large Inverted Waste

14<sup>RD</sup> x 16<sup>H</sup>

Form No: 2000-BO
No. Sold:

# Feature Baskets

## MARKET VALUES

| Photo | Description | | Original | Avg. | High |
|---|---|---|---|---|---|
| S. | 1987 | Med.Market™ (Natrl) | 41.95 | **50** | **78** |
| T. | 1987 | Med.Gathering™(Natrl) | 41.95 | **70** | **85** |
| U. | 1987 & 88 | Weekender™ | 54.95 | **96** | **150** |
| | *1988 Planters (with legs)* | | | | |
| V. | | Small Fern™ | 35.95 | **128** | **145** |
| W. | | Large Fern™ | 42.95 | **168** | **170** |
| X. | 1989 | Bed™ | 18.95 | **85** | **105** |
| | | with **L**iner | 29.95 | **89** | **110** |
| Y. | 1989 | Breakfast™ | 24.95 | **65** | **95** |
| | | with **L**iner | 37.95 | **82** | **110** |
| | | Bed / Breakfast Set | 43.90 | **140** | **150** |
| | | with **L**iner | 67.90 | **152** | **160** |
| Z. | 1989 | Friendship™ | 21.95 | **48** | **60** |
| A¹ | 1991 | Doll Cradle™ | 69.95 | **143** | **185** |
| | | with **P**rotector | 80.90 | — | — |
| | | with **L**iner | 86.90 | — | — |
| | | Combo (**P/L**) | 97.85 | — | — |
| | *Shades of Autumn Hostesses* | | | | |
| B¹ | 1991 | Small Hamper™ | 99.95 | **153** | **165** |
| | | with **P**rotector | 113.90 | — | — |
| B¹ | 1991 | Large Hamper™ | 149.95 | **227** | **295** |
| | | with **P**rotector | 169.90 | — | — |
| | 1993, 94 | Large Hamper™[WL] | 179.95 | **235** | **275** |
| | | Combo (**P**) | 185.95 | **244** | **280** |
| C¹ | 1994 | Hostess Appreciation | N/C | **39** | **65** |
| D¹ | 1996 | Hostess Appreciation | N/C | **39** | **65** |

**continued next page**

[WL] =Wish List™. It is similar to what is available today. Pictures can be found in a current Wish List™. See the Quick Find for dimensions and form numbers.

**S.**  1987  Medium Market
$15^L$ x $10^W$ x $7.5^H$
Form No:  500-
No. Sold:

*Hostess Only. Offered Natural or Natural with red, blue, green or brown accents.*

**W.**  1988  Large Planter
$13^{RD}$ x $8.5^H$
Form No:  3200-RO
No. Sold:

**A¹**  1991  Doll Cradle
$19^L$ x $12^W$ x $6^H$
Form No:  2500-LO
No. Sold:

*Featured for a short time during the 1991 Christmas season. Muslin liner and protector sold separately.*

**T.** 1987 Medium Gathering

18$^L$ x 11$^W$ x 4.5$^H$

Form No: 2400-C
No. Sold:

*Hostess Only. Offered Natural or Natural with red, blue, green or brown accents.*

**U.** 1987, 88 Weekender

10.5$^L$ x 9$^W$ x 8$^H$

Form No: 200-YO
No. Sold:

**V.** 1988 Small Planter

8.5$^{RD}$ x 7.5$^H$

Form No: 2900-RO
No. Sold:

**X.** 1989 Bed

11.5$^L$ x 5$^W$ x 3$^H$

Form No: 4500-AO
No. Sold:

**Y.** 1989 Breakfast

14.5$^L$ x 7.5$^W$ x 3.75$^H$

Form No: 4700-AO
No. Sold:

**Z.** 1989 Friendship

5.5$^L$ x 5.5$^W$ x 2.5$^H$

Form No: 13100-JO
No. Sold:

*Made using 1/2" weave.*

**B$^1$** 1991 Shades of Autumn

Sm: 12$^L$ x 12.25$^W$ x 16.25$^H$

Sm.Hamper: 1700-DS
Lg.Hamper: 1600-DS

*Large:* 16.5$^L$ x 16.5$^W$ x 21.5$^H$
*Only available to Hostesses during the Shades of Autumn campaign in 1991. Both hampers have detached lids, knob in center of lid and two hand slots.*

**C$^1$** 1994 Hostess Appreciation

8$^L$ x 4$^W$ x 2$^H$

Form No: unknown
No. Sold:

*Given to Hostesses with shows in both Oct. 93 and Jan. 94.*

**D$^1$** 1996 Hostess Appreciation

5.5$^L$ x 5.5$^W$ x 2.5$^H$

Form No: unknown
No. Sold: 181,337

*Given to Hostesses with shows in both Oct. 95 and Jan. 96. Liner was sold separately.*

## Feature Baskets

### MARKET VALUES

| Photo | Description | Original | Avg. | High |
|---|---|---|---|---|
| E¹ | 1998 Hostess Appreciation | N/C | 43 | 60 |
| | *1998 January Sale – Naturals* | | | |
| F¹ | 1998 Cake™ (Natrl) | 43.95 | — | — |
| | Combo (P/L) | 78.85 | 95 | 110 |
| G¹ | 1998–00 Gathering, Sm™ (Natrl) | 39.95 | 65 | 100 |
| | Combo (P/L) | 71.85 | — | — |
| | 1998 Market, Med™ (Natrl) | 53.95 | — | — |
| | Combo (P/L) | 91.85 | — | — |
| H¹ | 1998 Purse, Kiddie™ (Natrl) | 27.95 | 48 | 60 |
| | Combo (P/L) | 51.85 | 60 | 70 |
| I¹ | 1998,00 Spoon, Sm.™ (Natrl) | 19.95 | 26 | 38 |
| | Combo (P/L) | 39.85 | — | — |
| J¹ | 1998 Spring™ (Natrl) | 29.95 | 35 | 40 |
| | Combo (P/L) | 51.85 | — | — |
| K¹ | 1998 Tea™ (Natrl) | 19.95 | 29 | 45 |
| | Combo (P/L) | 37.85 | — | — |
| | 1998 Waste, Med.™ (Natrl)[np] | 71.95 | — | — |
| | Combo (P/L) | 111.85 | — | — |
| L¹ | 1998 Gma Bonnie's Two-Pie™ | 95.00 | 128 | 175 |
| | with Protector | 110.00 | 170 | 225 |
| | with Liner | 131.00 | 175 | 225 |
| | Combo (P/L) | 124.00 | 165 | 250 |
| | Full Set (C/Lid) | 182.00 | 170 | 260 |
| | *1999 January Sale – Naturals* | | | |
| M¹ | 1999 Berry, Large™ (Natrl) | 28.00 | 42 | 43 |
| | Combo (P/L) | 48.00 | — | — |
| N¹ | 1999 Darning™ (Natrl) | 31.00 | — | — |
| | Combo (P/L) | 57.00 | — | — |
| O¹ | 1999 Picnic, Large™ (Natrl) | 89.00 | 104 | 125 |
| | Combo (P/L) | 140.00 | — | — |
| P¹ | 1999 Pie™ (Natrl) | 39.00 | 41 | 60 |
| | Combo (P/L) | 68.00 | — | — |
| | **continued next page** | | | |

[np] = Not Pictured

**E¹** 1998 Hostess Appreciation

5.75$^L$ x 3.75$^W$ x 3$^H$

Form No:      unknown
No. Sold:

*Given to Hostesses with shows in both 10/97 and 1/98. Liner sold separately.*

**I¹** 1998 Natural Small Spoon

5.5$^L$ x 5.5$^W$ x 6$^H$

Form No:      10871
No. Sold:

*Offered in 1/98 and then again in 1/00.*

**M¹** 1999 Large Berry

8.5$^L$ x 8.5$^W$ x 5$^H$

Form No:      19844
No. Sold:

need help?

# Need help inventorying?

see page 158

**F¹** 1998 Natural Cake

12$^L$ x 12$^W$ x 6$^H$

Form No: 10481
No. Sold:

*Included riser.*

**G¹** 1998-00 Natural Small Gathering

14$^L$ x 9$^W$ x 4.5$^H$

Form No: 12572
No. Sold:

*Offered in 1/98, 2/99 and then again in the 1/00.*

**H¹** 1998 Natural Kiddie Purse

7$^L$ x 5$^W$ x 3.5$^H$

Form No: 10898
No. Sold:

**J¹** 1998 Natural Spring

11$^L$ x 8$^W$ x 5.5$^H$

Form No: 10880
No. Sold:

*First offered in 1/98, but then brought back during the 2/99 sale.*

**K¹** 1998 Natural Tea

7$^L$ x 5$^W$ x 3.5$^H$

Form No: 10847
No. Sold:

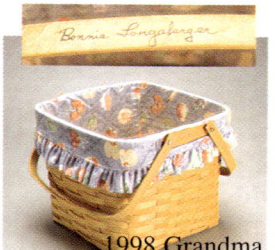

**L¹** 1998 Grandma Bonnie's Two-Pie

12$^L$ x 12$^W$ x 10$^H$

Form No: 19241
No. Sold:

*Basket features Grandma Bonnie's signature burned in on one handle. Created in celebration of her 90th Birthday.*

**N¹** 1999 Natural Darning

10$^{RD}$ x 4$^H$

Form No: 19640
No. Sold:

*Both a regular and divided protector were offered.*

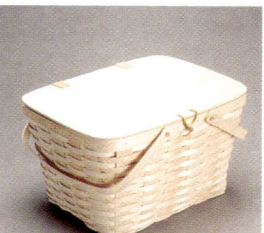

**O¹** 1999 Natural Large Picnic

17$^L$ x 14$^W$ x 11$^H$

Form No: 19755
No. Sold:

*Only available during January 1999. Included riser.*

**P¹** 1999 Natural Pie

12$^L$ x 12$^W$ x 4$^H$

Form No: 19441
No. Sold:

*Availability extended through Feb.28, 1999.*

| Photo | Description | Original | Avg. | High |
|---|---|---|---|---|
| | **MARKET VALUES** | | | |

| Photo | Description | Original | Avg. | High |
|---|---|---|---|---|
| Q¹ | 1999 Spoon, Med. (Natrl) | 28.00 | — | **43** |
| | Combo **(P/L)** | 51.00 | — | — |
| | *1999 January Sale – Naturals (con't)* | | | |
| R¹ | 1999 Vegetable, Lg. (Natrl) | 48.00 | — | — |
| | Combo **(P/L)** | 79.00 | — | — |
| R¹ | 2000 Vegetable, Med (Natrl) | 37.00 | **43** | **62** |
| | Combo **(P/L)** | 63.00 | — | — |
| S¹ | 2000 Berry, Small (Natrl) | 22.00 | **30** | **35** |
| | Combo **(P/L)** | 38.00 | — | — |
| S¹ | 2000 Fruit, Small (Natrl) | 25.00 | **37** | **39** |
| | Combo **(P/L)** | 45.00 | — | — |
| S¹ | 2000 Picnic, Small (Natrl) | 59.00 | **75** | **89** |
| | Combo **(P/L)** | 99.00 | — | — |
| T¹ | 2000 Bread, W. Traditions (Natrl) | 33.00 | — | — |
| | Combo **(P/L)** | 54.00 | — | — |
| U¹ | 2000 Dave Longaberger Founder's Basket | 189.00 | **200** | **250** |
| | with **P**rotector | 200.00 | **218** | **285** |
| | with **Lid** | 248.00 | **250** | **300** |
| | Combo **(P/Lid)** | 249.00 | **268** | **350** |
| V¹ | 2000 October Fields | 59.00 | **66** | **90** |
| | with **P**rotector | 68.00 | **79** | **90** |
| | with **Liner** | 81.00 | **100** | **110** |
| | Combo **(P/L)** | 79.00 | **102** | **149** |
| | Full Set **(C/Lid)** | 101.00 | **120** | **175** |
| V¹ | 2000 Double Leaf Tie-On | 10.00 | **14** | **18** |
| W¹ | 2001 Oval Laundry | 159.00 | **160** | **200** |
| | with **P**rotector | 177.00 | **170** | **203** |
| | with **Liner** | 204.00 | **180** | **210** |
| | Combo **(P/L)** | 198.00 | **200** | **250** |
| | Full Set **(C/Lid)** | 281.00 | — | — |
| X¹ | 2001 Card Keeper | 54.00 | **58** | **90** |
| | with **P**rotector | 70.00 | **70** | **95** |
| | with **Liner** | 72.00 | **75** | **95** |
| | Combo **(P/L)** | 69.00 | **79** | **99** |
| | Full Set **(C/Lid)** | 103.00 | **110** | **135** |
| Y¹ | 2001 Med Saddlebrook | 109.00 | **120** | **165** |
| | with **P**rotector | 116.00 | — | — |
| Z¹ | 2001 Pumpkin Patch | 49.00 | — | — |
| | with **P**rotector | 57.00 | — | — |
| | with **Liner** | 70.00 | — | — |
| | Combo **(P/L)** | 69.00 | **80** | **100** |
| | Full Set **(C/Lid)** | 109.00 | **110** | **130** |
| A² | 2002 Lucky Charm | 39.00 | **39** | **49** |
| | with **P**rotector | 43.00 | — | — |
| | with **Liner** | 51.00 | — | — |
| | Combo **(P/L)** | 55.00 | — | — |
| | Full Set **(C/Lid)** | 70.00 | — | — |

**Q¹** 1999 Natural Medium Spoon
6.5^L x 6.5^W x 8^H
Form No: 19658
No. Sold:

*Only available during January 1999.*

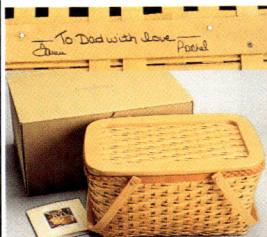

**U¹** 2000 Founder's Basket
15^L x 10^W x 7.5^H
Form No: 18791
No. Sold:

*Basket made in memory of Dave Longaberger.*

**Y¹** 2001 Med Saddlebrook
7.25^L x 4.5^W x 6.5^H
Form No: 12306
No. Sold:

**R¹** 1999 Natural Large Vegetable

16$^L$ x 9$^W$ x 3.5$^{FH}$ x 9$^{BH}$

Form No: 19551
No. Sold:

Med: 13$^L$ x 7.5$^W$ x 3$^{FH}$ x 8$^{BH}$

*Only available during January 1999.*

**S¹** 2000 Natural Baskets

see Quick Find

Form No.
Small Fruit: 17671
Small Berry: 17841
Small Picnic: 18040

*Only available Jan 2000.*

**T¹** 2000 Woven Traditions Bread

14.5$^L$ x 7.5$^W$ x 3.75$^H$

Form No: 18031
No. Sold:

*Only available Jan 2000.*

**V¹** 2000 October Fields

6.5$^{RD}$ x 9$^H$

Form No: 16951
Tie-On: 73393
No. Sold: 129,583

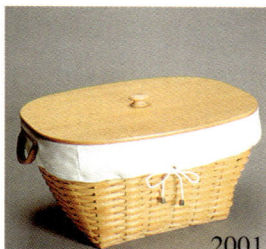

**W¹** 2001 Oval Laundry

21.25$^L$ x 14.25$^W$ x 10.5$^H$

Form No: 10893
No. Sold:

**X¹** 2001 Card Keeper

10.75$^L$ x 9$^W$ x 5$^{FH}$ x 7$^{BH}$

Form No: 12195
No. Sold:

**Z¹** 2001 Pumpkin Patch

6.5$^{RD}$ x 6.75$^H$

Form No: 10621
No. Sold:

**A²** 2002 Lucky Charm

5.25$^L$ x 4.25$^W$ x 1.75$^{FH}$ x 3$^{BH}$

Form No: 11482
No. Sold:

*Hostess Appreciation. Given to Hostesses with shows in both 10/01 and 1/02. Liner sold separately.*

## Feature Baskets

**B²**           2002
Pot of Gold

19.75^RD x 12.5^H

Form No:        11903
No. Sold:

*First time for this form. Available only to Hostesses in Jan.2002.*

### MARKET VALUES

| Photo | Description | | Original | Avg. | High |
|---|---|---|---|---|---|
| B² | 2002 | Pot of Gold™ | 198.00 | — | — |
| | | with **P**rotector | 237.00 | — | — |
| | | with **L**iner | 244.00 | — | — |
| | | Combo **(P/L)** | 278.00 | — | — |
| | | Full Set **(C/Lid)** | 357.00 | — | — |
| | 2002 | Window Box™ [np] | 89.00 | — | — |
| | | with **P**rotector | 101.00 | — | — |
| | | with **L**iner | 109.00 | — | — |
| | | Combo **(P/L)** | 118.00 | — | — |

[np] = Not Pictured.

f  u  n  **f a c t**

## Top Selling Feature Baskets:
## Jun 2000 – Jun 2001

2001 Inaugural™
2000 Horizon of Hope®
2001 Strawberry™
2000 Deck the Halls™
2000 October Fields™
2001 Vintage Blossoms™
2001 Peony™
2000 Let It Snow™

Candace Madura
Freedom, Pennsylvania

Candace knows a good product when she sees one. She signed up to be a Consultant in 1997 without ever having bought a single basket! Her first purchase was the Treasure Stand™ which she bought at her first show. As evidenced by her photo entry, Wrought Iron is one of Candace's favorite Longaberger Products®.

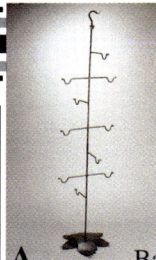

**A.** 95-97 Basket Tree

4'7" H

| Form No: | 74012 |
|---|---|
| Hanging | 70084 |

*The Tree is made up of the Hanging Tree [top part] and the Table Top Tree [lower section].*

## MARKET VALUES

| Photo | Description | Original | Avg. | High |
|---|---|---|---|---|
| | **Basket Tree** | | | |
| A. | (95-97)Ten Level Tree | 119.95 | **146** | **205** |
| | (95-97)Hanging Tree [np] | 69.95 | **75** | **105** |
| B. | (95-97)Table Top Tree | 64.95 | **75** | **110** |
| C. | (96-97)Hook Finial | 10.95 | — | — |
| C. | (95-97)Leaf Finial | 12.95 | **10** | **15** |
| | **Herb Markers** | | | |
| D. | (96-97)Gift Sets: | | | |
| | Basil & Chives | 19.95 | **17** | **25** |
| | Parsley & Thyme | 19.95 | **17** | **25** |
| | Dill & Cilantro | 19.95 | **17** | **25** |
| | Sage & Oregano | 19.95 | **17** | **25** |
| | **Stands/Tables** | | | |
| E. | (99-02)File Basket Stand | 189.00 | — | — |
| F. | (00-02)Side Table | 229.00 | — | — |
| G. | (99) Snowman Stand. Lg | 99.00 | **113** | **190** |
| | Combo **(w/baskets)** | 299.00 | **276** | **350** |
| G. | (00) Snowman Stand, Sm | 69.00 | **73** | **100** |
| | Combo **(w/basket)** | 129.00 | **144** | **185** |
| H. | (96-01)Treasure Stand | 149.00 | **167** | **207** |
| | **Tabletop Items** | | | |
| I. | (00-02)Easel, Large | 32.00 | — | — |
| J. | (98-02)Easel, Small | 19.00 | **19** | **20** |
| K. | (00) Heart to Heart Stand | 0.00 | **56** | **77** |
| | Combo **(w/baskets)** | 118.00 | **143** | **168** |
| L. | (99-02)Mug Rack | 54.00 | **54** | **70** |

**continued next page**

[np] = Not Pictured

**E.** 99-02 File Stand

20^L x 17.25^W x 22.5^H

| Form No: | 75906 |
|---|---|

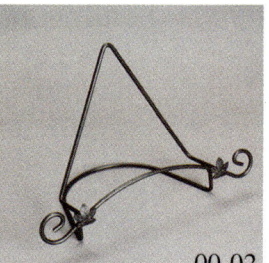

**I.** 00-02 Large Easel

12.75^L x 7.5^W x 9.5^H

| Form No: | 77992 |
|---|---|

FOUNDRY COLLECTION®

Foundry®

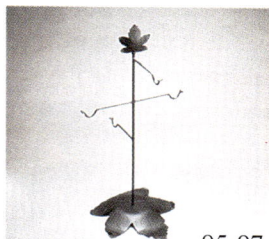

**B.** Table Top Tree
95-97

24 $^H$

Form No: 70068

**C.** Finials

N/A

Form No:
  Hook: 70254
  Leaf: 74039

**D.** Herb Markers
96-97

Form No:
  Basil & Chives 32905
  Parsley & Thyme 32808
  Dill & Cilantro 33006
  Sage & Oregano 33014

*Basket is for display only.*

**F.** Side Table
00-02

19$^L$x 19$^W$x 24$^H$

Form No: 76473 / 76481

*Choice of solid wood or glass tabletop.*

**G.** Snowman Stands

Sm: 11$^W$ x 12$^D$ x 22$^H$
17$^W$x 13.25$^D$x 31.5$^H$

Small: 77691
Large: 75795

*Shelves sold separately. Designed to hold the Christmas and Holiday Hostess baskets.*

**H.** Treasure Stand
96-01

24$^L$x 14$^W$x 15$^H$

Form No: 70327

*Shelves sold separately.*

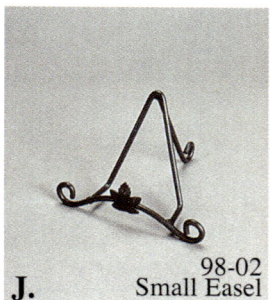

**J.** Small Easel
98-02

5.5$^W$x 4$^H$

Form No: 75604

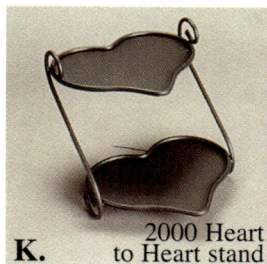

**K.** 2000 Heart to Heart stand

6.75$^L$ x 6.75$^W$ x 7.25$^H$

Form No: 78221

*Promoted along with the 2000 Sweetheart baskets.*

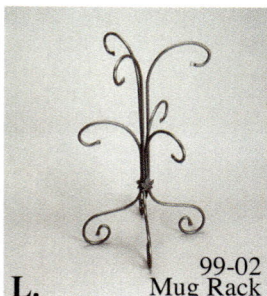

**L.** Mug Rack
99-02

9.75$^W$ x 16$^H$

Form No: 75892

## Foundry®

### MARKET VALUES

| Photo | Description | Original | Avg. | High |
|---|---|---|---|---|
| | *Tabletop Items (con't)* | | | |
| M. | (01) Pedestal, Large Star | 59.00 | — | — |
| M. | (01) Pedestal, Med Star | 49.00 | — | — |
| M. | (01) Pedestal, Small Star | 39.00 | — | — |
| N. | (95-98) Two-Pie Server | 59.95 | 60 | 77 |
| | *Wall Hangings* | | | |
| O. | (96-98) Plant Hanger | 39.95 | 45 | 50 |
| P. | (97-98) Spice Rack | 74.95 | 98 | 155 |
| P. | with Mug Rack | 104.90 | 105 | 135 |
| | with Shelf [np] | 139.90 | 110 | 135 |
| | Full Set | 169.85 | 224 | 350 |
| Q. | (96-98) Wall Arch | 29.98 | 33 | 50 |

**M.** 2001 Star Pedestals

Sm: 7.25$^W$ x 6.25$^H$
Md: 10.25$^W$ x 6.5$^H$
Lg: 13.25$^W$ x 4.25$^H$

Form No:
Small: 75931
Medium: 76635
Large: 76732

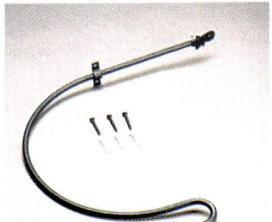

**Q.** 96-98 Wall Arch

15.5$^L$ x 11.5$^H$
Form No: 70297

*Discontinued after 8/31/98.*

need help?

Where is the Foundry
that is still available?

see page 10

**N.**  95-98
Two-Pie Server

10.5$^{RD}$ x 14$^{H}$

Form No:  74004

*There is still a Two-Pie Server in the Regular Line. It was made to be more decorative in 1998.*

**O.**  96-98
Plant Hanger

18$^{W}$ x 16$^{H}$

Form No:  70271

*Discontinued after 8/31/98.*

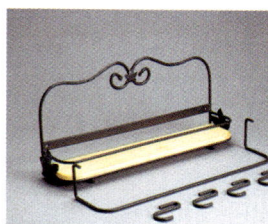

**P.**  97-98
Spice Rack

17$^{L}$ x 3.5$^{W}$ x 8.5$^{H}$

Form No:  71307

*The additional shelf is not pictured. Mug Rack included 4 "S" hooks.*

f  u  n  **f a c t**

## Two-Pie Server tip . . .

Increase the use of your Two-Pie Server by using it with Dinner Plates, the 2-Qt. Covered Casserole Dish, or Pie Plate. Or remove the knob from a 9" Measuring lid to use as a shelf.

# *Market Activity Report*

Throughout the year, The Bentley Collection has collected and reviewed over 26,000 actual selling transactions from the secondary market. Overall more than 26% of the items in the market have changed value in some way, up or down from last year. Below is a summary of the market activity reported to us during the 2001 – 2002 season.

## Top 10 Collections
### showing the highest market activity

| Collections with the greatest activity | % of Activity |
| --- | --- |
| #10 All-American® | 3.8% |
| #9 Retired Baskets | 4.2% |
| #8 Easter Series™ | 4.3% |
| #7 Regular Line Items | 4.5% |
| #6 May Series™ | 4.6% |
| #5 Pottery® | 4.9% |
| #4 Christmas Collection™ | 5.0% |
| #3 Booking/Promo Baskets™ | 5.4% |
| #2 Collectors Club™ | 7.7% |
| #1 Feature Baskets | 8.6% |

**Sharon Johnson**
*Mount Sterling, Ky.*

*Sharon's first basket was a 1995 Horizon of Hope®, which was given by a friend. Her second basket was a 1999 Popcorn™, which her husband Don won for her at a church auction. Ever since then, her husband has made it a habit to give her a Christmas™ basket each year.*

## Good Ol' Summertime™

**Series first introduced in 1998. Promoted during the month of July.**

**A.** 1998 Picnic Pal
$9.5^L$ x $9.5^W$ x $2.75^H$

Form No: 18643
No. Sold:

*Red and blue trim strip.*

### MARKET VALUES

| Photo | Description | Original | Avg. | High |
|---|---|---|---|---|
| A. | 1998 Picnic Pal™ | 37.00 | **50** | **60** |
| | with **P**rotector | 44.00 | **51** | **64** |
| | with **L**iner | 53.00 | **51** | **64** |
| | Combo (**P/L**) | 51.00 | **53** | **70** |
| B. | 1999 Seashell™ | 39.00 | **60** | **85** |
| | with **P**rotector | 46.00 | **60** | **85** |
| | with **L**iner | 55.00 | **60** | **85** |
| | Combo (**P/L**) | 49.00 | **75** | **129** |
| | Full Set (**C/Lid**) | 69.00 | **90** | **145** |
| C. | 1999 Beachcomber™ | 67.00 | **90** | **110** |
| | with **P**rotector | 83.00 | — | — |
| | with **L**iner | 91.00 | — | — |
| | Combo (**P/L**) | 97.00 | **111** | **156** |
| | Full Set (**C/Lid**) | 127.00 | **141** | **190** |
| C. | 1999 Seashell Tie-On | 8.00 | **13** | **22** |
| D. | 2000 Shaker Taker™ | 39.00 | **40** | **45** |
| | with **P**rotector | 43.00 | — | — |
| | with **L**iner | 54.00 | — | — |
| | Combo (**P/L**) | 49.00 | **50** | **92** |
| D. | 2000 Salt/Pepper Tie-On | 8.00 | **11** | **14** |
| D. | 2000 Barbeque Buddy™ | 49.00 | **63** | **90** |
| | with **P**rotector | 54.00 | **75** | **92** |
| | with **L**iner | 67.00 | **76** | **95** |
| | Combo (**P/L**) | 59.00 | **80** | **135** |
| D. | 2000 BBQ Buddy Tie-On | 10.00 | **11** | **16** |
| E. | 2001 Boardwalk, Small™ | 59.00 | **65** | **100** |
| | with **P**rotector | 67.00 | — | — |
| | with **L**iner | 83.00 | — | — |
| | Combo (**P/L**) | 79.00 | **83** | **125** |
| E. | 2001 Sand Dollar Tie-On | 8.00 | **11** | **14** |
| E. | 2001 Boardwalk, Med.™ | 89.00 | — | — |
| | with **P**rotector | 100.00 | **100** | **110** |
| | with **L**iner | 118.00 | — | — |
| | Combo (**P/L**) | 115.00 | **115** | **153** |
| E. | 2001 Surf's Up Tie-On | 8.00 | **10** | **14** |
| E. | 2001 Boardwalk, Large™ | 129.00 | — | — |
| | with **P**rotector | 148.00 | — | — |
| | with **L**iner | 168.00 | — | — |
| | Combo (**P/L**) | 169.00 | **170** | **195** |
| | 2002 Back Porch™ [np] | 59.00 | — | — |
| | with **P**rotector | 71.00 | — | — |
| | with **L**iner | 79.00 | — | — |
| | Combo (**P/L**) | 79.00 | — | — |
| | 2002 Bumblebee Pin[np] | 8.00 | — | — |

2001
**E.** Boardwalk Baskets
Sm:$9.25^L$ x $5^W$ x $6.25^H$
Md:$12.5^L$ x $6.75^W$ x $8.5^H$
Lg:$17.75^L$ x $10.5^W$ x $12^H$

Form No:
Small: 11393
Medium: 10552
Large: 10564
Sand Dollar: 39551
Surf's Up: 30088

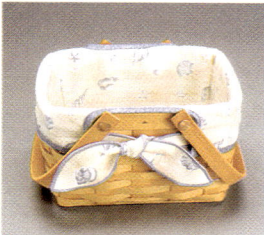

**B.** 1999 Seashell

7.75$^L$ x 5.75$^W$ x 5$^H$

Form No:          15296
  Tie-On:          36561
No. Sold:

*Both baskets in 1999 were offered to everyone. No Hostess Only.*

**C.** 1999 Beachcomber

10.5$^L$ x 9$^W$ x 8$^H$

Form No:          15342
No. Sold:

**D.** 2000

Sm: 7.5$^L$x 3.75$^W$x 2.75$^H$
Lg: 12$^L$ x 5.25$^W$ x 3$^H$

Shaker Taker:     17469
BBQ Buddy:        16284

f  u  n  **f a c t**

## Award-winning Longaberger Video Department

The Longaberger Video Services department began in September 1991 and provides video production services for all areas of the company. Covering all work shifts, the Video Services department's 18 employees provide around-the-clock company news, entertainment and general information. L-TV (Longaberger Television) broadcasts programming to over 600 televisions in 12 locations throughout the company, in four different counties.

# We Need You!

## Ever wonder where the values in the Bentley Guide come from?

? Ever look at a value and disagree with it?

? The Bentley Guide is based on *actual selling prices*.

? Most of the research we gather comes from Collectors like you!

? **We need you to accurately represent your area.**

? Whenever you buy, sell or trade, **SEND US YOUR RESULTS!**

? The more results we have, the more accurate your Guide will be.

## Call Us
1. 800. 837. 4394
Monday through Friday, 9am - 5pm (EST)

## Report Online  NEW!
www.bentleyguide.com
24 hours a day, 7 days a week

## Fax Us
1. 888. 275. 8484
24 hours a day, 7 days a week

**IT'S FUN!**

## E-mail Us
research@bentleyguide.com
24 hours a day, 7 days a week

## Mail Us
Bentley Guide Research
5870 Zarley Street, Suite C
New Albany, Ohio  43054

## The Info We Need
? Name of Basket and its Collection
? Year
? Did you buy, sell or trade it?
? Selling Price (not including shipping)
? Condition
? Accessories (liner, protector, tie-on, lid, divider, etc...)
? Signatures (who and how many)
? Which forum was used (internet, auction, etc...)
? Selling state and buying state

# Heartland Collection®

Heartland®

**Carroll Weinbroer**
**Valley City, Ohio**

*Carroll loves baskets with blue weaving: Collectors Club™, J.W.® & of course, Heartland®. She enjoys using her baskets as much as possible. She was even scolded by a well meaning friend for using her Heartland® Medium Chore to pick blueberries! Carroll has about 100 baskets in her collection and that's nothing to get blue about!*

## Heartland®

**Dresden Blue® shoestring weave. Series created in 1988, completed in 2001. Special burnt in logo on bottom.**

1990-01
A. Bakery

14.5$^L$ x 7.5$^W$ x 3.75$^H$

Form No: 14711
No.Sold:

## MARKET VALUES

| Photo | Description | Original | Avg. | High |
|-------|-------------|----------|------|------|
| A. | (90-01) Bakery™ | 30.95 | **42** | **55** |
| B. | (94-01) Button™ | 22.95 | **33** | **43** |
| C. | (99-00) Cake™ | 62.00 | **65** | **79** |
| D. | (88-97) Chore, Medium™ | 36.95 | **47** | **85** |
| E. | (89-97) Chore, Mini™ | 19.95 | **37** | **56** |
| F. | (89-97) Chore, Small™ | 22.95 | **43** | **65** |
| G. | (96-01) Darning™ | 39.95 | **44** | **70** |
| H. | (1990) Getaway™ | 65.95 | **154** | **190** |
| I. | (88-97) Key, Medium™ | 26.95 | **35** | **50** |
| J. | (94-97) Key, Small™ | 21.95 | **30** | **40** |
| K. | (88-97) Key, Tall™ | 34.95 | **44** | **70** |
| L. | (89-97) Market, Medium™ | 43.95 | **67** | **80** |

**continued next page**

1989-97
E. Mini Chore

7$^L$ x 5$^W$ 3.5$^H$

Form No: 10758
No.Sold:

collection **n o t e**

All Heartland Baskets® have this burned-in logo on the bottom, authenticating the collection.

1988-97
I. Medium Key

9$^L$ x 5$^W$ x 5$^H$

Form No: 11118
No.Sold:

*One of the first in the series.*

**B.** 1994-01
Button

7$^{RD}$ x 3$^H$

Form No: 15423
No.Sold:

**C.** 1999-00
Cake

12$^L$ x 12$^W$ x 6$^H$

Form No: 15148
No.Sold:

*Included a wood riser.*

**D.** 1988-97
Medium Chore

13$^L$ x 8$^W$ x 5$^H$

Form No: 13528
No.Sold:

*One of the first in the series.*

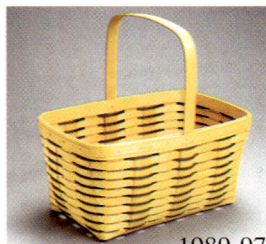

**F.** 1989-97
Small Chore

10$^L$ x 6$^W$ x 4$^H$

Form No: 13404
No.Sold:

**G.** 1996-01 Darning

10$^{RD}$ x 4$^H$

Form No: 15598
No. Sold:

**H.** 1990 Getaway

17$^L$ x 14$^W$ x 11$^H$

Form No: 300-CCS
No. Sold:

*Hostess only. Featured in 1990.*

**J.** 1994-97
Small Key

7$^L$ x 5$^W$ x 3.5$^H$

Form No: 10782
No.Sold:

*One of the first in the series.*

**K.** 1988-97
Tall Key

9.5$^L$ x 5$^W$ x 9.5$^H$

Form No: 11061
No.Sold:

*One of the first in the series.*

**L.** 1989-97
Medium Market

15$^L$ x 10$^W$ x 7.5$^H$

Form No: 10545
No.Sold:

## *Heartland*®

**Series completed in 2001.**

## MARKET VALUES

| Photo | Description | Original | Avg. | High |
|---|---|---|---|---|
| M | (90-00) Muffin™ | 25.95 | **36** | **55** |
| N. | (98-00) Pantry™ | 53.00 | **53** | **75** |
| O. | (89-97) Peg, Large™ | 28.95 | **40** | **70** |
| P. | (88-98) Purse, Small™ | 36.95 | **50** | **85** |
| Q | (98-01) Recipe™ | 39.00 | **40** | **40** |
| R. | (88-99) Spoon, Small™ | 23.95 | **34** | **55** |
| S. | (90-97) Spring™ | 34.95 | **48** | **75** |
| T. | (97-99) Vegetable, Med™ | 50.95 | **54** | **75** |

**M.**
1990-00
Muffin

$11.5^L$ x $5^W$ x $3^H$

Form No: 14516
No.Sold:

**Q.**
1998-01
Recipe

$8^L$ x $5.5^W$ x $4.5^{FH}$ x $6^{BH}$

Form No: 10596
No.Sold:

*need help?*

## How do we get our values?

see page 8

**N.** 1998-00 Pantry

$14^L$ x $9^W$ x $4.5^H$

Form No: 13951
No.Sold:

**O.** 1989-97 Large Peg

$6.5^L$ x $6.5^W$ x $8^H$

Form No: 11177
No.Sold:

**P.** 1988-98 Small Purse

$9.5^L$ x $6^W$ x $6^H$

Form No: 10839
No.Sold:

**R.** 1988-99 Small Spoon

$5.5^L$ x $5.5^W$ x $6^H$

Form No: 11096
No.Sold:

**S.** 1990-97 Spring

$11^L$ x $8^W$ x $5.5^H$

Form No: 10936
No.Sold:

**T.** 1997-99 Medium Vegetable

$13^L$ x $7.5^W$ x $3^{FH}$ x $8^{BH}$

Form No: 16713
No.Sold:

f  u  n  **f a c t**

## Nurses Inauguration Basket

This 1999 Heartland Button Basket™ was personalized by the Ohio Nurses Association to celebrate the Nurses' legacy at a 1999 Convention.

While they were not limited edition baskets created or sponsored by The Longaberger Company, they are a very nice keepsake.

**111**

# Oak Handles

## 1989: Handles changed from Oak to Maple

Oak handles
prior to 1989

Prior to 1989, all handles on Longaberger Baskets were made of Oak. This practice was handed down from J.W. himself. The smooth, worn finish of oak is a feature among most of his creations.

Maple handles
after 1989

In March 1989, a concern arose that the core from the maple logs used for making the veneer splints for the basket were just being thrown out. Instead, they could be used to make handles. Test marketing started immediately to compare oak versus maple.

Initially, these studies reported no real difference in durability, however the maple handles tended to be favored because they blended better with the baskets.

In May 1989, maple handles were implemented on all baskets, with the exception of the 1989 J.W. Banker's Waste™.

After the change, many wondered if the change was based on cost efficiency, rather than quality. Dave assured the Consultants that while there were many factors that affected the decision, the test studies eventually proved that maple handles were more durable than oak, not cracking with long term use, like oak has a tendency to do.

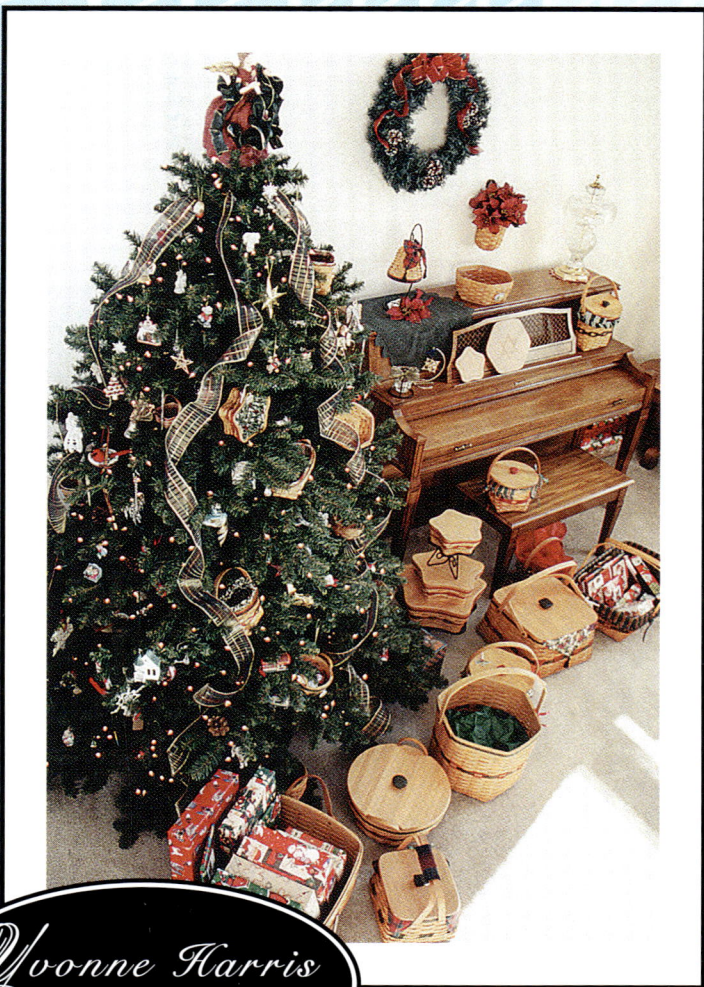

## *Yvonne Harris*
### *Auburn, Washington*

*Impressed by the fact that her consultant actually used all her baskets, Yvonne became a collector herself. Two years and over 100 baskets later, Yvonne and her husband are both avid collectors, making trips to The Homestead and Dresden.*

## Holiday Hostess™

**Red and Green Weave.
Red or Green Trim.**

### MARKET VALUES

| Photo | | Description | Original | Avg. | High |
|---|---|---|---|---|---|
| A. | 1987 | Tray™ | 32.95 | **76** | 135 |
| B. | 1988 | Tall Key™ | 30.95 | **84** | 115 |
| C. | 1988 | Weekender™ | 65.95 | **154** | 225 |
| D. | 1988 | Large Market™ | 49.95 | **119** | 135 |
| E. | 1988 | Small Laundry™ | 67.95 | **226** | 288 |
| F. | 1989 | Medium Gathering™ | 40.95 | **104** | 135 |
| G. | 1989 | Large Fruit™ | 49.95 | **90** | 140 |
| H. | 1989 | Magazine™ | 53.95 | **122** | 160 |
| I. | 1990 | 13" Measuring™ | 69.95 | **94** | 165 |
| J. | 1990 | Large Gathering™ | 65.95 | **95** | 125 |
| K. | 1991 | Tree Trimming™ | 79.95 | **90** | 190 |
| | | Combo (**P**) | 92.90 | **153** | 225 |
| L. | 1992 | Gift Giving™ | 124.95 | **124** | 200 |
| | | with **P**rotector | 137.90 | **140** | 200 |
| | | with **L**iner | 146.90 | **140** | 220 |
| | | Combo (**P/L**) | 169.85 | **170** | 225 |

**A.** 1987 Tray
$14^L$ x $9^W$ x $4.5^H$
Form No:  2300-JGRS
No. Sold:

**E.** 1988 Small Laundry
$24^L$ x $17^W$ x $10^H$
Form No:  2600-ORGS
No. Sold:

### collection **note**

Holiday Hostess baskets are only available to hostesses during the Holiday selling season. This season usually begins Sept.1 and goes through the end of the year. It is very common for the original collector to have purchased these baskets at half price, using their hostess benefits. This explains why some of the values in the market look as if they are below original retail.

**I.** 1990 13" Measuring
$13^{RD}$ x $12.5^H$
Form No:  4200-CGRS
No. Sold:

**B.** 1988 Tall Key

9.5$^L$ x 5$^W$ x 9.5$^H$

Form No: 1000-IRGS
No. Sold:

**C.** 1988 Weekender

10.5$^L$ x 9$^W$ x 8$^H$

Form No: 200-YRGS
No. Sold:

**D.** 1988 Large Market

16$^L$ x 11$^W$ x 9$^H$

Form No: 600-ARGS
No. Sold:

1989
**F.** Medium Gathering

18$^L$ x 11$^W$ x 4.5$^H$

Form No: 2400-AGRS
No. Sold:

1989
**G.** Large Fruit

13$^{RD}$ x 8.5$^H$

Form No: 3200-BGRS
No. Sold:

**H.** 1989 Magazine

16$^L$ x 8$^W$ x 11$^H$

Form No: 2100-CGRS
No. Sold:

1990
**J.** Large Gathering

19$^L$ x 12$^W$ x 6$^H$

Form No: 2500-CGRS
No. Sold:

1991
**K.** Tree Trimming

12.5$^{RD}$ x 13.5$^H$

Form No:
1900-BRGS/BGRS$^†$
No. Sold:

**L.** 1992 Gift Giving

20.5$^L$ x 15$^W$ x 10.5$^H$

Form No: 12700/12718$^†$
No. Sold:

† = Product numbers are stated:  Red weave / Green weave

## Holiday Hostess™

**M.** 1993 Homecoming
15$^L$ x 15$^W$ x 7.5$^H$

Form No:    12084/12092†
No. Sold:

### MARKET VALUES

| | Description | Original | Avg. | High |
|---|---|---|---|---|
| M. | 1993 Homecoming™ | 109.95 | **140** | **200** |
| | with Protector | 120.90 | **140** | **210** |
| | with Liner | 131.90 | **140** | **210** |
| | with Lid | 145.90 | **155** | **210** |
| | Combo (P/L/Lid) | 149.95 | **160** | **220** |
| N. | 1994 Sleigh Bell™ | 139.95 | **182** | **250** |
| | with Protector | 154.90 | **185** | **250** |
| | with Liner | 167.90 | **185** | **250** |
| | with Lid | 175.90 | **185** | **250** |
| | Combo (P/L/Lid) | 199.95 | **193** | **275** |
| O. | 1995 Evergreen™ | 139.95 | **148** | **215** |
| | with Protector | 154.90 | **153** | **220** |
| | with Liner | 167.90 | **155** | **220** |
| | with Lid | 179.90 | **160** | **230** |
| | Combo (P/L/Lid) | 199.95 | **165** | **235** |
| P. | 1996 Yuletide Treasures™ | 129.95 | **149** | **200** |
| | with Protector | 144.90 | **149** | **200** |
| | with Liner | 159.90 | **149** | **200** |
| | with Lid | 179.90 | **149** | **200** |
| | Combo (P/L/Lid) | 199.95 | **169** | **225** |
| Q. | 1997 Snowflake™ | 129.95 | **117** | **135** |
| | with Protector | 156.90 | **117** | **160** |
| | with Liner | 156.90 | **120** | **185** |
| | Combo (P/L) | 159.95 | **126** | **195** |
| | Full Set (C/Lid) | 204.90 | **141** | **200** |
| R. | 1998 Winter Wishes™ | 95.00 | **96** | **130** |
| | with Protector | 110.00 | **98** | **140** |
| | with Liner | 122.00 | **98** | **145** |
| | Combo (P/L) | 115.00 | **100** | **150** |
| | Full Set (C/Lid) | 149.00 | **105** | **168** |
| S. | 1999 Pinecone™ | 99.00 | **113** | **145** |
| | with Protector | 119.00 | — | — |
| | with Liner | 123.00 | — | — |
| | Combo (P/L) | 129.00 | **126** | **155** |
| | Full Set (C/Lid) | 174.00 | **160** | **178** |
| T. | 2000 12 Days of Christmas™ | 139.00 | **118** | **166** |
| | with Protector | 171.00 | — | — |
| | with Liner | 176.00 | — | — |
| | Combo (P/L) | 189.00 | **128** | **190** |
| | Full Set (C/Lid) | 234.00 | **141** | **195** |
| U. | 2001 Shining Star™ | 109.00 | — | — |
| | with Protector | 132.00 | — | — |
| | with Liner | 135.00 | — | — |
| | Combo (P/L) | 149.00 | **124** | **165** |
| | Full Set (C/Lid) | 198.00 | — | — |

**Q.** 1997 Snowflake
14$^L$ x 12.75$^W$ x 11.5$^H$

Form No:    12661/12653†
No. Sold:

*Three-level protector and wooden lid (with or without a knob) sold separately. Also features an open-weave bottom.*

**U.** 2001 Shining Star
13.5$^L$ x 14.5$^W$ x 4.75$^H$

Form No:    10753/10761†
No. Sold:

*Protector is a 2-piece, 5-way divided protector – sold separately.*

**116**  † = Product numbers are stated:  Red weave / Green weave

**N.** 1994 Sleigh Bell

$16.5^{RD}$ x $11.5^H$

Form No:    14427/14435†
No. Sold:

*Lid available with red or green knob.*

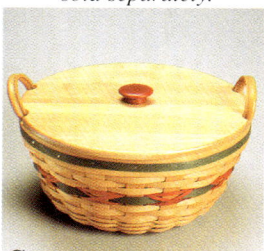

**O.** 1995 Evergreen

$15.5^L$ x $15.5^W$ x $12.25^H$

Form No:    19607/19615†
No. Sold:

*Lid available with red or green knob. Divider shelf sold separately.*

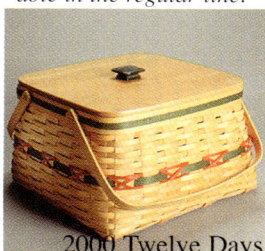

**P.** 1996 Yuletide Treasures

$20.25^L$ x $13.75^W$ x $7.5^H$

Form No:    18619/18627†
No. Sold:

*The lid that was introduced for this basket is still available in the regular line.*

**R.** 1998 Winter Wishes

$12.5^L$ x $8.25^W$ x $10.5^{FH}$ x $12^{BH}$

Form No:    12483/12491†
No. Sold:

*Lid available with red or green knob.*

**S.** 1999 Pinecone

$13^{RD}$ x $6.25^H$

Form No:  15253 / 15164†
No. Sold:

*Lid available with red or green knob. Divider shelf sold separately.*

**T.** 2000 Twelve Days of Christmas

$13^L$ x $13^W$ x $8.75^H$

Form No:  17833 / 17931†
No. Sold:

*Lid available with red or green knob. Has 20th Century logo on bottom.*

## DOUBLE TROUBLE!
### how could you ever tell them no?

**MINDY STOKER** Sunbury, Ohio

# The Bentley Collection wants to

## Feature YOUR Collection

### in the NEXT

## Edition BentleyGuide®

### Contest Details:

○ Only 35-40 collections will be featured – so send your entries right away! All entries must be received by March 15, 2003.

○ All winning photos will be featured in the 11th Edition, along with your name, city and state.

○ The Collector with the very best photo will receive $100 worth of Bentley products to supply friends with the special edition of the Bentley Guide or to use towards their own collection.

○ The other qualified winners will receive one *free* Bentley Collection 11th Edition Guide (at least a $30 value).

### Tips:

○ Vertical pictures work better than horizontal scenes.

○ Make sure that you have good lighting and no glares off of windows or mirrors. Also, be sure that the picture is clear with good focus.

○ Most rejected pictures are too dark or too blurry.

○ Sometimes choosing items all from one collection works best.

### Share your Collection with us today:

○ Send your photo entry to:  The Bentley Collection
c/o Nationwide Search 2003
5870 Zarley Street, Suite C
New Albany, Ohio 43054

○ Include your name, address and phone number on the back of the photo. Hold on to the negative because if selected, you may be contacted to arrange for the use of the negative. By entering this contest, you are granting J.Phillip, Inc. permission to use the photo in any forum without restitution. All photos sent become the property of The Bentley Collection and will not be returned. **Please send only one photo.** Entries limited to one per household.

## Millie Pearson
### Greentown, Indiana

*Wonderful surprises have come Millie's way recently. As a gift, her husband gave her the 1983 Bell™! On top of that, her friends gave her the Horizon of Hope® for her birthday! Now that would make anyone's day special!*

## Horizon of Hope ®

No color weave or trim. Each basket has the American Cancer Society logo on the bottom.

### MARKET VALUES

| | | Description | Original | Avg. | High |
|---|---|---|---|---|---|
| A. | 1995 | Horizon of Hope™ | 28.95 | **75** | **95** |
| | | with Protector | 31.90 | **78** | **110** |
| | | with Liner | 38.90 | **87** | **120** |
| | | Combo (P/L) | 41.85 | **108** | **145** |
| B. | 1996 | Horizon of Hope™ | 28.95 | **63** | **80** |
| | | with Protector | 31.90 | **63** | **85** |
| | | with Liner | 38.90 | **70** | **85** |
| | | Combo (P/L) | 41.85 | **71** | **115** |
| C. | 1997 | Horizon of Hope™ | 28.95 | **50** | **60** |
| | | with Protector | 31.90 | **62** | **85** |
| | | with Liner | 38.90 | **62** | **85** |
| | | Combo (P/L) | 41.85 | **64** | **90** |
| D. | 1998 | Horizon of Hope™ | 31.00 | **50** | **75** |
| | | with Protector | 34.00 | **53** | **78** |
| | | with Liner | 41.00 | **53** | **78** |
| | | Combo (P/L) | 44.00 | **67** | **95** |
| D. | 1998 | Oval Tie-On | 8.00 | **13** | **17** |
| E. | 1999 | Horizon of Hope™ | 31.00 | **60** | **75** |
| | | with Protector | 34.00 | **—** | **—** |
| | | with Liner | 44.00 | **—** | **—** |
| | | Combo (P/L) | 47.00 | **65** | **90** |
| | | Full Set (C/Lid) | 62.00 | **82** | **110** |
| E. | 1999 | Heart Tie-On | 8.00 | **12** | **16** |
| F. | 2000 | Horizon of Hope™ | 32.00 | **48** | **91** |
| | | with Protector | 35.00 | **—** | **—** |
| | | with Liner | 46.00 | **—** | **—** |
| | | Combo (P/L) | 49.00 | **58** | **100** |
| | | Full Set (C/Lid) | 65.00 | **71** | **105** |
| F. | 2000 | Hope Tie-On | 8.00 | **11** | **14** |
| G. | 2001 | Horizon of Hope™ | 34.00 | **38** | **60** |
| | | with Protector | 38.00 | **40** | **62** |
| | | with Liner | 48.00 | **40** | **62** |
| | | Combo (P/L) | 52.00 | **55** | **65** |
| | | Full Set (C/Lid) | 68.00 | **68** | **85** |
| G. | 2001 | Heart Tie-On | 8.00 | **12** | **14** |
| G. | 2001 | Votive w/Candle | 15.00 | **16** | **25** |

**A.** Horizon of Hope — 1995

5.75ᴸ x 3.75ᵂ x 3ᴴ

Form No: 17124
No. Sold: 181,506

*All Regular line fabrics were made available for this Liner.*

**E.** Horizon of Hope — 1999

6.25ᴸ x 5.25ᵂ x 3ᴴ

Form No: 14150
Tie-On: 36625
No. Sold: 368,719

*All Regular line fabrics were made available for this Liner. $1.3 Million was raised in 1999.*

**B.** 1996 Horizon of Hope

6.75$^L$ x 4.75$^W$ x 2.25$^H$

| | |
|---|---|
| Form No: | 15911 |
| No. Sold: | 226,292 |

*Each basket came with a set of 12 recipes. Liner offered in all regular line fabrics.*

**C.** 1997 Horizon of Hope

5.75$^L$ x 4$^W$ x 4$^H$

| | |
|---|---|
| Form No: | 18724 |
| No. Sold: | 278,689 |

*Liner available only as stand-up, but in all the regular line fabrics.*

**D.** 1998 Horizon of Hope

4$^L$ x 4$^W$ x 5.5$^H$

| | |
|---|---|
| Form No: | 10472 |
| Tie-On: | 33677 |
| No. Sold: | 372,941 |

*Each basket included a sheet of 12 breast self-exam reminder stickers. Liner offered in all regular line fabrics.*

**F.** 2000 Horizon of Hope

7.5$^L$ x 4.25$^W$ x 2.75$^H$

| | |
|---|---|
| Form No: | 17787 / 19194 |
| Tie-On: | 37036 |
| No. Sold: | 361,027 |

*Available in both classic stain and whitewash.*

**G.** 2001 Horizon of Hope

5.25$^{RD}$ x 4.25$^H$

| | |
|---|---|
| Form No: | 10591/11605 |
| Tie-On: | 77429 |
| Votive: | 74985 |
| No. Sold: | 332,258 |

*Available in both classic stain and whitewash. Tie-on and Votive sold separately.*

f u n **f a c t**

The annual Horizon of Hope Campaign is a two-month promotion during the months of July and August. Through this campaign over 11 million women have been reached with the early detection message and more than $7 million has been raised to further the cause.

## Large Hamper Basket History . . .

The Large Hamper™ is a form that has shown up in the Longaberger product line in many different variations. Following is a brief history time line describing the different looks of the Large Hamper.

### Prior to 1979 – July, 1986
- Available through the Regular Line.
- Attached Woven Lid with knob <u>at front</u> of Lid.
- No hand slots.
- Darker "old" stain, Natural or Natural with color.

### August, 1986 – 1990
- Available through the Hostess Collection.
- Attached Woven Lid with knob <u>at front</u> of Lid.
- No hand slots.
- Darker "old" stain, Natural or Natural with color.
- After 1987: Lighter "new' stain <u>only.</u>

### May 1986
- Available as a Feature Basket.
- No Lid.
- First time for two hand slots.
- Darker "old" stain <u>only.</u>

### 1991
- Featured for Shades of Autumn Hostesses only for one month.
- 3/8" Hostess Weaving.
- Detached Woven Lid with knob in <u>middle</u> of Lid.
- Two hand slots.
- Lighter "new' stain <u>only.</u>

### 1993 – 1994
- Available through the Regular Line.
- Detached Woven Lid with knob in middle of Lid.
- Two hand slots.
- Lighter "new' stain <u>only.</u>

### 1995 – 2000
- Available through the Hostess Collection.
- 3/8" Hostess Weaving.
- Detached Woven Lid with knob in middle of Lid.
- Two hand slots.
- Lighter "new' stain <u>only.</u>

### 2001 – present (See Wish List™)
- Same as 1995-2000 version, except with new lid.

Prior to 1979 – 1990
Large Hamper

1986 Feature Hamper

1991 Shades of Autumn
Hostess Hamper

*1993 – 1994 Hamper looks like this with, $1/2$" weave. Returned to $3/8$" weave in 1995 Hostess Collection.*

*A nn Newman*
*Farmington, Arkansas*

*When Ann is not selling baskets, she is working as a teacher. However, she is never seen without a basket from her collection of over 350! This has earned her the nick name of "The Basket Case!" Her favorite basket is the Hostess Wildflower™, which was given to her by 2 of her students.*

# *Hostess Collection*™

**Available only to Hostesses. Baskets from 1990 to present have 3/8" weave. Items listed in alphabetical order.**

## MARKET VALUES

| Photo | Description | Original | Avg. | High |
|---|---|---|---|---|
| A. | (99-02) Banker's Waste™ | 119.00 | **119** | **128** |
| | with **P**rotector | 139.00 | — | — |
| | with **L**iner | 148.00 | — | — |
| | Combo (**P/L**) | 168.00 | — | — |
| | Full Set (**C/Lid**) | 214.00 | — | — |
| B. | (95-99) Corn™ | 139.95 | **147** | **185** |
| | with **P**rotector | 158.90 | **171** | **250** |
| | with **L**iner | 169.90 | **180** | **260** |
| | Combo (**P/L**) | 193.85 | **212** | **265** |
| C. | (86-90) Cradle, Doll™ | 44.95 | **183** | **240** |
| D. | (86-90) Cradle, Large™(Infant) | 109.95 | **362** | **465** |
| E. | (96-99) Gathering, Large™ | 89.95 | **103** | **120** |
| | with **P**rotector | 102.90 | **110** | **125** |
| | with **L**iner | 118.90 | **110** | **130** |
| | Combo (**P/L**) | 131.85 | **153** | **200** |
| F. | (92-95) Gourmet Picnic™ | 99.95 | **100** | **140** |
| | with **P**rotector | 110.90 | **127** | **165** |
| | with **L**iner | 121.90 | **130** | **170** |
| | Combo (**P/L**) | 132.85 | **140** | **175** |
| G. | (86-90) Hamper, Large™ | 109.95 | **209** | **305** |
| | (95-01) Hamper, Large™[np] | 219.95 | **246** | **300** |
| | with **P**rotector | 249.90 | **258** | **300** |
| | (86-90) Hamper, Medium[np] | 69.95 | **131** | **175** |
| H. | (90-92) Harvest™ | 54.95 | **96** | **122** |
| | with Protector | 66.90 | **118** | **125** |
| I. | (90-92) Hearthside™ | 59.95 | **87** | **130** |
| | with Protector | 68.90 | **105** | **140** |
| J. | (90-92) Heirloom™ | 87.95 | **114** | **165** |
| K. | (99-02) Homecoming™ | 99.00 | — | — |
| | with **P**rotector | 127.00 | — | — |
| | with **L**iner | 130.00 | — | — |
| | Combo (**P/L**) | 158.00 | — | — |
| | Full Set (**C/Lid**) | 205.00 | — | — |
| L. | (86-90) Laundry, Large™ | 96.95 | **165** | **200** |

[np] = Not Pictured

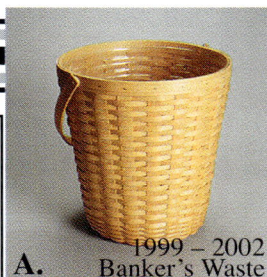

**A.** 1999 – 2002 Banker's Waste

12.5$^{RD}$ x 13.5$^{H}$

Form No: 14761
No. Sold:

**E.** 1996 – 1999 Large Gathering

19$^{L}$ x 12$^{W}$ x 6$^{H}$

Form No: 12564
No. Sold:

*Available at the $250 show level.*

**I.** 1990 – 1992 Hearthside

11.75$^{RD}$ x 6.5$^{H}$

Form No: 42000-AOS
No. Sold:

HOSTESS COLLECTION™

**B.** 1995 – 1999 Corn

$17^{RD}$ x $11.5^H$

Form No: 14443
No. Sold:

*Available at the $500 show level. Lid sold separately.*

**C.** 1986 - 1990 Doll Cradle

$19^L$ x $12^W$ x $6^H$

Form No: 2500-LO
No. Sold:

*Liner sold separately.*

**D.** 1986 - 1990 Large Cradle

$30^L$ x $20^W$ x $10.5^H$

Form No: 2800-M
No. Sold:

*Available Stained, Natural, or Natural with color. Available stained from 1990 – 1984, and then again from 8/89 - 1/90.*

**F.** 1992 – 1995 Gourmet Picnic

$13.25^L$ x $11.25^W$ x $9^H$

Form No: 10413
No. Sold:

**G.** 1986 - 1990 Large Hamper

$16.5^L$ x $16.5^W$ x $21.5^H$

Form No: 1600-DO
No. Sold:

Med: $12^L$ x $12.25^W$ x $16.25^H$
*Attached lid, knob towards front of lid, no handles.*

**H.** 1990 – 1992 Harvest

$16^L$ x $9^W$ x $6^H$

Form No: 3700-AOS
No. Sold:

**J.** 1990 – 1992 Heirloom

$15^L$ x $10^W$ x $7.5^H$

Form No: 500-HOS
No. Sold:

**K.** 1999 – 2002 Homecoming

$15^L$ x $15^W$ x $7.5^H$

Form No: 13081
No. Sold:

**L.** 1986 - 1990 Large Laundry

$30^L$ x $20^W$ x $10.5^H$

Form No: 2800-O
No. Sold:

*Available Stained, Natural, or Natural with color. Available stained from 1990 – 1984, and then again from 8/89 - 1/90.*

**125**

## Hostess Collection™

Hostesses were able to earn some of these baskets at half-price once their show totaled at least $250.

### MARKET VALUES

| Photo | Description | Original | Avg. | High |
|---|---|---|---|---|
| M. | (92-96) Mail™ | 79.95 | **118** | **160** |
| | with **P**rotector | 89.90 | **127** | **170** |
| | with **L**iner | 96.90 | **127** | **170** |
| | Combo (**P/L**) | 106.85 | **138** | **175** |
| N. | (95-02) Odds & Ends™ | 149.95 | **169** | **210** |
| | with **P**rotector | 169.90 | **175** | **235** |
| | with **L**iner | 183.90 | **184** | **235** |
| | Combo (**P/L**) | 204.85 | **205** | **250** |
| O. | (90-92) Remembrance™ | 79.95 | **125** | **175** |
| | with Protector | 88.90 | **134** | **179** |
| P. | (92-02) Serving Tray™ | 74.95 | **71** | **116** |
| | with **P**rotector | 89.90 | **84** | **125** |
| | with **L**iner | 96.90 | **92** | **130** |
| | Combo (**P/L**) | 116.85 | **100** | **175** |
| | (01-02) Serving Tray, Whitewash™ [np] | 95.00 | — | — |
| | with **P**rotector | 117.00 | — | — |
| | with **L**iner | 124.00 | — | — |
| | Combo (**P/L**) | 146.00 | — | — |
| Q. | (95-00) Sewing™ | 89.95 | **96** | **128** |
| | with **P**rotector | 105.90 | **111** | **130** |
| | with **L**iner | 113.90 | **130** | **140** |
| | Combo (**P/L**) | 129.85 | **137** | **230** |
| R. | (99-02) Sleeve, Sunroom™ | 210.00 | **209** | **231** |
| | with **P**rotector | 255.00 | **230** | **250** |
| S. | (95-99) Tea Pot | 59.95 | **68** | **144** |
| T. | (98-01) Treasure™ | 119.00 | **111** | **140** |
| | with **P**rotector | 134.00 | **120** | **150** |
| | with **L**iner | 149.00 | **120** | **150** |
| | Combo (**P/L**) | 164.00 | **130** | **175** |
| | Full Set (**C/Lid**) | 223.00 | — | — |
| U. | (92-98) Wildflower™ | 64.95 | **70** | **129** |
| | with **P**rotector | 75.90 | **90** | **140** |
| | with **L**iner | 84.90 | **97** | **155** |
| | Combo (**P/L**) | 95.85 | **103** | **160** |

[np] = Not Pictured.

**M.** 1992 – 1996 Mail

$12^L$ x $8^W$ x $11.5^H$

Form No: 10600
No. Sold:

**Q.** 1995 – 2000 Sewing

$13^{RD}$ x $8.5^H$

Form No: 13234
No. Sold:

*Available at the $500 show level. Accessories sold separately.*

**U.** 1992 – 1998 Wildflower

$13.5^{RD}$ x $8.5^H$

Form No: 10111
No. Sold:

*Available at the $250 show level.*

**N.** 1995 – 2002
Odds & Ends

18.75$^L$x 9$^W$x 12.75$^{FH}$x5.25$^{BH}$

Form No:                    18902
No. Sold:

**O.** 1990 – 1992
Remembrance

10.5$^L$ x 9$^W$x 8$^H$

Form No:          200-YOS
No. Sold:

**P.** 1992 – 2002
Serving Tray

20$^L$ x 14$^W$x 3.75$^H$

Form No:                    60011
No. Sold:

**R.** 1999 – 2002
Sunroom Sleeve

24.5$^L$ x 20$^W$ x 14$^H$

Form No:                    15261
No. Sold:

**S.** 1995 – 1998 Teapot

40 oz.

Form No:       32069/42/51
Ivory                        33782

*Available in red, blue,
green or ivory at the
$250 show level.*

**T.** 1995 – 2001
Treasure

20.25$^L$ x 13.75$^W$ x 7.5$^H$

Form No:                    18716
No.Sold:

n e e d  h e l p ?

Where are the
Hostess Baskets that
are still available?

see page 10

Implemented in 2000, the *Charitable Champs*™ program gives Longaberger Employees the chance to earn up to $500 for their local non-profit organizations by donating 25 hours of volunteer service within a six-month time period.

In the third year for the program, over 150 employees have raised more than $78,000 for local communities through the Charitable Champs™ Program.

Generosity has long since been a tradition at the Longaberger Company, named one of the "10 Most Generous Companies in America" by *George Magazine.*

The Longaberger Foundation, established in 1997, carries on the family tradition of generosity and provides funding for projects and programs aimed at strengthening communities, families and individuals, both locally and throughout the country.

In 1998, Dave Longaberger promised the Licking Valley school district, local to Dresden, a $2 Million donation if their levy passed. It passed and he made good on his promise.

Fund raising through the sale of their products has also become very common. The Horizon of Hope™ campaign has raised over $7 Million. One dollar from each sale of the 20th Century Basket™ went towards the preservation of American History and most recently, the sale of the American Pride™ liners gathered more than $700,000 in funds for the victims of the September 11th tragedies.

# Incentive/Award

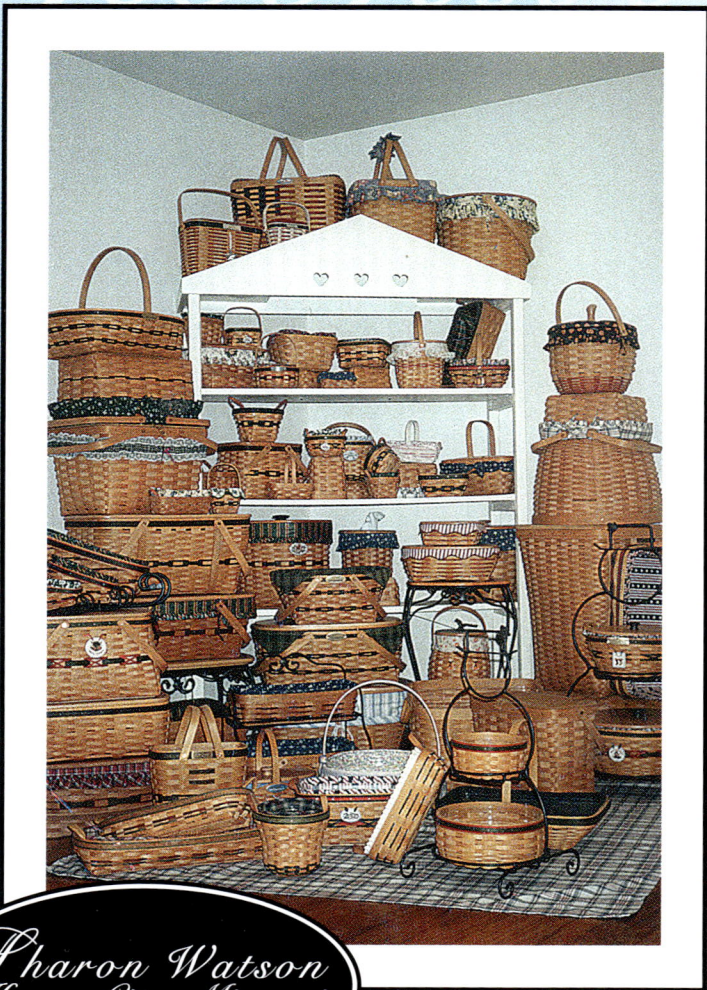

## Sharon Watson
### Kansas City, Missouri

Beginning with a Woven Traditions® Bread, Sharon now has about 100 baskets in her collection. Every year during Christmas, she holds a show in order to add to her favorite collection of Holiday Hostess™ baskets. Sharon enjoys attending basket auctions, flea markets, and second-hand shops, in search of good deals.

## *Incentive/Award*

**Available only to Consultants, Advisors, & Sales Directors. Most have commemorative tags. No original prices.**

### MARKET VALUES

**Photo** | **Description** | **Avg. High**

### *Recruit / Sponsor Baskets:*

| | | | Avg. | High |
|---|---|---|---|---|
| | 1988 | "Recruiting – Building Branches" | | |
| | | Sm.Fruit[WL] –1 recruit | — | 140 |
| | | Md. Fruit[WL] –2 recruits | — | 165 |
| | | Lg. Fruit[WL] –3+ recruits | — | — |
| | 1988 | "Share the Tradition" | | |
| A. | & 89 | Recruit | 119 | 175 |
| B. | | Sponsor | 207 | 325 |
| | | Set: | — | 425 |
| | 1990 | "Together – We're Growing" | | |
| C. | | Recruit | 169 | 180 |
| D. | | Sponsor | 175 | 200 |
| | 1990 | "Longaberger Rising Star" | | |
| E. | & 91 | Recruit | 185 | 195 |
| E. | | Sponsor | 185 | 230 |
| E. | | *Superstar Sponsor | 155 | 200 |
| | 1992 | "Flying High with Longaberger" | | |
| F. | | Recruit | 119 | 125 |
| G. | | Sponsor (Large) | 125 | 175 |
| F. | | *Sponsor (Small) | 118 | 175 |
| | 1993 | "All-Star Recruiting" | | |
| H. | | Recruit | 138 | 200 |
| I. | | Sponsor (Large) | 130 | 175 |
| H. | | *Sponsor (Small) | 113 | 160 |
| | 1996 | "Opportunity Reigns" | | |
| J. | | Recruit / Sponsor Umbrella | 63 | 75 |
| | 1996 | "Pegged for Your Success" | | |
| K. | | Recruit | 102 | 135 |
| | | with **P**rotector | — | — |
| | | with **L**iner | — | — |
| | | Combo (**P/L**) | — | — |
| K. | | Sponsor | 193 | 225 |
| | | with **P**rotector | — | — |
| | | with **L**iner | — | — |
| | | Combo (**P/L**) | — | — |
| | 1997 | "Watch Your Business Bloom" | | |
| L. | | Recruit / Sponsor | 90 | 125 |

\* Given to Sponsors with more than one recruit.

[WL] = See current *WishList*™ for picture.

**A.** 1988-89 Recruit

$5^L$ x $5^W$ x $2.5^H$

Form No: 13000-BBRS
No. Given:

*"Share the Tradition" No tag on basket.*

**E.** 1990-91 Recruit

$12^L$ x $12.25^W$ x $16.25^H$

Form No: 1700-DST
No. Given:

*Superstar Sponsor: Same as above, except tag is different. Sponsor (Lg.Hamper) 16.5L x 16.5W x 21.5H*

**I.** 1993 Sponsor (Large)

$8.5^L$ x $5^W$ x $3.5^H$

Form No: 13323
No. Given:

*"All-Star"*

**B.** 1988-89 Sponsor

$8.5^L$ x $8.5^W$ x $5^H$

Form No: 1500-BBRS
No. Given:

*"Share the Tradition"*
*No tag on basket.*

**C.** 1990 Recruit

$5.75^L$ x $3.75^W$ x $3^H$

Form No: 45000-ABRST
No. Given:

*Tag reads: "Together –*
*1990 Recruit".*

**D.** 1990 Sponsor

$9^L$ x $5^W$ x $5^H$

Form No: 1100-ABRST
No. Given:

*Tag reads: "Together –*
*1990 Sponsor".*

**F.** 1992 Recruit

$5^{RD}$ x $4.5^H$

Form No: 10154
No. Given:

**G.** 1992 Sponsor (Large)

$7^{RD}$ x $6.5^H$

Form No: 10162
No. Given:

**H.** 1993 Recruit

$8^L$ x $4^W$ x $2^H$

Form No: 16101
No. Given:

*"Flying High with Longaberger"*

1992 Sponsor (Small)
Looks the same as the 1992 Recruit, except tag is different.

*"All-Star"*

1993 Sponsor (Small)
Looks the same, except
tag is different.

**J.** 1996 Recruit/Sponsor

$34^H$

Form No: N/A
No. Given:

*"Opportunity Reigns"*
*Given to both the quali-*
*fied Recruit and Sponsor*
*between 1/27 – 3/29/96.*

**K.** 1996 Recruit & Sponsor

<u>Sm</u>: $5^L$ x $5^W$ x $4.5^H$
<u>Lg</u>: $6.5^L$ x $6.5^W$ x $8^H$

*"Pegged for Success"*
*Accessories could be earned*
*with additional recruits.*
*Available to both Recruit and*
*Sponsor from 4/22 – 5/31/96.*

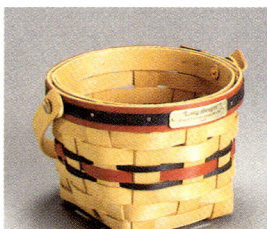

**L.** 1997 Recruit/Sponsor

$5^{RD}$ x $4.5^H$

Form No: unknown
No. Given:

*"Watch Your Business Bloom"*
*Given to both the qualified*
*Recruit and Sponsor from*
*3/22 – 6/27/97.*

| Photo | **MARKET VALUES** | | |
|---|---|---|---|
| | **Description** | **Avg.** | **High** |

### *Recruit / Sponsor (con't):*

| | | | |
|---|---|---|---|
| M. | 1997 Christmas Sponsoring Snowflake™ | **123** | **250** |
| N. | 1998 Flag Sponsoring | **213** | **225** |
| | 1998 Flag Recruit | **192** | **200** |
| O. | 1999 Make Your Dreams Recruit | **133** | **200** |
| | 1999 Recruit Tie-On[np] | — | — |
| | 2002 Red, White & You Basket [np] | — | — |
| | 2002 Red, White & You Ramekin[np] | — | — |

### *National Sponsoring Awards:*

| | | | |
|---|---|---|---|
| P. | 1992 Blue-Green Trim & Weave | — | — |
| Q. | 1993 Red Trim & Weave | | |
| | Sm.Gathering (5-9 recruits) | — | **250** |
| | Md. Gathering (10-14 recruits) | — | — |
| | Lg. Gathering (15-19 recruits) | — | — |
| | XLg. Gathering (20+ recruits) | — | — |
| R. | 1994 Pink/Purple Trim & Weave | | |
| | Sm.Gathering (5-9 recruits) | **200** | **220** |
| | Md. Gathering (10-14 recruits) | — | — |
| | Lg. Gathering (15-19 recruits) | — | — |
| | XLg. Gathering (20+ recruits) | — | — |
| S. | 1995 Purple/Green Trim & Weave | | |
| | Sm.Gathering (5-9 recruits) | **150** | **180** |
| | Md. Gathering (10-14 recruits) | — | — |
| | Lg. Gathering (15-19 recruits) | — | — |
| | XLg. Gathering (20+ recruits) | — | — |
| T. | 1996 Blue/Gold/Red Trim & Weave | | |
| | Sm.Gathering (5-9 recruits) | **108** | **120** |
| | Md. Gathering (10-14 recruits) | — | — |
| | Lg. Gathering (15-19 recruits) | — | — |
| U. | XLg. Gathering (20+ recruits) | — | — |
| V. | 1997 Red/Blue/Green Trim & Weave | | |
| | Sm.Gathering (5-9 recruits) | — | — |
| | Md. Gathering (10-14 recruits) | — | — |
| | Lg. Gathering (15-19 recruits) | — | — |
| | XLg. Gathering (20+ recruits) | — | — |
| W. | 1998 Green/Yellow/Blue/Red Trim & Weave | | |
| | Sm.Gathering (5-9 recruits) | — | — |
| | Md. Gathering (10-14 recruits) | — | — |
| | Lg. Gathering (15-19 recruits) | — | **117** |
| | XLg. Gathering (20+ recruits) | — | — |
| X. | 1999 Green, Rose, Blue, Purple Trim & Weave | | |
| | Small (6-10 recruits) | — | — |
| | Medium (11-15 recruits) | — | — |
| | Large (16-20 recruits) | — | — |
| | XLarge (21+ recruits) | — | — |

**continued next page**

**M.** 1997 Sponsor
10$^L$ x 9.25$^W$ x 6.5$^H$

Form No: unknown
No Given:

*Available to anyone sponsoring a recruit between 6/28 – 8/29/97. Accessories were not given with this award.*

1993
**Q.** Natl. Sponsoring
14$^L$ x 9$^W$ x 4.5$^H$

Form No: unknown
No Given:

*Woven by Larry Longaberger. Unique open-weave bottom and **personalized** brass tag. Engraved lid included.*

1996
**U.** XLg. Gathering
23$^L$ x 15$^W$ x 8$^H$

Form No: unknown
No. Given:

*The lid at this level is also engraved with recipient's name. First year for XLarge Size at the 20+ level.*

**N.** 1998 Recruit

7^L x 3.5^W x 4.75^H

Form No:        unknown
No. Given:

*The Recruit and Sponsor baskets are identical, except for the tag.*

**O.** 1999 Make Your Dreams Come True

5.5^RD x 4.5^H

Form No:        unknown
No. Given:

*Offered to both Consultants and their Recruits. A Tie-On was also available at a higher incentive level.*

**P.** 1992 Natl. Sponsoring

19.75^L x 12^W x 3.5^H

Form No:        unknown
No. Given:

*Woven by Larry Longaberger. The open-weave bottom is a unique and rare characteristic.*

**R.** 1994 Natl. Sponsoring

14^L x 9^W x 4.5^H

Form No:        unknown
No Given:

*Engraved lid included.*

**S.** 1995 Natl. Sponsoring

19^L x 12^W x 6^H

Form No:        unknown
No Given:

*Engraved lid included.*

**T.** 1996 Natl. Sponsoring

14^L x 9^W x 4.5^H

Form No:        unknown
No. Given:

*Engraved lid included.*

**V.** 1997 Natl. Sponsoring

14^L x 9^W x 4.5^H

Form No:        unknown
No. Given:

*Engraved lid included.*

**W.** 1998 Natl. Sponsoring

14^L x 9^W x 4.5^H

Form No:        unknown
No. Given:

*Engraved lid included.*

**X.** 1999 Natl. Sponsoring

14^L x 9^W x 4.25^H

Form No:        unknown
No. Given:

*First year for this new form. Engraved lid included.*

## Incentive/Award

**The V.I.P. Honorable Mention has been the only Tie-On given as an award.**

### MARKET VALUES

| Photo | Description | | Avg. | High |
|---|---|---|---|---|
| | *National Sponsoring Awards (con't)* | | | |
| Y. | 2000 | Blue Trim & Weave | | |
| | | Small (6-10 recruits) | — | — |
| | | Medium (11-15 recruits) | — | — |
| | | Large (16-20 recruits) | — | — |
| | | XLarge (21+ recruits) | — | — |
| | 2001 | Sage, Brown & Blue[np] | | |
| | | Small (6-10 recruits) | — | — |
| | | Medium (11-15 recruits) | — | — |
| | | Large (16-20 recruits) | — | — |
| | | XLarge (21+ recruits) | — | — |
| | *VIP – Honorable Mention:* | | | |
| | 1995 VIP Honorable Mention[np] | | | |
| Z. | 1996 VIP Honorable Mention | | — | — |
| A¹ | 1997 VIP Honorable Mention | | — | 33 |
| B¹ | 1998 VIP Honorable Mention | | — | — |
| C¹ | 1999 VIP Honorable Mention | | — | — |
| D¹ | 2000 VIP Honorable Mention | | — | — |
| E¹ | 2001 VIP Honorable Mention | | — | — |
| | *VIP – $30,000+ sales for the year:* | | | |
| F¹ | 1986 Blue weave & trim | | 375 | 400 |
| G¹ | 1987 Green or Red weave & trim | | 363 | 400 |
| H¹ | 1988 Blue weave & trim | | 310 | 400 |
| I¹ | 1989 Red/Blue weave; Red trim | | 313 | 370 ✍ |
| J¹ | 1990 Pink/Blue weave; Pink trim | | 367 | 450 ✍ |

**continued next page**

[np] = Not Pictured            ✍ = With Signatures

*need help?*

## Can't find something?
**Try the Quick Find**

**Y.** 2000 Natl. Sponsoring
$14^L$ x $9^W$ x $4.25^H$

Form No: unknown
No. Given:

*A miniature version of the award basket is given only at the top 3 levels.*

**C¹** 1999 Honorable Mention
$3^{RD}$ x $2.5^H$

Form No: N/A
No. Given:

*First time for this award to be personalized and printed on both sides.*

**G¹** 1987 VIP
$12^L$ x $7^W$ x $10^H$

Form No: N/A
No. Given:

*Selling Period:*
*Green: 1/86 – 6/86*
*Red:     7/86 – 6/87*

**Z.** Honorable Mention     1996
$3^{RD}$ x $2.5^{H}$

Form No:             N/A
No. Given:

*Given to Consultants who attain $20,000 - $34,999 in sales.*

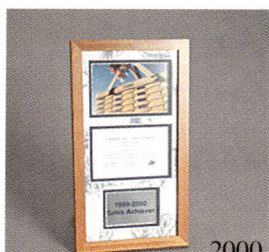

**A¹** Honorable Mention     1997
$3^{RD}$ x $2.5^{H}$

Form No:             N/A
No. Given:

*Given to Consultants who attain $20,000 - $34,999 in sales.*

**B¹** Honorable Mention     1998
$3^{RD}$ x $2.5^{H}$

Form No:             N/A
No. Given:        ≈ 2,800

*Given to Consultants who attain $20,000 - $34,999 in sales.*

**D¹** Honorable Mention     2000
$7^{W}$ x $13^{H}$

Form No:             N/A
No. Given:

*First time for a personalized plaque to be given.*

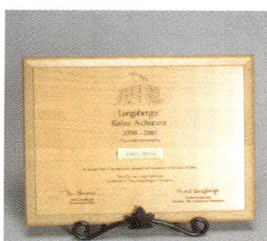

**E¹** Honorable Mention     2001
$10^{L}$ x $7.5^{W}$

Form No:             N/A
No. Given:

**F¹**             1986 VIP
$12^{L}$ x $7^{W}$ x $10^{H}$

Form No:             N/A
No. Given:            69

*Selling Period: Jan 1985 – Dec 1985*

**H¹**             1988 VIP
$12^{L}$ x $7^{W}$ x $10^{H}$

Form No:             N/A
No. Given:

*Selling Period:     July 1987 – June 1988*

**I¹**             1989 VIP
$12^{L}$ x $7^{W}$ x $10^{H}$

Form No:             N/A
No. Given:            163

*Selling Period: July 1988 – June 1989*

**J¹**             1990 VIP
$12^{L}$ x $7^{W}$ x $10^{H}$

Form No:             N/A
No. Given:            359

*Selling Period: July 1989 – June 1990*

## Incentive/Award

**Commemorative Plates, Pottery, Jewelry and Trips are examples of other awards given.**

### MARKET VALUES

| Photo | Description | Avg. | High |
|---|---|---|---|
| | *VIP – $30,000+ (con't)* | | |
| K[1] | 1991 Blue weave & trim | 310 | 425 |
| L[1] | 1992 Green weave & trim | 270 | 340 |
| M[1] | 1993 Teal/Pink weave; Teal trim | 230 | 350 |
| | *VIP – $35,000+ sales for the year:* | | |
| N[1] | 1994 Rose/Purple | 216 | 220 |
| O[1] | 1995 Purple/Green | 96 | 115 |
| P[1] | 1996 Red/Blue/Gold | 93 | 110 |
| Q[1] | 1997 Red/Blue/Green | 126 | 169 |
| R[1] | 1998 Green/Yellow/Blue/Red | 144 | 239 |
| S[1] | 1999 Green/Rose/Blue/Purple | 200 | 300 |
| T[1] | 2000 Blue | 132 | 250 |
| | 2001 Sage/Brown/Blue[np] | 125 | 150 |
| | *National Sales Awards:* | | |
| U[1] | 1983 Tin Punched Plaque | 400 | 500 |
| V[1] | 1984 Sketched Print | 275 | 350 |
| | **continued next page** | | |

[np] = Not Pictured.

**K[1]**  1991 VIP
$12^L$ x $7^W$ x $10^H$
Form No:   N/A
No. Given:
*Selling Period:
July 1990 – June 1991*

**O[1]**  1995 VIP
$12^L$ x $7^W$ x $10^H$
Form No:   N/A
No. Given:
*Selling Period:
July 1994 – June 1995*

**S[1]**  1999 VIP
$12^L$ x $7^W$ x $10^H$
Form No:   N/A
No. Given:
*Selling Period:
July 1998 – June 1999*

n e e d   h e l p ?

## How do we get our values?

see page 8

136

**L¹**          1992 VIP

$12^L$ x $7^W$ x $10^H$

Form No:           N/A
No. Given:

*Selling Period:    July
1991 – June 1992*

**M¹**          1993 VIP

$12^L$ x $7^W$ x $10^H$

Form No:           N/A
No. Given:

*Selling Period:
July 1992 – June 1993*

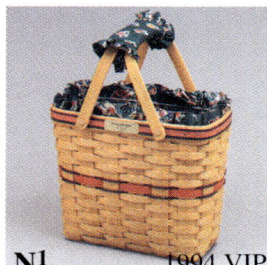

**N¹**          1994 VIP

$12^L$ x $7^W$ x $10^H$

Form No:           N/A
No. Given:

*Selling Period:
July 1993 – June 1994*

**P¹**          1996 VIP

$12^L$ x $7^W$ x $10^H$

Form No:           N/A
No. Given:        1356

*Selling Period:
July 1995 – June 1996*

**Q¹**          1997 VIP

$12^L$ x $7^W$ x $10^H$

Form No:           N/A
No. Given:

*Selling Period:
July 1996 – June 1997*

**R¹**          1998 VIP

$12^L$ x $7^W$ x $10^H$

Form No:           N/A
No. Given:      ≈ 1,800

*Selling Period:
July 1997 – June 1998*

**T¹**          2000 VIP

$12^L$ x $7^W$ x $10^H$

Form No:           N/A
No. Given:

*Selling Period:    July
1999 – June 2000*

**U¹**    1983 Tin
Punched Plaque

$8^L$ x $10^H$

Form No:           N/A
No. Given:         35

*Top selling consultants
in 1983.*

**V¹**    1984
Natl. High Sales

Form No:      unknown
No. Given:

*Given as a Top Sales
award.*

## Incentive/Award

**W¹**  1988 Coverlet
$16^L$ x $16^W$ x $8^H$

Form No:        unknown
No. Given:

*Top selling consultants in 1988.*

### MARKET VALUES

| Photo | Year | Description | | Avg. | High |
|---|---|---|---|---|---|
| | | **National Sales Awards:** *(con't)* | | | |
| W¹ | 1988 | Coverlet Basket™ | | — | — |
| X¹ | 1989 | Flag Basket™ | | — | — |
| Y¹ | 1993 | Red Accents | | | |
| | | Sm.Fruit [np] | (Level 1) | — | 190 |
| | | Md. Fruit | (Level 2) | — | 135 |
| | | Lg. Fruit [np] | (Level 3) | — | — |
| Z¹ | 1994 | Pink/Purple Accents | | | |
| | | 5" Measuring [np] | (Level 1) | — | 235 |
| | | 7" Measuring | (Level 2) | 168 | 185 |
| | | 9" Measuring [np] | (Level 3) | — | — |
| | | 11" Measuring [np] | (Level 4) | — | 400 |
| A² | 1995 | Purple/Green Accents | | | |
| | | 5" Measuring [np] | (Level 1) | — | 125 |
| | | 7" Measuring | (Level 2) | — | 110 |
| | | 9" Measuring | (Level 3) | — | 280 |
| | | 11" Measuring [np] | (Level 4) | — | — |
| B² | 1996 | Blue/Gold/Red Accents | | | |
| | | 5" Measuring | (Level 1) | 188 | 250 |
| | | 7" Measuring[np] | (Level 2) | — | 75 |
| | | 9" Measuring[np] | (Level 3) | — | — |
| | | 11" Measuring [np] | (Level 4) | — | 400 |
| C² | 1997 | Green/Red/Blue Accents | | | |
| | | 5" Measuring | (Level 1) | — | — |
| | | 7" Measuring [np] | (Level 2) | — | — |
| | | 9" Measuring[np] | (Level 3) | — | 100 |
| | | 11" Measuring [np] | (Level 4) | — | — |
| D² | 1998 | Green/Yellow/Blue/Red Accents | | | |
| | | 5" Measuring [np] | (Level 1) | — | — |
| | | 7" Measuring | (Level 2) | — | — |
| | | 9" Measuring [np] | (Level 3) | — | 100 |
| | | 11" Measuring [np] | (Level 4) | — | — |
| | | 13" Measuring [np] | (Level 4) | — | — |
| E² | 1999 | Green/Rose/Blue/Purple | | | |
| | | Level 1 | | — | — |
| | | Level 2 [np] | | — | — |
| | | Level 3 [np] | | — | — |
| | | Level 4 [np] | | — | — |
| F² | 2000 | Blue Accents | | | |
| | | Level 1 [np] | | — | — |
| | | Level 2 | | — | 75 |
| | | Level 3 [np] | | — | — |
| | | Level 4 [np] | | — | — |
| | 2001 | Sage/Brown/Blue[np] | | | |
| | | Level 1[np] | | — | 75 |
| | | Level 2 [np] | | — | — |
| | | Level 3 [np] | | — | — |
| | | Level 4 [np] | | — | — |

**A²**  1995 Natl. High Sales
$7^{RD}$ x $6.5^H$

Form No:        unknown
No. Given:

*$60,000 – 74,999 Sales in 1995.*

**E²**  1999 Natl. High Sales
$5^{RD}$ x $4.5^H$

Form No:        unknown
No. Given:

*First year for this new, exclusive form.*

**138**       [np] = Not Pictured

**X**[1]      1989 Flag

10.75[L] x 5.75[W] x 7.5[H]

Form No:      unknown
No. Given:      20

*Given to the Top selling Consultants during the "Weave Your American Dream" Bee in 1989.*

1993
**Y**[1]      Natl. High Sales

8[RD] x 6.5[H]

Form No:      unknown
No. Given:

*$60,000 – 74,999 Sales in 1993.*

1994
**Z**[1]      Natl. High Sales

7[RD] x 6.5[H]

Form No:      unknown
No. Given:

*$60,000 – 74,999 Sales in 1994.*

1996
**B**[2]      Natl. High Sales

5[RD] x 4.5[H]

Form No:      unknown
No. Given:

*$45,000 – 59,999 Sales in 1996.*

1997
**C**[2]      Natl. High Sales

5[RD] x 4.5[H]

Form No:      unknown
No. Given:

*$45,000 – 59,999 Sales in 1997.*

1998
**D**[2]      Natl. High Sales

7[RD] x 6.5[H]

Form No:      unknown
No. Given:

*$45,000 – 59,999 Sales in 1998.*

2000
**F**[2]      Natl. High Sales

5[RD] x 4.5[H]

Form No:      unknown
No. Given:

*$45,000 – 59,999 Sales in 2000.*

f u n **f a c t**

### Multi-Lingual Flyers

This year, the Longaberger Company made an improvement for their international fans. Product flyers are now available in both Japanese and Spanish.

## Incentive/Award

**Award baskets given during the Bee will have the same colors as that year's Bee Basket.**

### MARKET VALUES

| Photo | | Description | Avg. | High |
|---|---|---|---|---|
| | | *Miscellaneous Award and Incentives:* | | |
| | 1985 | Meadow Blossoms Pottery™ | | |
| G² | | Dinner Plate | — | 30 |
| G² | | Mug | — | 25 |
| G² | | Napkin Ring | — | 20 |
| H² | | Salad Plate | — | 20 |
| H² | | Sugar Bowl | 50 | 75 |
| H² | | Creamer | — | 35 |
| H² | | Pitcher | — | 125 |
| H² | | Honey Pot | 150 | 175 |
| I² | | Soup Tureen | 108 | 125 |
| I² | | Soup Bowl | — | 40 |
| I² | | Buffet Tray | — | 35 |
| J² | | Oval Bowl | 108 | 125 |
| J² | | Piepan w/ Lattice Cover | 150 | 175 |
| J² | | Hurricane Lamp | 82 | 175 |
| K² | | Pasta Bowl | — | 165 |
| | | Meat Platter[np] | — | — |
| L² | 1986 | December Special Recognition Bread Basket | 145 | 175 |
| M² | 1986 | Advisor Recognition Basket | 164 | 178 |
| | 1987 | 10th Anniversary Recruiting Award "We're Building New Traditions" | | |
| N² | | Medium Market™ | 175 | 200 |
| O² | | Plate | 154 | 200 |
| | | Candelabra [np] | — | — |
| P² | 1987 | May Basket Herb™ (5 shows + $1000 sales) | 80 | 80 |
| P² | 1988 | May Incentive Herb™ ($500 + 1 recruit) | 80 | 80 |
| | | Garden™ [np] ($1000 + 1 recruit) | 80 | 80 |
| | | Set: | 142 | 175 |
| Q² | 1991 | Basket Planter Sleeve | 445 | 500 |

[np] = Not Pictured

**G²** 1985 Grouping A

Form No: N/A
No. Given:

*Grouping A included 4 Dinner Plates, 4 Mugs and 4 Napkin Rings.*

**J²** 1985 Grouping D

Form No: N/A
No. Given:

*Grouping D included 1 Oval Bowl, 1 Piepan with Lattice Cover and 1 Hurricane Lamp with Globe.*

**N²** Tenth Anniversary 1987

$15^L$ x $10^W$ x $7.5^H$

Form No: 500-A
No. Given:

*Blue shoestring weave. Given for each new Recruit earned from 8/15 – 9/25/87.*

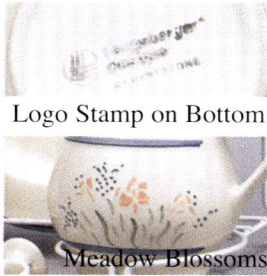

Logo Stamp on Bottom

Meadow Blossoms

*The design uses peach, navy and green. Stamp on the bottom says "Longaberger Pottery – by Heartstone".*

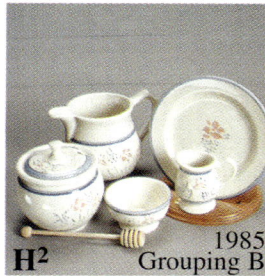

**H²**        1985
         Grouping B

Form No:        N/A
No. Given:

*Grouping B included 4 Salad Plates, 1 Sugar & Creamer, 1 Pitcher and 1 Honey Pot.*

**I²**        1985
         Grouping C

Form No:        N/A
No. Given:

*Grouping C included 1 Soup Tureen, 1 Soup Bowl and 1 Buffet Tray.*

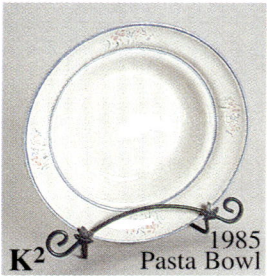

**K²**        1985
         Pasta Bowl
14$^{RD}$ x 3$^{H}$

Form No:        unknown
No. Given:

*Was not a part of the incentive groups. Could be purchased for $24.50. Stand not included.*

**L²**    1986 December
          Recognition
14.5$^{L}$ x 7.5$^{W}$ x 3.75$^{H}$

Form No:        4700-AO
No. Given:

*Sales of $500 or more for month of December. <u>Some</u> are signed by Dave.*

**M²**     1986 Advisor
           Recognition
14$^{L}$ x 9$^{W}$ x 4.5$^{H}$

Form No:        2300-
No. Given:

*Given to all Advisors during a 1986 Meeting.*

**O²**      1987 Plate

Form No:        N/A
No. Given:       660

*Three $1000 months from Sept. – Nov. Stand not included.*

**P²**    1987 & 88 Herb
11.5$^{L}$ x 5$^{W}$ x 3$^{H}$

Form No:        4500-
No. Given:

<u>Garden</u>:    15$^{L}$ x 8$^{W}$ x 2.25$^{H}$

**Q²**        1991
         Planter Sleeve
31.5$^{RD}$ x 18$^{H}$

Form No:        N/A
No. Given:       190

*"High Road to Success"*

## Incentive/Award

The Company's selling season runs from June to June. Most awards are given at The Bee™.

### MARKET VALUES

| Photo | Description | Avg. | High |
|---|---|---|---|
| | *Miscellaneous (con't)* | | |
| | 1992-98 "Success Start" | | |
| R² | Pencil Basket™ | **74** | **90** |
| R² | Paper Basket™ | **65** | **75** |
| | **Set:** | **123** | **138** |
| S² | 1993 "Holiday Basket of Thanks" | **38** | **76** |
| T² | 1996-97 Growing Strong Together | — | — |
| U² | 1998-P Growing Strong Together | — | — |
| V² | 1997 $500 Million Celebration | **230** | **275** |
| W² | 1997 Christmas Votive | — | — |
| X² | 1998 25th Anniversary Basket Sleeve | — | — |
| Y² | 1999 "Thanks a Million" Basket | **53** | **110** |
| | (99-00) "Success Start" | | |
| Z² | Pencil Basket™ | — | — |
| Z² | Note Paper Basket™ | — | — |
| Z² | Business Card Basket™ | — | **75** |
| Z² | Mini Waste Basket™ | — | — |
| Z² | Tapered Paper Tray™ | — | — |
| A² | 2000 January Advisors Meeting | **218** | **320** |
| B³ | (00-P) Associate Homestead Tour | — | — |
| | with **P**rotector | **134** | **195** |
| | with **L**iner | — | — |
| | Combo **(P/L)** | **160** | **250** |
| | Full Set **(C/Lid)** | **194** | **300** |
| C³ | 2000 Horizon of Hope™ | | |
| | Small Flower Pots | — | **60** |
| | Fabric Picture Frame | — | — |

**continued next page**

**R²** 1992 – 98 Success Start

| | |
|---|---|
| Pencil: | 15000- |
| Paper: | 16000- |
| Pen: | N/A |

*Consultants receive pen if reach $1000 in sales in first 90 days. Add Paper if achieve goal within 60 days, all three if within 30 days.*

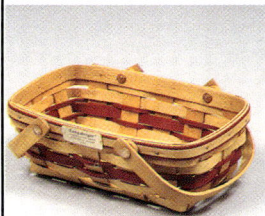

**V²** 1997 $500 Million

$10^L$ x $6^W$ x $4^H$

| | |
|---|---|
| Form No: | unknown |
| No. Given: | ≈ 1,225 |

*Given to all advisors at Jan 97 Advisor meeting to celebrate achieving $500 Million in Sales in Nov 96.*

**Z²** 1999 Success Start

| | |
|---|---|
| Pencil: | 15000 |
| Note Paper: | 16000 |
| Business Card: | 17361 |
| Mini Waste: | 11258 |
| Tapered Tray: | 19062 |

*These baskets can be earned exclusively by Consultants during their first 90 days. Each basket has a brass tag that reads "Longaberger – Success Start".*

**S²**    1993 Holiday
Basket of Thanks

$7^L$ x $5^W$ x $3.5^H$

Form No:      unknown
No. Given:

*Red and green trim.
Given for December
Sales.*

**T²**    1996-97 Growing
Strong Together

$9.5^L$ x $5^W$ x $9.5^H$

Form No:      unknown
No. Given:      ≈ 50

*Given to Regional
Advisors & Directors for
facilitating Branch
Advisor Trainings.*

**U²**    19xx Growing
Strong Together

$9.5^L$ x $5^W$ x $9.5^H$

Form No:      unknown
No. Given:

*Given to Regional
Advisors & Directors for
facilitating Branch
Advisor Trainings.*

**W²**    1997
Christmas Votive

$3^{RD}$ x $2.5^H$

Form No:      34932
No. Given:

*Given to all consultants
who hosted a Christmas
Open House by
September 12, 1997.*

**X²**    1998 25th
Anniversary Sleeve

$31.5^{RD}$ x $18^H$

Form No:      unknown
No. Given:      26

*Given as a surprise
thank you to all
Directors at the
1998 Bee.*

**Y²**    1999
Thanks-A-Million

$5.5^L$ x $4^W$ x $4^H$

Form No:      14940
No. Given:

*Given to all Advisors who
attended JAM 1999. This is
a 1997 Horizon of Hope basket that has been retagged.*

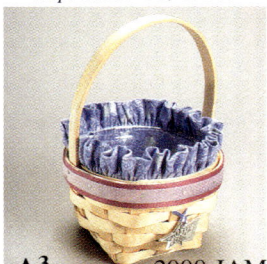

**A³**    2000 JAM

$5.5^{RD}$ x $3.75^H$

Form No:      unknown
No. Given:

*This basket, including
accessories & tie-on,
was given to all
Advisors who attended
JAM 2000.*

**B³**    2000 Associate
Homestead Tour

$10^{RD}$ x $6.25^H$

Form No:      unknown
No. Given:

*Dresden Blue accent
shoestring weaving.
Accessories sold
separately.*

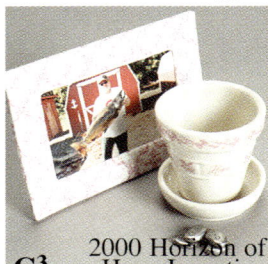

**C³**    2000 Horizon of
Hope Incentive

$7^L$ x $5^H$  /  $3.5^H$

Form No:      unknown
No. Given:

*Frame given with sales of
$700 - $1599. Flower Pot
with pebbles given when
sold 30+ 2000 Horizon of
Hope Baskets.* **143**

## Incentive/Award

Bee Speaker baskets are given to those who volunteer their time at the Bee to speak to other consultants about various topics.

### MARKET VALUES

| | Description | Avg. | High |
|---|---|---|---|
| | *Miscellaneous (con't)* | | |
| | (00-P) "Success Start" | | |
| D³ | Address™ | 75 | 100 |
| D³ | Business Card™ | — | 75 |
| D³ | Diskette™ | 54 | 57 |
| D³ | Catalog Caddy™ | — | — |
| | *Bee Speaker Baskets:* | | |
| E³ | 1988 Medium Market™ | 85 | 100 |
| F³ | 1990 Harvest™ | 120 | 130 |
| G³ | 1991 Spring™ | — | — |
| H³ | 1992 Spring™ | 145 | 189 |
| I³ | 1993 Spring™ | 235 | 260 |
| J³ | 1994 Spring™ | 230 | 250 |
| K³ | 1995 Spring™ | — | 270 |
| L³ | 1996 Spring™ | — | 200 |
| M³ | 1997 Spring™ | — | — |
| | 1998 Spring™ [np] | — | — |
| N³ | 1999 Spring™ | — | — |
| O³ | 2000 Spring™ | — | — |
| P³ | 2001 Spring™ | — | — |

[np] = Not Pictured

**D³** 2000 Success Start

Address: unknown
Business Card: 17361
Diskette: unknown
Catalog Caddy: unknown

*Each basket has a brass tag that reads "Success Start".*

**H³** 1992 Bee Speaker
11^L x 8^W x 5.5^H

Form No: unknown
No. Given:

*Green trim and weave.*

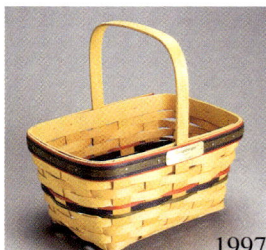

**L³** 1996 Bee Speaker
11^L x 8^W x 5.5^H

Form No: 900-
No. Given:

*Blue, gold and red trim and weave.*

**M³** 1997 Bee Speaker
11^L x 8^W x 5.5^H

Form No: 900-
No. Given:

*Green, red and blue weave and trim.*

**E³** 1988
Bee Speaker
$15^L$ x $10^W$ x $7.5^H$

Form No: 500-
No. Given: 15

*Blue shoestring weave.*

**F³** 1990
Bee Speaker
$16^L$ x $9^W$ x $6^H$

Form No: 3700-
No. Given:

*No color. Brass tag.*

**G³** 1991
Bee Speaker
$11^L$ x $8^W$ x $5.5^H$

Form No: 900-
No. Given:

*Blue trim and weave.*

**I³** 1993
Bee Speaker
$11^L$ x $8^W$ x $5.5^H$

Form No: 900-
No. Given:

*Teal and pink weave
and trim.*

**J³** 1994
Bee Speaker
$11^L$ x $8^W$ x $5.5^H$

Form No: 900-
No. Given:

*Pink and purple trim
and weave.*

**K³** 1995
Bee Speaker
$11^L$ x $8^W$ x $5.5^H$

Form No: 900-
No. Given:

*Purple and green trim
and weave.*

**N³** 1999
Bee Speaker
$11^L$ x $8^W$ x $5.5^H$

Form No: 900-
No. Given:

*Rose trim. Green, rose,
blue and purple accents.
Accessories sold separately.*

**O³** 2000
Bee Speaker
$11^L$ x $8^W$ x $5.5^H$

Form No: 900-
No. Given:

*Blue accent weave and
trim.*

**P³** 2001
Bee Speaker
$11^L$ x $8^W$ x $5.5^H$

Form No: 900-
No. Given:

*Sage, brwon and blue
trim and accents.*

INCENTIVE/AWARD

### MARKET VALUES

| Photo | Description | | Avg. | High |
|---|---|---|---|---|
| | *1988–P Consultant Advancement Baskets* | | | |
| Q³ | | MBA Basket™ | **69** | **160** |
| R³ | | Branch Basket™ | **300** | **312** |
| S³ | | Regional Basket™ | **250** | **250** |
| T³ | | Director Basket™ | **107** | **146** |
| | *Branch Sponsored Awards:* | | | |
| U³ | 1997 | Branch Bouquet | **61** | **129** |
| V³ | 1998 | Branch Excellence | **44** | **75** |
| V³ | 1998 | Branch Sponsoring Charm | — | — |
| W³ | 1999 | Branch Excellence | **56** | **60** |
| W³ | 1999 | Branch Sponsoring Excellence | **92** | **100** |
| X³ | 2000 | Branch Sales | **36** | **45** |
| X³ | 2000 | Branch Sponsoring | **41** | **53** |
| Y³ | 2001 | Branch Sales | — | — |
| Y³ | 2001 | Branch Sponsoring | — | — |
| Z³ | 2002 | Branch Sales | — | — |
| Z³ | 2002 | Branch Sponsoring | — | — |
| | *Regional Sponsored Awards:* | | | |
| A⁴ | 1991 | Small Chore | **188** | **225** |
| B⁴ | 1992 | Small Oval | **195** | **275** |
| C⁴ | 1993 | Potpourri with Lid | **111** | **160** |

**continued next page**

**Q³** MBA

$9.5^L$ x $5^W$ x $9.5^H$

Form No: 1000-FO
No. Given:

*No tag.*

**U³** 1997 Branch Bouquet

$10.5^L$ x $6^W$ x $4^H$

Form No: unknown
No. Given:

*First year for a Branch Advisor to sponsor an award.*

**Y³** 2001 Branch Awards

Lg: $8^L$ x $7.75^W$ x $3.5^H$
Sm: $7^L$ x $6.75^W$ x $3^H$

*Excellence (Lg):*
*$12,000 sales.*
*Sponsoring (Sm):*
*2+ recruits.*

**Z³** 2002 Branch Awards

Lg: $5.75^L$ x $5.25^W$ x $6.25^H$
Sm: $5.25^L$ x $5.25^W$ x $4.5^H$

*Excellence (Lg):*
*$12,000 sales.*
*Sponsoring (Sm):*
*2+ recruits.*

**R³** Branch Advisor

$15.75^L$ x $6.5^W$ x $11^H$

Form No: unknown
No. Given:

*Red trim and weave.*
*No tag.*

**S³** Regional Advisor

$15.75^L$ x $6.5^W$ x $11^H$

Form No: unknown
No. Given:

*Blue rim and weave.*
*No tag.*

**T³** Director Advisor

$15.75^L$ x $6.5^W$ x $11^H$

Form No: unknown
No. Given:

*Green trim and weave.*
*No tag.*

**V³** 1998 Branch Awards

$6.5^L$ x $6.5^W$ x $3^H$

Form No: unknown
No. Given:

*Excellence:*
*50+ shows*
*Sponsoring Excellence:*
*Charm given to all with at least one qualified recruit.*

**W³** 1999 Branch Awards

Lg: $9.5^L$ x $6^W$ x $6^H$
Sm: $7^L$ x $5^W$ x $3.5^H$

Form No:
No. Given:

*Red trim with green, red, blue weave.*
*Sponsoring (Lg):*
*2+ recruits.*
*Excellence (Sm): 50+ shows, or $12,000 sales.*

**X³** 2000 Branch Awards

Lg: $7.75^L$ x $3.75^W$ x $4.5^H$
Sm: $5.75^L$ x $3.75^W$ x $3^H$

*Red trim. Green, red, blue weave.*
*Sponsoring (Lg):*
*2+ recruits.*
*Excellence (Sm):*
*$12,000 sales.*

**A⁴** 1991 Regional Sponsored

$10^L$ x $6^W$ x $4^H$

Form No: 3400-
No. Given:

*Blue weave and trim.*
*Given for High Sales in the Region.*

**B⁴** 1992 Regional Sponsored

$8^L$ x $5^W$ x $3^H$

Form No: 33000-
No. Given:

*Green, blue and red shoestring weave.*

**C⁴** 1993 Regional Sponsored

$5^L$ x $5^W$ x $2.5^H$

Form No: 11321
No. Given:

*Blue weave and trim.*

## Incentive/Award

The Regional Sponsored Awards are funded and given out by each Regional Advisor. The number of awards given out is determined by the size of their Region.

### MARKET VALUES

| Photo | Description | Avg. | High |
|---|---|---|---|
| | **Regional Sponsored Awards** (con't) | | |
| D[4] | 1994 Small Purse, no Lid | **226** | **250** |
| E[4] | 1995 Medium Berry | **234** | **300** |
| F[4] | 1996 Darning | **190** | **210** |
| G[4] | 1997 Rose Garden | **65** | **79** |
| H[4] | 1998 Regional Excellence | **150** | **170** |
| H[4] | 1998 Reg. Sponsoring Excellence | — | **127** |
| I[4] | 1999 Regional Sales | — | **150** |
| I[4] | 1999 Reg. Sponsoring Excellence | — | **150** |
| J[4] | 2000 Regional Sales | — | — |
| J[4] | 2000 Regional Sponsored | **138** | **175** |
| K[4] | 2001 Regional Sales | — | **125** |
| L[4] | 2002 Regional Sales | — | — |
| | **Director Sponsored Awards:** | | |
| M[4] | 1988 Top Performer | — | — |
| N[4] | 1989 Top Performer | — | — |
| O[4] | 1990 Top Performer | — | — |
| P[4] | 1991 Top Performer | — | — |

**continued next page**

**D[4]** 1994 Regional Sponsored

$9.5^L$ x $6^W$ x $6^H$

Form No: 800-
No. Given:

*Blue trim and shoe-string weave. Two braided ears.*

**H[4]** 1998 Regional Sponsored

Lg: $8.5^L$ x $8.5^W$ x $5^H$
Sm:$4.25^L$ x $4.25^W$ x $3^H$

*Excellence (Lg): Top Regional performers. Sponsoring (Sm): 4+ recruits.*

**L[4]** 2002 Regional Sales

$6.5^L$ x $6.5^W$ x $6.5^H$

Form No: unknown
No. Given:

*Stained or Whitewash. Blue trim with blue accents.*

**M[4]** 1988 Top Performer

$10.5^L$ x $9^W$ x $8^H$

Form No: unknown
No. Given:

*Red weave and trim. Available both stained and natural.*

**E⁴** 1995 Regional Sponsored

7.5$^L$ x 7.5$^W$ x 3.5$^H$

Form No: 1400-
No. Given:

*Blue trim and shoestring weave.*

**F⁴** 1996 Regional Sponsored

10$^{RD}$ x 4$^H$

Form No: 500-
No. Given:

*Red trim and shoe-string weave at bottom.*

**G⁴** 1997 Regional Sponsored

12$^L$ x 7$^W$ x 4.5$^H$

Form No: unknown
No. Given:

*Green trim and shoe-string accent weave.*

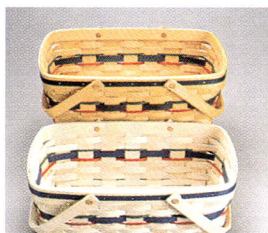

**I⁴** 1999 Regional Sponsored

15$^L$ x 9.5$^W$ x 5.5$^H$

Form No: unknown
No. Given:

*Stained:*
*Top Sales in Region.*
*Unstained:*
*Top Sponsors in Region.*

**J⁴** 2000 Regional Sponsored

9.25$^L$ x 5$^W$ x 6.5$^H$

Form No: unknown
No. Given:

*Natural or stained. Blue trim with green, blue, and red weave.*

**K⁴** 2001 Regional Sales

10$^L$ x 9.25$^W$ x 4$^H$

Form No: unknown
No. Given:

*Stained or Natural. Blue trim with blue, green and red accents.*

**N⁴** 1989 Top Performer

10.5$^L$ x 9$^W$ x 8$^H$

Form No: unknown
No. Given:

*Blue weave and trim. Available both stained and natural.*

**O⁴** 1990 Top Performer

10.5$^L$ x 9$^W$ x 8$^H$

Form No: unknown
No. Given:

*Red weave and trim. Available both stained and natural.*

**P⁴** 1991 Top Performer

10.5$^L$ x 9$^W$ x 8$^H$

Form No: unknown
No. Given:

*Purple weave and trim. Available both stained and natural.*

**149**

## Incentive/Award

The Director Sponsored award, Top Performer, is the same as the High Achiever. When the shape of the basket was changed in 1991, it was renamed as well.

**Q⁴** 1991 Pom Pom Peggy
12ᴴ

*Received doll for 50+ shows . The basket charm attached at her neck could be earned with 1 recruit.*

### MARKET VALUES

| Photo | Description | | Avg. | High |
|---|---|---|---|---|
| | *Director Sponsored Awards (con't)* | | | |
| Q⁴ | 1991 | Pom Pom Peggy™ | 73 | 100 |
| R⁴ | 1992 | Treasure Chest™ | 147 | 235 |
| S⁴ | 1992 | Top Performer | 198 | 200 |
| T⁴ | 1993 | Paint the Town™ | 100 | 150 |
| U⁴ | 1993 | Top Performer | 144 | 200 |
| V⁴ | 1994 | "Over the Rainbow" | | |
| | | Gold Nugget (Small) | 178 | 235 |
| | | Pot of Gold (Medium) | 110 | 160 |
| | | Gold Rush (Large) | 178 | 270 |
| W⁴ | | Top Performer | 267 | 380 |
| | 1995 | "Reach for the Stars" | | |
| X⁴ | | Star Bound (Small) | 215 | 300 |
| Y⁴ | | Shining Star (Medium) | 113 | 185 |
| Z⁴ | | Star Team (Large) | 219 | 300 |
| A⁵ | | High Achiever | 202 | 275 |
| | 1996 | "Our Business is Show Business" | | |
| B⁵ | | Associate Producer (Small) | 128 | 130 |
| C⁵ | | Show Star (Medium) | 118 | 160 |
| | | **continued next page** | | |

**U⁴** 1993 Top Performer
10.5ᴸ x 9ᵂ x 8ᴴ

Form No: unknown
No. Given:

*Green, blue, and red weave. Top 10 consultants in the Directorship.*

**Y⁴** 1995 Shining Star
5.75ᴸ x 3.75ᵂ x 3ᴴ

Form No: unknown
No. Given:

*Blue weave and trim. 50+ shows*

**Z⁴** 1995 Star Team
7ᴸ x 5ᵂ x 3.5ᴴ

Form No: unknown
No. Given:

*Available only to Branch Advisors when 30% of their Branch achieves the Shining Star.*

**R⁴**  1992 Treasure Chest

5.75$^L$ x 3.75$^W$ x 3$^H$

Form No:          45000-
No. Given:

*Given to consultants
with 50+ shows.*

**S⁴**  1992 Top Performer

10.5$^L$ x 9$^W$ x 8$^H$

Form No:          unknown
No. Given:

*Green, blue, and red weave.
Top 10 Consultants in the
Directorship.*

**T⁴**  1993 Paint the Town

5.75$^L$ x 3.75$^W$ x 3$^H$

Form No:          45000-
No. Given:

*Green, blue, and red
weave.  50+ shows.*

**V⁴**  1994 Over the Rainbow

*Small:*          4.5RD x 3H
*4+  recruits*
*Medium:*  5.5RD x 3.75H
*50+ shows*
*Large:*     6.5RD x 4.75H
*$40,000+ sales*

**W⁴**  1994 Top Performer

10.5$^L$ x 9$^W$ x 8$^H$

Form No:          unknown
No. Given:

*Teal Weave;  Top 10
consultants in the
Directorship.*

**X⁴**  1995 Star Bound

4.75$^L$ x 3.75$^W$ x 2.25$^H$

Form No:          unknown
No. Given:

*Blue weave and trim.
4+ recruits.*

**A⁵**  1995 High Achiever

12$^{RD}$ x 5.75$^H$

Form No:          unknown
No. Given:

*Blue weave and trim.
Top 10 consultants.*

**B⁵**  1996 Associate Producer

5.5$^{RD}$ x 2.5$^H$

Form No:          unknown
No. Given:

*Red weave and trim.
4+ Recruits*

**C⁵**  1996 Show Star

7$^{RD}$ x 3$^H$

Form No:          unknown
No. Given:

*Red weave and trim.
50+ shows*

**151**

## Incentive/Award

The "theme" for the Director Sponsored Awards
are developed by actual Consultants well over a
year before they are actually awarded.

**D⁵** 1996 Best
Supporting Role

8.5$^{RD}$ x 4$^H$

Form No:          unknown
No. Given:

*Awarded to Branch
Advisors when 30% of
their Branch achieves
the Show Star.*

### MARKET VALUES

| Photo Description | | Avg. | High |
|---|---|---|---|
| *Director Sponsored Awards (con't)* | | | |
| D⁵ | Best Supporting Role (Large) | 105 | 150 |
| E⁵ | High Achiever | 177 | 210 |
| | 1997 "Everything's Coming Up Roses" | | |
| F⁵ | Rose Bud (Small) | 124 | 150 |
| G⁵ | Rose Petal (Medium) | 66 | 119 |
| H⁵ | Rose Bud Flower Pots | 158 | 200 |
| I⁵ | American Beauty | 112 | 155 |
| J⁵ | 1998 Sales Excellence | 90 | 125 |
| J⁵ | 1998 Sponsoring Excellence | 108 | 130 |
| K⁵ | 1998 Team Excellence | 95 | 99 |
| L⁵ | 1999 Sales Excellence | — | — |
| L⁵ | 1999 Sponsoring Excellence | — | — |
| M⁵ | 1999 Team Excellence | 158 | 165 |
| N⁵ | 2000 Director Sponsored | — | — |
| O⁵ | 2000 Team Excellence | — | 100 |
| | **continued next page** | | |

**H⁵** 1997
Rose Bud Pots

2.5$^{RD}$ x 2.5$^H$

Form No:          33693
No. Given:

*Available only to Branch
Advisors when 30% of
their Branch achieves
the 50+ shows.*

f u n **f a c t**

## "Discover the Gift" Vase

This beautiful master-
piece was a gift for all
Directos at the 2001
Bee, in celebration of
the 20th Bee.

Wouldn't this make a
wonderful Mother's
Day basket!

**L⁵** 1999 Director
Sponsored

16$^L$ x 11$^W$ x 9$^H$

Form No:          unknown
No. Given:

*Green trim with blue,
green, and red weave.
Stained given to Top Sales
Performers. Unstained
given to Top Sponsors.*

**E⁵**      1996 High Achiever

$12^{RD} \times 5.75^{H}$

Form No:      unknown
No. Given:

*Red weave and trim. Top 10 Consultants in the Directorship.*

**F⁵**      1997 Rose Bud

$8^{L} \times 4^{W} \times 2^{H}$

Form No:      unknown
No. Given:

*Green weave and trim. 4+ recruits.*

**G⁵**      1997 Rose Petal

$8.5^{L} \times 5^{W} \times 3.5^{H}$

Form No:      unknown
No. Given:

*Green weave and trim. 50+ shows.*

**I⁵**      1997 American Beauty

$13.5^{L} \times 8.25^{W} \times 5.25^{H}$

Form No:      unknown
No. Given:

*Green weave and trim. Top 10 Consultants in the Directorship.*

**J⁵**      1998 Director Sponsored

$12^{L} \times 12^{W} \times 4^{H}$

Form No:      unknown
No. Given:

*Green trim with green, red and blue weave. Stained given to Top Sales Performers. Unstained given to Top Sponsors.*

**K⁵**      1998 Team Excellence

$8.25^{L} \times 8.25^{W} \times 3.5^{H}$

Form No:      unknown
No. Given:

*Green trim with green, red and blue weave. Available both stained and unstained.*

**M⁵**      1999 Team Excellence

$15^{L} \times 10^{W} \times 7.5^{H}$

Form No:      unknown
No. Given:

*Green trim with blue, green and red weave. Available both stained and unstained.*

**N⁵**      2000 Director Sponsored

$14.5^{L} \times 5.5^{W} \times 9.5^{H}$

Form No:      unknown
No. Given:

*Natural or stained. Green trim with green, red and blue weave.*

**O⁵**      2000 Team Excellence

$9.5^{L} \times 4.5^{W} \times 5^{H}$

Form No:      unknown
No. Given:

*Natural or stained. Green trim with green, red and blue weave.*

## Incentive/Award

**P⁵** 2001 Director

Sm: $12^L$ x $11^W$ x $4.5^H$
Lg: $14^L$ x $12.75^W$ x $5^H$

*Smaller = Team*
*Larger = Leadership*

### MARKET VALUES

| Photo | Description | Original | Avg. High |
|---|---|---|---|
| | *Director Sponsored Awards (con't)* | | |
| P⁵ | 2001 Directorship Team | — | — |
| P⁵ | 2001 Directorship Leadership | — | — |
| Q⁵ | 2002 Directorship Award | — | — |
| R⁵ | 2002 Team Award | — | — |

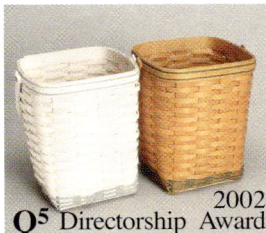

**Q⁵** 2002 Directorship Award
$8^L$ x $7.5^W$ x $10.5^H$

*It was up to the Director to decide how the different versions would be given.*

**R⁵** 2002 Team Award
$6.5^L$ x $6.5^W$ x $8.5^H$

*The stained version was given to Top Branch Advisors, while the whitewashed was given to Regional Advisors.*

f u n **f a c t**

# Mystery incentives . . .

Advisors now have a catalogue they can use to purchase incentive gifts with the Longaberger basket design or logo. Some of the items offered included a cross-stitched apron to wear at Home Shows, an umbrella, Cross pens, tote bags, jewelry, lamp shades and even Meadow Blossoms Pottery.

What a wonderful way to help Consultants get the Longaberger name out there!

## Peggy Elkins
### Toney, Alabama

*Somewhere in the process of buying a few old baskets from a friend and a few new ones, Peggy got hooked. She now has 100 baskets in her collection, her favorite being Traditions™. Peggy visited The Homestead and Dresden for the first time in April. She stayed at one of the Bed and Breakfasts in Dresden and had a FABULOUS time! But of course!*

# J.W. Collection®

**Blue Accent Weave and Trim.**
**Commemorative Brass Tag.**
**Series Retired in 1994.**

## MARKET VALUES

| | | Description | Original | Avg. | High |
|---|---|---|---|---|---|
| A. | 1983 | Market™ | 32.95 | **1257** | **1777** |
| | | with Liner (1993) | 52.90 | — | — |
| B. | 1984 | Waste™ | 34.95 | **1585** | **2100** |
| C. | 1985 | Apple™ | 45.95 | **572** | **750** |
| D. | 1986 | Two-Pie™ | 34.95 | **365** | **575** |
| E. | 1987 | Bread and Milk™ | 43.95 | **332** | **450** |
| | | with Protector | | **363** | **475** |
| | | with Liner (1993) | | **395** | **480** |
| | | Combo (P/L) | | **410** | **525** |
| F. | 1988 | Gathering™ | 36.95 | **280** | **425** |
| | | with Liner (1993) | 57.90 | **310** | **440** |
| G. | 1989 | Banker's Waste™ | 59.95 | **277** | **385** |
| H. | 1990 | Large Berry™ | 48.95 | **214** | **290** |
| | | Combo (P) | 53.90 | **222** | **290** |
| | | with Liner (1993) | 66.90 | **222** | **290** |
| | | Full Set (P/L) | 71.85 | **232** | **300** |
| I. | 1991 | Corn™ | 89.95 | **272** | **450** |
| | | Combo (P) | 103.90 | **341** | **520** |
| J. | 1992 | Cake™ | 55.95 | **117** | **225** |
| | | with Protector | 65.90 | **155** | **290** |
| | | with Liner | 67.90 | **163** | **290** |
| | | Combo (P/L) | 69.95 | **183** | **375** |
| K. | 1993 | Original Easter™ | 65.95 | **165** | **225** |
| | | with Protector | 71.90 | **169** | **225** |
| | | with Liner | 83.90 | **169** | **225** |
| | | Combo (P/L) | 82.95 | **176** | **250** |
| L. | 1994 | Umbrella™ | 74.95 | **177** | **250** |
| | | Combo (P) | 79.95 | **183** | **250** |
| L. | 1994 | JW Commemorative Book | 24.95 | **28** | **51** |
| | | **Full Set JW Collection:** | | **5492** | **7500** |

**A.** 1983 Market
$15^L$ x $10^W$ x $7.5^H$

Form No: 500-AT
No. Sold: 6,300

*A liner was made available in 1993.*

**E.** 1987 Bread and Milk
$16^L$ x $8^W$ x $11^H$

Form No: 2100-ABT
No. Sold: 17,818

*Did not originally sell with accessories. Liner first offered in 1993. Magazine protector used from the regular line.*

**I.** 1991 Corn
$17^{RD}$ x $11.5^H$

Form No: 4400-JBST
No. Sold: 48,332

*Box.*

## collection **note**

In May & June of 1993, Hostesses only were given the opportunity to purchase liners for four previous J.W. Baskets: Medium Market, Medium Gathering, Large Berry and Bread & Milk. A set of 4 Place Mats and 4 Napkins were also offered in the Classic Plaid™ fabric.

**B.** 1984 Waste

9.5$^L$ x 9.5$^W$ x 12$^H$

Form No: 1800-OT
No. Sold: 3,544

**C.** 1985 Apple

13$^{RD}$ x 8.5$^H$

Form No: 3200-BT
No. Sold: 10,467

*Also referred to as a Large Fruit.*

**D.** 1986 Two-Pie

12$^L$ x 12$^W$ x 10$^H$

Form No: 4800-BT
No. Sold: 44,363

**F.** 1988 Gathering

18$^L$ x 11$^W$ x 4.5$^H$

Form No: 2400-ABT
No. Sold: 49,495

*A liner was made available in 1993.*

**G.** 1989 Banker's Waste

12.5$^{RD}$ x 13.5$^H$

Form No: 1900-BBST
No. Sold: 53,328

*Came with box. First time for the company to offer a box.*

**H.** 1990 Large Berry

8.5$^L$ x 8.5$^W$ x 5$^H$

Form No: 1500-BBST
No. Sold: 37,009

*A liner was made available in 1993. Box.*

**J.** 1992 Cake

12$^L$ x 12$^W$ x 6$^H$

Form No: 100-CBST
No. Sold: 98,557

*Basket sold with divider. Box.*

**K.** 1993 Original Easter

16$^L$ x 9$^W$ x 6$^H$

Form No: 13722
No. Sold: ≈ 77,000

*Box.*

**L.** 1994 Umbrella

10$^{RD}$ x 17.5$^H$

Form No: 11215
Book: 72214
No. Sold: ≈ 95,000

*Book sold separately. Box.*

**157**

# J.W. Originals

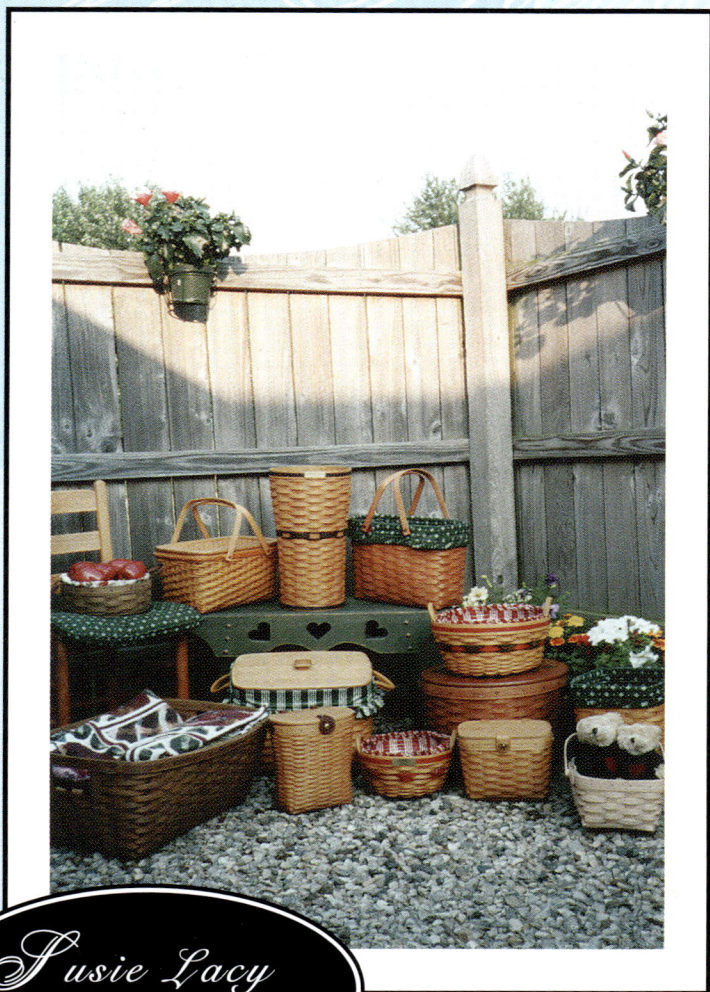

## Susie Lacy
### Chesterfield, Indiana

A collector since 1984, Susie has every one of the Christmas™ baskets beginning with the 1985 Cookie™. She favors smaller baskets and loves to display them on peg boards and basket trees. She loves to use her baskets for everything, everyday!

## J.W. Originals

**These baskets were woven by John Wendell Longaberger (J.W.), himself and are very rare in the secondary market.**

### MARKET VALUES

**Description**     **Original  Avg. High**

_Identifying features_:

A. Braided trim

Color weaving (red, green or blue)

B. Continuous weaving

Double weaving

Handles: very smooth, hand-carved

C. Open-weave or splinted bottom

Signatures: many have family signatures, to confirm its authenticity.

D. Stamp: "Made in Dresden, Ohio" on _inside_

E. Trim strip: Used metal tacks or staples

F. Upside down 'V' pattern at stationary handles

Weave: very tight basket with square corners

| _Common forms_: | _Market Estimates_ |
|---|---|
| Apple [np] | |
| Berry Baskets [np] | $ 350 – 500 |
| Bread & Milk / "Auto" [np] | $ 750 – 1200 |
| G. Cake | $ 700 – 1500 |
| H. Corn | $ 775 – 1200 |
| I. Gathering Baskets | $ 799 – 1000 |
| J. Hamper | $ 800 – 1400 |
| Key Baskets [np] | $ 300 – 400 |
| K. Laundry | $ 900 – 1300 |
| L. Market, Medium | $ 900 – 1300 |
| Market, Large [np] | $ 1255 – 1300 |
| Picnic, Large [np] | |
| M. Pool Basket | $ 500 – 1100 |
| Pottery Ware Basket [np] | $ 900 – 1500 |
| Purse [np] | |
| Two-Pie [np] | $ 750 – 1250 |
| Waste, Banker's [np] | |
| Waste, Square [np] | |
| Umbrella [np] | |

[np] = Not Pictured

160

### PLEASE NOTE

Reporting values based on actual selling transactions is difficult for this collection due to the fact that each one is so unique and there are not many being bought and sold in the market. The majority of J.W. Original transactions reported to us are findings at garage sales, in basements, attics, or at auctions for well below value. Therefore, the values listed here are based on market speculation, not on actual transactions.

**G.**    Cake Baskets

$12^L$ x $12^W$ x $6^H$

_These "blonde" baskets were most likely never stained, but would be considered "natural"._

**J.**    Hamper

$15^L$ x $15^W$ x $21^H$

_Notice the metal hinges on the back of this Hamper and the glass knob. Two unique features for this basket._

**A.** Braided Trim

*This is a smaller version of the braid used for trim. A wider, heavier material was also used.*

**B.** Continuous Weave

*This technique is evident by a "split upsplint", seen here on the front left corner.*

**C.** Open-weave bottom

*While this technique was common among J.W.'s baskets, he also closed the bottoms with filler splints.*

**D.** Stamp

*"Made in Dresden, Ohio" We are not clear when or for how long J.W. used this stamp on his baskets.*

**E.** Tacks vs. Staples

*J.W. started out using tacks for his trims. He received a staple gun for Christmas one year and used it on "everything". Later in his basketmaking, he returned to using tacks.*

**F.** Upside down 'V'

*Almost all of J.W.'s baskets with stationary handles have this trademark for added strength to the handle.*

**H.** Corn

19$^{RD}$ x 14$^{H}$

*This Corn basket is much larger than what was once offered in the regular line. He also made Corn baskets with leather handles.*

Bottom of Corn

*These metal reinforcements were common on Corn, Laundry and Pottery Ware Baskets. The nail in the center is another J.W. trademark.*

**I.** Gathering

19$^{L}$ x 12$^{W}$ x 6$^{H}$

**K.** Laundry

28$^{L}$ x 16.5$^{W}$ x 10.75$^{H}$

*This Laundry Basket also has the cutout handles and metal reinforcements, common for this big of a basket.*

**L.** Medium Market

16.5$^{L}$ x 11$^{W}$ x 8.75$^{H}$

*If you look closely, you can see that this Market had red accents. The inset shows the original price written in pencil on the handle.*

**M.** Pool Basket

22$^{L}$ x 14.5$^{W}$ x 6.25$^{H}$

*J.W. made these baskets for the Dresden Pool to hold visitors' clothes. This basket still has the metal rings used to hold the basket in place.*

# *Designs*

Many think that J.W. Longaberger was the basket pioneer of the family. However, basket-making skills actually started one generation earlier, with J.W.'s father, Daddy John.

Daddy John worked for the Dresden Basket Factory in the 1890's. J.W. often helped around the shop, making basket bottoms. But not until he was 17 did he join his father at the factory and quickly became very skilled at the art.

One of J.W.'s unique talents was to create shapes and sizes of baskets in response to the needs of his friends and family.

The tight square bottoms and round trim of the Measuring Baskets™ made them perfect for measuring feed and grain. Contraray to its name, the Umbrella™ basket was originally designed to dry Grandma Bonnie's tulip bulbs.

Fruit™ Baskets were designed with the inverted bottom to keep fruit from rotting and when local farmers asked for a basket that would stand up to the hard wear and tear on the farm, J.W. "downsized" the durable Pottery Ware™ basket he was so used to using, and created the Corn Basket™ to help carry field corn from silos to the wagons.

All of J.W.'s original basket forms have a "story" behind them. Just another reason to love each and every one!

162

## Cindy Derflinger
### Front Royal, Virginia

*Hooked on baskets through her sister since 1989, Cindy is a firm believer in putting her baskets to use. Thrilled to have the complete May Series™, Cindy is set to complete her favorite collection of J.W.®s.*

## Named after Grandma Bonnie's Favorite Flowers.

MAY SERIES™

May Series™

**A.** 1990 Violet

$5^L$ x $5^W$ x $4.5^H$

Form No: 14000-BVS
No. Sold: 49,591

*There were 28,791 Combos sold this year.*

**E.** 1994 Lilac

$6.5^{RD}$ x $6.5^H$

Form No: 16209
Tie-On: 31291
No. Sold:

*Tie-On sold separately.*

**I.** 1998 Snapdragon

$7.5^{RD}$ x $9.25^H$

Form No: 10863
Tie-On: 31658
No.Sold:

*Tie-On sold separately.*

| Photo | | Description | | MARKET VALUES | | |
|---|---|---|---|---|---|---|
| | | | | Original | Avg. | High |
| A. | 1990 | Violet™ | | 24.95 | **251** | **360** |
| | | with **P**rotector | | 28.90 | **228** | **365** |
| | | with **L**iner | | 34.90 | **285** | **365** |
| | | Combo (**P/L**) | | 34.95 | **363** | **400** |
| B. | 1991 | Rose™ | | 29.95 | **200** | **250** |
| | | with **P**rotector | | 34.90 | **213** | **250** |
| | | with **L**iner | | 41.90 | **213** | **285** |
| | | Combo (**P/L**) | | 39.95 | **246** | **295** |
| C. | 1992 | Pansy™ | | 29.95 | **113** | **155** |
| | | with **P**rotector | | 34.90 | **144** | **185** |
| | | with **L**iner | | 41.90 | **144** | **185** |
| | | Combo (**P/L**) | | 39.95 | **163** | **270** |
| D. | 1993 | Lily of the Valley™ | | 28.95 | **93** | **115** |
| | | with **P**rotector | | 32.90 | **108** | **126** |
| | | with **L**iner | | 41.90 | **108** | **126** |
| | | Combo (**P/L**) | | 39.95 | **106** | **145** |
| E. | 1994 | Lilac™ | | 34.95 | **85** | **115** |
| | | with **P**rotector | | 39.95 | **89** | **145** |
| | | with **L**iner | | 47.90 | **90** | **145** |
| | | Combo (**P/L**) | | 42.95 | **101** | **165** |
| E. | 1994 | Lilac™ Tie-On | | 5.95 | **29** | **44** |
| F. | 1995 | Tulip™ | | 42.95 | **100** | **105** |
| | | with **P**rotector | | 48.90 | **103** | **110** |
| | | with **L**iner | | 57.90 | **103** | **110** |
| | | Combo (**P/L**) | | 54.95 | **100** | **150** |
| F. | 1995 | Tulip™ Tie-On | | 6.95 | **29** | **39** |
| G. | 1996 | Sweet Pea™ | | 45.95 | **78** | **125** |
| | | with **P**rotector | | 52.90 | **80** | **130** |
| | | with **L**iner | | 61.90 | **80** | **130** |
| | | Combo (**P/L**) | | 59.95 | **105** | **158** |
| G. | 1996 | Sweet Pea™ Tie-On | | 6.95 | **25** | **39** |
| H. | 1997 | Petunia™ | | 45.95 | **80** | **110** |
| | | with **P**rotector | | 52.90 | **88** | **125** |
| | | with **L**iner | | 63.90 | **88** | **125** |
| | | Combo (**P/L**) | | 59.95 | **87** | **125** |
| | | Full Set (**C/Lid**) | | 88.90 | **110** | **148** |
| H. | 1997 | Petunia™ Tie-On | | 6.95 | **15** | **28** |
| I. | 1998 | Snapdragon™ | | 47.00 | **70** | **90** |
| | | with **P**rotector | | 55.00 | **78** | **105** |
| | | with **L**iner | | 63.00 | **78** | **105** |
| | | Combo (**P/L**) | | 59.00 | **82** | **125** |
| I. | 1998 | Snapdragon Tie-On | | 8.00 | **20** | **35** |
| J. | 1998 | Grandma Bonnie's Print | | 48.00 | **68** | **75** |
| K. | 1999 | Daisy™ | | 39.00 | **67** | **85** |
| | | with **P**rotector | | 44.00 | **70** | **85** |
| | | with **L**iner | | 53.00 | **70** | **85** |
| | | Combo (**P/L**) | | 49.00 | **72** | **109** |
| K. | 1999 | Daisy™ Tie-On | | 8.00 | **18** | **25** |
| L. | 2000 | Morning Glory™ | | 43.00 | **62** | **89** |
| | | with **P**rotector | | 49.00 | **—** | **—** |
| | | with **L**iner | | 60.00 | **—** | **—** |
| | | Combo (**P/L**) | | 59.00 | **65** | **95** |
| L. | 2000 | Morning Glory Tie-On | | 8.00 | **11** | **18** |

**B.** 1991 Rose

14.5<sup>L</sup> x 7.5<sup>W</sup> x 3.75<sup>H</sup>

Form No:      4700-CSS
No. Sold:

**C.** 1992 Pansy

7<sup>RD</sup> x 4.5<sup>H</sup>

Form No:      10006
No. Sold:

**D.** 1993 Lily of the Valley

5.5<sup>RD</sup> x 3.75<sup>H</sup>

Form No:      15717
No. Sold:

*3/8" Weaving. No color. Does not have an inverted bottom.*

**F.** 1995 Tulip

14.25<sup>L</sup> x 6.25<sup>W</sup> x 3.25<sup>H</sup>

Form No:      14648
Tie-On:      31542
No. Sold:

*Tie-On sold separately.*

**G.** 1996 Sweet Pea

8.25<sup>RD</sup> x 7<sup>H</sup>

Form No:      14915
Tie-On:      32883
No. Sold:      156,288

*Tie-On sold separately.*

**H.** 1997 Petunia

9.5<sup>RD</sup> x 5<sup>H</sup>

Form No:      12947
Tie-On:      34461
No. Sold:

*Tie-On sold separately.*

**J.** "Grandma Bonnie's Favorites" Print

20<sup>W</sup> x 24<sup>H</sup>

Form No:      84999
No. Sold:

*Frame not included.*

**K.** 1999 Daisy

6.75<sup>RD</sup> x 6<sup>H</sup>

Form No:      13056
Tie-On:      36544
No. Sold:

*Tie-On sold separately. Note cards only available free with Combo.*

**L.** 2000 Morning Glory

7.5<sup>L</sup> x 7.5<sup>W</sup> x 4.75<sup>H</sup>

Form No:      18899
Tie-On:      36226

*Grandma Bonnie's book, "Reflections on the Simple Life" included with every Combo.* **165**

## *May Series*™

### Series completed in 2002.

| Photo | Description | | Original | Avg. | High |
|---|---|---|---|---|---|
| M | 2001 | Peony™ | 39.00 | **47** | **56** |
| | | with **P**rotector | 43.00 | — | — |
| | | with **L**iner | 54.00 | — | — |
| | | Combo (**P/L**) | 49.00 | **57** | **102** |
| M | 2001 | Peony™ Tie-On | 8.00 | **13** | **16** |
| N. | 2002 | Geranium™[np] | 49.00 | — | — |
| | | with **P**rotector | 58.00 | — | — |
| | | with **L**iner | 66.00 | — | — |
| | | Combo (**P/L**) | 59.00 | — | — |
| N. | 2002 | Geranium™ Tie-On | 8.00 | — | — |
| | **Series complete** | | | | |

MARKET VALUES

[np] = Not Pictured.

**M.** 2001 Peony

12.75L x 6.25W x 2.75H

| Form No: | 10184 |
|---|---|
| Tie-On: | 39535 |
| No.Sold: | 108,820 |

*Tie-On sold separately.*

f   u   n   **f a c t**

## The Geranium basket . . . the final flower
A word from Longaberger on ending the May Series™:

Since 1990, the May Series has touched the hearts of collectors every where. What started as a way to share the love Grandma Bonnie has had for flowers since she was a little girl has blossomed into a celebration of spring and all the beauty and joy that is brings. And now, 13 years and 13 beautifully handcrafted baskets later, it is with mixed emotions that we bring the May Series to an end. We'll treasure the memories and the baskets that have become part of Grandma Bonnie's legacy.

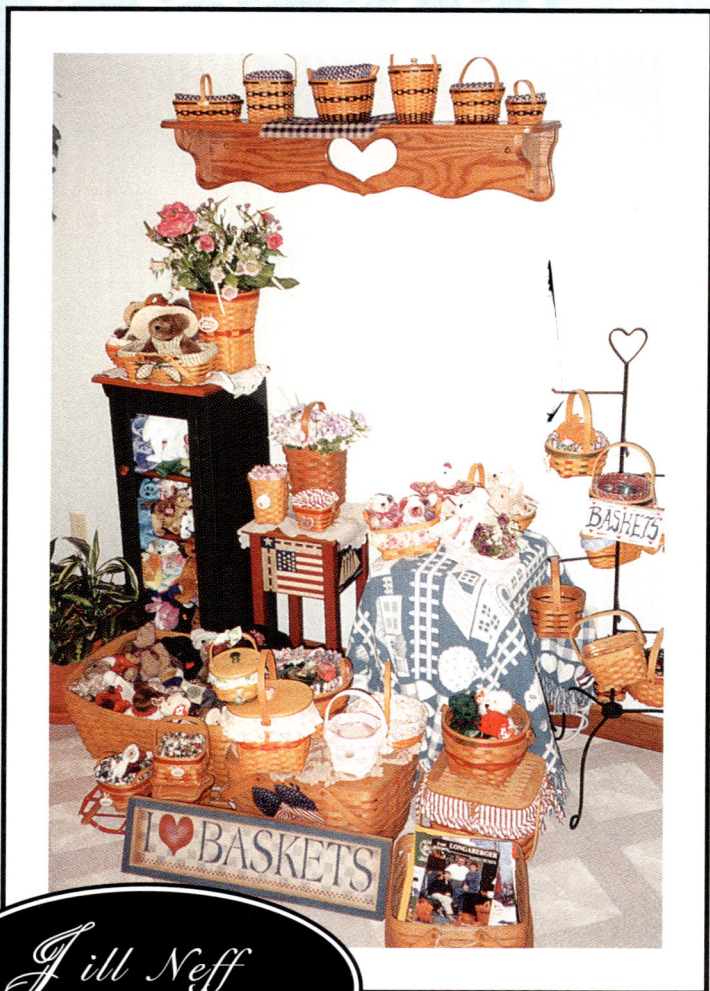

## Jill Neff
### Anderson, Indiana

Although Jill loves all the Longaberger Baskets®, she is especially fond of the May Series™ and Mother's Day™. She began collecting about 10 years ago, but took her first trip to Dresden last year. Needless to say, she LOVED it!

## Mother's Day ™

**Pink Weave and Trim, except in 1993.**

| Photo | | Description | Original | MARKET VALUES Avg. | High |
|---|---|---|---|---|---|
| A. | 1987 | Large Peg ™ | 26.95 | **100** | **165** |
| B. | 1988 | Spring ™ | 28.95 | **120** | **155** |
| | | Combo (**L**) | 39.90 | **154** | **185** |
| C. | 1989 | Mini Chore ™ | 21.95 | **93** | **100** |
| | | Combo (**L**) | 29.95 | **99** | **125** |
| D. | 1990 | Small Oval ™ | 28.95 | **51** | **80** |
| | | Combo (**L**) | 36.95 | **60** | **95** |
| E. | 1991 | Purse ™ | 34.95 | **108** | **130** |
| | | with **P**rotector | 39.90 | **110** | **130** |
| | | with **L**iner | 49.90 | **110** | **130** |
| | | Combo (**P/L**) | 54.85 | **114** | **170** |
| F. | 1991 | Potpourri ™ | 21.95 | **60** | **100** |
| | | Combo (**L**) | 30.90 | **75** | **125** |
| G. | 1992 | Mother's Day ™ | 34.95 | **68** | **100** |
| | | with **P**rotector | 40.90 | **70** | **100** |
| | | with **L**iner | 50.90 | **70** | **100** |
| | | Combo (**P/L**) | 49.95 | **74** | **105** |
| H. | 1993 | Mother's Day ™ | 44.95 | **60** | **100** |
| | | with **P**rotector | 50.90 | **65** | **100** |
| | | with **L**iner | 59.90 | **67** | **100** |
| | | Combo (**P/L**) | 57.95 | **70** | **117** |
| I. | 1994 | Mother's Day ™ | 37.95 | **50** | **85** |
| | | with **P**rotector | 42.90 | **50** | **87** |
| | | with **L**iner | 50.90 | **50** | **87** |
| | | Combo (**P/L**) | 49.95 | **54** | **100** |
| I. | 1994 | Mother's Journal | 5.95 | **10** | **21** |
| J. | 1995 | Basket of Love ™ | 37.95 | **45** | **75** |
| | | with **P**rotector | 43.90 | **50** | **85** |
| | | with **L**iner | 52.90 | **50** | **85** |
| | | Combo (**P/L**) | 49.95 | **54** | **95** |
| J. | 1995 | Mother's Day Tie-On | 6.95 | **18** | **25** |
| K. | 1996 | Vanity ™ | 44.95 | **52** | **105** |
| | | with **P**rotector | 56.90 | **68** | **105** |
| | | with **L**iner | 60.90 | **68** | **105** |
| | | Combo (**P/L**) | 59.95 | **70** | **125** |
| | | Full Set (**Combo/Lid**) | 82.90 | **85** | **130** |
| K. | 1996 | Mother's Day Tie-On | 6.95 | **14** | **23** |
| L. | 1997 | Timeless Memory ™ | 49.95 | **85** | **115** |
| | | with **P**rotector | 59.90 | **88** | **125** |
| | | with **L**iner | 69.90 | **88** | **125** |
| | | Combo (**P/L**) | 69.95 | **93** | **130** |
| | | Full Set (**Combo/Lid**) | 92.90 | **100** | **150** |
| L. | 1997 | Mother's Day Tie-On | 6.95 | **12** | **18** |

**A.** 1987 Large Peg

$6.5^L$ x $6.5^W$ x $8^H$

Form No: 11000-BPS
No. Sold:

**E.** 1991 Purse

$9.5^L$ x $6^W$ x $6^H$

Form No: 800-EPS
No. Sold:

**I.** 1994 Mother's Day

$6.75^L$ x $9.25^W$ x $3.75^H$

Form No: 16004
Journal: 72087
No. Sold:

*Journal sold separately.*

**B.** 1988 Spring

$11^L$ x $8^W$ x $5.5^H$

Form No: 900-APS
No. Sold:

*Promotion did not include a Combo.*

**C.** 1989 Mini Chore

$7^L$ x $5^W$ x $3.5^H$

Form No: 700-APS
No. Sold:

*Included note cards.*

**D.** 1990 Small Oval

$8.5^L$ x $5^W$ x $3.5^H$

Form No: 33000-JPS
No. Sold:

*Promotion did not include a Combo.*

**F.** 1991 Potpourri

$5^L$ x $5^W$ x $2.5^H$

Form No: 13000-APS
No. Sold:

*Hostess Only.
Sold as the "Touch of Pink Potpourri". Does not have color on trim.*

**G.** 1992 Mother's Day

$10.5^L$ x $10.5^W$ x $4.5^H$

Form No: 110-CPS
No. Sold:

**H.** 1993 Mother's Day

$8.5^L$ x $8^W$ x $6^H$

Form No: 12904
No. Sold:

*3/8" Weaving.
No color.*

**J.** 1995 Basket of Love

$8.5^{RD}$ x $4^H$

Form No: 18805
Tie-On: 31470
No. Sold:
  Tie-On: 90,515

*Tie-On sold separately.*

**K.** 1996 Vanity

$14.5^L$ x $7.5^W$ x $4.5^{FH}$ x $6.5^{BH}$

Form No: 14753
Tie-On: 32328
No. Sold: 224,278

*Tie-On & Lid sold separately.
Divided protector came with Combo. A regular protector also available for $5.95.*

**L.** 1997 Timeless Memory

$11.25^L$ x $9.25^W$ x $5.75^H$

Form No: 13030
Tie-On: 33995
No. Sold:

*Tie-On & Lid sold separately.*

**169**

## Mother's Day™

**These baskets are usually offered during March for Mother's Day gift giving.**

### MARKET VALUES

| Photo | Description | | Original | Avg. | High |
|---|---|---|---|---|---|
| M. | 1998 | Rings & Things™ | 34.00 | **40** | 65 |
| | | Combo (**Pouch**) | 45.00 | **56** | 80 |
| | | with **P**rotector | 40.00 | **45** | 65 |
| | | with **L**iner | 48.00 | **48** | 65 |
| | | Combo2 (**P/L**) | 54.00 | **65** | 95 |
| M. | 1998 | Mother's Day Tie-On | 8.00 | **14** | 15 |
| N. | 1999 | Tea for Two™ | 39.00 | **55** | 70 |
| | | with **P**rotector | 44.00 | — | — |
| | | with **L**iner | 53.00 | — | — |
| | | Combo (**P/L**) | 49.00 | **61** | 75 |
| | | Full Set (**Combo/Lid**) | 68.00 | **82** | 87 |
| N. | 1999 | Mother's Day Tie-On | 8.00 | **13** | 16 |
| O. | 2000 | Early Blossoms™ | 45.00 | **57** | 82 |
| | | with **P**rotector | 50.00 | — | — |
| | | with **L**iner | 60.00 | — | — |
| | | Combo (**P/L**) | 56.00 | **60** | 100 |
| O. | 2000 | Bonnet Tie-On | 8.00 | **13** | 16 |
| P. | 2001 | Vintage Blossoms™ | 49.00 | — | — |
| | | with **P**rotector | 56.00 | — | — |
| | | with **L**iner | 67.00 | — | — |
| | | Combo (**P/L**) | 59.00 | **82** | 105 |
| | | Full Set (**Combo/Lid**) | 81.00 | **88** | 110 |
| P. | 2001 | Vintage Tie-On | 8.00 | **12** | 14 |
| Q. | 2002 | Mom's Memories™ | 55.00 | **50** | 82 |
| | | with **P**rotector | 65.00 | — | — |
| | | with **L**iner | 70.00 | — | — |
| | | Combo (**P/L**) | 69.00 | — | — |
| | | Full Set (**C/Lid**) | 93.00 | **109** | 118 |
| Q. | 2002 | Photo Frame Tie-On | 10.00 | — | — |

**M.** 1998 Rings & Things
7$^{RD}$ x 3$^H$

Form No: 10383
Tie-On: 34002
No. Sold: 180,000

*Combo included the basket and jewelry pouch (not pictured).*

**Q.** 2002 Mom's Memories
9.5$^L$ x 7.75$^W$ x 6$^H$

Form No: 12136
Tie-On: 30806
No. Sold:

*Combo included the basket and jewelry pouch (not pictured). First time to use 2 accent colors.*

**N.** 1999
Tea for Two
$7.75^L$ x $5.75^W$ x $3.25^H$

Form No: 14931
Tie-On: 36251

*Liner was offered in both White Vine™ and Mother's Day Floral fabric.*

**O.** 2000
Early Blossoms
$11^L$ x $7.25^W$ x $2.75^H$

Form No: 19682
Tie-On: 37133

*First ever 3-D tie-on from Longaberger. Pottery sold separately. See Pottery Collection for details.*

**P.** 2001
Vintage Blossoms
$7.5^L$ x $5.75^W$ x $6.5^H$

Form No: 10222
Tie-On: 39527
No.Sold: 118,837

*Box included. Vintage Blossoms Soap Dish and soap promoted in same campaign. See Pottery Collection for details.*

f  u  n  **f a c t**

# Mother's Day Tea

May 11 and 12, 2002

Looking for a special way to show Mom that you love her? How about a day of shopping, eating and entertainment in basket heaven . . . The Homestead!

During this special weekend, Mom will also be treated to a fashion show and souvenirs for everyone. If that doesn't make up for all that you've put her through, nothing will!

## What are all those natural baskets with color?

That is a question we get more and more often. *Customized Baskets* are from the early Longaberger years, prior to 1990.

Customizing meant they were able to special order baskets with special features. Between 1977 and 1978, almost any combination could be ordered for a basket – stained, natural, with or without color weaving, lid, no lid, handle, no handle, 1 handle, 2 handles, etc. Because they were handmade and the orders were not as great as they are today, it was not hard to permit this policy.

In 1980, this policy was changed to only allow customers to choose between <u>two</u> special order options for an additional $5.00 charge: Natural or natural with color accent weave.

The colors available were *blue, green, red, and brown*. For a very short time prior to 1980, *yellow* was also an option.

### Here are the Exceptions . . .
Most baskets were included for this option, with the following exceptions:

**Natural** Only – No Color Weaving:

Button™                Cracker™                    Medium Vegetable™
Bread™                 Small Vegetable™           Wine™

**Stained** Only – No Special Order Options:

All promotional baskets

**Natural** or **Natural with Color** Only – No Stain:

1984 – 1989 :  Large (Infant) Cradle™, Large Laundry™

### Discontinued option . . .
The entire customizing option was discontinued for all Regular Line baskets in 1986. However, the option did continue for the Large Cradle and Large Laundry until August 1989.

### The Markets perception. . .
While there is an interest in the market for these baskets, there are others in the market that do not care for the option. Because it is a discontinued feature, it is realistic to expect a premium on the basket's value. Start by determining the value as if it were not customized. It is reasonable to consider the option worth at least $5.00 more valuable because that was the original cost for the option. However, the buyer's preference will ultimately determine if more than this can be collected.

# Pewter Ornaments

**Deborah Hanyka**
**Perry, Oklahoma**

Deborah purchased a basket on the secondary market from the cover winner of our 7th Edition Bentley®, and actually bought a basket that was featured in the photo! A SMALL WORLD INDEED! Deborah has about 200 baskets in her collection and was encouraged by her husband to collect the pottery as well.

# Pewter Ornaments

**Available individually or in sets of four.
Each ornament approximately 2" high.**

## MARKET VALUES

| | | Description | Original | Avg. | High |
|---|---|---|---|---|---|
| A. | 1993 | **Commemorative Santa Collection** | | | |
| | | Father Christmas™ | 8.95 | **10** | **12** |
| | | Kriss Kringle™ | 8.95 | **10** | **12** |
| | | Santa Claus™ | 8.95 | **10** | **15** |
| | | St. Nick™ | 8.95 | **10** | **12** |
| | | SET of Four Gift Set | 29.95 | **58** | **70** |
| B. | 1994 | **Commemorative Baskets Collection** | | | |
| | | 1981 Candle™ | 8.95 | **9** | **9** |
| | | 1982 Sleigh™ | 8.95 | **10** | **10** |
| | | 1983 Bell™ | 8.95 | — | — |
| | | 1984 Holly™ | 8.95 | — | — |
| | | SET of Four Gift Set | 29.95 | **37** | **60** |
| C. | 1995 | **Commemorative Baskets Collection** | | | |
| | | 1985 Cookie™ | 8.95 | **13** | **15** |
| | | 1986 Candy Cane™ | 8.95 | **13** | **17** |
| | | 1987 Mistletoe™ | 8.95 | **13** | **15** |
| | | 1988 Poinsettia™ | 8.95 | **13** | **15** |
| | | SET of Four Gift Set | 29.95 | **30** | **60** |
| D. | 1996 | **Commemorative Baskets Collection** | | | |
| | | 1989 Memory™ | 8.95 | — | — |
| | | 1990 Gingerbread™ | 8.95 | **10** | **10** |
| | | 1991 Yuletide Traditions™ | 8.95 | — | — |
| | | 1992 Season's Greetings™ | 8.95 | — | — |
| | | SET of Four Gift Set | 29.95 | **38** | **60** |
| E. | 1997 | **Commemorative Baskets Collection** | | | |
| | | 1993 Bayberry™ | 8.95 | — | — |
| | | 1994 Jingle Bell™ | 8.95 | — | — |
| | | 1995 Cranberry™ | 8.95 | — | — |
| | | 1996 Holiday Cheer™ | 8.95 | — | — |
| | | SET of Four Gift Set | 29.95 | **32** | **45** |
| F. | 1998 | **Commemorative Angels Collection** | | | |
| | | 1993 Peace™ | 9.00 | — | **14** |
| | | 1994 Hope™ | 9.00 | — | **15** |
| | | 1995 Love™ | 9.00 | — | **16** |
| | | 1996 Joy™ | 9.00 | — | **15** |
| | | SET of Four Gift Set | 30.00 | **34** | **45** |
| | 1999 | **Ornaments** | | | |
| G. | 1999 | Angel Set | 30.00 | **33** | **45** |
| H. | 1999 | Snow Friends Set | 15.00 | **16** | **27** |
| | 2000 | **Ornaments** | | | |
| I. | 2000 | Roger & Ginger Set | 19.00 | **20** | **24** |
| J. | 2000 | Snowflake Set | 19.00 | — | — |
| K. | 2000 | 12 Gifts of Christmas | 59.00 | — | — |
| | | **continued next page** | | | |

**1993**

**A.   Santa Ornaments**

Form No:
| | |
|---|---|
| Father Christmas | 70653 |
| Kriss Kringle | 70637 |
| Santa Claus | 70629 |
| St.Nick | 70645 |
| SET | 70661 |

**1997**

**E.   Basket Ornaments**

Form No:
| | |
|---|---|
| Bayberry | 71897 |
| Jingle Bell | 71960 |
| Cranberry | 71978 |
| Holiday Cheer | 71986 |
| SET | 71927 |

*Last year for the Basket
Ornaments.*

**2000**

**I.   Roger & Ginger**

Form No:          73369

*Sold only as a set of 2.*

PEWTER ORNAMENTS

Ornaments

**B.** Basket Ornaments 1994

Form No:

| | |
|---|---|
| Candle | 72273 |
| Sleigh | 72281 |
| Bell | 72290 |
| Holly | 72303 |
| SET | 72311 |

**C.** Basket Ornaments 1995

Form No:

| | |
|---|---|
| Cookie | 72141 |
| Candy Cane | 71838 |
| Mistletoe | 71943 |
| Poinsettia | 72460 |
| SET | 71803 |

**D.** Basket Ornaments 1996

Form No:

| | |
|---|---|
| Memory | 71951 |
| Gingerbread | 72028 |
| Yuletide Traditions | 72001 |
| Season's Greetings | 71935 |
| SET | 71901 |

**F.** Angel Ornaments 1998

Form No:

| | |
|---|---|
| Peace | 71765 |
| Hope | 71773 |
| Love | 71781 |
| Joy | 71790 |
| SET | 71757 |

*First year for the Angel Ornaments.*

**G.** Angel Ornaments 1999

Form No:

| | |
|---|---|
| Faith | |
| Friendship | |
| Gratitude | |
| Kindness | |
| SET | 71072 |

*Sold only as a set.*

**H.** 1999 Snow Friends Ornaments

Form No:

| | |
|---|---|
| Flurry | |
| Snowball | |
| SET | 72800 |

*Sold only as a set.*

**J.** Snowflakes 2000

Form No: 73431

*Sold only as a set of 2.*

**K.** 2000 Twelve Gifts of Christmas

Form No: 72931

*Sold only as a set of 12.*

## *Pewter Ornaments*

### MARKET VALUES

| Photo | Description | Original | Avg. | High |
|-------|-------------|----------|------|------|
| | **2001** **Pewter Items** | | | |
| | 2001 Baby's 1st Ornament[np] | 24.00 | — | — |
| L. | 2001 Santa's Key | 16.00 | **18** | **25** |
| M. | 2001 Star Ornament Set | 34.00 | — | — |

[np] = Not Pictured.

**L.** 2001 Santa's Key

1.5L x 4.25W

Form No: 77721

*Two-sided design.*

**M.** 2001 Star Ornament Set

Lg: 3W / Sm: 2.25W

Form No: 77623

*Set of 3. Not available separately.*

## f u n **f a c t**

# 2001 Bee Attendance Award

This striking basket was developed as an incentive to encourage attendance at the Bee™. This *Bee Attendance Basket* was presented by Rachel Longaberger to all Branch Advisors within the directorship having the highest Bee 2001 attendance.

9L x 5.5W x 6.5H

As an added special touch, each basket was also personally signed by Rachel.

## Julie Kokoszka
### Issaquah, Washington

*Julie, rather Julie's husband,
loves Longaberger Pottery®
since he does all the dishes and
has yet to break or chip a single piece! Julie
loves that they clean easily and keep their lustrous shine.
We think it has the family approval!*

# *Pottery*®

**Roseville:  Produced by Friendship Pottery from 1990 - 91.**

Roseville Embossing

## MARKET VALUES

| Photo | Description | Original | Avg. | High |
|---|---|---|---|---|
| | *Roseville Pottery – 1990–91* | | | |
| A. | Small Mixing Bowl | 17.95 | **48** | **65** |
| A. | Medium Mixing Bowl | 22.95 | **45** | **65** |
| A. | Large Mixing Bowl | 29.95 | **49** | **60** |
| B. | Grandma Bonnie's Apple Pie Plate | 23.95 | **50** | **65** |
| C. | Small Juice Pitcher | 21.95 | **60** | **75** |
| C. | Large Milk Pitcher | 27.95 | **56** | **80** |
| | FULL SET | | **213** | **250** |
| | *Bricks* | | | |
| D. | (90-01) Buffet | 14.95 | **—** | **—** |
| | (91-01) Button[np] | 9.95 | **11** | **15** |
| E. | (91–98) Cracker | 9.95 | **12** | **15** |
| | *Pottery, All-American* | | | |
| F. | (01) Baking, 8x8 | 39.00 | **43** | **53** |
| G. | (99-01) Bowl, Large Mixing | 39.00 | **49** | **70** |
| H. | (01) Crock, 1Pt. | 24.00 | **26** | **33** |
| I. | (98–01) Pie Plate | 30.00 | **37** | **56** |
| J. | (00-01) Pitcher, Milk | 42.00 | **53** | **60** |
| | **continued next page** | | | |

[np]  = Not Pictured.

**D.** (90-01) Buffet Brick
$7.25^L$ x $7.25^W$
Form No:          34568
No. Sold:

## collection **note**

Longaberger Pottery® was introduced in 1990 as the "Roseville Pottery", because it was made in Roseville, Ohio.  The demand was high, but the production had some problems and was eventually moved to East Liverpool, Ohio in late 1991.  The current line of pottery was reintroduced in 1991 in the Classic Blue™, Heritage Green™ and Traditional Red™.  Heirloom Ivory™ joined the options in 1996.

**H.** 2001 1 Pint Crock
$3.5^H$ / 1 Pt.
Form No:          39314
No. Sold:

**A.** Roseville Bowls

Form No:
| | |
|---|---|
| Small: | 30058 |
| Medium: | 30091 |
| Large: | 30023 |

**B.** Roseville Pie Plate

Form No: 30015
No.Sold:

*Came with a box and a recipe for Grandma Bonnie's famous Apple Pie.*

**C.** Roseville Pitchers

Form No:
| | |
|---|---|
| Small: | 30082 |
| Large: | 30031 |

**E.** 1991-98 Cracker Brick

$9^L$ x $2.25^W$

Form No: 30201
No. Sold:

**F.** 2001 8x8 Baking

$8^L$ x $8^W$ x $2^H$

Form No: 39306
No. Sold:

**G.** 1999-01 Lg Mixing Bowl

$10^{RD}$

Form No: 36200
No. Sold:

**I.** 1998-00 Pie Plate

$9^{RD}$ x $2^D$

Form No: 35801/35807
No. Sold:

*Red and blue design with stars around the edge. Only offered during the All-American campaign.*

**J.** 2000-01 Milk Pitcher

$7.5^H$ / 2 Qt.

Form No: 35491
No. Sold:

179

## *Pottery*®

**All Pottery pieces were originally sold with their own box and product card.**

### MARKET VALUES

| | Description | Original | Avg. | High |
|---|---|---|---|---|
| | **Pottery, American Holly** | | | |
| K. | (01) Bowl, Large Serving | 69.00 | — | — |
| K. | (01) Mug, Individual | 19.00 | — | — |
| K. | (01) Plate, Luncheon | 24.00 | — | — |
| K. | (01) Vase | 59.00 | — | — |
| | **Pottery, Christmas** | | | |
| L. | (97-01) Bowl, Serving | 41.95 | — | — |
| M. | (96-01) Candlesticks, pair | 39.95 | 40 | 60 |
| N. | (96–98) Casserole, 2Qt. | 59.95 | 73 | 80 |
| O. | (95–98) Covered Dish, Small | 29.95 | 33 | 40 |
| P. | (01) Dish, Shining Star | 39.00 | 42 | 51 |
| Q. | (98-01) Mug Cover | 9.00 | — | — |
| | (98–99) Plate & Tumbler, Snow Friends | | | |
| R. | (98) Cookies for Santa | 40.00 | 43 | 53 |
| S. | (99) Flurry & Snowball | 29.00 | 36 | 40 |
| T. | (00) Plate & Mug, Roger & Ginger | | | |
| | Mug | 19.00 | 19 | 25 |
| | Plate | 29.00 | — | — |
| U. | (97-01) Platter, Serving | 51.95 | — | — |
| V. | (98-01) Salt/Pepper Shakers | 28.00 | — | — |
| | **continued next page** | | | |

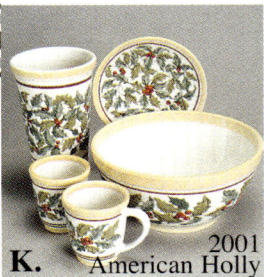

**K.** 2001 American Holly

Bowl: 30448
Mug: 30452
Plate: 30492
Vase: 30446

*First year for this exclusive design.*

**O.** 1995-98 Covered Dish
5.5RD

Form No: 31631
No. Sold:

*Traditional Holly. Only offered during the Christmas promotional period.*

n e e d   h e l p ?

## Where are the Regular Line items?

see page 10

**S.** 1999 Flurry & Snowball
9RD

Form No: 36927
No. Sold:

*Final year for the Snow Friends plate. No cup sold. Illustration by Richard Cowdrey.*

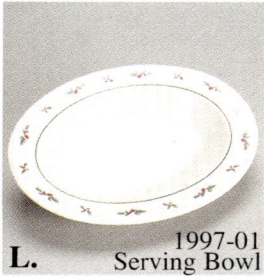

**L.** 1997-01 Serving Bowl

11.25$^L$ x 8.25$^W$

Form No: 34916
No. Sold:

*Traditional Holly.*

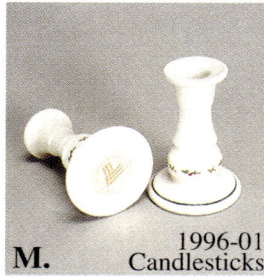

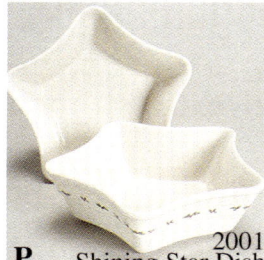

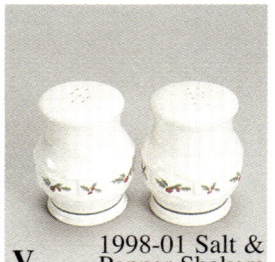

**M.** 1996-01 Candlesticks

3.25$^{RD}$ x 5$^H$

Form No: 32395
No. Sold:

*Traditional Holly.*

**N.** 1996-98 2 Qt. Casserole

10.5$^{RD}$

Form No: 33162
No. Sold:

*Traditional Holly.*

**P.** 2001 Shining Star Dish

9.5$^L$ x 9.5$^W$ x 3$^H$

Form No: 30592
No. Sold:

*Traditional Holly. First ever star-shaped pottery dish ever offered.*

**Q.** 1998-01 Mug Cover

3.5$^{RD}$

Form No: 33502
No. Sold:

*Traditional Holly not pictured.*

**R.** 1998 Cookies for Santa

9$^{RD}$ / 8$^{OZ}$

Form No: 36021
No. Sold:

*Sold as a Set only. Available in Nov. & Dec. 1998. Illustration by Richard Cowdrey.*

**T.** 2000 Roger & Ginger

9$^{RD}$ / 12$^{OZ}$

Mug: 36854
Plate: 36528

*Illustration by Richard Cowdrey.*

**U.** 1997-01 Serving Platter

12.75$^L$ x 10.5$^W$

Form No: 34908

*Traditional Holly.*

**V.** 1998-01 Salt & Pepper Shakers

3.25$^H$

Form No: 32549

*Traditional Holly. Set of 2.*

# Pottery®

## MARKET VALUES

| Description | Original | Avg. | High |
|---|---|---|---|
| *Pottery, Christmas* (con't) | | | |
| W. (95–98) Sauce Boat | 24.95 | **42** | **50** |
| X. (97–98) Tea Pot | 62.95 | **85** | **135** |
| Y. (96-01) Trivet | 19.95 | **27** | **34** |
| *Pottery, Feature* | | | |
| Z. (02) American Eagle Casserole Dish | 59.00 | — | — |
| A$^1$ (99-01) Candy Corn Crock | 17.00 | **22** | **36** |
| B$^1$ (00) Candy Corn Pillar | 23.00 | **23** | **35** |
| C$^1$ (00) Early Blossoms Flower Pots & Tray | 39.00 | **39** | **68** |
| D$^1$ (01) Falling Leaves Vase | 46.00* | **45** | **80** |
| E$^1$ (99) Homestead Crock | 45.00 | **84** | **120** |
| with Lid | 66.00 | **87** | **135** |
| F$^1$ (01-02) Matzah Tray | 49.00 | **52** | **61** |
| G$^1$ (01) Peony Flower Pots (2) | 39.00 | **48** | **55** |
| H$^1$ (02) Shamrock Ramekin | 19.00 | **24** | **28** |
| **continued next page** | | | |

* value listed for item

**W.**
**1995-98**
**Sauce Boat**

12$^{OZ}$

Form No:     31569
No. Sold:

*Traditional Holly. Only offered during the Christmas campaign.*

**A$^1$ Candy Corn Crock**
**1999-01**

1 Pint

Form No:     37516
No. Sold:

*Promoted during the in August 1999 and July 2000.*

**E$^1$ Homestead Crock**
**1999**

2 Quart

Form No:     37532
No. Sold:

*Features a sealable lid that sold separately.*

### f u n **f a c t**

**An Olympic Medal in the family!**

Lea Ann Parsley, winner of the Silver Medal in the Women's Skeleton at the 2002 Winter Olympics, is sister to Bob Parsley, Longaberger Director of Sales & Marketing Techonology. Lea Ann was also 1 of 7 USA Team members to carry the American Flag during opening ceremonies.

**X.** 1997-98 Tea Pot

40ᴼᶻ

Form No: 31615
No. Sold:

*Traditional Holly. Only offered during the Christmas campaign.*

**Y.** 1996-01 Trivet

8.5ᴿᴰ

Form No: 31941
No. Sold:

*Traditional Holly. Stand not included.*

**Z.** 2002 American Eagle Casserole

9.25ᴿᴰ x 5.25ᴴ

Form No: 30812
No. Sold:

*Promoted along with the All-American Casserole Basket.*

**B¹** 2000 Candy Corn Pillar Candle Holder

7.25ᴿᴰ

Form No: 36391
No. Sold:

*Promoted during July 2000.*

**C¹** 2000 Early Blossoms

Pots: 4ᴿᴰ x 3.5ᴴ
Tray: 8.75ᴸ x 5ᵂ x 1.75ᴴ
Form No: 38679

*Featured during the 2000 Mother's Day campaign.*

**D¹** 2001 Falling Leaves Vase

6.5ᴿᴰ x 8.5ᴴ

Form No: 30106
No. Sold:

*Sold only as a part of a set along with the Large Daily Blessings Basket.*

**F¹** 2001-02 Matzah Tray

9.5ᴸ x 9.5ᵂ x 1.25ᴴ

Form No: 35611

**G¹** 2001 Peony Flower Pots

3.75ᴿᴰ x 4ᴴ

Form No: 30028
No. Sold:

*Promoted along with the May Peony Basket.*

**H¹** 2002 Shamrock Ramekin

5.5ᴸ x 5.25ᵂ x 1.75ᴴ

Form No: 30540
No. Sold:

## Pottery®

**Most Pottery from the Regular Line was available in blue, green, red or ivory.**

## MARKET VALUES

| Photo | | Description | Original | Avg. | High |
|---|---|---|---|---|---|
| | | *Pottery, Feature (con't)* | | | |
| I¹ | (00) | Sweetheart Heart Dish | 19.00 | **23** | **35** |
| J¹ | (01) | Sweetheart Heart Plate | 19.00 | **22** | **30** |
| | | with Candle | 29.00 | — | — |
| U. | (01) | Vintage Blossoms Dish | 24.00 | **24** | **28** |
| | | with Soap | 29.00 | — | — |
| U. | (02) | Vintage Blossoms Vase | 26.00 | **31** | **42** |
| V. | | *Pottery, Fruit Medley* | | | |
| | (99) | Bowl, Pasta | 69.00 | **96** | **175** |
| | (99) | Mugs, set of 2 | 36.00 | **61** | **100** |
| | (99) | Pitcher | 49.00 | **99** | **175** |
| | (99) | Ramekin | 15.00 | **37** | **55** |
| | | *Pottery, Retired* | | | |
| W. | (94–98) | Bowl, Dessert | 13.95 | **25** | **35** |
| | (96–02) | Bowl, XLg Mixing[np] | 40.00 | — | — |
| X. | (97–01) | Butter Dish, | 39.95 | **40** | **43** |
| Y. | (96–99) | Candlesticks, pair | 39.95 | **50** | **75** |
| Z. | (00–02) | Crock, 1 Pint Crock | | | |
| | | 2 Crocks with lids | 44.00 | **50** | **55** |
| A¹ | (00–02) | Crock, Condiment | 13.00 | **19** | **25** |
| | | with Lid | 21.00 | — | — |
| | | 2 Crocks with lids | 39.00 | **39** | **46** |
| B¹ | (01) | Dish, Shining Star | 39.00 | **41** | **50** |
| C¹ | (97–98) | Flower Pot, Large | 29.95 | **41** | **73** |
| C¹ | (95–02) | Flower Pot, Medium | 17.95 | **18** | **30** |
| C¹ | (96–01) | Flower Pot, Small | 13.95 | **16** | **40** |
| D¹ | (97–02) | Lamp w/ shade | 74.95 | — | — |
| | | **continued next page** | | | |

[np] = Not Pictured.

**I¹** Sweetheart Dish
2000

5ᴸ x 4ᵂ x 2ᴴ

Form No: 37192 / 39730
39748 / 39756

*Available in blue, green, red or ivory. Promoted with the Sweetheart Little Love™. Box.*

**W.** Dessert Bowl
1994–98

6ᴼᶻ

Form No: 30147/30350
30236/33278

*Form numbers in order of blue, green, red, ivory. Box.*

**A¹** Condiment Crock
2000-02

2.75ᴴ

Form No: 38768/38776
38784/38792

*Form numbers in order of blue, green, red, ivory.*

**J¹** 2001
Sweetheart Plate

7ᴸ x 7.5ᵂ

Form No: 30506
Candle 62693

*Candle was sold
separately or in a set
with the plate. Box.*

**U.** 2001
Vintage Blossoms

5.25ᴸ x 4ᵂ

Form No: 36706

*Promoted along with
the Mother's Day
Vintage Blossoms. Box.*

**V.** 1999
Fruit Medley

Bowl: 37346
Mugs: 37320
Pitcher: 37338
Ramekin: 38521

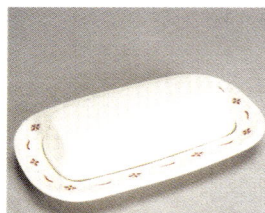

**X.** 1997-01
Butter Dish

8.25ᴸ x 5ᵂ x 2ᵂ

Form No: 33375/33383
33367/33391

*Form numbers in order of
blue, green, red, ivory.
Box.*

**Y.** 1996-99
Candlesticks

3.25ᴿᴰ x 5ᴴ

Form No: 32522/31/14/
34037

*Form numbers in order
of blue, green, red, ivory.
Sold as a Set of 2. Box.*

**Z.** 2000-02
1 Pint Crock Set

3.5ᴴ

Form No: 38890/38903
38911/38920

*Originally offered with the
Barbeque Buddy Basket.
The individual Pint Crock
is still available through
the Regular Line.*

**B¹** 2001
Shining Star Dish

9.5ᴸ x 9.5ᵂ x 3ᵂ

Form No: 30598/30586
30588/30600
No.Sold: 176,000

*Promoted to fit the
Shining Star Basket™.
Box.*

**C¹** Flower Pots

6.5ᴴ / 4.5ᴴ / 3.5ᴴ

Form No: various

*Sold individually.
Available in blue, green,
red, ivory. Box.*

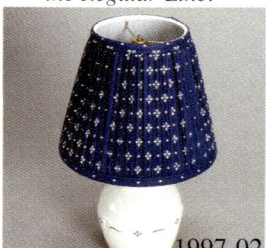

**D¹** 1997-02
Lamp with Shade

14.5ᴴ

Form No: 34266/34274
34282/34291

*Form numbers in order of
blue, green, red, ivory.
Shades were offered
in many regular line* **185**
*fabrics.*

# Pottery®

## MARKET VALUES

| Photo | Description | Original | Avg. | High |
|-------|-------------|----------|------|------|

### Pottery, Retired (con't)

| Photo | Description | Original | Avg. | High |
|-------|-------------|----------|------|------|
| E¹ (99-02) | Loaf Dish, Small | 29.00 | **29** | **31** |
| F¹ (98-02) | Mug Cover | 9.00 | **9** | **17** |
| G¹ (99–00) | Napkin Rings (2) | 19.00 | **20** | **35** |
| H¹ (00-02) | Quiche Dish | 39.00 | **39** | **48** |
| I¹ (02) | Roaster, 3-Qt. | 89.00 | **97** | **119** |
| J¹ (92-01) | Salt/Pepper Shakers | 26.95 | **28** | **38** |
| K¹ (93–99) | Sauce Boat | 24.95 | **52** | **87** |
| L¹ (99-01) | Soap Dish | 19.00 | **19** | **26** |
| L¹ (99-02) | Soap Dispenser | 26.00 | **26** | **35** |
| L¹ (99-01) | Tumbler | 15.00 | **16** | **21** |
| M¹ (96–98) | Spice Jar, indiv. | 19.95 | **25** | **45** |

**continued next page**

How do we
get our values?
see page 8

n e e d

**E¹** 1999-02 Small Loaf Dish

$8^L$ x $4^W$ x $2.25^W$

Form No:     37206/37214
37222/37231

*Form numbers in order of blue, green, red, ivory. Designed to fit the Small Loaf Basket.*

**I¹** 2002 3 Qt. Roaster

$14^L$ x $9.5^W$ x $6.25^H$

Form No:     37095/37915
37940/37982

*Form numbers in order of blue, green, red, ivory. Promoted with the 2002 Large Easter Basket.*

**M¹** 1996-98 Spice Jars

$4^H$

Form No:     various

*Form numbers vary based on the color and the type of spice.*

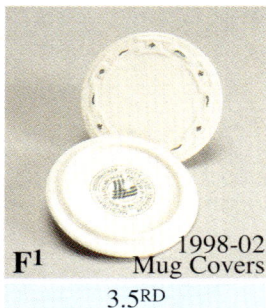

**F¹** 1998-02 Mug Covers

3.5$^{RD}$

Form No: 35823/35831
35840/35858

*Form numbers listed in order of blue, green, red and ivory. Also fits the Custard or Tea Cups.*

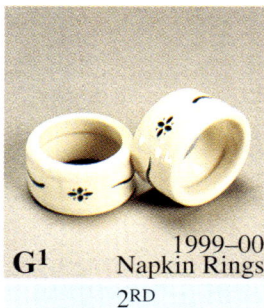

**G¹** 1999–00 Napkin Rings

2$^{RD}$

Form No: 37257/37265
37273/37281

*Form numbers listed in order of blue, green, red and ivory.*

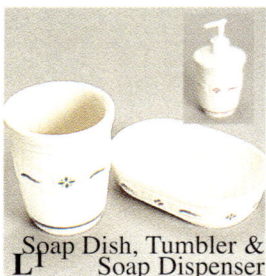

**H¹** 2000-02 Quiche Dish

11$^L$ x 9.25$^W$ x 1.5$^H$

Form No: 36889/36897
36901/36919

*Form numbers in order of blue, green, red, ivory. Originally promoted with the 2000 Easter Basket.*

**J¹** 1992-01 Salt & Pepper Shakers

3.25$^H$

Form No: 30627/30465
30783/33863

*Form numbers in order of blue, green, red, ivory.*

**K¹** 1993-99 Sauce Boat

12$^{OZ}$

Form No: 30767/30601
30929/34797

*Form numbers listed in order of blue, green, red and ivory.*

**L¹** Soap Dish, Tumbler & Soap Dispenser

Dish: 5.5$^L$ x 3.75$^W$
Tumbler: 4$^H$
Dispenser: 7$^H$

*Form numbers in order of blue, green, red, ivory. Originally promoted with the 2000 Easter Basket.*

f u n **f a c t**

## Did you know . . .

The best way to sniff a candle is from its bottom. The longer that it is exposed to air, the top can lose its scent.

# Pottery®

## MARKET VALUES

| | Description | Original | Avg. | High |
|---|---|---|---|---|
| | **Tie-Ons** | | | |
| $O^1$ | (96) Baby | 6.95 | **15** | **28** |
| $P^1$ | (97) Baby | 6.95 | **10** | **18** |
| $Q^1$ | (98) Baby | 8.00 | **9** | **13** |
| $Q^1$ | (99) Baby | 8.00 | **11** | **15** |
| $R^1$ | (00) Baby | 8.00 | **13** | **15** |
| $S^1$ | (01) Baby | 8.00 | — | — |
| | (02) Baby[np] | 8.00 | — | — |
| $T^1$ | (98-00) Coffee | 8.00 | **11** | **15** |
| $U^1$ | (96–97) Congratulations | 6.95 | **9** | **15** |
| $V^1$ | (98-00) Congratulations | 8.00 | **8** | **10** |
| $W^1$ | (01) Falling Leaves | 8.00 | **12** | **15** |
| $X^1$ | (99-01) From Our House to Yours | 8.00 | **10** | **14** |
| | (96–98) Happy Birthday[np] | 6.95 | **8** | **14** |
| $Y^1$ | (98-00) Happy Birthday | 6.95 | **8** | **10** |
| $Z^1$ | (99-00) Happy Halloween | 8.00 | **11** | **18** |
| $A^2$ | (00) Jack-O-Lantern Set | 19.00 | **22** | **34** |
| $B^2$ | (99-01) Postage Stamp | 12.00 | **17** | **18** |
| | **Provincial Cottage™** | | | |
| | (00-02) Bless You[np] | 8.00 | — | — |
| | (00-02) Cookbooks[np] | 8.00 | — | — |
| | (00-02) Mail[np] | 8.00 | — | — |
| | (00-02) Recipes[np] | 8.00 | — | — |
| | (00-02) Tissues[np] | 8.00 | — | — |
| | (00-02) Utensils[np] | 8.00 | — | — |
| $C^2$ | (01) Pumpkin Face Set | 19.00 | **23** | **27** |
| $D^2$ | (99-01) Teacher | 8.00 | — | — |
| $E^2$ | (96–98) Thank-You | 6.95 | **9** | **15** |
| $F^2$ | (97-00) Thinking of You | 6.95 | **8** | **9** |
| $G^2$ | (97-01) Welcome | 6.95 | — | — |

[np] = Not Pictured.

$O^1$ 1996 Baby Tie-On
$2.5^L$ x $1.75^W$
Form No: 32310

$S^1$ 2001 Baby Tie-On
$1.25^L$ x $2^H$
Form No: 39594

$W^1$ 2001 Falling Leaves
$2^L$ x $2^H$
Form No: 39411

$A^2$ 2000 Jack-O-Lantern
4 piece set
Form No: 37800

$E^2$ 1996-98 Thank You
$2.5^W$ x $1.75^H$
Form No: 32336

**P¹** 1997
Baby Tie-On

2.5ᴸ x 1.75ᵂ

Form No: 30503

**Q¹** 1998 & 99
Baby Tie-On

2.5ᴸ x 1.75ᵂ

Form No: 36099

*The 1998 Tie-On is the same design, except has "1998" in the center.*

**R¹** 2000
Baby Tie-On

2ᴿᴰ

Form No: 36293
No.Sold: 80,060

**T¹** 1998-00
Coffee

2.5ᴸ x 1.75ᵂ

Form No: 36030

**U¹** 1996-97
Congratulations

2.5ᴸ x 1.75ᵂ

Form No: 31496

**V¹** 1998-00
Congratulations

2.5ᴸ x 1.75ᵂ

Form No: 33685

**X¹** 1999-01
From Our House

1.75ᴸ x 2ᴴ

Form No: 35718

**Y¹** 1998-00
Happy Birthday

2ᴿᴰ

Form No: 31747

**Z¹** 1999-00
Happy Halloween

2.5ᴸ x 1.75ᵂ

Form No: 37559

**B²** 1999-01
Postage Stamp

1.75ᴸ x 1.5ᴴ

Form No: 36978

*Reversible.*

**C²** 2001
Pumpkin Face

4 piece set

Form No: 30096

**D²** 1999-01
Teacher

1.75ᴸ x 1.5ᴴ

Form No: 36617

**F²** 1997-00
Thinking of You

2.5ᴸ x 1.75ᵂ

Form No: 33464

**G²** 1997-01
Welcome

2.5ᴸ x 1.75ᵂ

Form No: 34096

# *ottery History*

## Introduction of Pottery . . .

The introduction of pottery to the Longaberger product line was a natural move for the company. The Longaberger family first made Ware Baskets for local pottery companies to use when carrying the pottery from the kilns. This introduction of pottery was promoted as "bringing two great American Classics back together again". The Roseville Pottery from 1990-1991was made by Friendship Pottery in Roseville, Ohio. The exclusive Woven Traditions design was hand decorated in <u>only</u> Classic Blue™. Each piece was dated and initialed. Due to problems in production, the production was moved to Sterling Pottery in East Liverpool, Ohio in late 1991. This pottery was not referred to as "Roseville Pottery" until after it was discontinued.

## Roseville vs. Current Pottery. . .

The difference between the pottery is hard to see at first glance. The best way to determine if a piece is Roseville, is by turning it over and looking for the unique Roseville embossing on the bottom (see page 156 for picture). The Roseville Pottery was only available in the Classic Blue™ and is cream in color. The current line of pottery is available in Classic Blue™, Heritage Green™, Traditional Red™ and Heirloom Ivory™. The body is more white in color. There is no difference in the quality and attributes.

## Embossing . . .

Current Longaberger Pottery® is made in East Liverpool, Ohio by Sterling Pottery and Hall China. This current pottery is neither signed nor dated. The only way to estimate its origination date iis by its embossing. The original trademark reads "Made in East Liverpool, Ohio". Sometime between 1994 and 1995, the embossing was changed to read "Made in the U.S.A".

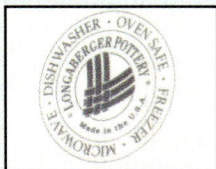

Starting with the Loaf Dish, released in August 1998, all pottery pieces now also have the product dimensions and capacity printed on the bottom of each piece.

## Pottery attributes . . .

Longaberger Pottery® is American Vitrified China, which means that it has less than .05% absorption. To the consumer, this means that it won't pick up contamination. It also has high impact and ship resistibility, a high gloss glaze, a glazed foot for safe stacking and is freezer, oven, microwave, and dishwasher safe.

# *Pumpkin Series*™

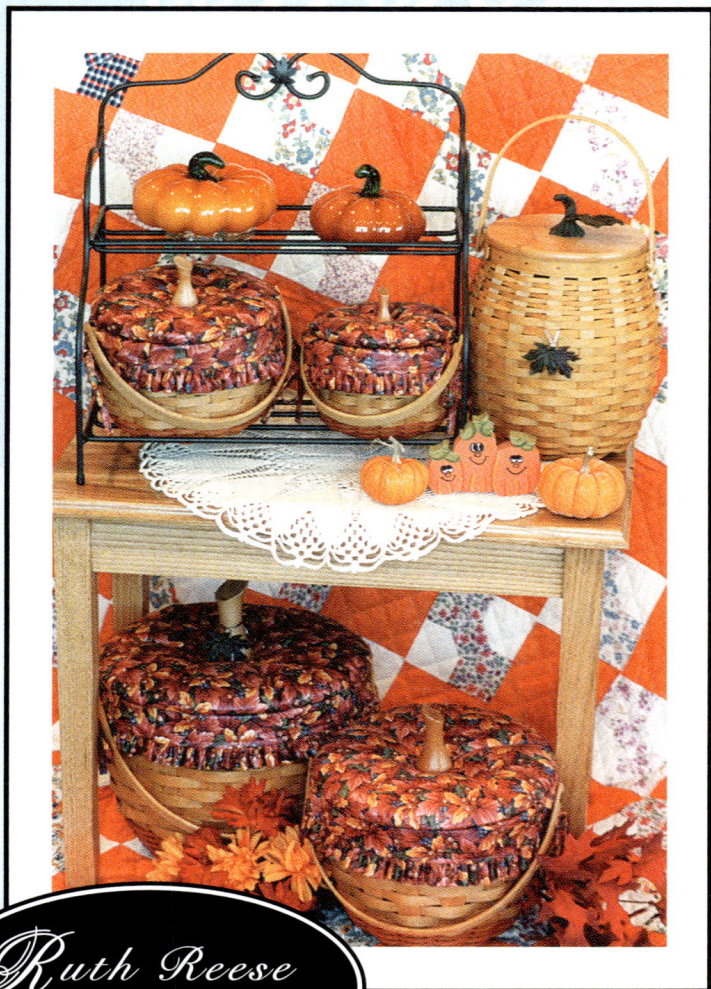

**Ruth Reese**
**Rochester, Indiana**

*A master gardener, Ruth's favorite collection is the May Series™. Although she received her first basket in 1983, she did not seriously collect until the Woven Traditons® came out. To this day, Ruth can't help but smile as she remembers a terrific deal she got on a Retired Corn™.*

Pumpkin™

191

## Pumpkin Series™

These baskets were not declared a series until 1997 when the last items were introduced.

### MARKET VALUES

| Photo | | Description | Original | Avg. | High |
|---|---|---|---|---|---|
| A. | 1995 | Pumpkin Basket™ | 47.95 | **103** | **135** |
| | | with **P**rotector | 54.90 | **103** | **145** |
| | | with **L**iner | 64.90 | **107** | **165** |
| | | Combo (**P/L**) | 59.95 | **107** | **176** |
| | | Full Set (**Combo/Lid**) | 84.90 | **123** | **185** |
| A. | 1995 | Pumpkin™ Tie-On | 6.95 | **14** | **28** |
| B. | 1996 | Small Pumpkin™ | 40.95 | **77** | **110** |
| | | with **P**rotector | 45.90 | **77** | **110** |
| | | with **L**iner | 55.90 | **77** | **110** |
| | | Combo (**P/L**) | 52.95 | **84** | **130** |
| | | Full Set (**Combo/Lid**) | 72.90 | **89** | **160** |
| C. | 1997 | Little Pumpkin™ | 34.95 | **65** | **90** |
| | | with **P**rotector | 39.90 | **70** | **100** |
| | | with **L**iner | 49.90 | **75** | **120** |
| | | Combo (**P/L**) | 46.95 | **82** | **125** |
| | | Full Set (**Combo/Lid**) | 64.90 | **89** | **140** |
| C. | 1997 | Pumpkin™ Tie-On | 6.95 | **16** | **24** |
| C. | 1997 | Large Pumpkin™ | | | |
| | | Combo (**P/L/Lid**) | 117.95 | **142** | **210** |

collection **n o t e**

Liners also available in Fall Foliage™ fabrics.

**A.** 1995 Pumpkin
$9.25^{RD}$ x $7.25^{H}$

Form No: 19402
Tie-On: 31763
No. Sold:

**B.** 1996 Small Pumpkin
$7.25^{RD}$ x $5.25^{H}$

Form No: 16012
No. Sold: 134,914

**C.** 1997 Pumpkin
Ltl: $5.75^{RD}$ x $4.25^{H}$
Lg: $11.25^{RD}$ x $9^{H}$

Form No:
Little: 16021
No. Sold: 177,000
Large: 16039
No. Sold:
Tie-On: 34517

*The Large Pumpkin was available to Hostesses only.*

# Retired Baskets

**Valerie Smith**
Blandon, Pennsylvania

Valerie has such love for Longaberger® that her mother used going to a home show as an excuse to get her to her bridal shower! And of course, 3 of her gifts were Longaberger Baskets®! The beautiful hutch pictured above belonged to her step-father's great grandmother.

## Retired Baskets

Offered at one time through the Regular Line. Baskets are listed in alphabetical order. The years offered are noted in parenthesis. Unless otherwise noted, the Original price listed is from the first year the basket was offered.

### MARKET VALUES

| Photo | Description | Original | Avg. | High |
|---|---|---|---|---|
| | ***Barbeque Buddy:*** | | | |
| A. | (01-02) BBQ Buddy, Large | 69.90 | — | — |
| | (01-02) BBQ Buddy, Med[np] | 49.00 | — | — |
| | (01-02) BBQ Buddy, Small[np] | 39.00 | — | — |
| | ***Berry Baskets (no handles):*** | | | |
| B. | (79–99) Berry, Large | 8.95 | **34** | **51** |
| B. | (79–99) Berry, Medium | 7.95 | **41** | **70** |
| B. | (79–99) Berry, Small | 6.95 | **29** | **41** |
| C. | (99-01) Bread (Natural) | 34.00 | **43** | **50** |
| D. | (82–88) Bread (Old) | 11.95 | **38** | **53** |
| E. | (99-01) Button (Natural) | 27.00 | **27** | **50** |
| F. | (79–94) Cake (1st/h) | 15.95 | **52** | **90** |
| G. | (94) Cake (Natural) | 46.95 | **62** | **105** |
| H. | (99-02) Candle | 36.00 | **41** | **75** |
| I. | (79–80) Canister Set | 39.95 | **246** | **351** |
| | 5" Measuring, w/lid | | | |
| | 7" Measuring, w/lid | | | |
| | 9" Measuring, w/lid | | | |
| J. | (86-02) Chore, Medium | 18.95 | **49** | **65** |
| K. | (79–94) Corn | 29.95 | **95** | **200** ✍ |
| | with Protector | 39.95 | **121** | **250** |
| L. | (94) Cracker (Natural) | 20.95 | **39** | **55** |

**continued next page**

[np] = Not Pictured          ✍ = With Signatures

*need help?*

## How do we get our values?

see page 8

**A.** 2001-02
Large BBQ Buddy
See pg. 246 for dimensions

Form No:
Large:        16381
Medium:       10801
Small:        10702

**E.** 1999-01
Natural Button

7RD x 3H

Form No:        19526
No. Sold:

**I.** 1979–80
Canister Set

5", 7" & 9" Measuring

5" Measuring:  5RD x 4.5H
7" Measuring:  7RD x 6.5H
9" Measuring:  9RD x 8.5H

*Only sold as a set. No handles, included lids.*

**B.** 1979–99 Berry Baskets

See pg. 252 for dimensions

Form No:
Small: 11304/1300-O
Medium: 11410/1400-O
Large: 11509/1500-O

**C.** 1999-01 Natural Bread

14.5$^L$ x 7.5$^W$ x 3.75$^H$

Form No: 14974
No. Sold:

**D.** 1982–88 "Old" Bread

15$^L$ x 8$^W$ x 2.25$^H$

Form No: 4600-OO
No. Sold:

*Replaced by a deeper Bread basket in 1988.*

**F.** 1979–94 Cake

12$^L$ x 12$^W$ x 6$^H$

Form No: 11002
No. Sold:

*1 st/h, included divider.*

**G.** 1994 Natural Cake

12$^L$ x 12$^W$ x 6$^H$

Form No: 16144
No. Sold:

*Available from Feb. 1 through Aug. 31, 1994. Divider sold with basket.*

**H.** 1999–02 Candle

9$^L$ x 5$^W$ x 5$^H$

Form No: 19739
No. Sold:

**J.** 1986–02 Medium Chore

13$^L$ x 8$^W$ x 5$^H$

Form No: 13510
No. Sold:

**K.** 1979–94 Corn

17$^{RD}$ x 11.5$^H$

Form No: 14401
No. Sold:

*Inverted bottom, two hand slots. Reintroduced through the Hostess Collection with two braided ears in 1995.*

**L.** 1994 Natural Cracker

11.5$^L$ x 5$^W$ x 3$^H$

Form No: 17198
No. Sold:

*Available from Feb. 1 through Aug. 31, 1994.*

**195**

## Retired Baskets

**All baskets prior to 1985 will have the older, darker stain and all baskets after 1987 will have the newer, lighter stain. The stain was changed sometime between 1986 and 1987.**

### MARKET VALUES

| Photo | Description | Original | Avg. | High |
|---|---|---|---|---|
| | *Cradles:* | | | |
| | (79–86) Cradle, Doll [pg.124] | 25.95 | **131** | **185** |
| | (79–86) Cradle, Large [pg.124] | 39.95 | **323** | **500** |
| M. | (79–83) Cradle, Medium | 37.95 | — | **200** |
| N. | (79–93) Cradle, Mini | 9.95 | **66** | **160** |
| | (79–80) Cradle, Small [np] | 35.95 | — | **105** |
| O. | (94) Darning (Natural) | 30.95 | **64** | **110** |
| | *Easter Baskets: (Renamed to Chore Baskets in 1987)* | | | |
| P. | (79–87) Easter, Baby (st/h) [np] | 8.95 | **52** | **82** |
| P. | (79–87) Easter, Baby (sw/h) | 9.95 | **56** | **85** |
| Q. | (79–87) Easter, Large (st/h) | 11.95 | **52** | **80** |
| Q. | (79–87) Easter, Large (sw/h) [np] | 12.95 | **58** | **93** |
| R. | (79–87) Easter, Med. (st/h) [np] | 10.95 | **73** | **95** |
| R. | (79–87) Easter, Med. (sw/h) | 11.95 | **50** | **75** |
| S. | (79–87) Easter, Small (st/h) | 9.95 | **64** | **95** |
| S. | (79–87) Easter, Small (sw/h) [np] | 10.95 | **60** | **75** |
| T. | (99-02) 8x8 Serving Solutions | 37.00 | **44** | **59** |
| U. | (94–98) Flower Pot Basket | 47.95 | **52** | **125** |
| V. | (96–01) Flower Pot Basket, Small | 34.95 | **35** | **50** |
| | *Fruit Baskets – with Splint Hangers:* | | | |
| W. | (79–80) Hanging, Large | 21.95 | **100** | **140** |
| W. | (79–80) Hanging, Medium | 15.95 | **50** | **50** |
| W. | (79–80) Hanging, Small | 11.95 | **77** | **125** |
| W. | (79–80) Hanging, Tall | 18.95 | — | — |
| X. | (79–95) Fruit, Tall | 15.95 | **68** | **110** |

**continued next page**

[np] = Not Pictured

[pg.xx] = This item is also featured in another section. Go to the page noted for a photo.

1979–83
**M.** Medium Cradle

28.5$^L$ x 17.75$^W$ x 9.75$^H$

Form No: 2700–M
No. Sold:

Doll: 19$^L$ x 12$^W$ x 6$^H$
Large: 30$^L$ x 20$^W$ x 10.5$^H$
Small: 24$^L$ x 17$^W$ x 10$^H$

1979–87
**Q.** Large Easter

14$^L$ x 7.75$^W$ x 5.25$^H$

Form No: 3600-AO
No. Sold:

*Also available with 1 sw/h. (Form No. 3600-BO)*

1995–98
**U.** Flower Pot Basket

17$^L$ x 7.5$^W$ x 4.75$^H$

Form No: 16306
No. Sold:

*Retired after 8/31/98, along with its liner, protector and riser.*

**N.** 1979–93
Mini Cradle

$7^L$ x $5^W$ x $3.5^H$

Form No: 10715/700-K
No. Sold:

*Had 2 wooden loops
prior to 1984.*

**O.** 1994 Natural
Darning

$10^{RD}$ x $4^H$

Form No: 15521
No. Sold:

*Available from Feb. 1
through Aug. 31, 1994.*

**P.** 1979–87
Baby Easter

$7^L$ x $5^W$ x $3.5^H$

Form No: 700-BO
No. Sold:

*Also available with 1 st/h.
(Form No. 700-AO)*

**R.** 1979–87
Medium Easter

$13^L$ x $8^W$ x $5^H$

Form No: 3500-BO
No. Sold:

*Also available with 1 st/h.
(Form No. 3500-AO)*

**S.** 1979–87
Small Easter

$10^L$ x $6^W$ x $4^H$

Form No: 3400-AO
No. Sold:

*Also available with 1 sw/h.
(Form No. 3400-BO).*

**T.** 1999–02 8x8
Serving Solutions

$9.5^L$ x $9.5^W$ x $2.75^H$

Form No: 15393
No. Sold:

*Designed to fit the 8x8
Baking Dish.*

**V.** 1996–01
Small Flower Pot

$14^L$ x $6^W$ x $3^H$

Form No: 18414
No. Sold:

*Riser sold separately.*

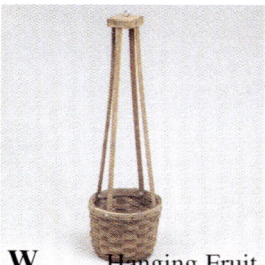

**W.** Hanging Fruit

$8^{RD}$ x $6.5^H$

| | |
|---|---|
| Small: | 3000-P |
| Medium: | 3100-P |
| Large: | 3200-P |
| Tall: | 3300-P |

**X.** 1979–95
Tall Fruit

$8^{RD}$ x $9^H$

Form No: 13307/3300-BO
No. Sold:

*Inverted Bottom*

## Retired Baskets

From 1980 – 1986, most Regular Line baskets could be "customized" with color accent weaving and trim. See page 172 for more information.

**Photo** **Description**

### MARKET VALUES

| | Description | Original | Avg. | High |
|---|---|---|---|---|
| | **Gathering Baskets:** | | | |
| Y. | (83–93) Gathering, Lg. (1st/h) | 26.95 | **89** | **125** |
| Z. | (79–94) Gathering, Lg. (2sw/h) | 19.95 | **71** | **130** |
| | (80–93) Gathering, Med.(1st/h) | 41.95 | **83** | **120** |
| A¹ | (86–93) Gathering, Sm. (1st/h) | 22.95 | **103** | **120** |
| | **Hampers:** | | | |
| | (79–86) Hamper, Lg. [pg.124] | 59.95 | **153** | **300** |
| | (79–86) Hamper, Sm./Med. [np] | 31.95 | **140** | **175** |
| B¹ | **Hanging Baskets – with Rawhide Hangers:** | | | |
| | (80–86) 5" Square bottom | 14.95 | **37** | **70** |
| | (80–86) 7" Square bottom | 15.95 | **67** | **75** |
| | (80–86) 9" Square bottom | 22.95 | **40** | **40** |
| | (80–86) 11" Square bottom | 29.95 | **45** | **75** |
| | (80–86) 13" Square bottom | 35.95 | **40** | **90** |
| C¹ | (79–86) Woven bottom | 14.95 | **39** | **55** |
| | **Inverted Waste:** | | | |
| | (79–84) Lg. Round (no/h) [np] | 26.95 | **95** | **130** |
| | (79–84) Lg. Round (1sw/h) [pg.88] | 28.95 | **114** | **120** |
| | (79–84) Sm. Round (no/h) [np] | 21.95 | **90** | **100** |
| D¹ | (79–84) Sm. Round (1sw/h) | 23.95 | **75** | **125** |
| E¹ | (94) Key, Tall (Natural) | 31.95 | **50** | **60** |
| | **Laundry:** | | | |
| | (79–86) Laundry, Large [pg.124] | 34.95 | **208** | **300** |
| F¹ | (79–83) Laundry, Medium | 31.95 | **93** | **150** |
| G¹ | (79–98) Laundry, Small | 29.95 | **127** | **250** |
| H¹ | (99-02) Loaf, Small | 32.00 | **37** | **40** |
| | **Magazine:** | | | |
| I¹ | (79–95) Magazine (1sw/h, legs) | 21.95 | **58** | **85** |
| J¹ | (79–98) Magazine (1sw/h, legs, lid) | 25.95 | **82** | **160** |

[np] = Not Pictured

[pg.xx] = This item is also featured in another section. Go to the page noted for a photo.

**Y.** 1983–93 Large Gathering

$19^L$ x $12^W$ x $6^H$

Form No: 12505/2500-A
No. Sold:

Medium: $18^L$ x $11^W$ x $4.5^H$
12408

*All Gathering baskets with 1st/h are currently retired.*

**C¹** 1979–86 Woven bottom

$8.25^{RD}$ x $7.75^H$

Form No: 3700-PO
No. Sold:

**G¹** 1979–98 Sm Laundry

$24^L$ x $17^W$ x $10^H$

Form No: 12602
No. Sold:

**Z.** 1979–94 Large Gathering

$19^L$ x $12^W$ x $6^H$

Form No: 12513/2500-C
No. Sold:

*This basket was brought back into the regular line through the Hostess Collection in 1996.*

**A¹** 1986–93 Small Gathering

$14^L$ x $9^W$ x $4.5^H$

Form No: 12301/2300-AO
No. Sold:

*Only the Small Gathering with 1 st/h has been retired. This basket with 2 sw/h is still available.*

**B¹** 1980–86 Hanging Baskets

| | |
|---|---|
| 5" : | $5^{RD}$ x $4.5^H$ |
| 7" : | $7^{RD}$ x $6.5^H$ |
| 9" : | $9^{RD}$ x $8.5^H$ |
| 11": | $11^{RD}$ x $10.5^H$ |
| 13": | $13^{RD}$ x $12.5^H$ |

**D¹** 1979–84 Small Inverted

$12.5^{RD}$ x $13.5^H$

Form No: 1900-BO
No. Sold:

Large: $14^{RD}$ x $16^H$
2000-OO/BO

*Both available with 1 sw/h or without a handle.*

**E¹** 1994 Natural Tall Key

$9.5^L$ x $5^W$ x $9.5^H$

Form No: 14630
No. Sold:

*Available from Feb. 1 through Aug. 31, 1994.*

**F¹** 1979–83 Medium Laundry

$28.5^L$ x $17.75^W$ x $9.75^H$

Form No: 2700-O
No. Sold:

Large: $30^L$ x $20^W$ x $10.5^H$
2800-OO

**H¹** 1999-02 Small Loaf

$7.5^L$ x $4.75^W$ x $2.5^H$

Form No: 12823
No. Sold:

*Designed to hold the Small Loaf Baking Dish.*

**I¹** 1979–95 Magazine

$16^L$ x $8^W$ x $11^H$

Form No: 12122/2100-U
No. Sold:

*1 sw/h, legs, no lid*

**J¹** 1979–98 Magazine

$16^L$ x $8^W$ x $11^H$

Form No: 12214
No. Sold:

*1 sw/h, legs, attached lid*

## Retired Baskets

**All baskets listed were offered at one time through the Regular Line.**

### MARKET VALUES

| Photo | Description | Original | Avg. | High |
|---|---|---|---|---|
| | **Mail** | | | |
| K[1] | (00-02) Mail, Large | 115.00 | — | — |
| K[1] | (00-02) Mail, Medium[np] | 99.00 | — | — |
| K[1] | (01-02) Mail, Small | 79.00 | — | — |
| | **Market:** | | | |
| L[1] | (79–93) Market, Large (1st/h) | 19.95 | **93** | **100** |
| M[1] | (79–98) Market, Med (1st/h) | 16.95 | **56** | **89** |
| N[1] | (79–93) Market, Small (1st/h) | 14.95 | **101** | **140** |
| | **Measuring** | | | |
| O[1] | (79–98) 5" Measuring | 7.95 | **37** | **68** |
| P[1] | (79–98) 7" Measuring | 10.95 | **35** | **65** |
| Q[1] | (79–98) 9" Measuring | 13.95 | **52** | **80** |
| R[1] | (79–98) 11" Measuring | 17.95 | **60** | **85** |
| S[1] | (79–98) 13" Measuring | 20.95 | **78** | **115** |
| | (99-02) 9x13 Serving Solutions[np] | 49.00 | — | — |
| T[1] | (86-02) Pantry | 21.95 | **43** | **65** |
| | **Peg Baskets:** | | | |
| U[1] | (85–99) Peg, Large | 19.95 | **48** | **85** |
| U[1] | (85–99) Peg, Medium | 17.95 | **38** | **65** |
| U[1] | (85–99) Peg, Small | 15.95 | **38** | **55** |
| | **continued next page** | | | |

[np] = Not Pictured

**K[1]** Mail Baskets

Lg:     $12^L$ x $8.75^W$ x $11^H$
Med: $10.75^L$ x $7.75^W$ x $10.25^H$
Small:  $9.75^L$ x $6.25^W$ x $8.5^H$

**O[1]** 1979–98 5" Measuring

$5^{RD}$ x $4.5^H$

Form No:    13803/3800-B
No. Sold:

**S[1]** 1979–98 13" Measuring

$13^{RD}$ x $12.5^H$

Form No:    14206/4200-B
No. Sold:

*Reintroduced into the Regular Line in 2000.*

### Can't find something?
**Try the Quick Find**

**L¹** 1979–93 Large Market

16$^L$ x 11$^W$ x 9$^H$

Form No:  10626/600-AO
No. Sold:

*This basket is still available with 2 sw/h. Only the 1 st/h option has been retired.*

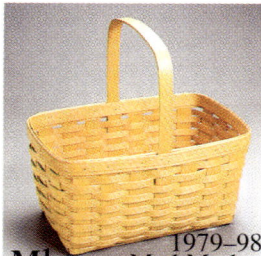

**M¹** 1979–98 Med Market

15$^L$ x 10$^W$ x 7.5$^H$

Form No:  10529/500-AO
No. Sold:

*This basket is still available with 2 sw/h. Only the 1 st/h option has been retired.*

**N¹** 1979–93 Small Market

15$^L$ x 9.5$^W$ x 5.5$^H$

Form No:  10421/400-AO
No. Sold:

*This basket is still available with 2 sw/h. Only the 1 st/h option has been retired.*

**P¹** 1979–98 7" Measuring

7$^{RD}$ x 6.5$^H$

Form No:  13901/3900-B
No. Sold:

*Reintroduced into the Regular Line in 2000.*

**Q¹** 1979–98 9" Measuring

9$^{RD}$ x 8.5$^H$

Form No:  14001/4000-B
No. Sold:

*Reintroduced into the Regular Line in 2000.*

**R¹** 1979–98 11" Measuring

11$^{RD}$ x 10.5$^H$

Form No:  14109/4100-B
No. Sold:

**T¹** 1986-02 Pantry

14$^L$ x 9$^W$ x 4.5$^H$

Form No:  12327
No. Sold:

**U¹** 1985–99 Peg Baskets

Large:  6.5$^L$ x 6.5$^W$ x 8$^H$
Medium: 5.5$^L$ x 5.5$^W$ x 6$^H$
Small:  5$^L$ x 5$^W$ x 4.5$^H$

*Retired after 2/28/99, along with accessories.*

## MARKET VALUES

| Photo | Description | | Original | Avg. | High |
|---|---|---|---|---|---|
| | **Picnic:** | | | | |
| V[1] | (83–86) | Picnic, Family | 98.95 | **330** | **390** |
| | | with Liner | 135.90 | **346** | **390** |
| W[1] | (79–84) | Picnic, Medium | 26.95 | **195** | **240** |
| X[1] | (79-02) | Picnic, Small | 21.95 | **68** | **100** |
| Y[1] | (86-02) | Pie Basket | 22.95 | **47** | **58** |
| | **Planters:** | | | | |
| Z[1] | (82–86) | Fern, Lg. (w/feet) | 27.95 | **63** | **85** |
| | (79–86) | Fern, Lg. (13" stand)[np] | 23.95 | **121** | **200** |
| | (79–86) | Fern, Lg. (20" stand)[np] | 26.95 | **105** | **190** |
| A[2] | (82–86) | Fern, Sm. (w/feet) | 21.95 | **108** | **175** |
| | (79–86) | Fern, Sm. (13" stand)[np] | 21.95 | **102** | **115** |
| B[2] | (79–86) | Fern, Sm. (20" stand) | 24.95 | **138** | **150** |
| | **Purse:** | | | | |
| C[2] | (94) | Purse, Kiddie(Natural) | 28.95 | **40** | **60** |
| D[2] | (79–97) | Purse, Medium | 16.95 | **56** | **119** |
| E[2] | (82–86) | Purse, Med.(Split Lid) | 24.95 | **120** | **255** |
| F[2] | (96–99) | Purse, Shoulder | 84.95 | **90** | **175** |
| G[2] | (79–99) | Purse, Small | 14.95 | **54** | **110** |
| H[2] | (79–89) | Purse, Tall | 27.95 | **62** | **90** |
| | **continued next page** | | | | |

[np] = Not Pictured

**V[1]** 1983–86 Family Picnic

24$^L$ x 17$^W$ x 10$^H$

Form No: 2600-HO
No. Sold:

*Red Gingham liner also available. Most Family Picnic Baskets will look darker than this one.*

**Z[1]** 1982–86 Large Fern

13$^{RD}$ x 8.5$^H$

Form No: 3200-RO
No. Sold:

**D[2]** 1979-97 Medium Purse

11$^L$ x 8$^W$ x 5.5$^H$

Form No: 10901/900-E
No. Sold:

**E[2]** 1982–86 Medium Purse

11$^L$ x 8$^W$ x 5.5$^H$

Form No: 900-QO
No. Sold:

*Split-lid option retired.*

**W¹** 1979–84
Medium Picnic

15$^L$ x 15$^W$ x 7.5$^H$

Form No: 200-H
No. Sold:

**X¹** 1979-02
Small Picnic

12$^L$ x 12$^W$ x 6$^H$

Form No: 11029
No. Sold:

**Y¹** 1986-02
Pie Basket

12$^L$ x 12$^W$ x 4$^H$

Form No: 12203
No. Sold:

**A²** 1982–86
Small Fern

8.5$^{RD}$ x 7.5$^H$

Form No: 2900-RO
No. Sold:

*These baskets are sometimes referred to as "Floor Planters" or planters with "feet".*

**B²** 1979–86
Small Fern

8.5$^{RD}$ x 7.5$^H$ (20" stand)

Form No: 2900-TO
No. Sold:

*Available for either Large or Small Fern baskets, 13" or 20" stand. No feet on baskets. Not available without a stand.*

**C²** 1994 Natural
Kiddie Purse

87$^L$ x 5$^W$ x 3.5$^H$

Form No: 17019
No. Sold:

*Available from Feb. 1 through Aug. 31, 1994.*

**F²** 1996-99
Shoulder Purse

9.5$^L$ x 5.75$^W$ x 7$^H$

Form No: 18210
No. Sold:

**G²** 1979-99
Small Purse

9.5$^L$ x 6$^W$ x 6$^H$

Form No: 10821 / 800-E
No. Sold:

**H²** 1979-89
Tall Purse

9.5$^L$ x 5$^W$ x 9.5$^H$

Form No: 1000-EO
No. Sold:

# Retired Baskets

## MARKET VALUES

| Photo | Description | Original | Avg. | High |
|---|---|---|---|---|
| I² | (99-01) Recipe (Natural) | 25.00 | **34** | **45** |
| | *Sewing:* | | | |
| J² | (78–86) Sewing, Round | | | |
| | with 13"stand | 29.95 | **128** | **250** |
| | without stand[pg.88] | | **111** | **187** |
| K² | (78–83) Sewing, Rectangular | 26.95 | **381** | **400** |
| | *Spoon* | | | |
| L² | (00-01) Spoon, Lg (Natrl) | 45.00 | — | — |
| L² | (00-01) Spoon, Med (Natrl) | 34.00 | — | — |
| L² | (00-01) Spoon, Sm (Natrl) | 26.00 | — | — |
| | (99-01) Tea (Natural)[pg.92] | 25.00 | **33** | **40** |
| M² | (00-01) Teaspoon (Natural) | 25.00 | — | **30** |
| N² | (99-01) Tissue (Natural) | 32.00 | — | — |
| O² | (79–94) Umbrella | 18.95 | **77** | **153** |
| | with Protector | | **127** | **160** |
| | *Vegetable Baskets* | | | |
| P² | (87-00) Vegetable, Large | 26.95 | **74** | **100** |
| P² | (82-02) Vegetable, Medium | 14.95 | **47** | **65** |
| Q² | (94) Vegetable, Med(Ntrl) | 38.95 | **60** | **75** |
| P² | (82-02) Vegetable, Small | 12.95 | **32** | **45** |
| | *Waste Baskets* | | | |
| R² | (79–00) Waste, Medium | 21.95 | **84** | **170** |
| R² | (79–00) Waste, Small | 16.95 | **66** | **90** |
| S² | (83-86) Wine, Large | 29.95 | **95** | **135** |

[pg.xx] = This item is also featured in another section. Go to the page noted for a photo.

**I²** 1999-01 Natural Recipe

8^L x 5.5^W x 4.5^FH x 6^BH

Form No: 19542
No. Sold:

**M²** 2000-01 Natural Teaspoon

5^L x 5^W x 4.5^H

Form No: 17868
No. Sold:

**Q²** 1994 Natural Med. Vegetable

13^L x 7.5^W x 3^FH x 8^BH

Form No: 15113
No. Sold:

*Available from Feb. 1 through Aug. 31, 1994.*

204

**J²**  Round Sewing  1978–86

13$^{RD}$ x 8.5$^{H}$ (13" stand)

Form No:  3200-NO
No. Sold:

*Split attached lid, 1 sw/h.
Metal hinges changed to
leather in 1979. Available
with or without a stand.*

**K²**  Rectangular Sewing  1978–83

16$^{L}$ x 11$^{W}$ x 9$^{H}$

Form No:  600-F
No. Sold:

*Split attached lid, 2 sw/h.
Had metal hinges in
1978, only.*

**L²**  Natural Spoon  2000-01

| | |
|---|---|
| Large: | 7.5$^{L}$x7.5$^{W}$x10$^{H}$ |
| Med: | 6.5$^{L}$x6.5$^{W}$x8$^{H}$ |
| Small: | 5.5$^{L}$x5.5$^{W}$x6$^{H}$ |

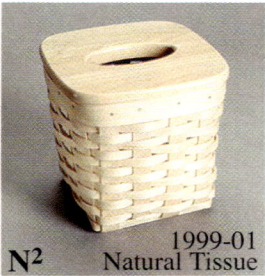

**N²**  Natural Tissue  1999-01

6.5$^{L}$ x 6.5$^{W}$ x 6.25$^{H}$

Form No:  14184
No. Sold:

**O²**  Umbrella  1979–94

10$^{RD}$ x 17.5$^{H}$

Form No: 11207/1200-OO
No. Sold:

*Brought back in 1999 as
a Hostess Only item.*

**P²**  Vegetable Baskets

| | |
|---|---|
| Large: | 16$^{L}$x9$^{W}$x3.5$^{FH}$x9$^{BH}$ |
| Med: | 13$^{L}$x7.5$^{W}$x3$^{FH}$x8$^{BH}$ |
| Small: | 10.5$^{L}$x6.5$^{W}$x3$^{FH}$ 7$^{BH}$ |

**R²**  Waste Baskets  1979–00

Md:  13.5$^{L}$ x 13.5$^{W}$ x 16$^{H}$
Sm:  9.5$^{L}$ x 9.5$^{W}$ x 12$^{H}$

| | |
|---|---|
| Med: | 11703/1700-O |
| Small: | 11801/1800-O |

**S²**  Large Wine  1983–86

16$^{L}$ x 9$^{W}$x 3.5$^{FH}$ x 9$^{BH}$

Form No:  5200-CO
No. Sold:

*Included dividers
(wine rack).*

There are many different weaving techniques, some of which have become popular in the secondary market. While it is hard to determine if there is an added value for these features, it is becoming a trend that some Collectors are starting to look specifically for these unique features, and thus are willing to pay a premium for them.

## Continuous Weaving:

This is the practice of using the same splint to weave the entire basket. While it makes the basket very strong, it is a very time-consuming and difficult technique. It was one of J.W. Longaberger's trademarks and was a common feature for Longaberger Baskets, until sometime after May 1989. It is evident on a basket by a split upsplint which was done to allow for the weave pattern to continue.

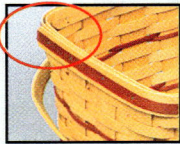

## Left-handed Weaving:

This feature is evident by looking at the trim strip. When you hold the basket in front of you, with the end of the trim strip facing up, look at which direction the trim "turn" is pointing. If it is pointing towards your left hand, it is a left-handed basket, meaning that a left-handed weaver made the basket. If the turn points towards your right hand, it was made by a more common right-hander.

## Hardest Baskets to Make

According to a few weavers, the hardest baskets to make are the small baskets with inverted bottoms, such as the Button™ or Tree-Trimming™. The most difficult one, before the Founder's Basket™, was the 1992 Discovery Basket™. Because the basket was not made with double splints, if a mistake was made, it was difficult to correct.

# Shades of Autumn ®

*Kelly Stamm*
*Washington, Kansas*

It took a while for Kelly to catch the "basket fever". She bought her first basket in 1989, but did not buy again until almost 10 years later! Kelly says her Bentley Guide® helps her to know what baskets to buy. Her collection of 250+ baskets includes the complete Shades of Autumn® collection.

# Shades of Autumn®

**Rust trim. Green, Rust and Deep Blue weave. Series completed in 1998.**

**A.** 1990 Pie

$12^L$ x $12^W$ x $4^H$

Form No: 2200-AGUBS
No. Sold:

## MARKET VALUES

| Photo | Year | Description | Original | Avg. | High |
|---|---|---|---|---|---|
| A. | 1990 | Pie™ | 31.95 | 67 | 135 |
| B. | 1990 | Small Vegetable™ | 35.95 | 145 | 280 |
| C. | 1991 | Small Gathering™ | 36.95 | 138 | 185 |
| | | with Protector | 45.90 | 140 | 200 |
| | | with Liner | 49.90 | 140 | 200 |
| | | Combo (P/L) | 48.95 | 146 | 245 |
| D. | 1991 | Acorn™ | 24.95 | 109 | 125 |
| | | with Protector | 28.90 | 110 | 130 |
| | | with Liner | 35.90 | 115 | 130 |
| | | Combo (P/L) | 35.95 | 128 | 165 |
| E. | 1992 | Bittersweet™ | 24.95 | 52 | 70 |
| | | with Protector | 29.90 | 52 | 75 |
| | | with Liner | 33.90 | 54 | 75 |
| | | Combo (P/L) | 29.95 | 56 | 85 |
| F. | 1993 | Harvest™ | 39.95 | 75 | 100 |
| | | with Protector | 45.90 | 83 | 125 |
| | | with Liner | 52.90 | 86 | 130 |
| | | Combo (P/L) | 49.95 | 94 | 145 |
| F. | 1993 | Table runner | 34.95 | — | — |
| G. | 1994 | Recipe™ | 29.95 | 66 | 75 |
| | | with Protector | 34.90 | 67 | 81 |
| | | with Lid | 42.90 | 73 | 100 |
| | | Combo (P/Lid/Cards) | 44.95 | 81 | 125 |
| H. | 1995 | Basket of Plenty™ | 53.95 | 70 | 118 |
| | | with Protector | 61.90 | 71 | 131 |
| | | with Liner | 73.90 | 75 | 140 |
| | | Combo (P/L) | 69.95 | 80 | 140 |
| | | Full Set (Combo/Lid) | 101.85 | 87 | 150 |
| H. | 1995 | Fall Foliage Tie-On | 6.95 | 17 | 23 |
| I. | 1996 | Maple Leaf™ | 40.95 | 45 | 83 |
| | | with Protector | 46.90 | 50 | 95 |
| | | with Liner | 56.90 | 58 | 95 |
| | | Combo (P/L) | 54.95 | 65 | 115 |
| | | Full Set (Combo/Lid) | 74.90 | 80 | 125 |
| I. | 1996 | Maple Leaf™ Tie-On | 6.95 | 11 | 17 |
| J. | 1997 | Bountiful Harvest™ | 44.95 | 53 | 84 |
| | | with Protector | 53.90 | 65 | 90 |
| | | with Liner | 64.90 | 65 | 90 |
| | | Combo (P/L) | 61.95 | 66 | 100 |
| | | Full Set (Combo/Lid) | 86.90 | 90 | 120 |
| K. | 1998 | Baker's Bounty™ | 39.00 | 53 | 75 |
| | | with Protector | 44.00 | 55 | 77 |
| | | with Liner | 55.00 | 60 | 77 |
| | | Combo (P/L) | 49.00 | 63 | 90 |
| | | Full Set (Combo/Lid) | 71.00 | 65 | 100 |
| K. | 1998 | Baker's Bounty Tie-On | 8.00 | 9 | 12 |

**E.** 1992 Bittersweet

$5.5^L$ x $5.5^W$ x $6^H$

Form No: 10804
No. Sold:

**I.** 1996 Maple Leaf

$7^{RD}$ x $6.5^H$

Form No: 13935
Tie-On: 32999
No. Sold:

**B.** 1990 Small Vegetable

$10.5^L$ x $6.5^W$ x $3^{FH}$ x $7^{BH}$

Form No:     5000-CGUBS
No. Sold:

*Hostess Only*

**C.** 1991 Small Gathering

$14^L$ x $9^W$ x $4.5^H$

Form No:   2300-CGUBS
No. Sold:

**D.** 1991 Acorn

$7^L$ x $5^W$ x $3.5^H$

Form No:     700-BGUBS
No. Sold:

**F.** 1993 Harvest

$7^L$ x $4.75^W$ x $7.75^H$

Form No:              14303
Tablerunner:         20150
No. Sold:

*Liner is Autumn™.
Reversible Table
runner is Sunset™.*

**G.** 1994 Recipe

$8^L$ x $5.5^W$ x $4.5^{FH}$ x $6^{BH}$

Form No:              17400
No. Sold:

*Basket included set of
Recipe Cards.*

**H.** 1995 Basket of Plenty

$12^{RD}$ x $5.75^H$

Form No:              15563
Tie-On:               31755
No. Sold:

*Tie-On and Fabric Lid
sold separately.*

**J.** 1997 Bountiful Harvest

$10.25^L$ x $10.25^W$ x $4.5^H$

Form No:              12254
No. Sold:

*Also promoted with
1 Quart Casserole Dish,
which was then added
to the regular line.*

**K.** 1998 Baker's Bounty

$10^L$ x $6.25^W$ x $3.75^H$

Form No:              11771
Tie-On:               33669
No. Sold:

*Promoted with the Loaf
Dish, which was
then added to the
regular line.*

## Lesley DeTitta
### Park Ridge, New Jersey

How many baskets can some-
one collect in 7 months?  How
about 85!  Lesley and her huband
George love that their baskets go so well with their antiques.
Their 22 lb. cat loves that she can take naps in their Shining
Star™ basket. Lesley makes sure she never leaves home without a basket.  She keeps the Road Trip™ basket in her car,
and always carries around a Saddlebrook Purse™.

## Special Events

Baskets produced in honor of a special
event.  Listed by year within its own
category.  Commemorative Tag.

### MARKET VALUES

| Photo | Description | Original | Avg. | High |
|---|---|---|---|---|
| | *Bob & Dolores Hope:* | | | |
| A. | 1989  Bob & Dolores Hope | N/A | **696** | **857** |
| B. | 1990  Bob & Dolores Hope | N/A | **597** | **733** |
| C. | 1991  Bob & Dolores Hope | N/A | **650** | **750** |
| D. | 1992  Bob & Dolores Hope | N/A | **622** | **753** |
| E. | 1993  Bob & Dolores Hope | N/A | **558** | **804** |
| F. | 1994  Bob & Dolores Hope | N/A | **714** | **774** |
| G. | 1995  Bob & Dolores Hope | N/A | **613** | **625** |
| H. | 1996  Bob & Dolores Hope | N/A | **677** | **729** |
| | [Series completed in 1996] | | | |
| | *Inaugural:* | | | |
| I. | 1989  Inaugural™ | 19.89 | **247** | **475** ✍ |
| J. | 1993  Inaugural™ | 24.95 | **58** | **102** |
| | with **P**rotector | 28.90 | **68** | **115** |
| | with **L**iner | 34.90 | **70** | **115** |
| | Combo **(P/L)** | 34.95 | **74** | **120** |
| K. | 1997  Inaugural™ | 32.95 | **60** | **85** |
| | with **P**rotector | 36.90 | **65** | **86** |
| | with **L**iner | 44.90 | **65** | **90** |
| | Combo **(P/L)** | 42.95 | **65** | **110** |
| K. | 1997  Inaugural™ Tie-On | 6.95 | **15** | **28** |
| L. | 2001  Inaugural™ | 39.00 | **44** | **50** |
| | with **P**rotector | 42.00 | **49** | **53** |
| | with **L**iner | 53.00 | **49** | **60** |
| | Combo **(P/L)** | 49.00 | **58** | **116** |
| | Full Set **(C/Lid)** | 63.00 | **65** | **130** |
| L. | 2001  Inaugural Tie-On | 8.00 | **14** | **18** |

✍ = With Signatures

**A.** 1989 Bob & Dolores Hope

11$^L$ x 8$^W$ x 5.5$^H$

*Form No:* 900-
*No. Sold:* ≈ 500

*First Edition
Brown trim and center
weave with blue shoe-
string weave.*

**E.** 1993 Bob & Dolores Hope

11$^L$ x 8$^W$ x 5.5$^H$

*Form No:* 900-
*No. Sold:* ≈ 500

*Fifth Edition* Blue
*trim with brown, blue,
brown center weave.
No shoestring weaving.*

**I.** 1989 Inaugural

5$^{RD}$ x 4.5$^H$

*Form No:* 3800-ABRST
*No. Sold:*

*In honor of President
Bush's Inauguration.*

**B.** 1990 Bob & Dolores Hope

$11^L$ x $8^W$ x $5.5^H$

| Form No: | 900- |
|---|---|
| No. Sold: | ≈ 500 |

*Second Edition*
*Blue trim and center weave with brown shoestring weave.*

**C.** 1991 Bob & Dolores Hope

$11^L$ x $8^W$ x $5.5^H$

| Form No: | 900- |
|---|---|
| No. Sold: | ≈ 500 |

*Third Edition*
*Blue trim with brown, blue, brown center weave. No shoestring weaving.*

**D.** 1992 Bob & Dolores Hope

$11^L$ x $8^W$ x $5.5^H$

| Form No: | 900- |
|---|---|
| No. Sold: | ≈ 500 |

*Fourth Edition*
*Brown trim with blue, brown, blue center weave. No shoestring weaving.*

**F.** 1994 Bob & Dolores Hope

$11^L$ x $8^W$ x $5.5^H$

| Form No: | 900- |
|---|---|
| No. Sold: | ≈ 500 |

*Sixth Edition*
*Blue trim and center weave. Brown shoe-string weave.*

**G.** 1995 Bob & Dolores Hope

$11^L$ x $8^W$ x $5.5^H$

| Form No: | 900- |
|---|---|
| No. Sold: | ≈ 250 |

*Seventh Edition*
*Blue trim and center weave. Brown shoe-string weave.*

**H.** 1996 Bob & Dolores Hope

$11^L$ x $8^W$ x $5.5^H$

| Form No: | 900- |
|---|---|
| No. Sold: | ≈ 250 |

*Eighth Edition*
*Blue trim and center weave. Brown shoe-string weave.*

**J.** 1993 Inaugural

$5^L$ x $5^W$ x $4.5^H$

| Form No: | 11461 |
|---|---|
| No. Sold: | |

*In honor of President Clinton's Inauguration.*

**K.** 1997 Inaugural

$5.5^{RD}$ x $3.25^H$

| Form No: | 15326 |
|---|---|
| Tie-On: | 71609 |
| No. Sold: | 298,318 |

*In honor of President Clinton's Inauguration.*

**L.** 2001 Inaugural

$5.5^L$ x $4^W$ x $4^H$

| Form No: | 16080 |
|---|---|
| Tie-On: | 73903 |
| No. Sold: | 227,763 |

*In honor of President Bush's Inauguration.*

**213**

## Special Events

This collection does not always have an addition each year. Only when The Company chooses to honor an event.

**M.** 1992 Discovery
5.5^{RD} x 3.5^{H}

*Form No:* 5700-AO
*No. Sold:*

*In honor of the Discovery of America. Does not have double weaving. Protector not offered.*

### MARKET VALUES

| Photo | Description | Original | Avg. | High |
|---|---|---|---|---|
| | *Miscellaneous Events:* | | | |
| M. | 1992 Discovery™ | 19.92 | **62** | **100** |
| | Combo (**L**) | 29.87 | **68** | **140** ✍ |
| N. | 1996 Ohio Statehouse Opening | N/C | — | **80** |
| O. | 1998 25th Anniversary™ | 49.95 | **76** | **130** |
| | with **P**rotector | 55.90 | **81** | **150** |
| | with **L**iner | 65.90 | **90** | **180** |
| | Combo (**P/L**) | 71.85 | **102** | **205** |
| P. | 1998 Barn Raising™ | | **141** | **161** |
| | with **P**rotector | | **150** | **180** |
| | with **L**iner | | **158** | **183** |
| | Combo (**P/L**) | 59.95 | **161** | **200** |
| | Full Set (**C/Lid**) | 85.95 | **170** | **275** |
| P. | 1998 Barn Raising Tie-On | 7.00 | **18** | **25** |
| | *Heisey Horses:* | | | |
| Q. | 1998 Red Heisey Horse | 95.00 | **1967** | **2125** |
| R. | 1999 Cobalt Heisey Horse | 98.00 | **188** | **250** |
| | Blue Balking Colt | 50.00 | **105** | **110** |
| | Blue Kicking Colt | 50.00 | **93** | **96** |
| | Blue Standing Colt | 50.00 | **68** | **75** |
| S. | 2000 Emerald Heisey Horse | 98.00 | **188** | **250** |
| | Green Balking Colt | 50.00 | — | — |
| | Green Kicking Colt | 50.00 | — | — |
| | Green Standing Colt | 50.00 | — | — |

1998 Heisey Horse

**Q.** 6.5^{W} x 6.75^{H}

*Form No:* unknown
*No. Given:* 900

*This is the first of three horses that will be produced over the next 3 years.*

✍ = With Signatures

**N.** 1996 Statehouse

$11^L$ x $8^W$ x $5.5^H$

*Form No:* 900-
*No. Given:* 400

Received at the Ohio
Statehouse reopening
in 1996.

**O.** 1998
25th Anniversary

$8.75^L$ x $4.75^W$ x $6.5^H$

*Form No:* 17612
*No. Given:*

Available to all customers
in celebration of
The Company's 25th
Anniversary: 1973 – 1998.

**P.** 1998
Barn Raising

$7^{RD}$ x $6.5^H$

*Form No:* 222806
*No. Given:*

Sold at the Crawford Barn
Raising Event. Sold only as a
Combo. Other accessories
offered through the mail.

**R.** 1999
Heisey Horses

$6.5^W$ x $6.75^H$

*Form No:* unknown

*Balking:* $3.5^H$
*Kicking:* $4^H$
*Standing:* $5^H$

Second in the series of
three. First year for the
Colts to be offered.

**S.** 2000
Heisey Horse

$6.5^W$ x $6.75^H$

*Form No:* unknown
*No. Given:*

Final horse for this
series.

n e e d

# How do we
get our values?

see page 8

# *entley History*

## Thank you for 10 wonderful years!

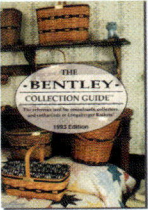
**1993**

**1994**

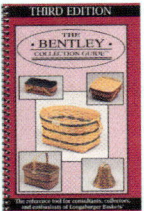
**1995**

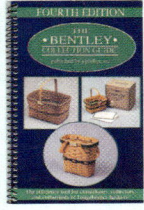
**1996**

**1997**

### First Edition – 1993
- 72 pages
- Group photos
- 7,000 copies sold

### Second Edition – 1994
- 85 pages
- Group photos
- 12,000 copies sold

### Third Edition – 1995
- 121 pages
- Added individual pictures
- Added Dimensional Search

### Fourth Edition – 1996
- 157 pages
- Moved to both Avg and High

### Fifth Edition – 1997
- 200 pages
- First time for Binder format

### Sixth Edition – 1998
- 241 pages
- Introduced Photo Contest

### Seventh Edition – 1999
- 269 pages
- Quick Find grows to be bigger than the entire First Edition!

### Eighth Edition – 2000
- 298 pages
- Added J.W. Originals

### Ninth Edition – 2001
- 321 pages
- 35,000 copies sold

### Tenth Edition – 2002
- 366 pages
- 1500 full-color photos
- Servicing over 65,000 Collectors

**1998**

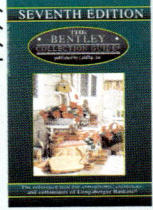
**1999**

**2000**

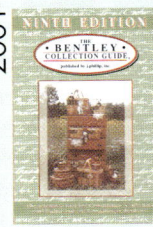
**2001**

**2002**

**Deloris Alexander**
*Friendsville, Tennessee*

*Deloris' favorite collection is the Sweetheart™ since she was married 26 years ago on Valentine's Day. As a hairdresser, Deloris displays the baskets at her station and just takes orders while she styles hair!*

## Sweetheart Collection™

### Red Shoestring Weaving.
### Red Ticking Liners Starting in 1993.

**A.** 1990 Sweetheart

$5.75^L$ x $3.75^W$ x $3^H$

*Form No:* 45000-ARS
*No. Sold:*

## MARKET VALUES

| Photo | | Description | Original | Avg. | High |
|---|---|---|---|---|---|
| A. | 1990 | Sweetheart™ | 24.95 | **129** | **180** |
| | | Combo (**L**) | 32.95 | **169** | **185** |
| B. | 1990 | Getaway™ | 79.95 | **119** | **195** |
| C. | 1993 | Sweetheart™ | 25.95 | **60** | **100** |
| | | with **P**rotector | 28.90 | **60** | **100** |
| | | with **L**iner | 35.90 | **60** | **100** |
| | | Combo (**P/L**) | 29.95 | **71** | **132** |
| C. | 1993 | Pewter Tie-On | 8.95 | **21** | **42** |
| D. | 1993 | Getaway™ | 119.95 | **130** | **175** |
| | | with **P**rotector | 131.90 | **150** | **200** |
| | | with **L**iner | 149.90 | **155** | **215** |
| | | Combo (**P/L**) | 139.95 | **178** | **260** |
| E. | 1994 | Be Mine™ | 27.95 | **66** | **90** |
| | | with **P**rotector | 32.90 | **66** | **90** |
| | | with **L**iner | 39.90 | **66** | **90** |
| | | Combo (**P/L**) | 36.95 | **67** | **100** |
| F. | 1994 | Forever Yours™ | 109.95 | **158** | **170** |
| | | with **P**rotector | 123.90 | **162** | **200** |
| | | with **L**iner | 139.90 | **162** | **200** |
| | | Combo (**P/L**) | 139.95 | **168** | **203** |
| E. | 1994 | Fabric Heart Tie-On | 6.95 | **14** | **25** |
| G. | 1995 | Sweet Sentiments™ | 28.95 | **46** | **70** |
| | | with **P**rotector | 31.90 | **50** | **73** |
| | | with **L**iner | 38.90 | **52** | **73** |
| | | Combo (**P/L**) | 33.95 | **55** | **80** |
| G. | 1995 | Small Heart Tie-On | 5.95 | **14** | **23** |
| H. | 1995 | Precious Treasures™ | 89.95 | **168** | **200** |
| | | with **P**rotector | 100.90 | **—** | **—** |
| | | with **L**iner | 116.90 | **—** | **—** |
| | | Combo (**P/L**) | 99.95 | **170** | **200** |
| | | Full Set (**C/Lid**) | 129.95 | **175** | **225** |
| H. | 1995 | Large Heart Tie-On | 6.95 | **15** | **20** |
| I. | 1996 | Bouquet™ | 34.95 | **45** | **65** |
| | | with **P**rotector | 40.90 | **55** | **67** |
| | | with **L**iner | 47.90 | **60** | **89** |
| | | Combo (**P/L**) | 44.95 | **67** | **89** |
| I. | 1996 | Bouquet™ Tie-On | 6.95 | **11** | **17** |
| J. | 1997 | Sweet Treats™ | 32.95 | **45** | **70** |
| | | with **P**rotector | 37.90 | **47** | **82** |
| | | with **L**iner | 43.90 | **52** | **85** |
| | | Combo (**P/L**) | 42.95 | **58** | **87** |
| J. | 1997 | Sweet Treats Tie-On | 6.95 | **12** | **18** |
| J. | 1997 | Gourmet Gathering™ | 74.95 | **85** | **120** |
| | | with **P**rotector | 92.90 | **90** | **125** |
| | | with **L**iner | 98.90 | **100** | **130** |
| | | Combo (**P/L**) | 99.95 | **101** | **130** |
| | | Full Set (**C/Lid**) | 144.90 | **115** | **150** |
| K. | 1997 | Ticking Trivets | 13.95 | **18** | **20** |

**E.** 1994 Be Mine

$8.5^L$ x $5^W$ x $3.5^H$

*Form No:* 18601
*No. Sold:*

**I.** 1996 Bouquet

$6.5^{RD}$ x $6.5^H$

*Form No:* 11240
*Tie-On:* 33596
*No. Sold:*

**B.** 1990 Getaway

17$^L$ x 14$^W$ x 11$^H$

Form No: 300-CRS
No. Sold:

*Hostess Only*

**C.** 1993 Sweetheart

5$^L$ x 5$^W$ x 2.5$^H$

Form No: 11347
Tie-On: 72036
No. Sold:

*Tie-On sold separately.*

**D.** 1993 Getaway

17$^L$ x 14$^W$ x 11$^H$

Form No: 10359
No. Sold:

*Hostess Only*

**F.** 1994 Forever Yours

20.5$^L$ x 15$^W$ x 10.5$^H$

Form No: 10367
Tie-On: 22659
No. Sold:

*Hostess Only.*
*Tie-On sold separately.*

**G.** 1995 Sweet Sentiments

4.25$^L$ x 4.25$^W$ x 3$^H$

Form No: 19046
Tie-On: 31780
No. Sold:

*Tie-On sold separately.*

**H.** 1995 Precious Treasures

13.25$^L$ x 11.25$^W$ x 9$^H$

Form No: 10456
Tie-On: 31798
No. Sold:

*Hostess Only.*
*Tie-On sold separately.*

**J.** 1997 Sweet Treats & Gourmet Gathering

Sm: 8$^L$ x 5$^W$ x 3$^H$
Lg: 18$^L$ x 11$^W$ x 4.5$^H$

| Form No: | Small | Large |
|----------|-------|-------|
| Red | 15938 | 15946 |
| Green | 15962 | 16063 |
| Blue | 15954 | 16055 |
| Purple | 15971 | 16071 |
| Tie-On: | | 71617 |

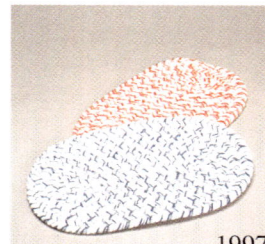

**K.** 1997 Ticking Trivets

14$^L$ x 9$^W$

Form No:
Red: 2366390
Green: 2366391
Blue: 2366392
Purple: 2366393

*Promoted along with*
*the Gourmet Gathering.*

collection **note**

**Sweetheart & Friends**

Starting in 1997, Longaberger introduced colors to the Sweetheart Collection. Baskets and Ticking liners were available in red, green, blue, purple or even classic stain (1998 only). These options were promoted as "Sweetheart & Friends", but did not reappear with the 1999 Sweetheart™ baskets.

**219**

## Sweetheart Collection™

**1998**
**L.** Sweetheart Baskets

<u>Sm</u>: 7.25$^L$ x 4$^W$ x 4.5$^H$
<u>Lg</u>: 14.25$^L$ x 6.25$^W$ x 9.5$^H$

| Form No: | Small | Large |
|---|---|---|
| Red | 17523 | 17531 |
| Blue | 16250 | 16268 |
| Green | 16357 | 16365 |
| Purple | 16454 | 16462 |
| Classic | 16551 | 16560 |
| Lapel Pin: | | 72761 |
| Frame: | | 72770 |

### MARKET VALUES

| | | Description | Original | Avg. | High |
|---|---|---|---|---|---|
| L. | 1998 | Picture Perfect™ | 39.00 | **52** | **75** |
| | | with **P**rotector | 43.00 | **56** | **90** |
| | | with **L**iner | 54.00 | **58** | **100** |
| | | Combo (**P/L**) | 49.00 | **65** | **120** |
| | | Full Set(**C/HTie**) | 55.00 | **77** | **130** |
| L. | 1998 | Pewter Lapel Pin/Tie-On | 8.00 | **12** | **23** |
| L. | 1998 | Cherished Memories™ | 89.00 | **120** | **150** |
| | | with **P**rotector | 99.00 | **125** | **150** |
| | | with **L**iner | 118.00 | **130** | **155** |
| | | Combo (**P/L**) | 119.00 | **130** | **165** |
| | | Full Set(**C/Lid/HT**) | 153.00 | **135** | **175** |
| L. | 1998 | Pewter Frame/Tie-On | 10.00 | **14** | **18** |
| M. | 1999 | Love Letters™ | 44.00 | **60** | **90** |
| | | with **P**rotector | 49.00 | **62** | **92** |
| | | with **L**iner | 61.00 | **62** | **95** |
| | | Combo (**P/L**) | 56.00 | **65** | **105** |
| | | Full Set(**C/Lid**) | 82.00 | **90** | **110** |
| M. | 1999 | Love Tie-On | 8.00 | **10** | **17** |
| M. | 1999 | Love Treasures™ | 68.00 | **96** | **120** |
| | | with **P**rotector | 84.00 | **90** | **130** |
| | | with **L**iner | 90.00 | **100** | **135** |
| | | Combo (**P/L**) | 89.00 | **103** | **155** |
| | | Full Set(**C/Lid**) | 137.00 | **133** | **170** |
| N. | 1999 | Love Stationary | 14.00 | **—** | **—** |
| O. | 2000 | Little Love™ | 34.00 | **41** | **45** |
| | | with **P**rotector | 38.00 | **—** | **—** |
| | | with **L**iner | 44.00 | **—** | **—** |
| | | Combo (**P/L**) | 39.00 | **46** | **75** |
| | | Full Set(**C/Lid**) | 58.00 | **65** | **96** |
| O. | 2000 | Heart Pillow[np] | 12.00 | **13** | **15** |
| P. | 2001 | Love Notes™ | 39.00 | **51** | **56** |
| | | with **P**rotector | 43.00 | **—** | **—** |
| | | with **L**iner | 53.00 | **—** | **—** |
| | | Combo (**P/L**) | 49.00 | **52** | **75** |
| P. | 2001 | Bouquet Heart Tie-On | 8.00 | **11** | **14** |
| Q. | 2001 | Bouquet Wall Hook | 16.00 | **18** | **25** |

[np] = Not Pictured

**2001**
**P.** Love Notes

5.75$^L$ x 3.75$^W$ x 5$^H$

| Form No: | 12055 / 10826 |
|---|---|
| Tie-On: | |
| | 78328 |

*Available Classic stain
or Classic with red
accents. Tie-On sold
separately.*

**M.** Sweetheart Baskets  
1999

Sm: 8.75$^L$ x 7.75$^W$ x 2.75$^H$  
Lg: 13.25$^L$ x 12.5$^W$ x 4.25$^H$

*Form No:*
| | |
|---|---|
| *Small:* | *12963* |
| *Large:* | *13064* |
| *Tie-On:* | *37184* |

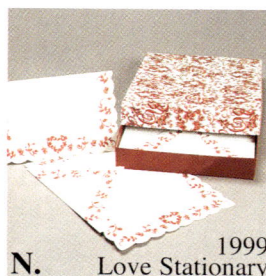

**N.**  
1999  
Love Stationary

*Form No:    73245*

*Sold separately.*  
*Included 10 note cards,*  
*10 stationary sheets and*  
*21 envelopes.*

**O.**    2000 Little Love

6.25$^L$ x 4.75$^W$ x 2.25$^H$

*Form No:    17728 / 10874*  
*18062 / 10850*  
*10885*

*Available red, blue,*  
*green, purple or classic.*  
*See Foundry for info on*  
*the stand also promoted.*

**Q.** Bouquet Wall Hook  
2001

1.5$^L$ x 1.5$^W$ x 2.5$^H$

*Form No:    78123*

*Designed to hold the*  
*Love Notes basket.*

**WHAT A SWEETHEART!**    with a beautiful  
collection like that, she should stand proud.

**BARB STRAIGHT** Westerville, Ohio

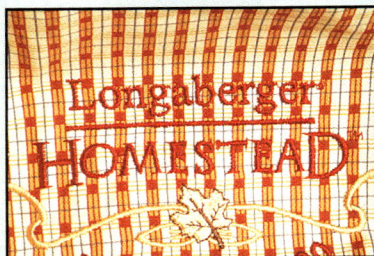

The Longaberger Homestead® continues to grow in popularity and attendance.

Named as one of Ohio's "Great Ohio Adventures in Learning Destinations" in 2001 by the Ohio Division of Travel and Tourism, The Homestead® continues to add wonderful experiences for collectors of all ages.

The newest addition is the *Longaberger Farms* for the "Look, Think and Do Club". This club gives the kids visiting The Homestead activities to keep them busy discovering new things around the area. The *Longaberger Farm* covers approximately 700 acres of diverse habitats, including a natural wetland, lush forests, open grassy fields, cultivated fields and various fence row areas which can attract many different kinds of birds.

Kids will also get a chance to meet "Matt" and "Pete", two resident percheron horses, as well as many of their other farm friends! Hands-on activities are also planned throughout the adventure, such as cooking lunch in a solar oven, learning how to measure distance without a tape measure, making sun prints and much more!

The cost for a "Look, Think and Do" Adventure is $25 per child for the whole day of fun. Reservations are required and can be made by calling Guest Relations at 740-322-5588.

## Lisa Moodie
### Dayton, Ohio

*Lisa loves traveling to The Homestead and Dresden, because it places her right in the heart of basket comaraderie! She says being at a place where EVERYONE truly loves baskets lends a sense of belonging. For Lisa, the trip to "basket country" has become an eagerly anticipated yearly excursion.*

**A.** Dresden Tour

8.75$^L$ x 4.75$^W$ x 6.5$^H$

*Form No:5600-BO / 15601*

*Basket pictured is the actual first Tour Basket ever sold in Dresden in 1988.*

## Tour Baskets

The only baskets that cannot be purchased through a Consultant. Available only at Dresden, The Homestead or Hartville.

### MARKET VALUES

| Photo | Description | Original | Avg. | High |
|---|---|---|---|---|
| A. | *Dresden:* | | | |
| | (88) Tour™ | | — | — |
| | (89) Tour™ | | 35 | 75 |
| | (90) Tour™ | | 70 | 70 |
| | (91) Tour™ | | 44 | 83 |
| | (92) Dresden Tour™ | | 38 | 69 |
| | (93) Dresden Tour™ | 24.95 | 53 | 60 |
| | with Protector | 30.90 | 63 | 80 |
| | (94) Dresden Tour™ | 29.95 | 44 | 75 |
| | with Protector | 35.90 | 48 | 80 |
| | (95-99) Dresden Tour™ | 34.95 | 43 | 70 |
| | with Protector | 40.90 | 47 | 100 |
| | (99) Dresden Basket™ | 29.95 | — | — |
| B. | (00) Dresden Basket™ | 29.95 | 59 | 63 |
| C. | (01-P) Dresden Basket™ | 34.95 | 50 | 60 |
| D. | *Dresden II:* | | | |
| | (96-99) Dresden Tour II™ | 29.95 | 66 | 70 |
| | with Protector | 33.90 | 70 | 75 |
| | *Golf:* | | | |
| E. | (00) Golf™ | 39.95 | 62 | 84 |
| | with **P**rotector | 43.90 | — | — |
| | with **L**iner | 55.95 | — | — |
| | Combo (**P/L**) | 59.90 | 98 | 162 |
| | Full Set (**C/Lid**) | 89.90 | 100 | 175 |
| F. | (01) Golf™ | 44.95 | — | — |
| | with **P**rotector | 49.90 | — | — |
| | with **L**iner | 59.95 | — | — |
| | Combo (**P/L**) | 65.90 | — | — |
| | Full Set (**C/Lid**) | 95.90 | — | — |
| G. | *Hartville:* | | | |
| | (95-99) Hartville Tour™ | 34.95 | 50 | 60 |
| | with Protector | 40.90 | 60 | 60 |
| H. | *Hartville II:* | | | |
| | (96-99) Hartville Tour II™ | 29.95 | — | 45 |
| | with Protector | 33.90 | — | — |
| | *Miscellaneous:* | | | |
| I. | (97-99) 20th Century™ | 49.95 | 64 | 105 |
| | with Protector | 55.90 | 67 | 125 |
| | with **L**iner | 64.95 | 83 | 125 |
| | Combo (**P/L**) | 70.90 | 84 | 125 |
| J. | (00) Homestead Tie-On | 0.00 | 10 | 10 |

**E.** 2000 Golf

6.75$^{RD}$ x 6$^H$

*Form No:        unknown*

*Special burned-in logo on the bottom. Also sold at the Golf Course.*

**H.** Hartville Tour II

7$^L$ x 3.5$^W$ x 4.75$^H$

*Form No:        15814*

**B.** 2000 Dresden Basket

$7^L$ x $3.5^W$ x $4.75^H$

Form No: unknown

*This is the same form as what used to be known as the Tour II.*

**C.** 2001-P Dresden Basket

$7^L$ x $3.5^W$ x $4.75^H$

Form No: unknown

*This same basket was brought back in 2002, just with a different tag.*

**D.** Dresden Tour II

$7^L$ x $3.5^W$ x $4.75^H$

Form No: 15814

*This new form first appeared in Dresden & Hartville stores in Jan. 96.*

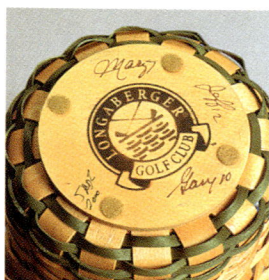

Golf Basket Logo

*These baskets do not come with signatures.*

**F.** 2001 Golf

$6.75^{RD}$ x $6^H$

Form No: unknown

*Special burned-in logo on the bottom. Also sold at the Golf Course.*

**G.** Hartville Tour

$8.75^L$ x $4.75^W$ x $6.5^H$

Form No: 15661

*Same as the Dresden Tour, except different tag. First appeared in the Hartville factory store in 1995.*

**I.** 20th Century

$8.75^L$ x $4.75^W$ x $6.5^H$

Form No: 17575
No.Sold:

collection **n o t e**

### 20th Century Basket

First offered in at the 1997 Bee General Session. More than 9,500 were sold prior to being available to the public. In Sept. 1998, it was moved to the Basket Village Preview Center for sale to the public. All 1997 baskets are marked as "First Edition". Starting in 1998, this notation was removed from the tag.

**J.** 2000 Homestead Tie-On

$2^{RD}$ x $1.5^H$

Form No: unknown

*Postcards were sent to Collectors Club Members and Consultants inviting them to visit the Homestead. They could redeem the postcard for this free Tie-On.*

**225**

## Tour Baskets

**Most Longaberger stores in Dresden were closed once the Homestead opened. Only the Dresden Basket is still available in Dresden.**

### MARKET VALUES

| | | Description | Original | Avg. | High |
|---|---|---|---|---|---|
| | | *Woven Memories:* | | | |
| K. | (99) | Blue Chore Basket | 39.95 | **83** | **128** |
| | | with **P**rotector | 45.90 | **88** | **140** |
| | | with **L**iner | 55.95 | — | — |
| | | Combo (**P/L**) | 61.90 | **97** | **175** |
| L. | (00) | Red Chore Basket | 39.95 | **63** | **65** |
| | | with **P**rotector | 45.90 | — | — |
| | | with **L**iner | 55.95 | — | — |
| | | Combo (**P/L**) | 61.90 | **84** | **134** |
| M. | (01) | Green Chore Basket | 44.95 | **62** | **65** |
| | | with **P**rotector | 50.95 | **73** | **75** |
| | | with **L**iner | 60.95 | — | — |
| | | Combo (**P/L**) | 66.90 | **118** | **150** |
| N. | (02) | Red Apple Basket | 44.95 | — | — |
| | | with **P**rotector | 52.90 | — | — |
| | | with **L**iner | 64.95 | — | — |
| | | Combo (**P/L**) | 72.90 | — | — |

1999
**K.** Woven Memories
10$^L$ x 6$^W$ x 4$^H$
*Form No:* *unknown*

*Classic Stain or blue accent weaving. Accessories sold separately.*

2000
**L.** Woven Memories
10$^L$ x 6$^W$ x 4$^H$
*Form No:* *unknown*

*Also available in Classic stain. Inset picture shows special embroidered liner sold separately.*

2001
**M.** Woven Memories
10$^L$ x 6$^W$ x 4$^H$
*Form No:* *unknown*

*Also available in Classic stain. Accessories sold separately.*

2002
**N.** Woven Memories
7.5$^{RD}$ x 4.5$^H$
*Form No:* *unknown*

*Also available in Classic stain. Accessories sold separately.*

**Purdue Troy**
*Greentown, Indiana*

*2002 Photo Winner!*

*A collector since 1995, Purdue became interested in baskets through his mom. His favorite collection is the Father's Day™. The above photo was taken in his back yard. We thought it was absolutely beautiful and selected it as the Grand Prize Winner of this year's National Photo Search Contest. We think you'll agree!*

Traditions™

## Traditions Collection™

**Heritage Green™ Weave and Trim.
Commemorative Brass Tag.
Series completed in 1999.**

**A.** 1995 Family

$15.25^L$ x $11^W$ x $7.75^H$

*Form No:* 19101
*No. Sold:*

*3/8" Weaving. Liner added in 1996, not originally available. Box.*

### MARKET VALUES

| | Description | Original | Avg. | High |
|---|---|---|---|---|
| A. | 1995 Family™ | 89.95 | **96** | **180** |
| | Combo (P) | 95.95 | **100** | **195** |
| | with Liner (1996) | 119.90 | **135** | **250** |
| | Full Set (P/L) | 125.90 | **167** | **290** |
| B. | 1996 Community™ | 84.95 | **84** | **125** |
| | with Protector | 93.95 | **100** | **160** |
| | with Liner | 114.90 | **100** | **180** |
| | Combo (P/L) | 109.95 | **110** | **202** |
| | Full Set (C/Div) | 117.90 | **168** | **250** |
| C. | 1997 Fellowship™ | 69.95 | **90** | **115** |
| | with Protector | 81.90 | **100** | **150** |
| | with Liner | 92.90 | **106** | **160** |
| | Combo (P/L) | 89.95 | **108** | **160** |
| | Full Set: (C/Lid/Grip) | 129.95 | **110** | **180** |
| D. | 1998 Hospitality™ | 89.00 | **77** | **120** |
| | with Protector | 110.00 | **105** | **130** |
| | with Liner | 115.00 | **108** | **147** |
| | Combo (P/L) | 114.00 | **111** | **200** |
| E. | 1999 Generosity™ | 119.00 | **112** | **170** |
| | with Protector | 150.00 | **120** | **180** |
| | with Liner | 147.00 | **143** | **200** |
| | Combo (P/L) | 159.00 | **147** | **225** |
| | Full Set (C/Lid) | 218.00 | **180** | **300** |
| **Complete Set** | | 705.75 | **588** | **800** |

**B.** 1996 Community

$14.75^L$ x $13.5^W$ x $6.25^H$

*Form No:* 19119
*No. Sold:* 171,381

*Divider sold separately. Box.*

**C.** 1997 Fellowship

$12.5^L$ x $6.5^W$ x $7.75^H$

*Form No:* 15920
*No. Sold:*

*Handle Gripper not shown. Box.*

**D.** 1998 Hospitality

$18.5^L$ x $13.5^W$ x $5.25^H$

*Form No:* 10669
*No. Sold:*

*Did not come with a box.*

**E.** 1999 Generosity

$19.25^L$ x $13.5^W$ x $7.75^H$

*Form No:* 13358
*No. Sold:*

*Did not come with a box.*

## Diane Jay
### Arcanum, Ohio

*Diane has been collecting since 1987 and has been a Consultant for 3 years. Her favorite is the Cake™ basket. Every year for Christmas, she loves to put up Christmas trees and decorate them with Longaberger Products®.*

## Tree-Trimming™

**Smaller replica versions of the Christmas Collection Baskets. Box included with each.**

### MARKET VALUES

| Photo | Description | Original | Avg. | High |
|---|---|---|---|---|
| A. | Peppermint™ | 45.00 | **54** | **75** |
| | with **P**rotector | 48.00 | **60** | **79** |
| | with **L**iner | 56.00 | **67** | **80** |
| | Combo **(P/L)** | 59.00 | **73** | **95** |
| B. | Let it Snow™ | 45.00 | **59** | **81** |
| | with **P**rotector | 48.00 | **60** | **83** |
| | with **L**iner | 56.00 | **61** | **85** |
| | Combo **(P/L)** | 59.00 | **63** | **85** |
| | Full Set **(C/Lid)** | 74.00 | **68** | **90** |
| C. | Twinkle Twinkle™ | 49.00 | **65** | **80** |
| | with **P**rotector | 53.00 | **70** | **82** |
| | with **L**iner | 61.00 | **70** | **85** |
| | Combo **(P/L)** | 65.00 | **75** | **90** |
| | Full Set **(C/Lid)** | 82.00 | **82** | **95** |

**A.** 1999 Peppermint
5.5RD x 2.75H

*Form No:* 19364/16837
*No.Sold:*

*All baskets included Tie-On. Basket available in red or green. Box.*

**B.** 2000 Let It Snow
4.75L x 5W x 3.25H

*Form No:* 18147 / 18155
*No.Sold:* 200,500

*All baskets included Tie-On. Basket available in red or green. Box.*

collection **note**

This special burned-in logo is present on the *inside* of all Tree-Trimming Baskets, authenticating the collection.

**C.** 2001 Twinkle Twinkle
5.5L x 6W x 2.25H

*Form No:* 10664 / 10672
*No.Sold:*

*All baskets included Tie-On. Basket available in red or green. Box.*

# Wood Products

*Cathy Burr*
*Deerfield, Ohio*

Cathy has been collecting
Wood Products for the past
5 years. She has all the
shelves and cupboards, and
eventually hopes to complete the col-
lection. The piece she treasures the most is the Wood Scoop
which she found at a sale.

## Wood Products

**Decorative handcrafted Wood Products. Years listed in parenthesis are the years the items were available.**

### MARKET VALUES

| Photo | Description | Original | Avg. | High |
|---|---|---|---|---|
| | *Cupboards:* | | | |
| A. | (80) 2-Door (Pine) | | **588** | 600 |
| B. | (84–85) 1-Door (Maple) | 119.95 | **434** | 500 |
| C. | (84–85) 2-Door (Oak) | 189.95 | **538** | 550 |
| D. | (85–86) 1-Door (bottom shelf) | 139.95 | **378** | 525 |
| | *Dividers:* | | | |
| | (99) 4-way, Ntrl (Spring)[np] | 12.00 | — | — |
| | (00-01) 4-way, Ntrl (S.Spoon)[np] | 11.00 | — | — |
| E. | (92-99) 6-way (Chore, Med.) | 18.00 | **10** | 23 |
| E. | (92-99) 6-way (Gathering, Med) | 20.00 | **13** | 15 |
| F. | (92-99) 8-way (Pantry) | 19.00 | **12** | 22 |
| | (99) 8-way, Ntrl (Pantry)[np] | 19.00 | — | — |
| G. | (99-01) Bread | 8.00 | — | — |
| | *Lids:* | | | |
| H. | (95-99) Corn Lid | 37.95 | **55** | 94 |
| | (95-98) Fabric Lids: | | | |
| I. | Cake | 24.95 | **20** | 31 |
| J. | Fruit, Large | 24.95 | — | — |
| J. | Fruit, Medium | 21.95 | — | — |
| J. | Fruit, Small | 19.95 | **13** | 18 |
| J. | Magazine | 21.95 | **16** | 24 |
| J. | Sewing | 24.95 | **16** | 20 |
| K. | (83–86) Measuring Baskets: | | | |
| | 5" Measuring | 6.95 | — | 21 |
| | 7" Measuring | 7.95 | — | — |
| | 9" Measuring | 8.95 | — | — |
| | 11" Measuring | 9.95 | **27** | 33 |
| | 13" Measuring | 10.95 | — | 20 |
| L. | (97–98) Measuring Baskets: | | | |
| | 5" Measuring | 13.95 | **17** | 21 |
| | 11" Measuring | 34.95 | **31** | 35 |

**[continued next page]**

[np] = Not Pictured

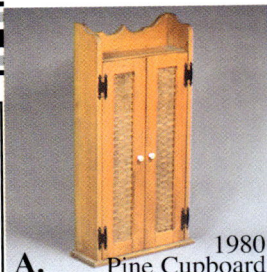

**A.** 1980 Pine Cupboard
$15.5^L$ x $5^W$ x $32.75^H$

*Form No:* unknown
*No. Sold:*

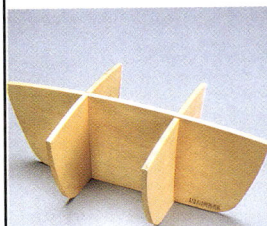

**E.** 1992-99 6-way Divider
$\approx 13^L$ x $8^W$ x $5^H$

*Form No:* 50172
*No. Sold:*

*Fits the Medium Chore.*

**I.** 1995-98 Cake Fabric Lid
$12^L$ x $12^W$

*Form No:* 51021
*No. Sold:*

*All regular line fabrics offered.*

**B.** 1984–85 Maple Cupboard

$27.5^L$ x $13^W$ x $5.25^H$

Form No: 8101-OO
No. Sold:

**C.** 1984–85 Oak Cupboard

$22.5^L$ x $17.5^W$ x $6.25^H$

Form No: 8100-O
No. Sold:

**D.** 1985–86 Cupboard

$27.25^L$ x $15.5^W$ x $5.25^H$

Form No: 8100-OO
No. Sold:

*Also featured in 1988.*

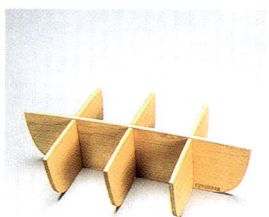

**F.** 1992-99 8-way Divider

$\approx 13^L$ x $8^W$ x $5^H$

Form No: 50164
No. Sold:

*Fits either the Pantry or Small Gathering.*

**G.** 1999-01 Bread Divider

$\approx 14.5^L$ x $7.5^W$ x $3.75^H$

Form No: 59315
No. Sold:

**H.** 1995-99 Corn Lid

$17^{RD}$

Form No: 54429
No. Sold:

**J.** 1995-98 Fabric Lids

*Left to right, back row first*
Sewing          53210
Fruit, Large    53236
Fruit, Small    53015
Fruit, Medium   53112
Magazine        52108

*All regular line fabrics offered. The Sewing lid has a quilted underside, to be used as a pin cushion.*

**K.** 1983-86 Measuring Lids

5", 7", 9", 11", 13"

5" Lid    8300-OO
7" Lid    8301-OO
9" Lid    8302-OO
11" Lid   8303-OO
13" Lid   8304-OO

**L.** 1997-98 Measuring Lids

5", 7", 9", 11", 13"

5" Lid    53848
11" Lid   53864

*7", 9", and 13" lids returned to the Regular Line in 2000.*

## Wood Products

The WoodCrafts® lids have been offered in a variety of ways:  center wood or painted knobs, no knobs or covered in fabric.

### MARKET VALUES

| | Description | Original | Avg. | High |
|---|---|---|---|---|
| | *Lids (con't):* | | | |
| | Natural Lids | | | |
| M. | (99-P)  Spoon, Medium | 16.00 | — | — |
| | *Paddles:* | | | |
| | **Butter Paddles:** | | | |
| | (83–85) 28$^L$ x 4.5$^W$ [np] | 14.95 | **33** | **55** |
| N. | (85–94) 28$^L$ x 6.25$^W$ | 16.95 | **38** | **55** |
| O. | **Stencil-Cut Paddles:** | | | |
| | (87–88) Heart™ | 14.95 | **50** | **65** |
| | (87–88) Goose™ | 14.95 | **36** | **65** |
| | (87–88) Gingerbread Man™ | 14.95 | **53** | **65** |
| | *Wall Hangings:* | | | |
| | **Rectangular, with shelf:** | | | |
| P. | (79–84) 10$^L$ x 14$^H$ | 16.95 | **68** | **115** |
| Q. | (85–86) 12$^L$ x 16$^H$ | 39.95 | **103** | **110** |
| | (79–80) 12$^L$ x 24$^H$ [np] | 21.95 | **160** | **175** |
| | **Square, with shelf:** | | | |
| R. | (79–80) Square, 20" | 26.95 | **168** | **180** |
| S. | (79–80) Square, 10" | 12.95 | **43** | **90** |
| | **Triangle, with shelf:** | | | |
| | (79–80) Triangle, 12$^L$ x 10$^H$ [np] | 15.95 | **90** | **120** |
| T. | (79–80) Triangle, 24$^L$ x 21$^H$ | 23.95 | **95** | **125** |
| | **Wall Brackets:** | | | |
| U. | (79–85) Large | 6.95 | **33** | **33** |
| U. | (79–85) Small | 5.95 | **30** | **30** |
| | (85–86) Small [np] | 12.95 | **55** | **90** |
| | **Miscellaneous Hangings:** | | | |
| W. | (80)  Cathedral Mirror | 19.95 | **263** | **300** |

**continued next page**

[np] = Not Pictured

**M.** 1999-P
Med.Spoon Lid
6.5$^L$ x 6.5$^W$

Form No:  58611
No. Sold:

*Fits Medium Spoon and all other baskets with its form, such as Large Peg.*

**Q.** 1985–86
Rectangular
12$^L$ x 16$^H$

Form No:  7800-O
No. Sold:

LONGABERGER ™
DESIGN
BY THE W.C. MOCK FAMILY

Wood Product Logo

*Logo appears on all wood products starting in 1985.  Unknown when the logo was changed to the current WoodCrafts® logo.*

**N.** 1985–94 Butter Paddle

$28^L$ x $6.25^W$

Form No: 8000-O
No. Sold:

1983–85 Butter Paddle
28L x 4.5W    8010-O

**O.** 1987–88 Stencil Paddles

$12.5^L$ x $4.5^H$

Form No:
Heart         8020-OO
Goose         8030-OO
Gingerbread   8040-OO

**P.** 1979–84 Rectangular

$10^L$ x $14^H$

Form No: 7800-OO
No. Sold:

$12^L$ x $24^W$    7801-O
Same style as the one above, only larger.

**R.** 1979–80 Square

$20^L$ x $20^H$

Form No: 7701-O
No. Sold:

**S.** 1979–80 Square

$10^L$ x $10^H$

Form No: 7700-O
No. Sold:

**T.** 1979–80 Triangular

$24^L$ x $21^H$

Form No: 7901-O
No. Sold:

$12^L$ x $10^W$    7900-OO
Same style as the one above, only smaller.

**U.** 1979–85 Wall Brackets

Lg: $4.5^W$ x $13.5^H$ x $11.5^{EXT}$
Sm: $4.5^W$ x $8^H$ x $6.5^{EXT}$

Form No:
 Large:    8902-O
 Small:    8900-O

**V.** 1979-85 Wall Brackets

Both the "X" shaped brackets to the left and the "Hourglass" design above were offered from the company. When the change in design occurred is unknown. It was redesigned again in 1985, shaped like an upside down "L".

**W.** 1980 Cathedral Mirror

$9^W$ x $25^H$

Form No: 8060-0
No. Sold:

## Wood Products

**While lids are made from hardwood maple, to match the baskets, the other wood crafts were made from hardwood poplar.**

### MARKET VALUES

| Photo | Description | Original | Avg. | High |
|---|---|---|---|---|
| | **Wall Hangings: (con't)** | | | |
| X. | (80) Framed Clock | 39.95 | **353** | **455** |
| | (80) Framed Mirror[np] | 32.95 | **383** | **400** |
| Y. | (99-02) Fruit Medley prints | 219.00 | — | — |
| | Blueberries | 59.00 | — | — |
| | Blackberries | 59.00 | — | — |
| | Grapes | 59.00 | — | — |
| | Cherries | 59.00 | — | — |
| Z. | (N/A) Nail Board | | — | — |
| A[1] | (80) Picture Frame | 29.95 | **250** | **325** |
| B[1] | (85–94) Peg Board | 21.95 | **40** | **45** |
| C[1] | (94–99) Peg Board | 39.95 | **34** | **45** |
| D[1] | (94-97) Wood Shelf | 89.95 | **108** | **110** |
| | **Misc. Wood Crafts:** | | | |
| E[1] | (80) Bread Box | N/A | **420** | **450** |
| F[1] | (80) Carpenter Box | N/A | **318** | **380** |
| G[1] | (80) Cheese Board | N/A | — | **260** |
| H[1] | (80) Cookbook Nook | N/A | **245** | **310** |
| I[1] | (79–82) Toilet Paper Holder | 6.95 | **48** | **50** |

**continued next page**

[np] = Not Pictured

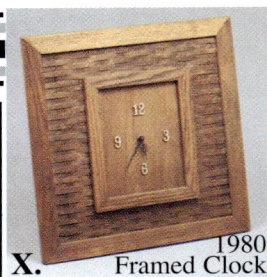

**X.** 1980 Framed Clock
$20^L$ x $20^H$
*Form No:* 7701-X
*8 x 10 face.*

**B[1]** 1985–94 Peg Board
$23^L$ x $5^W$ x $5^H$
*Form No:* 7900-
*Often promoted along with the Peg Baskets.*

**F[1]** 1980 Carpenter Box
$8^L$ x $6^W$ x $10^H$
*Form No:* unknown
*No. Sold:*
*Came with divider.*

n e e d   h e l p?

## How do we get our values?

see page 8

**Y.** Fruit Medley Prints
1999-02

$12.5^L$ x $12.5^H$

*Blueberries:* 72877
*Blackberries:* 72869
*Grapes:* 72855
*Cherries:* 72851

*Sold individually or as
a set of 4.*

**Z.** Nail Board

Approx. $16^L$ – $18^L$

*Form No:* unknown
*No. Sold:*

**A$^1$** Picture Frame
1980

$20^L$ x $20^H$

*Form No:* 7701-Z

**C$^1$** Peg Board
1994-99

$23.5^L$ x $5^W$ x $3.5^H$

*Form No:* 51101

*Made of hardwood
poplar.*

**D$^1$** Wood Shelf
1994-97

$32^L$ x $5.75^W$ x $5^H$

*Form No:* 50601
*No. Sold:*

**E$^1$** Bread Box
1980

$18.5^L$ x $12.75^W$ x $13.5^H$

*Form No:* unknown
*No. Sold:*

**G$^1$** Cheese Board

$15^L$ x $10^W$

*Form No:* unknown
*No. Sold:*

**H$^1$** Cookbook Nook
1980

$13^W$ x $17^H$

*Form No:* unknown
*No. Sold:*

**I$^1$** Toilet
Paper Holder
1979–82

$8^L$ x $3.5^W$

*Form No:* 8800-O
*No. Sold:*

## *Wood Products*

Many of the earlier wood crafts were made by a Dresden, family-owned cabinet company called Mock Woodworking.

**J[1]** 1979–80 12" Towel Holder
15.5$^L$ x 3.5$^W$

*Form No:* 8801-O

18" Holder: 19.5$^L$ x 3.5$^W$
8802-O
21" Holder: 22.5$^L$ x 3.5$^W$
8803-O
24" Holder: 25.5$^L$ x 3.5$^W$
8804-O

### MARKET VALUES

| Photo | Description | Original | Avg. | High |
|---|---|---|---|---|
| | **Misc. Wood Crafts (con't):** | | | |
| J[1] | (79–80) Towel Holder, 12" | 8.95 | **48** | **50** |
| | (79–80) Towel Holder, 18"[np] | 10.95 | **35** | **35** |
| | (79–80) Towel Holder, 21"[np] | 11.95 | **73** | **110** |
| | (79–80) Towel Holder, 24"[np] | 12.95 | — | — |
| K[1] | (94-97) Wood Mug Tree | 34.95 | **35** | **45** |
| L[1] | (81) Wood Scoop | N/A | **667** | **800** |

[np] = Not Pictured.

**K[1]** 1994-97 Mug Tree
14.75$^H$

*Form No:* 51306
*No. Sold:*

### f u n **f a c t**

## On the move . . .

The Hartville basket-making facilities are being moved to Springfield Township near Akron, Ohio. This move is scheduled to take place sometime this year, moving over 300 employees.

**L[1]** Wood Scoop
Dimensions – N/A

*Form No:* unknown
*No. Sold:*

# *Woven Traditions*®

## Connie Uhle
### Massillon, Ohio

Connie began collecting when she moved to New Mexico in 1992. The baskets reminded her of home (Ohio). The 1996 Easter holds a special place in her heart, because it was given to her when she gave birth to her first child. Connie's children have been featured in the Guide® in smaller insert photos, but now MOM has hit the big time!

## Woven Traditions®

**Red, blue, green shoestring weaving.**
**Series created in 1992, completed in 2001.**

**A.** 1992-97
Large Berry

$8.5^L$ x $8.5^W$ x $5^H$

*Form No:* 11533
*No.Sold:*

*One of the original three pieces introduced during the 1992 Holiday Season.*

### MARKET VALUES

| Photo | | Description | Original | Avg. | High |
|---|---|---|---|---|---|
| A. | (92-97) | Berry, Large™ | 30.95 | **40** | **55** |
| B. | (92-01) | Bread™ | 36.95 | **36** | **65** |
| C. | (99-01) | Button™ | 33.00 | **35** | **50** |
| D. | (96-00) | Cake™ | 59.95 | **65** | **85** |
| E. | (92-00) | Cracker™ | 26.95 | **31** | **45** |
| F. | (94-01) | Darning™ | 39.95 | **40** | **55** |
| G. | (98-00) | Pantry™ | 53.00 | **57** | **75** |
| H. | (95-99) | Peg, Large™ | 39.95 | **49** | **70** |
| I. | (1994) | Pie™ | 37.95 | **56** | **86** |
| | | with **P**rotector | 45.90 | **62** | **80** |
| | | with **L**iner | 55.90 | **65** | **85** |
| | | Combo (**P/L/Plate**) | 79.95 | **66** | **100** |
| J. | (98-01) | Recipe™ | 39.00 | — | — |
| K. | (95-97) | Spring™ | 41.95 | **51** | **65** |
| L. | (95–99) | Tea™ | 28.95 | **36** | **48** |
| M. | (95-99) | Vegetable, Small™ | 35.95 | **40** | **55** |

**Series complete**

**E.** 1992-00
Cracker

$11.5^L$ x $5^W$ x $3^H$

*Form No:* 14532
*No.Sold:*

*One of the original three pieces introduced during the 1992 Holiday Season.*

**I.** 1994 Pie

$12^L$ x $12^W$ x $4^H$

*Form No:* 12211
*No. Sold:*

*Combo included Liner, Protector and Pie Plate. Featured in 1994.*

**J.** 1998-01
Recipe

$8^L$x $5.5^W$x $4.5^{FH}$x $6^{BH}$

*Form No:* 10499
*No. Sold:*

*Retired after 8/01/01.*

**B.** 1992-01
Bread

14.5<sup>L</sup> x 7.5<sup>W</sup> x 3.75<sup>H</sup>

Form No: 14737
No.Sold:

*One of the original three pieces introduced during the 1992 Holiday Season.*

**C.** 1999-01
Button

7<sup>RD</sup> x 3<sup>H</sup>

Form No: 12971
No.Sold:

*Retired after 8/01/01.*

**D.** 1996-00
Cake

12<sup>L</sup> x 12<sup>W</sup> x 6<sup>H</sup>

Form No: 11657
No.Sold:

*Retired after 8/31/00.*

**F.** 1994-01
Darning

10<sup>RD</sup> x 4<sup>H</sup>

Form No: 15539
No.Sold:

*Retired after 8/01/01.*

**G.** 1998-00
Pantry

14<sup>L</sup> x 9<sup>W</sup> x 4.5<sup>H</sup>

Form No: 13854
No.Sold:

*Retired after 8/31/00.*

**H.** 1995-99
Large Peg

6.5<sup>L</sup> x 6.5<sup>W</sup> x 8<sup>H</sup>

Form No: 11142
No. Sold:

*Retired after 2/28/99 along with its accessories.*

**K.** 1995-97 Spring

11<sup>L</sup> x 8<sup>W</sup> x 5.5<sup>H</sup>

Form No: 10936
No.Sold:

*Retired after 8/31/99.*

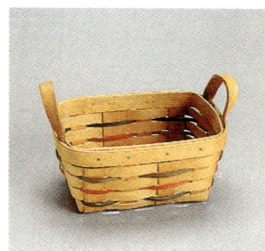

**L.** 1995-99 Tea

7<sup>L</sup> x 5<sup>W</sup> x 3.5<sup>H</sup>

Form No: 10710
No. Sold:

*Retired after 8/31/99.*

**M.** 1995-99
Small Vegetable

10.5<sup>L</sup> x 6.5<sup>W</sup> x 3<sup>FH</sup> x 7<sup>BH</sup>

Form No: 15016
No.Sold:

*Retired after 2/28/99.*

# *Spy...Longaberger!*

Have you noticed any of your favorite TV stars using Longaberger Products?  Well, keep watching because it might not be long until you do!

The Longaberger Company has been working very hard to get more of their product into the "secular" world.

Here is a list of just a few places where they've been seen:

### *Friends*, **Feb 2002**
Many items have debuted in this season.  Monica and Chandler received many items as wedding gifts and most recently Ross' girlfriend showed up at the door with a Larger Boardwalk Basket™.

### *The Rosie O'Donnell Show*, **March 2002**
Medium Berry Baskets™ holding a Cornflower Small Mixing Bowl were given to everyone in the audience during a show this past March.

### *Taste of Home* **Magazine, March/April 2002**
A two-page article featuring a kitchen remodel displayed a Barbeque Buddy Basket™.

### *Gilmore Girls*, **Feb 2002**
Several items have been sighted in this series, including the Large Picnic™, and a Whitewash Sewing Basket™.

### *Yes, Dear*, **Feb 2002**
A Large Picnic was also seen on this show as the family picnicked in a park.

Other special sightings have included the Oscars, the Emmys, the Blockbuster Awards, the NAACP Image Awards, and the LPGA tour.  Each basket given away has a postcard asking the recipient to send the card back to the basket-maker.

# Quick Find index

## How To Use:

This quick-reference index was designed to help collectors easily find information concerning their baskets.

The "Quick Find" is divided into six columns; **Basket, Collections (Year), Original Price, Market Value, Page in Guide, Form No., and Other Baskets Using Same Form.**

### Basket

Each basket is listed alphabetically by name, not by collection. For example, the *J.W. Corn®* basket is found under *'C'* for *Corn*, <u>not</u> *"J"* for the *J.W. Collection®*. If you want to see the baskets by collection, the front part of the Guide is what you should use. Also listed in this column are the basket's dimensions.

### Collections

This column lists all the different collections of which the basket has been a part. The number in parenthesis represents the year(s) that the basket was available. The letter 'P' in this parenthesis stands for 'Present' and means that the item is still available directly from the Company.

### Original Price

The price that the basket originally sold for is listed in this column. The values listed are for **Basket Only**, unless otherwise noted by the following letters: **C** (Combo), **L** (basket sold with liner), **P** (basket sold with protector), or **F** (full set).

### Market Price

Both the **Average and the High Market Values** are listed in this column. In addition, if a collection has ** listed, this indicates that the basket may have several different market values, usually dependent on the year it was produced. When this notation is used, you will need to go to its location in the Guide or Checklist to find its value. If this column has been left blank or has dashes, a market value has not been determined.

### Page in Guide

Refer to the listed page number or reference in order to obtain additional information on the basket or to find a picture of the basket. If "checklist" is noted, this item is still available directly in the Regular Line and can only be found in the checklist. If the page number is green in color, a picture is not featured in the Guide.

### Form No./Other Baskets Using Same Form

Listed is the basket's form number(s) and then a compilation of the different baskets made with this same form and the same dimensions. This information is very useful when trying to identify what basket you have or when looking for an accessory to fit a discontinued basket.

### Disclaimer

**All basket names listed in this index are trademarks registered and owned by The Longaberger Company® and J. Phillip Inc. has no interest therein.**

243

Quick Find

| Basket | Collection(Year) | Orig.Price | AVG | HIGH |
|---|---|---|---|---|
| **Acorn** | Shades of Autumn(91) | 24.95 | **109** | **125** |
| 7L x 5W x 3.5H | | | | |
| **Address** | Father's Day(96) | 29.95 | **42** | **80** |
| | Incentive (00-P) | 0.00 | **75** | **100** |
| | Regular Line(98-P) | 34.00 | **35** | **60** |
| | Regular Line, W.Wash(01-P) | 35.00 | **35** | **35** |
| 8.25L x 6.25W x 3.75H | | | | |
| **Advisor Recognition** | Incentive(86) | N/A | **164** | **178** |
| 14L x 9W x 4.5H | | | | |
| **All-Star Trio** | Feature(93) | 29.95 | **48** | **80** |
| 5.75L x 3.75W x 3H | | | | |
| **Ambrosia** | Booking(92-96) | 22.95 | **32** | **58** |
| | Employee Christmas(95) | N/A | **75** | **95** |
| 5.5L x 4W x 4H | | | | |
| **American Beauty** | Incentive(97) | N/A | **112** | **155** |
| 13.5L x 8.25W x 5.25H | | | | |
| **Apple** | J.W. Collection(85) | 45.95 | **572** | **750** |
| see **Large Fruit** | | | | |
| 13RD x 8.5H | | | | |
| **Apple, Miniature** | Collectors Club(98) | 139.95 | **148** | **210** |
| 5.25RD x 3.25H | | | | |
| **Associate Homestead Tour** | Incentive(00-P) | N/A | **—** | **—** |
| 13RD x 8.5H | | | | |
| **Associate Producer** | Incentive(96) | N/A | **128** | **130** |
| 5.5RD x 2.5H | | | | |

Quick Find

| Page in Guide | Form No. | Other Baskets Using Same Form |
|---|---|---|
| page 208 | 700-BGUBS | Basket of Thanks, Mini Berry, Mini Chore, Mistletoe, Mini Cradle, Baby Easter, 91 Hostess Easter, 93 Small Easter, 94 Employee Christmas, Kiddie Purse, Star Team, Small Key, Tea, Patriot |
| page 78<br>page 144<br>checklist<br>checklist | 12611<br>unknown<br>18546<br>10983 | None |
| page 140 | 2300- | 92 Bee, 90 Employee Christmas Small Gathering, Tray, Pantry |
| page 82 | 64408 | 89 Employee Birthday, Keepsake, Paint the Town, 90 Recruit, Shining Star, Rosemary, Sugar and Spice, 90 Sweetheart, Treasure Chest, 95 Horizon of Hope, 98 Hostess Appreciation, 00 Branch Sales, Salt & Pepper |
| page 32<br>page 74 | 10120<br>10120 | 97 Horizon of Hope, Thanks-A-Million, 01 Hostess Appreciation 01 Inaugural |
| page 152 | unknown | 94 Easter |
| page 156 | 3200-BT | Large Fruit |
| page 46 | 13749 | None |
| page 142 | unknown | Homestead |
| page 150 | unknown | None |

| Basket | Collection(Year) | Orig.Price | AVG | HIGH |
|---|---|---|---|---|
| **Back Porch** 13.25$^L$ x 9.5$^W$ x 3$^H$ | Good Ol' Summertime $^{(02)}$ | 59.00 | — | — |
| **Baker's Bounty** 10$^L$ x 6.25$^W$ x 3.75$^H$ | Shades of Autumn$^{(98)}$ | 39.00 | 53 | 75 |
| **Bakery** 14.5$^L$ x 7.5$^W$ x 3.75$^H$ | Feature$^{(87)}$ Heartland$^{(90-01)}$ | 19.95 30.95 | 48 42 | 50 55 |
| **Baking** 14.5$^L$ x 7.5$^W$ x 3.75$^H$ | Crisco® $^{(93)}$ | 39.95 | 105 | 120 |
| **Banker's Waste** 12.5$^{RD}$ x 13.5$^H$ | Hostess $^{(99-02)}$ J.W. Collection$^{(89)}$ | 119.00 59.95 | 119 277 | 128 385 |
| **Banker's Waste Miniature** 5.25$^{RD}$ x 5.25$^H$ | Collectors Club$^{(00-01)}$ | 150.00 | — | — |
| **Barbeque Buddy** 12$^L$ x 5.25$^W$ x 3$^H$ | Good Ol' Summertime$^{(00)}$ Retired $^{(01-02)}$ | 49.00 49.00 | 63 — | 90 — |
| **Barbeque Buddy Large** 12.5$^L$ x 6.25$^W$ x 7$^H$ | Retired$^{(01-02)}$ | 69.00 | — | — |
| **Barbeque Buddy Small** 7.5$^L$ x 3.75$^W$ x 2.75$^H$ | Retired$^{(01-02)}$ | 39.00 | — | — |
| **Barn Raising** 7$^{RD}$ x 6.5$^H$ | Special Event $^{(98)}$ | 59.95 C | 141 | 161 |
| **Basket Bin, Large** 16.5$^L$ x 12.5$^W$ x 5$^{FH}$ x 7.75$^{BH}$ | Regular Line$^{(00-P)}$ | 79.00 | 79 | 81 |
| **Basket Bin, Small** 12$^L$ x 11.75$^W$ x 3$^{FH}$ x 5.55$^{BH}$ | Regular Line$^{(00-P)}$ | 54.00 | 54 | 54 |
| **Basket O' Luck** 5.5$^{RD}$ x 3.75$^H$ | Feature$^{(90)}$ | N/A | 89 | 150 |

**KEY:**

**Values listed are for BASKET ONLY, unless otherwised noted.** **(-P)** = to present

| Page in Guide | Form No. | Other Baskets Using Same Form |
|---|---|---|
| page 104 | 12381 | None |
| page 208 | 11771 | None |
| page 88<br>page 108 | 4700-JO<br>14711 / 4700-JCS | Bread (new), Breakfast, Baking, Rose |
| page 60 | 14745 | Bakery, Bread (new), Breakfast, Rose |
| page 124<br>page 156 | 14761<br>1900-BBST | Master Employee, Waste (Small Round Inverted), Tree Trimming |
| page 48 | 16578 | None |
| page 104<br>page 194 | 16284<br>10801 | None |
| page 194 | 16381 | None |
| page 194 | 10702 | Shaker Taker |
| page 214 | 222806 | 7" Hanging, 7" Measuring, 90 Bee, 92 Sponsor (Lg), Maple Leaf, Poinsettia, 97 Perfect Attendance, Canister Set |
| checklist | 17850 | None |
| checklist | 17752 | None |
| page 82 | 17000-AGS | Laurel |

| Basket | Collection(Year) | Orig.Price | AVG | HIGH |
|--------|------------------|------------|-----|------|
| **Basket of Love** $8.5^{RD} \times 4^{H}$ | Mother's Day (95) | 37.95 | **45** | **75** |
| **Basket of Plenty** $12^{RD} \times 5.75^{H}$ | Shades of Autumn(95) | 53.95 | **70** | **118** |
| **Basket of Thanks** | Incentive(93) | N/A | **38** | **76** |
| $7^{L} \times 5^{W} \times 3.5^{H}$ | | | | |
| **Bayberry** $9^{L} \times 9^{W} \times 4.5^{H}$ | Christmas(93) | 42.95 | **65** | **90** |
| **Be Mine** $8.5^{L} \times 5^{W} \times 3.5^{H}$ | Sweetheart(94) | 27.95 | **66** | **90** |
| **Beachcomber** $10.5^{L} \times 9^{W} \times 8^{H}$ | Good Ol' Summertime(99) | 67.00 | **90** | **110** |
| **Bed** $11.5^{L} \times 5^{W} \times 3^{H}$ | Feature(89) | 18.95 | **85** | **105** |
| **Bee, Large** **1988** $14^{L} \times 7.75^{W} \times 5.25^{H}$ | Bee(88) | N/A | **145** | **165** |
| **Bee, Medium** **1988** $13^{L} \times 8^{W} \times 5^{H}$ | Bee(88) | N/A | **100** | **100** |
| **Bee** **1989** | Bee(89) | N/A | **145** | **180** |
| $8.75^{L} \times 4.75^{W} \times 6.5^{H}$ | | | | |
| **Bee** **1990** $7^{RD} \times 6.5^{H}$ | Bee(90) | 19.90 | **44** | **70** |
| **Bee** **1991** $8.5^{L} \times 8.5^{W} \times 5^{H}$ | Bee(91) | 19.91 | **56** | **80** |

| Page in Guide | Form No. | Other Baskets Using Same Form |
|---|---|---|
| page 168 | 18805 | Best Supporting Role, 98 Renewal |
| page 208 | 15563 | High Achiever, Quilting |
| page 142 | 700- | Acorn, Mini Berry, Mini Chore, Tea Mistletoe, Mini Cradle, Patriot, Baby Easter, 91 Hostess Easter, 93 Small Easter, 94 Employee Christmas, Kiddie Purse, Star Team, Small Key, 99 Branch Excellence |
| page 40 | 11584$^R$/11592$^G$ | 98 Large Easter |
| page 218 | 18601 | 92 Regional Sponsored Award, Small Oval, 93 Sponsor (Large), 97 Small Easter, Rose Petal |
| page 104 | 15342 | Weekender, Remembrance, Top Performer |
| page 90 | 4500-AO | Liberty, Cracker, Muffin, Herb, 96 Employee Christmas |
| page 26 | 3600-AO | Large Chore, 88 Large Easter |
| page 26 | 3500-AN | Medium Chore, 88 Medium Easter, 93 Bee |
| page 26 | 5600-BRST | Dresden, Tour, Hartville, Memory, 92 Employee Birthday, Sophomore – Senior Recognition, 20th Century, 25th Anniversary (Sm) |
| page 26 | 3900-AO | 7" Hanging, 7" Measuring, Barn Raising, Poinsettia, 92 Sponsor (Lg), Maple Leaf, 97 Perfect Attendance |
| page 26 | 1500- | Large Berry, 88-89 Sponsor, 96 Bee 98 Regional Sales Excellence |

**KEY:** In blue = Not pictured in the Guide. **S** = Stained, **U** = Unstained, **W** = Whitewash
**HL** = Heartland® Collection, **WT** = Woven Traditions®, **R** = Red, **G** = Green

| Basket | Collection(Year) | Orig.Price | AVG | HIGH |
|---|---|---|---|---|
| **Bee** <br> **1992** <br> $14^L$ x $9^W$ x $4.5^H$ | Bee$^{(92)}$ | 20.00 | **69** | **90** |
| **Bee** <br> **1993** <br> $13^L$ x $8^W$ x $5^H$ | Bee$^{(93)}$ | 25.00 | **100** | **125** |
| **Bee** <br> **1994** <br> $6.5^L$ x $6.5^W$ x $8^H$ | Bee$^{(94)}$ | 25.00 | **155** | **200** |
| **Bee** <br> **1995** <br> $10^L$ x $6^W$ x $4^H$ | Bee$^{(95)}$ | 25.00 | **55** | **75** |
| **Bee** <br> **1996** <br> $8.5^L$ x $8.5^W$ x $5^H$ | Bee$^{(96)}$ | 25.00 | **53** | **75** |
| **Bee** <br> **1997** <br> $5.5^L$ x $5.5^W$ x $6^H$ | Bee$^{(97)}$ | 27.95 | **57** | **100** |
| **Bee** <br> **1998** <br> $5.25^L$ x $5.25^W$ x $4^H$ | Bee$^{(98)}$ | 25.00 | **75** | **80** |
| **Bee** <br> **1999** <br> $7^L$ x $3^W$ x $4.75^H$ | Bee$^{(99)}$ | 29.00 | **81** | **100** |
| **Bee** <br> **2000** <br> $5.5^{RD}$ x $4^H$ | Bee$^{(00)}$ | 0.00 | **72** | **100** |
| **Bee** <br> **2001** <br> $7.5^L$ x $4.75^W$ x $2.5^H$ | Bee$^{(01)}$ | 0.00 | **53** | **85** |
| **Bee, Speaker** <br> **1988** <br> $15^L$ x $10^W$ x $7.5^H$ | Incentive$^{(88)}$ | N/A | — | — |

| Page in Guide | Form No. | Other Baskets Using Same Form |
|---|---|---|
| page 26 | 12335 | Advisor Recognition, Tray, Pantry 90 Employee Christmas, Small Gathering |
| page 26 | 13501 | Medium Chore, Medium Easter 88 Medium Bee |
| page 26 | unknown | Large Peg, Medium Spoon, 96 Sponsor, 98 Perfect Attendance |
| page 28 | unknown | 93 Lg Easter, 88 Sm Easter, Gingerbread, 91 Regional Sponsored, $500 Million, Small Chore, Woven Memories |
| page 28 | unknown | 91 Bee, 88-89 Sponsor, Large Berry 98 Regional Sales Excellence |
| page 28 | unknown | Bittersweet, Carry Along, Medium Peg, Small Spoon, 96 Sponsor, Shaker Peg |
| page 28 | unknown | None |
| page 28 | unknown | Tour II, 98 Flag Sponsoring, Hartville II |
| page 28 | unknown | None |
| page 28 | 10643 | Small Loaf |
| page 144 | 500- | 87 Employee Christmas, Heirloom, Medium Market, 77-87 Tenth Anniversary, 99 Team Excellence, Founder's |

| Basket | Collection(Year) | Orig.Price | AVG | HIGH |
|---|---|---|---|---|
| **Bee, Speaker**<br>**1990**<br>16$^L$ x 9$^W$ x 6$^H$ | Incentive$^{(90)}$ | N/A | 120 | 130 |
| **Bee, Speaker**<br>**1991-P**<br><br>11$^L$ x 8$^W$ x 5.5$^H$ | Incentive$^{(91-P)}$ | N/A | ** | ** |
| **Bell**<br>6.5$^{RD}$ x 7$^H$ | Christmas$^{(83)}$ | 22.95 | 598 | 850 |
| **Berry, Large**<br><br><br><br><br><br>8.5$^L$ x 8.5$^W$ x 5$^H$ | Feature (1st/h)$^{(85, 88)}$<br>Feature (Natrl)$^{(99)}$<br>J.W. Collection$^{(90)}$<br>Regular Line (1sw/h)$^{(79-P)}$<br>Retired (no/h) $^{(79-99)}$<br>Woven Traditions$^{(92-97)}$ | 18.95<br>28.00<br>48.95<br>10.95<br>8.95<br>30.95 | 68<br>42<br>214<br>38<br>34<br>40 | 85<br>43<br>290<br>60<br>51<br>55 |
| **Berry, Medium**<br><br><br><br><br>7.5$^L$ x 7.5$^W$ x 3.5$^H$ | All-American$^{(87)}$<br>Feature (1st/h)$^{(85, 88)}$<br>Feature $^{(96-97)}$<br>Regular Line (1sw/h)$^{(79-P)}$<br>Retired (no/h)$^{(79-99)}$ | 19.95<br>17.95<br>29.95<br>9.95<br>7.95 | 95<br>53<br>41<br>32<br>41 | 145<br>58<br>50<br>50<br>70 |
| **Berry, Mini**<br>(see Tea)<br>7$^L$ x 5$^W$ x 3.5$^H$ | | 7.95 | 47 | 85 |
| **Berry, Miniature**<br>3.5$^L$ x 3.5$^W$ x 3$^H$ | Collectors Club$^{(01-02)}$ | 85.00 | 85 | 100 |
| **Berry, Small**<br><br><br><br><br>6.5$^L$ x 6.5$^W$ x 3$^H$ | Employee Christmas$^{(98)}$<br>Feature(1st/h)$^{(85, 88)}$<br>Feature (Natrl)$^{(00)}$<br>Regular Line(1sw/h)$^{(79-P)}$<br>Retired (no/h)$^{(79-99)}$ | N/A<br>16.95<br>22.00<br>8.95<br>6.95 | 73<br>55<br>30<br>29<br>29 | 85<br>60<br>35<br>50<br>41 |
| **Best Supporting**<br>**Role**<br>8.5$^{RD}$ x 4$^H$ | Incentive $^{(96)}$ | N/A | 105 | 150 |
| **Bittersweet**<br>5.5$^L$ x 5.5$^W$ x 6$^H$ | Shades of Autumn$^{(92)}$ | 24.95 | 52 | 70 |

| Page in Guide | Form No. | Other Baskets Using Same Form |
|---|---|---|
| page 144 | 3700- | Harvest, Original Easter, Senior Employee |
| page 144 | 900- | Bob and Dolores Hope, Boo Basket, 91 Customer Easter, Medium Purse, Red Pottery Thank You, Spring, 96 Statehouse, 99 Perfect Attendance, Sparkler |
| page 38 | 4901-OO | None |
| page 88<br>page 92<br>page 156<br>checklist<br>page 194<br>page 240 | 1500-AO<br>19844<br>1500-BBST<br>11517/1500-BO<br>11509/ 1500-OO<br>11533 | 91 Bee, 88-89 Sponsor, 96 Bee, 98 Regional Sales Excellence |
| page 18<br>page 88<br>page 82<br>checklist<br>page 194 | 1400-ABRS<br>1400-AO<br>16241/25/33<br>11428/1400-AO<br>11410/1400-O | 95 Regional Sponsored |
| checklist | | Renamed Tea as of May 1, 1991 |
| page 50 | 10842 | None |
| page 74<br>page 88<br>page 94<br>checklist<br>page 194 | unknown<br>1300-AO<br>17841<br>11312/1300-AO<br>11304/1300-O | Spare Change, 98 Branch Excellence |
| page 152 | unknown | Basket of Love, 98 Renewal |
| page 208 | 10804 | Carry Along, Md Peg, Sm Spoon 97 Bee, Shaker Peg, 96 Sponsor |

| Basket | Collection(Year) | Orig.Price | AVG | HIGH |
|---|---|---|---|---|
| **Block Party**<br>20.5^L x 12.5^W x 11.5^H | All-American (02) | 178.00 | — | — |
| **Blue Ribbon Bread**<br>10.5^L x 8.75^W x 4^H | All-American (99) | 39.00 | 56 | 80 |
| **Boardwalk, Large**<br>17.75^L x 10.5^W x 12^H | Good Ol' Summertime(01) | 129.00 | — | — |
| **Boardwalk, Medium**<br>12.5^L x 6.75^W x 8.5^H | Good Ol' Summertime(01) | 89.00 | — | — |
| **Boardwalk, Small**<br><br>9.25^L x 5^W x 6.25^H | Employee Christmas(01)<br>Good Ol' Summertime(01) | N/A<br>59.00 | 98<br>65 | 100<br>100 |
| **Bob and**<br>   **Dolores Hope**<br><br>11^L x 8^W x 5.5^H | Special Events(89-96) | N/A | ** | ** |
| **Boo**<br><br><br>11^L x 8^W x 5.5^H | Feature(94) | 34.95 | 93 | 135 |
| **Book Keeper**<br>15^L x 16^W x 3.5^FH x 10.25^BH | Regular Line(00-P) | 109.00 | 109 | 109 |
| **Bountiful Harvest**<br>10.25^L x 10.25^W x 4.5^H | Shades of Autumn(97) | 44.95 | 53 | 84 |
| **Bouquet**<br>6.5^RD x 6.5^H | Sweetheart (96) | 34.95 | 45 | 65 |
| **Branch Basket**<br>15.75^L x 6.5^W x 11^H | Incentive(88-P) | N/A | 300 | 312 |
| **Branch Bouquet**<br>10.5^L x 6^W x 4^H | Incentive(97) | N/A | 61 | 129 |
| **Branch Excellence**<br>   **1998**<br>6.5^L x 6.5^W x 3^H | Incentive(98) | N/A | 44 | 75 |

| Page in Guide | Form No. | Other Baskets Using Same Form |
|---|---|---|
| page 22 | 12421 | None |
| page 20 | 14346 | None |
| page 104 | 10564 | None |
| page 104 | 10552 | None |
| page 74<br>page 104 | unknown<br>11393 | None |
| page 212 | 900- | 91-P Bee Speaker, Boo Basket, 91 Customer Easter, Medium Purse, Red Pottery Thank You, Spring, 96 Statehouse, 99 Perfect Attendance, Sparkler |
| page 82 | 10987 | 91-P Bee Speaker, Bob & Dolores Hope, 91 Customer Easter, Medium Purse, Red Pottery Thank You, Spring, 96 Statehouse, 99 Perfect Attendance, Sparkler |
| checklist | 10516 | None |
| page 208 | 12254 | None |
| page 218 | 11240 | Lilac |
| page 146 | unknown | Director Basket, Regional Basket |
| page 146 | unknown | None |
| page 146 | unknown | Small Berry, Spare Change |

| Basket | Collection(Year) | Orig.Price | AVG | HIGH |
|--------|------------------|-----------|-----|------|
| **Branch Excellence 1999**<br>$7^L$ x $5^W$ x $3.5^H$ | Incentive$^{(99)}$ | N/A | 56 | 60 |
| **Branch Sales 2000**<br>$5.75^L$ x $3.75^W$ x $3^H$ | Incentive$^{(00)}$ | N/A | 36 | 45 |
| **Branch Sales 2001**<br>$8^L$ x $7.75^W$ x $3.5^H$ | Incentive$^{(01)}$ | N/A | — | — |
| **Branch Sales 2002**<br>$5.75^L$ x $5.25^W$ x $6.25^H$ | Incentive$^{(02)}$ | N/A | — | — |
| **Branch Sponsoring, 1999**<br>$9.5^L$ x $6^W$ x $6^H$ | Incentive(99) | N/A | 92 | 100 |
| **Branch Sponsoring, 2000**<br>$7.75^L$ x $3.75^W$ x $4.5^H$ | Incentive(00) | N/A | 41 | 53 |
| **Branch Sponsoring, 2001**<br>$7.75^L$ x $3.75^W$ x $4.5^H$ | Incentive(01) | N/A | — | — |
| **Branch Sponsoring, 2002**<br>$5.25^L$ x $5.25^W$ x $4.5^H$ | Incentive(02) | N/A | — | — |
| **Bread (new)**<br>$14.5^L$ x $7.5^W$ x $3.75^H$ | Feature, WT(Natrl)$^{(00)}$ | 33.00 | — | — |
| | Incentive$^{(86)}$ | N/A | 145 | 175 |
| | Regular Line$^{(88-P)}$ | 20.95 | 36 | 60 |
| | Regular Line (WWash) $^{(01-P)}$ | 36.00 | 36 | 36 |
| | Retired (Natrl) $^{(99-01)}$ | 34.00 | 43 | 50 |
| | Woven Traditions$^{(92-01)}$ | 36.95 | 36 | 65 |
| **Bread (old)**<br>$15^L$ x $8^W$ x $2.25^H$ | Retired$^{(82-88)}$ | 11.95 | 38 | 53 |

**KEY:**
Values listed are for **BASKET ONLY, unless otherwised noted**, **(-P)** = to present

| Page in Guide | Form No. | Other Baskets Using Same Form |
|---|---|---|
| page 146 | unknown | Basket of Thanks, Mini Berry, Mini Chore, Mistletoe, Mini Cradle, Baby Easter, 91 Hostess Easter, 93 Small Easter, 94 Employee Christmas, Kiddie Purse, Star Team, Small Key, Tea, Patriot |
| page 146 | unknown | Rosemary, All-Star Trio, Keepsake, Sugar and Spice, 95 Horizon of Hope, 98 Hostess Appreciation, Treasure Chest, 90 Sweetheart, Paint the Town, Shining Star, 89 Employee Birthday, Salt & Pepper |
| page 146 | unknown | 8″ Generation |
| page 146 | unknown | None |
| page 146 | unknown | Small Purse, Season's Greetings, 94 Regional Sponsored |
| page 146 | unknown | None |
| page 146 | unknown | 7″ Generations |
| page 146 | unknown | None |
| page 94<br>page 140<br>checklist<br>checklist<br>page 194<br>page 240 | 18031<br>4700-AO<br>14702 / 4700-OO<br>10370<br>14974<br>14737 | Bakery, Breakfast, Crisco Baking, Rose |
| page 194 | 4600-OO | Holly, Garden |

| Basket | Collection(Year) | Orig.Price | AVG | HIGH |
|---|---|---|---|---|
| **Bread & Milk** | Feature[81] | unknown | 675 | 850 |
| | J.W. Collection[87] | 43.95 | 332 | 450 |
| 16L x 8W x 11H | J.W. Originals | N/A | ** | ** |
| **Bread & Milk** | Collectors Club[00] | 130.00 | 140 | 175 |
| **Miniature** | | | | |
| 6L x 3.25W x 4.5H | | | | |
| **Breakfast** | Feature[89] | 24.95 | 65 | 95 |
| 14.5L x 7.5W x 3.75H | | | | |
| **Business Card** | Father's Day[94] | 22.95 | 49 | 70 |
| | Incentive [99-P] | N/A | — | 75 |
| | Regular Line[97-P] | 22.95 | 28 | 50 |
| 4.75L x 3.75W x 2.25H | | | | |
| **Button** | Booking [xx-84] | 6.43 | 58 | 65 |
| | Employee Christmas[93] | N/A | 99 | 125 |
| | Heartland[94-01] | 22.95 | 33 | 43 |
| | Regular Line[84-P] | 24.95 | 27 | 45 |
| | Retired (Natrl) [99-01] | 27.00 | 27 | 50 |
| 7RD x 3H | Woven Traditions [99-01] | 33.00 | 35 | 50 |
| **Cake** | All-American[88] | 39.95 | 119 | 165 |
| | Employee [92] | N/A | — | 150 |
| | Employee Christmas[88] | N/A | 143 | 180 |
| | Feature[83-84] | 20.95 | — | — |
| | Feature(Natrl) [98] | 43.95 | — | — |
| | Heartland [99-00] | 62.00 | 65 | 79 |
| | J.W. Collection[92] | 55.95 | 117 | 225 |
| | J.W. Originals | N/A | ** | ** |
| | Regular Line (2sw/h)[85-P] | 26.95 | 56 | 100 |
| | Retired (1st/h)[79-94] | 15.95 | 52 | 90 |
| | Retired (Natrl)[94] | 46.95 | 62 | 105 |
| 12L x 12W x 6H | Woven Traditions [96-00] | 59.95 | 65 | 85 |
| **Cake, Miniature** | Collectors Club[02-03] | 125.00 | — | — |
| 4.75L x 4.75W x 2.5H | | | | |
| **Candle** | All-American[94] | 34.95 | 56 | 85 |
| | Booking[84-90] | N/A | 41 | 65 |
| | Christmas[81] | 14.95 | 895 | 1100 |
| | Employee Christmas[89] | N/A | 132 | 150 |
| 9L x 5W x 5H | Retired [99-02] | 36.00 | 41 | 75 |

| Page in Guide | Form No. | Other Baskets Using Same Form |
|---|---|---|
| page 86 | 2100- | Magazine, 25th Anniversary (Lg) |
| page 156 | 2100-ABT | |
| page 160 | N/A | |
| page 48 | 13391 | None |
| page 90 | 4700-AO | Bakery, Bread (new), Crisco Baking, Rose |
| page 78 | 17477 | Star Bound |
| page 142, 144 | 17361 | |
| checklist | 17361 | |
| page 32 | 5400-JO | Stitching, Cookie, Show Star, |
| page 74 | 5400- | Rings & Things, Frosty Jr., Nurses |
| page 108 | 15423 | Inaugural |
| checklist | 15407 | |
| page 194 | 19526 | |
| page 240 | 12971 | |
| page 18 | 100-GBRS | Crisco Pie, Oak Lid Picnic, |
| page 70 | 100- | Small Picnic |
| page 72 | 100- | |
| page 86 | 100-CO | |
| page 92 | 10481 | |
| page 108 | 15148 | |
| page 156 | 100-CBST | |
| page 160 | unknown | |
| checklist | 11011/100-GO | |
| page 194 | 11002/100-A | |
| page 194 | 16144 | |
| page 240 | 11657 | |
| not in this edition | 11474 | None |
| page 20 | 11134 | 90 Sponsor, Medium Key, 96 Perfect |
| page 32 | 1100-AO | Attendance, 89 Employee Christmas, |
| page 38 | 1100- | 97 Collectors Club Renewal |
| page 72 | 1100- | |
| page 194 | 19739 | |

**259**

| Basket | Collection(Year) | Orig.Price | AVG | HIGH |
|---|---|---|---|---|
| **Candy Cane** $5^L$ x $5^W$ x $4.5^H$ | Christmas(86) | 26.95 | **159** | **245** |
| **Candy Corn** $7.75^L$ x $4^W$ x $3.75^H$ | Feature(99) | 29.00 | **46** | **53** |
| **Canister Set** Set of 3 Baskets | Retired (79-80) | 39.95 | **246** | **351** set |
| **Card Keeper** $10.75^L$ x $9^W$ x $5^{FH}$ x $7^{BH}$ | Feature(01) | 54.00 | **58** | **90** |
| **Carry Along** $5.5^L$ x $5.5^W$ x $6^H$ | All-American(95) | 34.95 | **55** | **85** |
| **Casserole** $10.25^{RD}$ x $3.5^H$ | All-American(02) | 59.00 | — | — |
| **Catalog Caddy** $12^L$ x $6^W$ x $4.5^{FH}$ x $11.5^{BH}$ | Incentive(00-P) | 0.00 | — | — |
| **Catch-All, Large** $12^{RD}$ x $3.5^H$ | Regular Line(01-P) | 45.00 | **45** | **45** |
| **Catch-All, Medium** $9^{RD}$ x $3^H$ | Regular Line(01-P) | 37.00 | **37** | **37** |
| **Catch-All, Small** $7.25^{RD}$ x $2.25^H$ | Regular Line(00-P) Regular Line (W.Wash)(01-P) | 32.00 34.00 | **34** **34** | **78** **34** |
| **Century Celebration** $10.5^L$ x $6.25^W$ x $4.75^H$ | Collectors Club(00) | 59.00 | **75** | **80** |
| **Century Celebration** **Hostess Appreciation** $7.5^L$ x $4.5^W$ x $3.5^H$ | Feature(00) | 44.00 | **42** | **60** |
| **Checkerboard** $15^L$ x $15^W$ x $6^H$ | Father's Day(01) | 139.00 | **160** | **175** |
| **Cheers** $7.5^L$ x $4.5^W$ x $3.5^H$ | Feature(00) | 39.00 | **61** | **71** |
| **Cherished Memories** $14.25^L$ x $6.25^W$ x $9.5^H$ | Sweetheart (98) | 89.00 | **120** | **150** |

**KEY:**
**Values listed are for BASKET ONLY, unless otherwised noted, (-P)** = to present

| Page in Guide | Form No. | Other Baskets Using Same Form |
|---|---|---|
| page 38 | 14000-ART / AGT | 93 Inaugural, Violet, Small Peg, 96 Recruit, Teaspoon |
| page 84 | 14354 | None |
| page 194 | 4700 / 4800 / 4900-O | See Measuring (5", 7" and 9") |
| page 94 | 12195 | None |
| page 20 | 14656 | Bittersweet, Med Peg, Small Spoon 96 Sponsor, 97 Bee, Shaker Peg |
| page 22 | 12144 | None |
| page 144 | unknown | None |
| checklist | 15890 | None |
| checklist | 15792 | None |
| checklist | 15083 | None |
| checklist | 10382 | |
| page 48 | 15385 | None |
| page 86 | 13498 | Cheers |
| page 80 | 10036 | None |
| page 86 | 18945 | Century Celebration (Hostess) |
| page 218 | 17531$^R$ / 16268$^B$ 16365$^G$ / 16462$^P$ / 16560$^C$ | None |

| Basket | Collection(Year) | Orig.Price | AVG | HIGH |
|---|---|---|---|---|
| **Chives** | Booking [96-01] | 25.95 | **30** | **35** |
| $4^L$ x $4^W$ x $4^H$ | Employee Christmas(97) | N/A | **115** | **130** |
| **Chore, Large** | Feature[86] | 23.95 | **68** | **85** |
| $14^L$ x $7.75^W$ x $5.25^H$ | | | | |
| **Chore, Medium** | Easter[87] | 28.95 | **198** | **300** |
| | Feature[85-86] | 18.95 | **53** | **69** |
| | Heartland[88-97] | 36.95 | **47** | **85** |
| | Retired [86-02] | 18.95 | **49** | **65** |
| $13^L$ x $8^W$ x $5^H$ | | | | |
| **Chore, Mini** | Heartland[89-97] | 19.95 | **37** | **56** |
| | Mother's Day[89] | 21.95 | **93** | **100** |
| $7^L$ x $5^W$ x $3.5^H$ | | | | |
| **Chore, Small** | Feature [86] | 17.95 | **55** | **60** |
| | Heartland[89-97] | 22.95 | **43** | **65** |
| $10^L$ x $6^W$ x $4^H$ | | | | |
| **Christmas Sponsoring** | Incentive[97] | N/A | **123** | **250** |
| $10^L$ x $9.25^W$ x $6.5^H$ | | | | |
| **Community** | Traditions [96] | 84.95 | **84** | **125** |
| $14.75^L$ x $13.5^W$ x $6.25^H$ | | | | |
| **Cookie** | Christmas [85] | 24.95 | **151** | **300** |
| $7^{RD}$ x $3^H$ | | | | |
| **Cookie, Crisco** | Crisco® [92] | 29.95 | **93** | **175** |
| $10^{RD}$ x $4^H$ | | | | |
| **Corn** | Hostess[95-99] | 139.95 | **147** | **185** |
| | J.W. Collection[91] | 89.95 | **272** | **450** |
| | J.W. Originals | N/A | ** | ** |
| | Retired [79-94] | 29.95 | **95** | **200** |
| $17^{RD}$ x $11.5^H$ | | | | |
| **Corn, Miniature** | Collectors Club[01-02] | 185.00 | — | — |
| $7.75^{RD}$ x $4.25^H$ | | | | |
| **Coverlet** | Incentive [88] | N/A | — | — |
| $16^L$ x $16^W$ x $8^H$ | | | | |

| Page in Guide | Form No. | Other Baskets Using Same Form |
|---|---|---|
| page 32<br>page 74 | 15211<br>unknown | None |
| page 88 | 3600-CO | 88 Large Bee, 88 Large Easter,<br>Large Easter (Retired) |
| page 62<br>page 88<br>page 108<br>page 194 | 3500-CX<br>3500-CO<br>13528 / 3500-CCS<br>13510 / 3500-CO | 93 Bee, 88 Medium Easter,<br>88 Medium Bee, Med Easter (Retired) |
| page 108<br>page 168 | 10758 / 700-ACS<br>700-APS | Acorn, Basket of Thanks, Tea, Mini<br>Berry, Mistletoe, Mini Cradle, Baby<br>Easter, 91 Hostess Easter, 93 Small<br>Easter, 94 Employee Christmas,<br>Patriot, Kiddie Purse, Star Team,<br>Small Key, 99 Branch Excellence |
| page 88<br>page 108 | 3400-CO<br>13404 / 3400-ACS | 93 Lg Easter, 88 Sm Easter, 95 Bee<br>Gingerbread, 91 Regional Sponsored,<br>$500 Million, Woven Memories |
| page 132 | unknown | Snowflake (Small) |
| page 228 | 19119 | None |
| page 38 | 5400-AR / G | Stitching, Button, 93 Employee<br>Christmas, Rings & Things, Frosty Jr,<br>Nurses Inaugural |
| page 60 | 10081 | Daisy, Darning, 89 Easter, Frosty<br>96 Regional Sponsored |
| page 124<br>page 156<br>page 160<br>page 194 | 14443<br>4400-JBST<br>unknown<br>14401 / 4400-OO | None |
| page 50 | 11466 | None |
| page 138 | unknown | None |

| Basket | Collection(Year) | Orig.Price | AVG | HIGH |
|---|---|---|---|---|
| **Cracker** | Employee Christmas(96) | N/A | **65** | **95** |
| | Regular Line(82-P) | 9.95 | **25** | **50** |
| | Retired (Natrl) (94) | 20.95 | **39** | **55** |
| 11.5$^L$ x 5$^W$ x 3$^H$ | Woven Traditions (92-00) | 26.95 | **31** | **45** |
| **Cradle, Doll** | Feature (91) | 69.95 | **143** | **185** |
| | Hostess (86-90) | 44.95 | **183** | **240** |
| 19$^L$ x 12$^W$ x 6$^H$ | Retired (79-86) | 25.95 | **131** | **185** |
| **Cradle, Large** | Hostess(86-90) | 109.95 | **362** | **465** |
| **(Infant)** | Retired(79-86) | 39.95 | **323** | **500** |
| 30$^L$ x 20$^W$ x 10.5$^H$ | | | | |
| **Cradle, Medium** | Retired(79-83) | 37.95 | **—** | **200** |
| 28.5$^L$ x 17.75$^W$ x 9.75$^H$ | | | | |
| **Cradle, Mini** | Retired(79-93) | 9.95 | **66** | **160** |
| 7$^L$ x 5$^W$ x 3.5$^H$ | | | | |
| **Cradle, Small** | Retired(79-80) | 35.95 | **—** | **105** |
| 24$^L$ x 17$^W$ x 10$^H$ | | | | |
| **Craft Keeper** | Regular Line, HC (02-P) | 169.00 | **169** | **169** |
| 18$^L$ x 13.75$^W$ x 9.25$^H$ | | | | |
| **Cranberry** | Christmas(95) | 47.95 | **56** | **90** |
| 8.5$^L$ x 8.5$^W$ x 7$^H$ | | | | |
| **Daddy's Caddy** | Father's Day (02) | 49.00 | **—** | **—** |
| 8$^L$ x 7.75$^W$ x 7$^H$ | | | | |
| **Daily Blessings** | Autumn Reflections (01) | 49.00 | **69** | **89** |
| **Large** | | | | |
| 12.75$^L$ x 9.75$^W$ x 5.25$^H$ | | | | |
| **Daily Blessings** | Autumn Reflections (01) | 39.00 | **52** | **60** |
| **Small** | | | | |
| 10$^L$ x 7.25$^W$ x 3.75$^H$ | | | | |
| **Daisy (new)** | May (99) | 39.00 | **67** | **85** |
| 6.75$^{RD}$ x 6$^H$ | | | | |

| Page in Guide | Form No. | Other Baskets Using Same Form |
|---|---|---|
| page 74 checklist page 194 page 240 | 4500- 14508 /4500-OO 17198 14532 | Liberty, Bed, Muffin, Herb |
| page 90 page 124 page 196 | 2500-LO 2500-LO 2500-LO | Large Gathering |
| page 124 page 196 | 2800-M 2800-MO | Large Laundry |
| page 196 | 2700-M | Medium Laundry |
| page 176 | 10715/700-K | Acorn, Basket of Thanks, Tea, Mini Berry, Mini Chore, Mistletoe, Baby Easter, 91 Hostess Easter, 93 Small Easter, 94 Employee Christmas, Kiddie Purse, Star Team, Small Key, Patriot, 99 Branch Excellence |
| page 196 | 2600-M | Small Laundry, Family Picnic |
| checklist, Hostess | 12535 | None |
| page 40 | 19500$^R$ / 19518$^G$ | None |
| page 80 | 11854 | None |
| page 24 | 10656 | None |
| page 24 | 11404 | None |
| page 164 | 13056 | Golf |

**KEY:** In blue = Not pictured in the Guide. **S** = Stained, **U** = Unstained, **W** = Whitewash
**HL** = Heartland® Collection, **WT** = Woven Traditions®, **R** = Red, **G** = Green

| Basket | Collection(Year) | Orig.Price | AVG | HIGH |
|---|---|---|---|---|
| **Daisy**<br>10$^{RD}$ x 4$^H$ | Feature(Stained) (86, 87)<br>Feature(Natrl) (86) | 25.95<br>27.95 | **62**<br>**63** | **85**<br>**70** |
| **Darning**<br><br><br><br><br>10$^{RD}$ x 4$^H$ | Feature (Natrl) (99)<br>Heartland (96-01)<br>Regular Line (83-P)<br>Retired(Natrl)(94)<br>Woven Traditions (94-01) | 31.00<br>39.95<br>15.95<br>30.95<br>39.95 | —<br>**44**<br>38<br>**64**<br>40 | —<br>**70**<br>55<br>**110**<br>55 |
| **Dash Away Sleigh**<br>7.75$^L$ x 4.5$^W$ x 2.25$^{FH}$ x 4.5$^{BH}$ | Feature (98-99) | 36.00 | 50 | 84 |
| **Deck the Halls**<br>8.5$^L$ x 8.5$^W$ x 6$^H$ | Christmas(00) | 64.00 | 67 | 80 |
| **Director Basket**<br>15.75$^L$ x 6.5$^W$ x 11$^H$ | Incentive (88-P) | N/A | 107 | 146 |
| **Director Sales**<br>**Excellence 1998**<br>12$^L$ x 12$^W$ x 4$^H$ | Incentive(98) | N/A | 90 | 125 |
| **Director Sales**<br>**Excellence 1999**<br>16$^L$ x 11$^W$ x 9$^H$ | Incentive(99) | N/A | — | — |
| **Director Sponsoring**<br>**Excellence 1998**<br>12$^L$ x 12$^W$ x 4$^H$ | Incentive (Natrl) (98) | N/A | 108 | 130 |
| **Director Sponsoring**<br>**Excellence 1999**<br>16$^L$ x 11$^W$ x 9$^H$ | Incentive (Natrl) (99) | N/A | — | — |
| **Director Sponsored**<br>**2000**<br>14.5$^L$ x 5.5$^W$ x 9.5$^H$ | Incentive(00) | N/A | — | — |
| **Directorship**<br>**Award (02)**<br>8$^L$ x 7.5$^W$ x 10.5$^H$ | Incentive (02) | N/A | — | — |
| **Directorship**<br>**Leadership**<br>14$^L$ x 12.75$^W$ x 5$^H$ | Incentive (01) | N/A | — | — |

| Page in Guide | Form No. | Other Baskets Using Same Form |
|---|---|---|
| page 88 | 5500-AO | Crisco Cookie, Darning, 89 Easter |
| page 88 | 5500-AN | 96 Regional Sponsored, Frosty |
| page 92 | 19640 | Crisco Cookie, Daisy (Feature), |
| page 108 | 15598 | 96 Regional Sponsored, 89 Easter, |
| checklist | 15504 / 500-JO | Frosty |
| page 196 | 15521 | |
| page 240 | 15539 | |
| page 84 | 13943 | Summertime |
| page 42 | 17639$^R$ / 17736$^G$ | None |
| page 136 | unknown | Branch Basket, Regional Basket |
| page 152 | unknown | Pie, Director Sponsoring Excellence |
| page 152 | unknown | Large Market, Rectangular Sewing 99 Director Sponsoring Excellence |
| page 152 | unknown | Pie, Director Sales Excellence |
| page 152 | unknown | Large Market, Rectangular Sewing 99 Director Sales Excellence |
| page 152 | unknown | None |
| page 154 | unknown | None |
| page 154 | unknown | 14" Generations |

**KEY:** In blue = Not pictured in the Guide. **S** = Stained, **U** = Unstained, **W** = Whitewash
**HL** = Heartland® Collection, **WT** = Woven Traditions®, **R** = Red, **G** = Green   **267**

| Basket | Collection(Year) | Orig.Price | AVG | HIGH |
|---|---|---|---|---|
| **Directorship Team 2001** $12^L$ x $11^W$ x $4.5^H$ | Incentive(01) | N/A | — | — |
| **Directorship Team 2002** $6.5^L$ x $6.5^W$ x $8.5^H$ | Incentive(02) | N/A | — | — |
| **Discovery** $5.5^{RD}$ x $3.5^H$ | Special Event (92) | 19.92 | 62 | 100 |
| **Diskette** $6^L$ x $6^w$ x $4.25^{FH}$ x $5.25^{BH}$ | Incentive (00-P) | 0.00 | 54 | 57 |
| **Dresden Basket** see also **Tour** $8.75^L$ x $4.75^W$ x $6.5^H$ | Tour (88-P) | | ** | ** |
| **Dresden Basket II** see also **Tour II** $7^L$ x $3.5^W$ x $4.75^H$ | Tour (96-99) | 29.95 | 66 | 70 |
| **Early Blossoms** $11^L$ x $7.25^W$ x $2.75^H$ | Mother's Day (00) | 45.00 | 57 | 82 |
| **Easter (1989)** $10^{RD}$ x $4^H$ | Easter (89) | 29.95 | ** | ** |
| **Easter (1992)** $10.5^L$ x $7.5^W$ x $4.5^H$ | Easter (92) | 27.95 | 50 | 75 |
| **Easter (1994)** $13.5^L$ x $8.25^W$ x $5.25^H$ | Easter (94) | 49.95 | 51 | 75 |
| **Easter (1995)** $10.75^L$ x $8.75^W$ x $5.25^H$ | Easter (95) | 49.95 | 55 | 80 |
| **Easter (1996)** $7.5^L$ x $5^W$ x $6^H$ | Easter (96) | 39.95 | 60 | 83 |
| **Easter, Baby** | Easter (88) | 18.95 | 74 | 117 |
| | Retired(1st/h) (79-87) | 8.95 | 52 | 82 |
| | Retired(1sw/h) (79-87) | 9.95 | 56 | 85 |

$7^L$ x $5^W$ x $3.5^H$

| Page in Guide | Form No. | Other Baskets Using Same Form |
|---|---|---|
| page 154 | unknown | 12" Generations |
| page 154 | unknown | None |
| page 214 | 5700-AO | None |
| page 144 | unknown | Finder's Keepers |
| page 224 | 100114/5600- | 89 Bee, 92 Employee Birthday, Sophomore - Senior Recognition, Tour, Memory, 25th Anniversary (Sm), Hartville, 20th Century |
| page 224 | unknown | Tour II |
| page 170 | 19682 | None |
| page 62 | 5500-ABS/AO/APS | Crisco Cookie, Daisy, Darning 96 Regional Sponsored, Frosty |
| page 64 | 34000-APVCNK | None |
| page 64 | 16926$^S$/34$^U$/00/18 | American Beauty |
| page 64 | 18708 | None |
| page 64 | 12912$^S$/12939$^U$ | None |
| page 62<br>page 196<br>page 196 | 700-AN<br>700-AO<br>700-BO | Acorn, Basket of Thanks, Tea, Mini Berry, Mini Chore, Mistletoe,  Small Key, Mini Cradle, 91 Hostess Easter, 93 Small Easter, Kiddie Purse, Patriot, 94 Employee Christmas, Star Team, 99 Branch Excellence |

**KEY:** In blue = Not pictured in the Guide.  **S** = Stained, **U** = Unstained, **W** = Whitewash
**HL** = Heartland® Collection, **WT** = Woven Traditions®, **R** = Red, **G** = Green

## Quick Find Index

| Basket | Collection(Year) | Orig.Price | AVG | HIGH |
|---|---|---|---|---|
| **Easter, Customer (1991)** | Easter (91) | 26.95 | **36** | **60** |
| $11^L \times 8^W \times 5.5^H$ | | | | |
| **Easter, Hostess (1991)** | Easter (91) | 21.95 | **35** | **70** |
| $7^L \times 5^W \times 3.5^H$ | | | | |
| **Easter, Large** | Easter (88) | 32.95 | **87** | **110** |
| | Retired(1st/h) (79-87) | 11.95 | **52** | **80** |
| | Retired(1sw/h) (79-87) | 12.95 | **58** | **93** |
| $14^L \times 7.75^W \times 5.25^H$ | | | | |
| **Easter, Large (1990)** $9.5^{RD} \times 5^H$ | Easter (90) | 43.95 | **63** | **110** |
| **Easter, Large (1993)** $10^L \times 6^W \times 4^H$ | Easter (93) | 27.95 | **60** | **80** |
| **Easter, Large (1997)** $12^L \times 7^W \times 4.5^H$ | Easter (97) | 42.95 | **55** | **60** |
| **Easter, Large (1998)** $9^L \times 9^W \times 4.5^H$ | Easter (98) | 43.95 | — | — |
| **Easter, Large (1999)** $7.5^L \times 7.5^W \times 3.75^H$ | Easter (99) | 39.00 | **50** | **60** |
| **Easter, Large (2000)** $12.5^{RD} \times 6^H$ | Easter (00) | 65.00 | **70** | **85** |
| **Easter, Large (2001)** $12.75^{RD} \times 4^H$ | Easter (01) | 65.00 | **84** | **95** |
| **Easter, Large (2002)** $12.5^L \times 10.25^W \times 4.25^H$ | Easter (02) | 69.00 | — | — |

| Page in Guide | Form No. | Other Baskets Using Same Form |
|---|---|---|
| page 64 | 900-ATMS / ATMN | 91-P Bee Speaker, Bob & Dolores Hope Boo Basket, Medium Purse, Red Pottery Thank You, Spring, 96 Statehouse, 99 Perfect Attendance, Sparkler |
| page 64 | 700-ATMS / ATMN | Acorn, Basket of Thanks, Tea, Mini Berry, Mini Chore, Mistletoe, Mini Cradle, Baby Easter, 93 Small Easter, Patriot, 94 Employee Christmas, Kiddie Purse, Star Team, Small Key, 99 Branch Excellence |
| page 62 <br> page 196 <br> page 196 | 3600-AN <br> 3600-AO <br> 3600-BO | 88 Large Bee, Large Chore |
| page 62 | 41000-APVBS | Petunia |
| page 64 | 13439$^S$/13412$^U$ | Gingerbread, Small Chore, 88 Small Easter, 91 Regional Sponsored, 95 Bee, $500 Million, Woven Memories |
| page 64 | 13447$^S$/13455$^U$ | Rose Garden |
| page 64 | 11851$^S$/11860$^U$ | Bayberry |
| page 66 | 14061$^S$ / 14265$^U$ | None |
| page 66 | 19283$^S$ / 19186$^U$ | None |
| page 66 | 10915$^S$ / 11016$^U$ | None |
| page 66 | 12233$^S$ / 12411$^W$ | None |

| Basket | Collection(Year) | Orig.Price | AVG | HIGH |
|---|---|---|---|---|
| **Easter, Medium** | Easter (88) | 28.95 | 84 | 105 |
| | Retired(1st/h) (79-87) | 10.95 | 73 | 95 |
| 13L x 8W x 5H | Retired(1sw/h) (79-87) | 11.95 | 50 | 75 |
| **Easter, Medium** **(1990)** 8RD x 4.5H | Easter (90) | 38.95 | 55 | 100 |
| **Easter, Small** | Easter (88) | 22.95 | 68 | 90 |
| | Retired(1st/h) (79-87) | 9.95 | 64 | 95 |
| 10L x 6W x 4H | Retired(1sw/h) (79-87) | 10.95 | 60 | 75 |
| **Easter, Small** **(1993)** 7L x 5W x 3.5H | Easter (93) | 24.95 | 44 | 60 |
| **Easter, Small** **(1997)** 8.5L x 5W x 3.5H | Easter (97) | 29.95C | 41 | 65 C |
| **Easter, Small** **(1998)** 6L x 6W x 3H | Easter (98) | 32.95 | 45 | 55 |
| **Easter, Small** **(1999)** 5.75L x 5.75W x 3H | Easter (99) | 33.00 | 50 | 60 |
| **Easter, Small** **(2001)** 6RD x 2.75H | Easter (01) | 35.00 | 47 | 66 |
| **Easter, Small** **(2002)** 7.75L x 6.25W x 2.75H | Easter (02) | 44.00 | — | — |
| **8 x 8 Basket** 9.5L x 9.5W x 2.75H | Retired (99-02) | 37.00 | 44 | 59 |
| **Envelope** 12L x 5.25W x 3.75FH x 5BH | Regular Line(99-P) | 43.00 | 44 | 55 |
| **Evergreen** 15.5L x 15.5W x 12.25H | Holiday Hostess (95) | 139.95 | 148 | 215 |

**KEY:**
**272** **Values listed are for BASKET ONLY, unless otherwised noted, (-P) = to present**

| Page in Guide | Form No. | Other Baskets Using Same Form |
|---|---|---|
| page 62<br>page 196<br>page 196 | 3500-AN<br>3500-AO<br>3500-BO | 93 Bee, Medium Chore, 88 Md Bee |
| page 62 | 40000-APVBS | None |
| page 62<br>page 196<br>page 196 | 3400-AN<br>3400-AO<br>3400-BO | Gingerbread, Small Chore, 95 Bee<br>93 Lg Easter, 91 Regional Sponsored<br>$500 Million, Woven Memories |
| page 64 | 10774$^S$/10766$^U$ | Acorn, Basket of Thanks, Tea, Mini Berry, Mini Chore, Mistletoe, Mini Cradle, Baby Easter, Patriot, 91 Hostess Easter, 94 Employee Christmas, Kiddie Purse, Star Team, Small Key, 99 Branch Excellence |
| page 64 | 63541$^S$/63550$^U$ | Be Mine, 93 Sponsor (All-Star), 92 Regional Sponsored Award, Small Oval, Rose Petal |
| page 64 | 11959$^S$/11967$^U$ | None |
| page 66 | 14052$^S$/14168$^U$ | None |
| page 66 | 10023$^S$/10125$^U$ | None |
| page 66 | 12093/12111<br>12101/12123 | None |
| page 196 | 15393 | Picnic Pal |
| checklist | 14311 | Picnic Pal |
| page 116 | 19607$^R$/19615$^G$ | None |

| Basket | Collection(Year) | Orig.Price | AVG | HIGH |
|---|---|---|---|---|
| **Everything's Coming Up Roses (small)**<br>see **Rose Bud** | | | | |
| **Everything's Coming Up Roses (medium)**<br>see **Rose Petal** | | | | |
| **Everything's Coming Up Roses (large)**<br>see **American Beauty** | | | | |
| **Family**<br>15.25$^L$ x 11$^W$ x 7.75$^H$ | Traditions [95] | 89.95 | 96 | 180 |
| **Fellowship**<br>12.5$^L$ x 6.5$^W$ x 7.75$^H$ | Traditions [97] | 69.95 | 90 | 115 |
| **File**<br>20$^L$ x 17.5$^W$ x 12.5$^H$ | Regular Line, Hostess[99-P] | 189.00 | 199 | 248 |
| **Finders' Keepers**<br>6$^L$ x 6$^W$ x 4.25$^{FH}$ x 5.25$^{BH}$ | Father's Day[97] | 34.00 | 48 | 65 |
| **$500 Million**<br>10$^L$ x 6$^W$ x 4$^H$ | Incentive [97] | N/A | 230 | 275 |
| **5-Yr Anniversary**<br><br>6$^L$ x 5$^W$ x 8.25$^H$ | Collectors Club, Charter[01]<br>Collectors Club[02-P] | 99.00<br>99.00 | —<br>— | —<br>— |
| **Flag**<br>10.75$^L$ x 5.75$^W$ x 7.5$^H$ | Incentive [89] | N/A | — | — |
| **Flag Recruit**<br>7$^L$ x 3.5$^W$ x 4.75$^H$ | Incentive [98] | N/A | 192 | 200 |
| **Flag Sponsoring**<br>7$^L$ x 3.5$^W$ x 4.75$^H$ | Incentive [98] | N/A | 213 | 225 |
| **Flower Pot Basket**<br>17$^L$ x 7.5$^W$ x 4.75$^H$ | Retired [95-98] | 47.95 | 52 | 125 |
| **Flower Pot Basket, Small**<br>14$^L$ x 6$^W$ x 3$^H$ | Retired [96-01] | 34.95 | 35 | 50 |

KEY:
**Values listed are for BASKET ONLY, unless otherwised noted, (-P)** = to present

| Page in Guide | Form No. | Other Baskets Using Same Form |
|---|---|---|
| page 152 | unknown | 93 Recruit, 93 Sponsor (Small), Lavender, 94 Hostess Appreciation |
| page 152 | unknown | Small Oval, Be Mine, 93 Sponsor (All-Star), 92 Regional Sponsored Award, 97 Small Easter |
| page 152 | unknown | 94 Easter |
| page 228 | 19101 | None |
| page 228 | 15920 | None |
| checklist, Hostess | 12769 | None |
| page 78 | 12777 | Diskette |
| page 142 | 900- | Gingerbread, 95 Bee, 93 Lg Easter, 88 Sm Easter, 91 Regional Sponsored, Small Chore, Woven Memories |
| page 50 page 44 | 17345 12020 | None |
| page 138 | unknown | None |
| page 132 | unknown | Tour II, Hartville II |
| page 132 | unknown | Tour II, Hartville II |
| page 196 | 16306 | None |
| page 196 | 18414 | Personal Organizer |

| Basket | Collection(Year) | Orig.Price | AVG | HIGH |
|--------|------------------|------------|-----|------|
| **Forever Yours** | Sweetheart (94) | 109.95 | **158** | **200** |
| 20.5$^L$ x 15$^W$ x 10.5$^H$ | | | | |
| **Forget-Me-Not** | Booking(86-87) | N/A | **52** | **74** |
| 5$^{RD}$ x 4.5$^H$ | | | | |
| **Founder's** | Feature (00) | 189.00 | **200** | **250** |
| 15$^L$ x 10$^W$ x 7.5$^H$ | | | | |
| **Friendship** 5.5$^L$ x 5.5$^W$ x 2.5$^H$ | Feature (89) | 21.95 | **48** | **60** |
| **Frosty** 10$^{RD}$ x 4$^H$ | Feature (00) | 43.00 | **47** | **54** |
| **Frosty, Jr.** | Feature (00) | 33.00 | **35** | **52** |
| 7$^{RD}$ x 3$^H$ | | | | |
| **Fruit, Large** **(Apple)** | Holiday Hostess (89) | 49.95 | **90** | **140** |
| | Incentive, Recruit (88) | N/A | — | — |
| | Incentive, N.Sales (93) | N/A | — | — |
| | Regular Line (79-P) | 18.95 | **68** | **100** |
| 13$^{RD}$ x 8.5$^H$ | Retired, hanging (79-80) | 21.95 | **100** | **140** |
| **Fruit, Medium** | Incentive, Recruit (88) | N/A | — | **165** |
| | Incentive, N.Sales (93) | N/A | — | **135** |
| | Regular Line (79-P) | 12.95 | **37** | **65** |
| 8$^{RD}$ x 6.5$^H$ | Retired, hanging (79-80) | 15.95 | **50** | **50** |
| **Fruit, Small** | Feature(00) (Natrl) | 25.00 | **37** | **39** |
| | Incentive, Recruit (88) | N/A | — | **140** |
| | Incentive, N.Sales (93) | N/A | — | **190** |
| | Regular Line (79-P) | 9.95 | **31** | **55** |
| 6.5$^{RD}$ x 5$^H$ | Retired, hanging (79-80) | 11.95 | **77** | **125** |
| **Fruit, Tall** | Retired, hanging (79-80) | 18.95 | — | — |
| 8$^{RD}$ x 9$^H$ | Retired (79-95) | 15.95 | **68** | **110** |

**KEY:**
**276** **Values listed are for BASKET ONLY, unless otherwised noted, (-P) = to present**

| Page in Guide | Form No. | Other Baskets Using Same Form |
|---|---|---|
| page 218 | 10367 | Gift Giving |
| page 32 | 3800-AO | 89 Inaugural, 88 Employee Birthday, 5" Hanging, 92 Sponsor (Small), 92 Employee Christmas, Resolution, 5" Measuring, 92 Recruit, Watch Your Business Bloom, 5" Canister, 99 Recruit |
| page 94 | 500- | Medium Market, 87 Employee Christmas, Heirloom, 77-87 Tenth Anniversary, 99 Team Excellence, 88 Bee Speaker |
| page 90 | 13100-JO | 91 Employee Birthday, Ivy, 96 Hostess Appreciation, Tarragon |
| page 86 | 10242 | Darning, Crisco Cookie, 89 Easter, Daisy (Feature), 96 RegSponsored |
| page 86 | 10230 | Button, Stitching, Cookie, ShowStar Rings & Things, 93 EmployChristmas Nurses Inaugural |
| page 114<br>page 130<br>page 138<br>checklist<br>page 196 | 3200-BGRS<br>3200-BO<br>3200-<br>13200/3200-BO<br>3200-P | Apple |
| page 130<br>page 138<br>checklist<br>page 196 | 3100-BO<br>3100-<br>13102/3100-BO<br>3100-P | Master Employee2 (97-P) |
| page 94<br>page 130<br>page 138<br>checklist<br>page 196 | 17671<br>3000-BO<br>3000-<br>13005/3000-BO<br>3000-P | 94 Perfect Attendance, Senior Employee2 |
| page 196<br>page 196 | 3300-P<br>13307/3300-BO | None |

| Basket | Collection(Year) | Orig.Price | AVG | HIGH |
|---|---|---|---|---|
| **Garden** 15L x 8W x 2.25H | Feature (86) | N/A | 78 | 85 |
| | Incentive (88) | N/A | 80 | 80 |
| **Gatehouse, Extra Small** 3.75RD x 3.75H | Regular Line (01-P) | 29.00 | 29 | 29 |
| **Gatehouse, Large** 6.5RD x 10.5H | Regular Line (01-P) | 59.00 | 59 | 59 |
| **Gatehouse, Small** 4.75RD x 7.5H | Regular Line (01-P) | 39.00 | 39 | 39 |
| **Gathering Event** 12L x 6.75W x 3.5W | Collectors Club(01-02) | 55.00 | — | — |
| **Gathering, Large** | Holiday Hostess (90) | 65.95 | 95 | 125 |
| | Hostess(96-99) | 89.95 | 103 | 120 |
| | Incentive, N.Sponsor (93-98) | N/A | ** | ** |
| | Retired(1st/h) (83-93) | 26.95 | 89 | 125 |
| 19L x 12W x 6H | Retired(2sw/h) (79-94) | 19.95 | 71 | 130 |
| **Gathering, Medium** | Feature (Natrl) (87) | 41.95 | 70 | 85 |
| | Holiday Hostess (89) | 40.95 | 104 | 135 |
| | Incentive, N.Sponsor (93-98) | N/A | ** | ** |
| | J.W. Collection (88) | 36.95 | 280 | 425 |
| | J.W. Original | N/A | ** | ** |
| | Regular Line(2sw/h) (79-P) | 17.95 | 64 | 100 |
| 18L x 11W x 4.5H | Retired(1st/h) (80-93) | 41.95 | 83 | 120 |
| **Gathering, Mini** 7L x 4.5W x 2H | Collectors Club(00-01) | 130.00 | 137 | 164 |
| **Gathering, Small** | Easter (87) | 28.95 | 172 | 225 |
| | Employee Christmas(90) | N/A | 110 | 140 |
| | Feature (Natrl)(98-00) | 39.95 | 65 | 100 |
| | Incentive, N.Sponsor (93-98) | N/A | ** | ** |
| | Regular Line(2sw/h) (79-P) | 15.95 | 50 | 85 |
| | Regular Line(WWash) (01-P) | 54.00 | 54 | 54 |
| | Retired(1st/h) (86-93) | 22.95 | 103 | 120 |
| 14L x 9W x 4.5H | Shades of Autumn(91) | 36.95 | 138 | 185 |

| Page in Guide | Form No. | Other Baskets Using Same Form |
|---|---|---|
| page 88 | 4600-AO | Bread (old), Holly |
| page 140 | 4600- | |
| checklist | 12433 | None |
| checklist | 11763 | None |
| checklist | 11751 | None |
| page 50 | 11222 | None |
| page 114 | 2500-CGRS | Doll Cradle |
| page 124 | 12564 | |
| page 132 | 2500- | |
| page 198 | 12505/2500-A | |
| page 198 | 12513/2500-CO | |
| page 90 | 2400-C | Gourmet Gathering |
| page 114 | 2400-AGRS | |
| page 132 | 2400- | |
| page 156 | 2400-ABT | |
| page 160 | unknown | |
| checklist | 12416/2400-CO | |
| page 198 | 12408/2400-AO | |
| page 48 | 18941 | None |
| page 62 | 2300-AX | Advisor Recognition, 92 Bee, Tray, |
| page 72 | 2300- | Pantry, 90 Employee Christmas |
| page 92 | 12572 | |
| page 132 | 2300- | |
| checklist | 12319/2300-CO | |
| checklist | 11052 | |
| page 198 | 12301/2300-AO | |
| page 208 | 2300-CGUBS | |

| Basket | Collection(Year) | Orig.Price | AVG | HIGH |
|---|---|---|---|---|
| **Gathering, XLarge** $23^L$ x $15^W$ x $8^H$ | Incentive$^{(96-98)}$ | N/A | ** | ** |
| **Generations, 7"** $7^L$ x $6.75^W$ x $3^H$ | Regular Line $^{(98-P)}$ | 28.95 | 29 | 55 |
| **Generations, 8"** $8^L$ x $7.75^W$ x $3.5^H$ | Regular Line $^{(98-P)}$ | 35.00 | 36 | 65 |
| **Generations, 10"** $10^L$ x $9.25^W$ x $4^H$ | Regular Line $^{(98-P)}$ | 38.95 | 39 | 55 |
| **Generations, 12"** $12^L$ x $11^W$ x $4.5^H$ | Regular Line $^{(98-P)}$ | 54.00 | 56 | 75 |
| **Generations, 14"** $14^L$ x $12.75^W$ x $5^H$ | Regular Line $^{(98-P)}$ | 57.95 | 59 | 85 |
| **Generosity** $19.25^L$ x $13.5^W$ x $7.75^H$ | Traditions $^{(99)}$ | 119.00 | 112 | 170 |
| **Geranium** $10.25^L$ x $6.25^W$ x $7.5^H$ | May $^{(02)}$ | 49.00 | — | — |
| **Getaway** $17^L$ x $14^W$ x $11^H$ | Heartland $^{(90)}$ Sweetheart $^{(90)}$ Sweetheart $^{(93)}$ | 65.95 79.95 119.95 | 154 129 60 | 190 180 100 |
| **Gift Giving** $20.5^L$ x $15^W$ x $10.5^H$ | Holiday Hostess $^{(92)}$ | 124.95 | 124 | 200 |
| **Gingerbread** $10^L$ x $6^W$ x $4^H$ | Christmas $^{(90)}$ | 32.95 | 69 | 125 |
| **Glad Tidings** $8.75^L$ x $6^W$ x $2^{FH}$ x $5.5^{BH}$ | Christmas$^{(98)}$ | 49.00 | 66 | 88 |
| **Gold Nugget** $4.5^{RD}$ x $3^H$ | Incentive $^{(94)}$ | N/A | 178 | 235 |
| **Gold Rush** $6.5^{RD}$ x $4.75^H$ | Incentive $^{(94)}$ | N/A | 178 | 270 |
| **Golf** $6.75^{RD}$ x $6^H$ | Tour $^{(00-P)}$ | 39.95 | ** | ** |

**KEY:**
**Values listed are for BASKET ONLY, unless otherwised noted**, **(-P)** = to present

| Page in Guide | Form No. | Other Baskets Using Same Form |
|---|---|---|
| page 132 | unknown | None |
| checklist | 13757 | Branch Sponsoring (01) |
| checklist | 13765 | None |
| checklist | 13773 | Regional Sales (01) |
| checklist | 13790 | Director Sponsored (01) |
| checklist | 13781 | Leadership Award |
| page 228 | 13358 | None |
| page 166 | 12373 | None |
| page 108<br>page 218<br>page 218 | 300-CCS<br>300-CRS<br>10359 | Large Picnic |
| page 114 | 12700$^R$ / 12718$^G$ | Forever Yours |
| page 38 | 3400-ARST / AGST | 88 Sm Easter, 93 Lg Easter, Small Chore, 91 Regional Sponsored, 95 Bee, $500 Million, Woven Memories |
| page 40 | 12386$^R$ / 12394$^G$ | None |
| page 150 | unknown | Thyme |
| page 150 | unknown | None |
| page 224 | unknown | Daisy (new) |

| Basket | Collection(Year) | Orig.Price | AVG | HIGH |
|---|---|---|---|---|
| **Gourmet Gathering** $18^L$ x $11^W$ x $4.5^H$ | Sweetheart (97) | 74.95 | 85 | 120 |
| **Grandad's Sleigh** $9.25^L$ x $5.5^W$ x $2^{FH}$ x $5.5^{BH}$ | Christmas (82) | 19.95 | 818 | 1000 |
| **Growing Strong Together** $9.5^L$ x $5^W$ x $9.5^H$ | Incentive (96-97) Incentive (98-P) | N/A N/A | — — | — — |
| **Hamper, Large** $16.5^L$ x $16.5^W$ x $21.5^H$ | Feature (86) Feature (93-94) Feature, SOA (91) Hostess (86-90) Retired (79-86) | 79.95 179.95 149.95 109.95 59.95 | 223 235 227 209 153 | 295 275 295 305 300 |
| **Hamper, Large** (1995 – 01) $17^L$ x $17^W$ x $22^H$ | Hostess(95-01) Regular Line, Hostess(01-P) | 219.95 259.00 | 246 259 | 300 259 |
| **Hamper, Medium** $12^L$ x $12.25^W$ x $16.25^H$ | Hostess(86-90) Retired (79-86) | 69.95 31.95 | 131 140 | 175 175 |
| **Hamper, Small** $12^L$ x $12.25^W$ x $16.25^H$ | Feature, SOA (91) | 99.95 | 153 | 165 |
| **Hanging, 13" Sq. Bottom** $13^{RD}$ x $12.5^H$ | Retired (80-86) | 35.95 | 40 | 90 |
| **Hanging, 11" Sq. Bottom** $11^{RD}$ x $10.5^H$ | Retired (80-86) | 29.95 | 45 | 75 |
| **Hanging, 9" Sq. Bottom** $9^{RD}$ x $8.5^H$ | Retired (80-86) | 22.95 | 40 | 40 |
| **Hanging, 7" Sq. Bottom** $7^{RD}$ x $6.5^H$ | Retired (80-86) | 15.95 | 67 | 75 |

| Page in Guide | Form No. | Other Baskets Using Same Form |
|---|---|---|
| page 218 | 15946<sup>R</sup> / 16063<sup>G</sup><br>16055<sup>B</sup> / 16071<sup>P</sup> | Medium Gathering |
| page 38 | 4900-Z | None |
| page 142<br>page 142 | unknown<br>unknown | Tall Key, MBA, Tall Purse, Two-Quart, Membership, 91 Employee Christmas |
| page 88<br>page 90<br>page 90<br>page 124<br>page 198 | 1600-OO<br>11622<br>1600-DS<br>1600-DO<br>1600-DO | 90-91 Sponsor |
| page 124<br>checklist, Hostess | 11631<br>11362 | None |
| page 124<br>page 198 | 1700-DO<br>1700-DO | Small Hamper, 90-91 Recruit, 90-91 Sponsor (Superstar), |
| page 90 | 1700-DS | Medium Hamper, 90-91 Recruit, 90-91 Sponsor (Superstar), |
| page 198 | 4200-PO | 13" Measuring |
| page 198 | 4100-PO | 11" Measuring |
| page 198 | 4000-PO | 9" Measuring, 9" Canister |
| page 198 | 3900-PO | 90 Bee, Poinsettia, 7" Measuring, 92 Sponsor (Large), Maple Leaf, 97 Perfect Attendance, 7" Canister, Barn Raising |

**KEY:** In blue = Not pictured in the Guide.   **S** = Stained, **U** = Unstained, **W** = Whitewash
**HL** = Heartland® Collection, **WT** = Woven Traditions®, **R** = Red, **G** = Green      **283**

| Basket | Collection(Year) | Orig.Price | AVG | HIGH |
|---|---|---|---|---|
| **Hanging,** <br> **5" Sq. Bottom** <br><br><br> $5^{RD}$ x $4.5^{H}$ | Retired (80-86) | 14.95 | **37** | **70** |
| **Hanging,** <br> **Woven Bottom** <br> $8.25^{RD}$ x $7.75^{H}$ | Retired (79-86) | 14.95 | **85** | **100** |
| **Harbor** <br> $10^{L}$ x $8.25^{W}$ x $8.25^{H}$ | Collectors Club (98) | 85.00 | **98** | **110** |
| **Hartville Basket** <br> see also **Tour** <br> $8.75^{L}$ x $4.75^{W}$ x $6.5^{H}$ | Tour (95-99) | 34.95 | **50** | **60** |
| **Hartville II Basket** <br> see also **Tour II** <br> $7^{L}$ x $3.5^{W}$ x $4.75^{H}$ | Tour (96-99) | 29.95 | — | **45** |
| **Harvest** <br> $16^{L}$ x $9^{W}$ x $6^{H}$ | Hostess(90-92) | 54.95 | **96** | **122** |
| **Harvest (1993)** <br> $7^{L}$ x $4.75^{W}$ x $7.75^{H}$ | Shades of Autumn (93) | 39.95 | **75** | **100** |
| **Harvest Blessings** <br> **Large** <br> $19.5^{L}$ x $8^{W}$ x $3.25^{H}$ | Autumn Reflections(00) | 54.00 | **60** | **86** |
| **Harvest Blessings** <br> **Small** <br> $15.25^{L}$ x $5.75^{W}$ x $2.5^{H}$ | Autumn Reflections(00) | 42.00 | **56** | **64** |
| **Hearthside** <br> $11.75^{RD}$ x $6.5^{H}$ | Hostess(90-92) | 59.95 | **87** | **130** |
| **Heirloom** <br><br> $15^{L}$ x $10^{W}$ x $7.5^{H}$ | Hostess(90-92) | 87.95 | **114** | **165** |

**KEY:** <br> **Values listed are for BASKET ONLY, unless otherwised noted, (-P)** = to present

| Page in Guide | Form No. | Other Baskets Using Same Form |
|---|---|---|
| page 198 | 3800-PO | 88 Employee Birthday, Resolution 92 Employee Christmas, Forget-Me-Not, 5" Hanging, 5" Measuring, 92 Recruit, 92 Sponsor (Small), Watch Your Business Bloom, 5" Canister, 99 Recruit |
| page 178 | 3700-PO | None |
| page 46 | 10677 | None |
| page 224 | 15661 | Tour, 89 Bee, 92 Employee Birthday Sophomore - Senior Recognition, 20th Century, Dresden Basket, Memory, 25th Anniversary (Sm) |
| page 224 | 15814 | Tour II, 98 Flag Sponsoring, 99 Bee |
| page 124 | 3700-AOS | Original Easter, Senior Employee, 90 Bee Speaker |
| page 208 | 14303 | None |
| page 24 | 14397 | None |
| page 24 | 18058 | None |
| page 124 | 42000-AOS | None |
| page 124 | 500-HOS | 88 Bee Speaker, 87 Employee Christmas, Medium Market, 99 Team Excellence, (77-87) Tenth Anniversary, Founder's |

| Basket | Collection(Year) | Orig.Price | AVG | HIGH |
|---|---|---|---|---|
| Herb<br>11.5L x 5W x 3H | Feature (86)<br>Incentive (87-88) | 32.90 set<br>N/A | 59<br>80 | 75<br>80 |
| High Achiever<br>12RD x 5.75H | Incentive (95-96) | N/A | ** | ** |
| Holiday Cheer<br><br>12L x 8W x 4.25H | Christmas(96)<br>Employee Christmas(00) | 47.95<br>0.00 | 68<br>93 | 90<br>100 |
| Holiday Sleigh<br>13L x 7.5W x 3FH x 8BH | Feature (97-99) | 47.95 | 58 | 97 |
| Holly<br>15L x 8W x 2.25H | Christmas (84) | 24.95 | 272 | 355 |
| Homecoming<br><br>15L x 15W x 7.5H | Holiday Hostess (93)<br>Hostess (99-02) | 109.95<br>99.00 | 140<br>— | 200<br>— |
| Homestead<br><br>10RD x 6.25H | Collectors Club(99)<br>Feature(99) | 79.00C<br>59.00 | 101<br>84 | 149  C<br>95 |
| Hope Chest<br>23L x 14W x 11.25H | Regular Line, Hostess(98-P) | 189.00 | 209 | 285 |
| Horizon of Hope<br>(1995)<br><br><br>5.75L x 3.75W x 3H | Horizon of Hope (95) | 28.95 | 75 | 95 |
| Horizon of Hope<br>(1996)<br>6.75L x 4.75W x 2.25H | Horizon of Hope (96) | 28.95 | 63 | 80 |
| Horizon of Hope<br>(1997)<br>5.5L x 4W x 4H | Horizon of Hope (97) | 28.95 | 50 | 60 |
| Horizon of Hope<br>(1998)<br>4L x 4W x 5.5H | Horizon of Hope (98) | 31.00 | 50 | 75 |

<u>**KEY:**</u>
**Values listed are for BASKET ONLY, unless otherwised noted, (-P)** = to present

| Page in Guide | Form No. | Other Baskets Using Same Form |
|---|---|---|
| page 88 | 4500-AO | Liberty, Bed, Cracker, Muffin |
| page 140 | 4500- | 96 Employee Christmas |
| page 150-152 | unknown | Basket of Plenty, Quilting |
| page 40 | $18511^R$ / $18520^G$ | None |
| page 74 | unknown | |
| page 84 | 16811 | Medium Vegetable, Yuletide Traditions |
| page 38 | 4600-AZ | Bread (old), Garden |
| page 116 | $12084^R$/ $12092^G$ | Medium Picnic |
| page 124 | 13081 | |
| page 48 | 13871 | Associate Homestead Tour |
| page 84 | 6609596 | |
| checklist, Hostess | 18431 | None |
| page 120 | 17124 | All-Star Trio, Keepsake, Paint the Town, 90 Recruit, Shining Star, Rosemary, Sugar and Spice, Treasure Chest, 90 Sweetheart, 95 Horizon of Hope, 98 Hostess Appreciation, 00 Branch Sales, Salt & Pepper |
| page 120 | 15911 | None |
| page 120 | 18724 | Ambrosia, Thanks-A-Million, 01 Hostess Appreciation, 01 Inaugural |
| page 120 | 10472 | None |

| Basket | Collection(Year) | Orig.Price | AVG | HIGH |
|---|---|---|---|---|
| **Horizon of Hope (1999)** 6.25$^L$ x 5.25$^W$ x 3$^H$ | Horizon of Hope (99) | 31.00 | **60** | **75** |
| **Horizon of Hope (2000)** 7.5$^L$ x 4.25$^W$ x 2.75$^H$ | Horizon of Hope (00) | 32.00 | **48** | **91** |
| **Horizon of Hope (2001)** 5.25$^{RD}$ x 4.25$^H$ | Horizon of Hope (01) | 34.00 | **38** | **60** |
| **Hospitality** 18.5$^L$ x 13.5$^W$ x 5.25$^H$ | Traditions (98) | 89.00 | **77** | **120** |
| **Hostess Appreciation (94)** 8$^L$ x 4$^W$ x 2$^H$ | Feature (94) | N/A | **39** | **65** |
| **Hostess Appreciation (96)** 5.5$^L$ x 5.5$^W$ x 2.5$^H$ | Feature (96) | N/A | **39** | **65** |
| **Hostess Appreciation (98)** 5.75$^L$ x 3.75$^W$ x 3$^H$ | Feature (98) | 29.95 | **43** | **60** |
| **Hostess Appreciation (01)** 5.5$^L$ x 4$^W$ x 4$^H$ | Feature (01) | 39.00 | **44** | **50** |
| **Inaugural, (1989)** 5$^{RD}$ x 4.5$^H$ | Special Event (89) | 19.89 | **247** | **475** |
| **Inaugural, (1993)** 5$^L$ x 5$^W$ x 4.5$^H$ | Special Event (93) | 24.95 | **58** | **102** |

| Page in Guide | Form No. | Other Baskets Using Same Form |
|---|---|---|
| page 120 | 14150 | None |
| page 120 | 17787$^S$ / 19194$^W$ | None |
| page 120 | 10591$^S$/11605$^W$ | None |
| page 228 | 10669 | None |
| page 90 | unknown | 93 Recruit, 93 Sponsor (Small), Lavender, Rose Bud |
| page 90 | unknown | Ivy, 91 Employee Birthday, Friendship, Tarragon |
| page 92 | unknown | All-Star Trio, 89 Employee Birthday, Keepsake, Paint the Town, 00 Branch Sales, Reach for the Stars (Med), Sugar and Spice, 90 Sweetheart, Treasure Chest, 95 Horizon of Hope Rosemary, 98 Hostess Appreciation, Salt & Pepper |
| page 86 | 15873 | Ambrosia, 97 Horizon of Hope, Thanks-A-Million, 01 Inaugural |
| page 212 | 3800-ABRST | 88 Employee Birthday, 92 Sponsor (Small), 92 Employee Christmas, Forget-Me-Not, 5" Hanging, 5" Measuring, 92 Recruit, Resolution, Watch Your Business Bloom, 5" Canister, 99 Recruit |
| page 212 | 11461 | Candy Cane, Violet, Small Peg 96 Recruit, Teaspoon |

**KEY:** In blue = Not pictured in the Guide.  **S** = Stained, **U** = Unstained, **W** = Whitewash
**HL** = Heartland® Collection, **WT** = Woven Traditions®, **R** = Red, **G** = Green          **289**

| Basket | Collection(Year) | Orig.Price | AVG | HIGH |
|--------|------------------|------------|-----|------|
| **Inaugural,** (1997) 5.5$^{RD}$ x 3.25$^H$ | Special Event $^{(97)}$ | 32.95 | **60** | 85 |
| **Inaugural,** (2001) 5.5$^L$ x 4$^W$ x 4$^H$ | Special Event $^{(01)}$ | 39.00 | **44** | 50 |
| **Ivy** 5.5$^L$ x 5.5$^W$ x 2.5$^H$ | Booking $^{(90-92)}$ Employee $^{(91)}$ | N/A N/A | **50** **90** | 72 130 |
| **JAM 2000** 5.5$^{RD}$ x 3.75$^H$ | Incentive$^{(00)}$ | N/A | **218** | 320 |
| **Jelly Bean** 5.5$^{RD}$ x 3.75$^H$ | Easter $^{(00)}$ | 34.00 | **45** | 52 |
| **Jingle Bell** 8$^{RD}$ x 6$^H$ | Christmas$^{(94)}$ | 47.95 | **58** | 95 |
| **Junior Recognition** 8.75$^L$ x 4.75$^W$ x 6.5$^H$ | Employee $^{(xx-97)}$ | N/A | **79** | 85 |
| **Keepsake** 5.75$^L$ x 3.75$^W$ x 3$^H$ | Booking $^{(88-90)}$ | 16.95 | **55** | 77 |
| **Key, Medium** 9$^L$ x 5$^W$ x 5$^H$ | Feature $^{(94)}$ Heartland$^{(88-97)}$ Regular Line $^{(79-P)}$ | 29.95 26.95 9.95 | **38** **35** **34** | 50 50 64 |
| **Key, Small** 7$^L$ x 5$^W$ x 3.5$^H$ | Feature $^{(94)}$ Heartland$^{(94-97)}$ Regular Line $^{(79-P)}$ | 27.95 21.95 7.95 | **36** **30** **29** | 46 40 75 |

| Page in Guide | Form No. | Other Baskets Using Same Form |
|---|---|---|
| page 212 | 15326 | None |
| page 212 | 16080 | Ambrosia, Thanks-A-Million, 97 Horizon of Hope, 01 Hostess Appreciation |
| page 32 <br> page 70 | 13100-JOS <br> 13100- | 91 Employee Birthday, Friendship, 96 Hostess Appreciation, Tarragon |
| page 142 | unknown | Lily of the Valley, Pot of Gold, Jelly Bean |
| page 66 | 19488 | Lily of the Valley, Pot of Gold, JAM 2000 |
| page 40 | $17906^R$ / $17914^G$ | None |
| page 70 | unknown | 89 Bee, Dresden Basket, Tour, 92 Employee Birthday, Memory, Sophomore – Senior Recognition, Hartville, 25th Anniversary (Sm), 20th Century |
| page 32 | 45000-IO | All-Star Trio, 89 Employee Birthday Paint the Town, 90 Recruiting, Shining Star, Rosemary, Sugar and Spice, 90 Sweetheart, Treasure Chest, 95 Horizon of Hope, 98 Hostess Appreciation, 00 Branch Sales, Salt & Pepper |
| page 82 <br> page 108 <br> checklist | $15172^R$/$99^B$/$81^G$ <br> 11118/1100-ICS <br> 11100/1100-IO | Candle, Collectors Club 97 Renewal, 89 Employee Christmas, 90 Sponsor, 96 Perfect Attendance |
| page 82 <br> page 108 <br> checklist | $17078^R$/$51^B$/$60^G$ <br> 10782 <br> 10723/700-IO | Acorn, Basket of Thanks, Tea, Mini Berry, Mini Chore, Mistletoe, Mini Cradle, Tea, Baby Easter, 91 Hostess Easter, 93 Small Easter, 94 Employee Christmas, Kiddie Purse, Star Team, Patriot, 99 Branch Excellence |

| Basket | Collection(Year) | Orig.Price | AVG | HIGH |
|--------|------------------|-----------|-----|------|
| **Key, Tall** | Employee Christmas(91) | N/A | **98** | **125** |
| | Feature (94) | 40.95 | **52** | **75** |
| | Heartland (88-97) | 34.95 | **44** | **70** |
| | Holiday Hostess (88) | 30.95 | **84** | **115** |
| | Regular Line (79-P) | 11.95 | **44** | **90** |
| 9.5$^L$ x 5$^W$ x 9.5$^H$ | Retired(Natrl) (94) | 31.95 | **50** | **60** |
| **Laundry, Large** | Hostess (86-90) | 96.95 | **165** | **200** |
| 30$^L$ x 20$^W$ x 10.5$^H$ | Retired (79-86) | 34.95 | **208** | **300** |
| **Laundry, Medium** | J.W. Original | N/A | ** | ** |
| | Retired (79-83) | 31.95 | **93** | **150** |
| 28.5$^L$ x 17.75$^W$ x 9.75$^H$ | | | | |
| **Laundry, Oval** | Feature(01) | 159.00 | **160** | **200** |
| | Regular Line, Hostess (02-P) | 159.00 | **159** | **159** |
| 21.25$^L$ x 14.25$^W$ x 10.5$^H$ | | | | |
| **Laundry, Small** | Holiday Hostess (88) | 67.95 | **226** | **288** |
| 24$^L$ x 17$^W$ x 10$^H$ | Retired (79-98) | 29.95 | **127** | **250** |
| **Laurel** 5.5$^{RD}$ x 3.75$^H$ | Booking (90-92) | N/A | **39** | **50** |
| **Lavender** 8$^L$ x 4$^W$ x 2$^H$ | Booking (92-99) | 22.95 | **30** | **58** |
| **Let It Snow** 4.75$^L$ x 5$^W$ x 3.25$^H$ | Tree-Trimming(00) | 45.00 | **59** | **81** |
| **Liberty** 11.5$^L$ x 5$^W$ x 3$^H$ | All-American (93) | 29.95 | **60** | **75** |
| **Lilac** 6.5$^{RD}$ x 6.5$^H$ | May (94) | 34.95 | **85** | **115** |
| **Lily of the Valley** 5.5$^{RD}$ x 3.75$^H$ | May (93) | 28.95 | **93** | **115** |
| **Little Bin, bottom** 7.25$^L$ x 8$^W$ x 2.5$^{FH}$ x 3.75$^{BH}$ | Regular Line (00-P) | 37.00 | **37** | **37** |
| **Little Bin, top** 7.25$^L$ x 7.5$^W$ x 2$^{FH}$ x 3$^{BH}$ | Regular Line (00-P) | 34.00 | **34** | **34** |

**KEY:**
**Values listed are for BASKET ONLY, unless otherwised noted, (-P)** = to present

| Page in Guide | Form No. | Other Baskets Using Same Form |
|---|---|---|
| page 72 | 1000- | MBA, Tall Purse, Two-quart, |
| page 82 | 14672$^R$/99$^B$/81$^G$ | Collectors Club Membership, |
| page 108 | 11061/1000-ICS | 91 Employee Christmas |
| page 114 | 1000-IRGS | |
| checklist | 11053/1000-IO | |
| page 198 | 14630 | |
| page 124 | 2800-O | Large Cradle |
| page 198 | 2800-OO | |
| page 160 | 2700-O | Medium Cradle |
| page 198 | unknown | |
| page 94 | 10893 | None |
| checklist, Hostess | 10893 | |
| page 114 | 2600-ORGS | Family Picnic, Small Cradle |
| page 198 | 12602 /2600-OO | |
| page 32 | 17000-JOS | Basket 'O Luck |
| page 32 | 10138 | 94 Hostess Appreciation, 93 Recruit 93 Sponsor (Small) |
| page 230 | 18147 / 18155 | None |
| page 20 | 14541 | Bed, Cracker, Herb, Muffin, 96 Employee Christmas |
| page 164 | 16209 | Bouquet |
| page 164 | 15717 | Pot of Gold, JAM 2000, Jelly Bean |
| checklist | 16586 | None |
| checklist | 16489 | None |

| Basket | Collection(Year) | Orig.Price | AVG | HIGH |
|---|---|---|---|---|
| **Little Joy**<br>$5^L$ x $3.75^W$ x $4.5^H$ | Feature (99) | 38.00 | **53** | **69** |
| **Little Love**<br>$6.25^L$ x $4.75^W$ x $2.25^H$ | Sweetheart (00) | 34.00 | **41** | **45** |
| **Little Star**<br>$7.5^L$ x $8^W$ x $3^H$ | Feature (01) | 49.00 | **51** | **60** |
| **Loaf, Small**<br>$7.5^L$ x $4.75^W$ x $2.5^H$ | Retired (99-02) | 32.00 | **37** | **40** |
| **Lots of Luck**<br>$4.25^L$ x $4.25^W$ x $3^H$ | Feature (99) | 29.00 | **90** | **130** |
| **Love Letters**<br>$8.75^L$ x $7.75^W$ x $2.75^H$ | Sweetheart(99) | 44.00 | **60** | **90** |
| **Love Notes**<br>$5.75^L$ x $3.75^W$ x $5^H$ | Sweetheart(01) | 39.00 | **51** | **56** |
| **Love Treasures**<br>$13.25^L$ x $12.5^W$ x $4.25^H$ | Sweetheart(99) | 68.00 | **96** | **120** |
| **Lucky Charm**<br>$5.25^L$ x $4.25^W$ x $1.75^{FH}$ x $3^{BH}$ | Feature (02) | 39.00 | **39** | **49** |
| **Lucky You**<br>$4.75^{RD}$ x $3^H$ | Feature (02) | 34.00 | **40** | **50** |
| **Magazine**<br><br><br><br>$16^L$ x $8^W$ x $11^H$ | Employee (92)<br>Holiday Hostess (89)<br>Regular Line(2sw/h) (79-P)<br>Retired(1sw/h, legs) (79-98)<br>Retired(1sw/h, legs, no lid) (79-95) | N/A<br>53.95<br>21.95<br>25.95<br>21.95 | —<br>**122**<br>**75**<br>**82**<br>**58** | —<br>**160**<br>**150**<br>**160**<br>**85** |
| **Mail**<br>$12^L$ x $8^W$ x $11.5^H$ | Hostess (92-96) | 79.95 | **118** | **160** |
| **Mail, Large**<br>$12^L$ x $8.75^W$ x $11^H$ | Retired (00-02) | 115.00 | — | — |
| **Mail, Medium**<br>$10.75^L$ x $7.75^W$ x $10.25^H$ | Retired (00-02) | 99.00 | — | — |
| **Mail, Small**<br>$9.75^L$ x $6.25^W$ x $8.5^H$ | Retired (01-02) | 79.00 | — | — |

**KEY:**
**294** **Values listed are for BASKET ONLY, unless otherwise noted. (-P)** = to present

| Page in Guide | Form No. | Other Baskets Using Same Form |
|---|---|---|
| page 84 | 19445 | None |
| page 218 | 17728/10874/18062 10850/10885 | None |
| page 86 | 12202$^R$ / 12214$^G$ | None |
| page 198 | 12823 | Bee (01) |
| page 84 | 18465 | Regional SponsExc (98), Sweet Sweet Sentiments |
| page 229 | 12963 | None |
| page 220 | 12055 / 10826 | None |
| page 220 | 13084 | None |
| page 94 | 11482 | None |
| page 86 | 11911 | None |
| page 70 page 114 checklist page 198 page 198 | 12106 2100-CGRS 12106/2100-CO 12114/2100-W 12122/2100-U | Bread & Milk, 25th Anniversary (Lg) |
| page 126 | 10600 | None |
| page 200 | 16373 | None |
| page 200 | 16969 | None |
| page 200 | 11271 | None |

| Basket | Collection(Year) | Orig.Price | AVG | HIGH |
|---|---|---|---|---|
| **Make Your Dreams Come True** see Recruit 1999 | | | | |
| **Maple Leaf** | Shades of Autumn (96) | 40.95 | **45** | **83** |
| 7$^{RD}$ x 6.5$^{H}$ | | | | |
| **Market, Large** | Feature (96-97) | 77.95 | **94** | **135** |
| | Holiday Hostess (88) | 49.95 | **119** | **135** |
| | J.W. Originals | N/A | ** | ** |
| | Regular Line(2sw/h) (83-P) | 29.95 | **79** | **100** |
| 16$^{L}$ x 11$^{W}$ x 9$^{H}$ | Retired(1st/h) (79-93) | 19.95 | **93** | **100** |
| **Market, Little** 7.75$^{L}$ x 5.5$^{W}$ x 4.5$^{H}$ | Regular Line (02-P) | 44.00 | **44** | **44** |
| **Market, Medium** | Employee Christmas(87) | N/A | **248** | **310** |
| | Feature (Natrl) (87) | 41.95 | **50** | **78** |
| | Feature (Natrl) (98) | 53.95 | — | — |
| | Heartland (89-97) | 43.95 | **67** | **80** |
| | J.W. Collection (83) | 32.95 | **1257** | **1777** |
| | J.W. Originals | N/A | ** | ** |
| | Regular Line (2sw/h) (83-P) | 24.95 | **69** | **85** |
| | Regular Line(WWash) (00-P) | 69.00 | **69** | **69** |
| 15$^{L}$ x 10$^{W}$ x 7.5$^{H}$ | Retired (1st/h) (79-98) | 16.95 | **56** | **89** |
| **Market, Miniature** 5.75$^{L}$ x 4$^{W}$ x 3$^{H}$ | Collectors Club (96) | 125.00 | **233** | **465** |
| **Market, Small** | All-American (92) | 39.95 | **97** | **100** |
| | Regular Line(2sw/h)(93-P) | 45.95 | **59** | **59** |
| 15$^{L}$ x 9.5$^{W}$ x 5.5$^{H}$ | Retired(1st/h)(79-93) | 14.95 | **101** | **140** |
| **Master Employee** 12.5$^{RD}$ x 13.5$^{H}$ | Employee (xx-97) | N/A | **232** | **275** |
| **Master Employee2** 8$^{RD}$ x 6.5$^{H}$ | Employee (97-P) | N/A | — | **175** |
| **MBA Basket** 9.5$^{L}$ x 5$^{W}$ x 9.5$^{H}$ | Incentive (88-P) | N/A | **169** | **160** |
| **Meadow Blossoms Pottery** | Incentive (85) | N/A | ** | ** |

**KEY:**

**Values listed are for BASKET ONLY, unless otherwised noted, (-P) = to present**

| Page in Guide | Form No. | Other Baskets Using Same Form |
|---|---|---|
| page 132 | unknown | None |
| page 208 | 13935 | 7" Measuring, 90 Bee, Poinsettia, 92 Sponsor (Large), 7" Hanging, 7" Canister, 97 Perfect Attendance, Barn Raising |
| page 84 | 16641$^R$/24$^B$/32$^G$ | Rectangular Sewing, 99 Director |
| page 114 | 600-ARGS | Sales & Sponsoring Excellence |
| page 160 | N/A | |
| checklist | 10634/600-CO | |
| page 200 | 10626/600-AO | |
| checklist | 12500 | None |
| page 72 | 500 | 88 Bee Speaker, Heirloom, |
| page 90 | 500- | 77-87 Tenth Anniversary, |
| page 92 | 10588 | 87 Employee Christmas, 99 Team |
| page 108 | 10545/500-ACS | Excellence, Founder's |
| page 156 | 500-AT | |
| page 160 | unknown | |
| checklist | 10537 | |
| checklist | 11301 | |
| page 200 | 10529/500-AO | |
| page 44 | 15024/150240 | None |
| page 18 | 10707 | Welcome Home, 99 Regional |
| checklist | 10430/400-CO | Sales & Sponsoring Excellence |
| page 200 | 10421/400-AO | |
| page 70 | 1900- | Banker's Waste, Waste (Inverted, Small Round) , Tree-Trimming |
| page 70 | unknown | Medium Fruit |
| page 146 | 1000-FO | 91 Employee Christmas, Tall Key, Tall Purse, Two-Quart, Growing Strong Together, Membership |
| page 140 | unknown | None |

**297**

| Basket | Collection(Year) | Orig.Price | AVG | HIGH |
|---|---|---|---|---|
| **Measuring, 13"** | Holiday Hostess (90) | 69.95 | **94** | **165** |
| | Incentive, N.Sales (98) | N/A | — | — |
| | Regular Line (00-P) | 89.00 | **89** | **89** |
| 13$^{RD}$ x 12.5$^H$ | Retired (79-98) | 20.95 | **78** | **115** |
| **Measuring, 11"** | Incentive, N.Sales (94-98) | N/A | ** | ** |
| 11$^{RD}$ x 10.5$^H$ | Retired (79-98) | 17.95 | **60** | **85** |
| **Measuring, 9"** | Incentive, N.Sales (94-98) | N/A | ** | ** |
| | Regular Line (00-P) | 56.00 | **56** | **80** |
| 9$^{RD}$ x 8.5$^H$ | Retired (79-98) | 13.95 | **52** | **80** |
| **Measuring, 7"** | Incentive, N.Sales (94-98) | N/A | ** | ** |
| | Regular Line (00-P) | 44.00 | **44** | **80** |
| 7$^{RD}$ x 6.5$^H$ | Retired (79-98) | 10.95 | **35** | **65** |
| **Measuring, 5"** | Booking (xx-84) | N/A | **30** | **35** |
| | Employee Birthday(88) | N/A | **77** | **105** |
| | Employee Christmas(92) | N/A | **94** | **120** |
| | Incentive, N.Sales (94-98) | N/A | ** | ** |
| | Regular Line (01-P) | 34.00 | **34** | **45** |
| 5$^{RD}$ x 4.5$^H$ | Retired (79-98) | 7.95 | **37** | **68** |
| **Membership** | Collectors Club(95-96) | 75.00 | **105** | **178** |
| | Collectors Club(97-P) | 75.00 | — | — |
| 9.5$^L$ x 5$^W$ x 9.5$^H$ | | | | |
| **Memory** | Christmas (89) | 34.95 | **87** | **155** |
| | Feature (88-89) | 39.95 | **112** | **165** |
| 8.75$^L$ x 4.75$^W$ x 6.5$^H$ | | | | |
| **Mistletoe** | Christmas (87) | 19.95 | **87** | **155** |
| 7$^L$ x 5$^W$ x 3.5$^H$ | | | | |
| **Mom's Memories** | Mother's Day (02) | 55.00 | **50** | **82** |
| 9.5$^L$ x 7.75$^W$ x 6$^H$ | | | | |
| **Morning Glory** | May(00) | 43.00 | **62** | **89** |
| 7.5$^L$ x 7.5$^W$ x 4.75$^H$ | | | | |

**KEY:**
**Values listed are for BASKET ONLY, unless otherwised noted**, **(-P)** = to present

| Page in Guide | Form No. | Other Baskets Using Same Form |
|---|---|---|
| page 114 | 4200-CGRS | 13" Hanging |
| page 138 | unknown | |
| checklist | 19968 | |
| page 200 | 14206 / 4200-B | |
| | | |
| page 138 | unknown | 11" Hanging |
| page 200 | 14109 / 4100-B | |
| | | |
| page 138 | unknown | 9" Hanging, 9" Canister |
| checklist | 19763 | |
| page 200 | 14001 / 4000-B | |
| | | |
| page 138 | unknown | 90 Bee, Maple Leaf, Poinsettia, |
| checklist | 19861 | 92 Sponsor (Large), 7" Hanging, |
| page 200 | 13901 / 3900-B | 97 Perfect Attendance, 7" Canister, |
| | | Barn Raising |
| | | |
| page 32 | 3800-BO | 89 Inaugural, Forget-Me-Not, |
| page 70 | 3800- | 5" Hanging, 92 Recruit, Resolution, |
| page 72 | 3800- | 92 Sponsor (Small), 5" Canister, |
| page 138 | unknown | Watch Your Business Bloom, |
| checklist | 11415 | 99 Recruit |
| page 200 | 13803 / 3800-B | |
| | | |
| page 44 | 62839 | 91 Employee Christmas, MBA, |
| page 44 | 62847 | Tall Purse, Two-Quart, Tall Key, |
| | | Growing Strong Together |
| | | |
| page 38 | 5600-BRST / BGST | 89 Bee, Dresden Basket, Hartville, |
| page 82 | 5600-BBS | Tour, 92 Employee Birthday, |
| | | Sophomore - Senior Recognition, |
| | | 25th Anniversary(Sm), 20th Century |
| | | |
| page 38 | 700-ART / AGT | Acorn, Basket of Thanks, Tea, Mini |
| | | Berry, Mini Chore, Patriot, Mini Cradle, |
| | | Baby Easter, 91 Hostess Easter, Small |
| | | Key, 93 Small Easter, 94 Employee |
| | | Christmas, Kiddie Purse, Star Team, 99 |
| | | Branch Excellence |
| | | |
| page 170 | 12136 | None |
| | | |
| page 164 | 18899 | None |

| Basket | Collection(Year) | Orig.Price | AVG | HIGH |
|---|---|---|---|---|
| **Mother's Day (1992)** 10.5$^L$ x 10.5$^W$ x 4.5$^H$ | Mother's Day $^{(92)}$ | 34.95 | **68** | **100** |
| **Mother's Day (1993)** 8.5$^L$ x 8$^W$ x 6$^H$ | Mother's Day $^{(93)}$ | 44.95 | **60** | **100** |
| **Mother's Day (1994)** 6.75$^L$ x 9.25$^W$ x 3.75$^H$ | Mother's Day $^{(94)}$ | 37.95 | **50** | **85** |
| **Muffin** 11.5$^L$ x 5$^W$ x 3$^H$ | Heartland $^{(90-00)}$ | 25.95 | **36** | **55** |
| **National High Sales Level 1** 5$^{RD}$ x 4.5$^H$ | Incentive$^{(99-P)}$ | N/A | ** | ** |
| **National High Sales Level 2** 7$^{RD}$ x 5.5$^H$ | Incentive$^{(99-P)}$ | N/A | ** | ** |
| **National High Sales Level 3** | Incentive$^{(99-P)}$ | N/A | ** | ** |
| **National High Sales Level 4** | Incentive$^{(99-P)}$ | N/A | ** | ** |
| **National High Sales Level 5** | Incentive$^{(99-P)}$ | N/A | ** | ** |
| **National Sponsoring Large** | Incentive$^{(99-P)}$ | N/A | ** | ** |
| **National Sponsoring Medium** | Incentive$^{(99-P)}$ | N/A | ** | ** |
| **National Sponsoring Small** 14$^L$ x 9$^W$ x 4.25$^H$ | Incentive$^{(99-P)}$ | N/A | ** | ** |
| **Newspaper** 15.75$^L$ x 10.5$^W$ x 2.75$^H$ | Regular Line$^{(99-P)}$ | 124.00 | **129** | **129** |

<u>KEY:</u>
**Values listed are for BASKET ONLY, unless otherwised noted, (-P)** = to present

| Page in Guide | Form No. | Other Baskets Using Same Form |
|---|---|---|
| page 168 | 110-CPS | None |
| page 168 | 12904 | None |
| page 168 | 16004 | None |
| page 110 | 14516/4500-JCS | Liberty, Bed, Cracker, Herb, 96 Employee Christmas |
| page 138 | unknown | None |
| page 138 | unknown | None |
| page 138 | unknown | None |
| page 138 | unknown | None |
| page 138 | unknown | None |
| page 132-134 | unknown | None |
| page 132-134 | unknown | None |
| page 132-134 | unknown | None |
| checklist | 17329 | None |

| Basket | Collection^(Year) | Orig.Price | AVG | HIGH |
|---|---|---|---|---|
| **9 x 13 Basket**<br>9.5$^L$ x 14.5$^W$ x 2.75$^H$ | Retired $^{(99-02)}$ | 49.00 | — | — |
| **Noel Bell**<br>5.5$^{RD}$ x 5.5$^H$ | Feature$^{(01)}$ | 43.00 | 46 | 80 |
| **Note Pal**<br><br>7.5$^L$ x 5.5$^W$ x 2$^{FH}$ x 3.5$^{BH}$ | Regular Line$^{(00-P)}$<br>Regular Line(WWash)$^{(01-P)}$ | 32.00<br>34.00 | 34<br>34 | 34<br>34 |
| **October Fields**<br>6.5$^{RD}$ x 9$^H$ | Feature $^{(00)}$ | 59.00 | 66 | 90 |
| **Odds & Ends**<br>18.75$^L$ x 9$^W$ x 12.75$^{FH}$ x 5.25$^{BH}$ | Hostess$^{(95-02)}$ | 149.95 | 169 | 210 |
| **Oregano**<br>5$^L$ x 3$^W$ x 3.5$^H$ | Booking$^{(98-01)}$ | 27.00 | 27 | 40 |
| **Original Easter**<br>16$^L$ x 9$^W$ x 6$^H$ | J.W. Collection $^{(93)}$ | 65.95 | 165 | 225 |

**Our Business is Show Busines (small)**
see **Associate Producer**

**Our Business is Show Busines (medium)**
see **Show Star**

**Our Business is Show Busines (large)**
see **Best Supporting Role**

**Over the Rainbow (small)**
see **Gold Nugget**

**Over the Rainbow (medium)**
see **Pot of Gold**

**Over the Rainbow (large)**
see **Gold Rush**

| | | | | |
|---|---|---|---|---|
| **Paint the Town** | Incentive $^{(93)}$ | N/A | 100 | 150 |

5.75$^L$ x 3.75$^W$ x 3$^H$

**KEY:**
Values listed are for BASKET ONLY, unless otherwise noted, (-P) = to present

| Page in Guide | Form No. | Other Baskets Using Same Form |
|---|---|---|
| page 200 | 15491 | None |
| page 86 | 16845 | None |
| checklist<br>checklist | 11606<br>11003 | Paper |
| page 94 | 16951 | None |
| page 126 | 18902 | None |
| page 32 | 13145 | None |
| page 156 | 13722 | Harvest, Senior Employee, 90 Bee Speaker |
| page 150 | unknown | None |
| page 150 | unknown | Button, Stitching, Rings & Things, Cookie, 93 Employee Christmas, Frosty Jr. |
| page 150 | unknown | Basket of Love, 98 Renewal |
| page 150 | unknown | None |
| page 150 | unknown | Lily of the Valley, Jelly Bean, JAM 2000 |
| page 150 | unknown | None |
| page 150 | 45000- | All-Star Trio, 89 Employee Birthday, Keepsake, 90 Recruit, Shining Star, Rosemary, Sugar and Spice, 90 Sweetheart, Treasure Chest, 95 Horizon of Hope, 98 Hostess Appreciation, 00 Branch Sales, Salt & Pepper |

**KEY:** In blue = Not pictured in the Guide.   **S** = Stained, **U** = Unstained, **W** = Whitewash
**HL** = Heartland® Collection, **WT** = Woven Traditions®, **R** = Red, **G** = Green

| Basket | Collection(Year) | Orig.Price | AVG | HIGH |
|---|---|---|---|---|
| **Pansy**<br>7RD x 4.5H | May (92) | 29.95 | **113** | **155** |
| **Pantry**<br><br><br><br>14L x 9W x 4.5H | Feature (85)<br>Feature (96-97)<br>Heartland (98-00)<br>Retired (86-02)<br>Woven Traditions (98-00) | 21.95<br>46.95<br>53.00<br>21.95<br>53.00 | 62<br>59<br>53<br>43<br>57 | 70<br>80<br>75<br>65<br>75 |
| **Paper**<br><br><br>7.5L x 5.5W x 2FH x 3.5BH | Father's Day (92)<br>Incentive (92-98)<br>Incentive (99-00) | 23.95<br>N/A<br>N/A | 70<br>65<br>— | 95<br>75<br>— |
| **Paper Tray**<br>**(Bottom)**<br>12L x 14.5W x 3H | Regular Line (99-P) | 50.00 | 50 | 50 |
| **Paper Tray**<br>**(Tapered)**<br>12L x 14.5W x 3FH x 5.5BH | Incentive (99-00)<br>Regular Line (99-P) | N/A<br>55.00 | —<br>57 | —<br>110 |
| **Parsley**<br>6L x 4.5W x 2.5H | Booking(99-02) | 27.00 | 27 | 35 |
| **Patriot**<br><br><br>7L x 5W x 3.5H | All-American (97) | 32.95 | 55 | 70 |
| **Peg, Large**<br><br><br><br><br>6.5L x 6.5W x 8H | Bee (88)<br>Heartland (89-97)<br>Mother's Day (87)<br>Retired (85-99)<br>Woven Traditions (95-99) | N/A<br>28.95<br>26.95<br>19.95<br>39.95 | —<br>40<br>100<br>48<br>49 | —<br>70<br>165<br>85<br>70 |
| **Peg, Medium**<br><br>5.5L x 5.5W x 6H | Bee (88)<br>Feature (shaker) (84)<br>Retired (85-99) | N/A<br>14.95<br>17.95 | —<br>45<br>36 | —<br>60<br>65 |
| **Peg, Small**<br><br>5L x 5W x 4.5H | Bee (88)<br>Retired (85-99) | N/A<br>15.95 | —<br>38 | —<br>55 |

**KEY:**

| Page in Guide | Form No. | Other Baskets Using Same Form |
|---|---|---|
| page 164 | 10006 | 95 Perfect Attendance |
| page 86 | 2300-JO | Advisor Recognition, 92 Bee, |
| page 82 | 16446$^R$/20$^B$/38$^G$ | 90 Employee Christmas,Tray, |
| page 110 | 13951 | Small Gathering |
| page 200 | 12327/ 2300-JO | |
| page 250 | 13854 | |
| page 78 | 16000 | Note Pal |
| page 142 | 16000 | |
| page 142 | 16000 | |
| checklist | 18961 | None |
| page 142 | 19062 | None |
| checklist | 19062 | |
| page 32 | 12882 | None |
| page 20 | 10651 | Acorn, Basket of Thanks, Mini Berry, Mini Chore, Mistletoe, Mini Cradle, Baby Easter, 91 Hostess Easter, 93 Small Easter, Star Team, 94 Employee Christmas, Kiddie Purse, Small Key, Tea, 99 Branch Excellence |
| page 26 | 11000-AO | Medium Spoon, 94 Bee, 96 Large |
| page 110 | 11177/11000-ACS | Sponsor, 98 Perfect Attendance |
| page 168 | 11000-BPS | |
| page 200 | 11151 /11000-AO | |
| page 240 | 11142 | |
| page 26 | 10000-AO | Bittersweet, Carry Along, Small |
| page 86 | 10000-AO | Spoon, 96 Sponsor, 97 Bee |
| page 200 | 11070 /10000-AO | Shaker Peg |
| page 26 | 14000-AO | 93 Inaugural, Candy Cane, Violet |
| page 200 | 11452 /14000-ART | 96 Recruit, Teaspoon |

| Basket | Collection(Year) | Orig.Price | AVG | HIGH |
|---|---|---|---|---|
| **Pen Pal** <br> 4RD x 4.25H | Regular Line(00-P) <br> Regular Line(WWash)(01-P) | 29.00 <br> 29.00 | **29** <br> **29** | **29** <br> **29** |
| **Pencil** <br><br><br> 4RD x 4.25H | Father's Day (92) <br> Incentive (92-98) <br> Incentive (99-00) | 20.95 <br> N/A <br> N/A | **70** <br> **74** <br> — | **95** <br> **90** <br> — |
| **Peony** <br> 12.75L x 6.25W x 2.75H | May (01) | 39.00 | **47** | **56** |
| **Peppermint** <br> 5.5RD x 2.75H | Tree-Trimming(99) | 45.00 | **54** | **75** |
| **Perfect Attendance (1994)** <br> 6.5RD x 5H | Employee (94) | N/A | **433** | **475** |
| **Perfect Attendance (1995)** <br> 7RD x 4.5H | Employee (95) | N/A | **425** | **475** |
| **Perfect Attendance (1996)** <br> 9L x 5W x 5H | Employee (96) | N/A | **400** | **425** |
| **Perfect Attendance (1997)** <br><br> 7RD x 6.5H | Employee (97) | N/A | **388** | **425** |
| **Perfect Attendance (1998)** <br> 6.5L x 6.5W x 8H | Employee (98) | N/A | **405** | **425** |
| **Perfect Attendance (1999)** <br><br><br><br> 11L x 8W x 5.5H | Employee (99) | N/A | **--** | **425** |
| **Personal Organizer** <br> 14L x 6W x 3H | Father's Day (97) | 39.95 | **66** | **80** |
| **Petunia** <br> 9.5RD x 5H | May (97) | 45.95 | **80** | **110** |

**KEY:** <br> Values listed are for **BASKET ONLY, unless otherwised noted**, **(-P)** = to present

| Page in Guide | Form No. | Other Baskets Using Same Form |
|---|---|---|
| checklist | 11541 | Pencil |
| checklist | 10931 | |
| page 78 | 15000 | Pen Pal |
| page 142 | 15000- | |
| page 142 | 15000- | |
| page 166 | 10184 | None |
| page 230 | $19364^R/16837^G$ | Saffron |
| page 72 | unknown | Small Fruit, Senior Employee2 |
| page 72 | unknown | Pansy |
| page 72 | unknown | Candle, 90 Sponsor, Medium Key, 97 Collectors Club Renewal, 89 Employee Christmas |
| page 72 | unknown | 90 Bee, Maple Leaf, Poinsettia, 92 Sponsor (Large), 7" Hanging, 7" Canister, 7" Measuring, Barn Raising |
| page 72 | unknown | Large Peg, Medium Spoon, 94 Bee, 96 Sponsor |
| page 72 | unknown | Spring, Bob & Dolores Hope, 91-P Bee Speaker, Sparkler, Boo, Red Pottery Thank You, 91 Customer Easter, Medium Purse, Ohio Statehouse, Sparkler |
| page 78 | 13137 | Flower Pot (Small) |
| page 164 | 12947 | 90 Large Easter |

| Basket | Collection[(Year)] | Orig.Price | AVG | HIGH |
|---|---|---|---|---|
| **Picnic, Family** 24[L] x 17[W] x 10[H] | Retired [(83-86)] | 98.95 | 330 | 390 |
| **Picnic, Family Collectors Club** 20[L] x 14[W] x 9.5[H] | Collectors Club[(99)] | 255.00 | 288 | 300 |
| **Picnic, Gourmet** 13.25[L] x 11.25[W] x 9[H] | Hostess [(92-95)] | 99.95 | 100 | 140 |
| **Picnic, Large** 17[L] x 14[W] x 11[H] | All-American [(87)] Feature (Natrl) [(99)] Regular Line [(79-P)] | 64.95 89.00 29.95 | 255 104 106 | 365 125 153 |
| **Picnic, Medium** 15[L] x 15[W] x 7.5[H] | Retired [(79-84)] | 26.95 | 195 | 240 |
| **Picnic, Oak Lid** 12[L] x 12[W] x 6[H] | Feature [(82)] | N/A | 600 | 650 |
| **Picnic Pal** 9.5[L] x 9.5[W] x 2.75[H] | Good Ol' Summertime[(98)] | 37.00 | 50 | 60 |
| **Picnic, Small** 12[L] x 12[W] x 6[H] | All-American [(88)] Feature (Natrl)[(00)] Retired [(79-02)] | 65.95 59.00 21.95 | 186 75 68 | 300 89 100 |
| **Picture Perfect** 7.25[L] x 4[W] x 4.5[H] | Sweetheart [(98)] | 39.00 | 52 | 75 |
| **Pie** 12[L] x 12[W] x 4[H] | All-American [(98)] Easter [(87)] Feature [(85)] Feature (Natrl) [(99)] Retired [(86-02)] Shades of Autumn [(90)] Woven Tradition [(94)] | 55.00 28.95 19.95 39.00 22.95 31.95 37.95 | 75 193 — 41 47 67 56 | 105 300 50 60 58 135 86 |
| **Pie, Crisco** 12[L] x 12[W] x 6[H] | Crisco® [(91)] | 79.95 | 303 | 400 |
| **Pinecone** 13[RD] x 6.25[H] | Holiday Hostess[(99)] | 99.00 | 113 | 145 |

**KEY:**
**308** Values listed are for BASKET ONLY, unless otherwised noted, (-P) = to present

| Page in Guide | Form No. | Other Baskets Using Same Form |
|---|---|---|
| page 202 | 2600-HO | Small Laundry, Small Cradle |
| page 48 | 13561 | None |
| page 124 | 10413 | Precious Treasures |
| page 18<br>page 92<br>checklist | 300-HBRS<br>19755<br>10324 / 300-HO | Getaway |
| page 202 | 200-H | Homecoming |
| page 86 | unknown | Cake, Crisco Pie, 88 Employee Christmas, Small Picnic |
| page 104 | 18643 | 8 x 8 Basket |
| page 18<br>page 94<br>page 202 | 100-HBRS<br>18040<br>10324 / 300-HO | Cake, Crisco Pie, 88 Employee Christmas, Oak Lid Picnic |
| page 220 | 17523$^R$ / 16250$^B$<br>16357$^G$ / 16454$^P$ / 16551$^C$ | None |
| page 20<br>page 62<br>page 86<br>page 92<br>page 202<br>page 208<br>page 240 | 12289<br>2200-AX<br>2200-AO<br>19941<br>12203 / 2200-AO<br>2200-AGUBS<br>12211 | Director Sales Excellence, Director Sponsoring Excellence |
| page 60 | 100-DBRS | Cake, 88 Employee Christmas, Small Picnic, Oak Lid Picnic |
| page 116 | 15253$^R$ / 15164$^G$ | None |

| Basket | Collection(Year) | Orig.Price | AVG | HIGH |
|---|---|---|---|---|
| **Planter,** | Feature(feet) (88) | 42.95 | 168 | 170 |
| **Large Fern** | Retired(feet) (82-86) | 27.95 | 63 | 85 |
| | Retired(13") (79-86) | 23.95 | 121 | 200 |
| 13$^{RD}$ x 8.5$^H$ | Retired(20") (79-86) | 26.95 | 105 | 190 |
| **Planter, Patio** | Feature (84) | 21.95 | 90 | 135 |
| 10$^{RD}$ x 5.5$^H$ | | | | |
| **Planter, Sleeve** | Incentive (91) | N/A | 445 | 500 |
| | Incentive (25th) (98) | N/A | — | — |
| 31.5$^{RD}$ x 18$^H$ | | | | |
| **Planter,** | Feature(feet) (88) | 35.95 | 128 | 145 |
| **Small Fern** | Retired(feet) (82-86) | 21.95 | 108 | 175 |
| | Retired(13") (79-86) | 21.95 | 102 | 115 |
| 8.5$^{RD}$ x 7.5$^H$ | Retired(20") (79-86) | 24.95 | 138 | 150 |
| **Poinsettia** | Christmas(88) | 26.95 | 70 | 155 |
| 7$^{RD}$ x 6.5$^H$ | | | | |
| **Pom Pom Peggy** | Incentive (91) | N/A | 73 | 100 |
| 12$^H$ | | | | |
| **Pool** | J.W. Originals | N/A | ** | ** |
| 22$^L$ x 14.5$^W$ x 6.25$^W$ | | | | |
| **Popcorn** | Christmas(99) | 59.00 | 68 | 90 |
| 10.5$^{RD}$ x 5$^H$ | | | | |
| **Pot of Gold** | Feature (02) | 198.00 | — | — |
| 19.75$^{RD}$ x 12.5$^H$ | | | | |
| **Pot of Gold, Small** | Incentive (94) | N/A | 110 | 160 |
| 5.5$^{RD}$ x 3.75$^H$ | | | | |
| **Potpourri** | Booking(85-90) | 3.00 | 46 | 80 |
| | Employee Birthday(90) | N/A | 87 | 112 |
| 5$^L$ x 5$^W$ x 2.5$^H$ | Mother's Day (91) | 21.95 | 60 | 100 |
| **Pottery Ware** | J.W. Originals | N/A | ** | ** |
| 25$^{RD}$ x 13$^H$ | | | | |
| **Precious Treasures** | Sweetheart (95) | 89.95 | 168 | 200 |
| 13.25$^L$ x 11.25$^W$ x 9$^H$ | | | | |

| Page in Guide | Form No. | Other Baskets Using Same Form |
|---|---|---|
| page 90 | 3200-RO | Sewing (Round) |
| page 202 | 3200-RO | |
| page 202 | 3200-SO | |
| page 202 | 3200-TO | |
| page 86 | 6000-R | None |
| page 140 | unknown | None |
| page 142 | unknown | |
| page 90 | 2900-RO | None |
| page 202 | 2900-RO | |
| page 202 | 2900-SO | |
| page 202 | 2900-TO | |
| page 38 | 3900-BRST / BGST | 90 Bee, 7" Hanging, 7" Measuring, 92 Sponsor (Large), Maple Leaf, 97 Perfect Attendance, 7" Canister, Barn Raising |
| page 150 | unknown | None |
| page 160 | unknown | None |
| page 40 | $15156^R / 15351^G$ | None |
| page 96 | 11903 | None |
| page 150 | unknown | Lily of the Valley, Jelly Bean, JAM 2000 |
| page 32 | 13000-AO | 88-89 Recruit, 90 Employee Birthday, |
| page 70 | 13000- | 93 Regional Sponsored Award, Sweet |
| page 168 | 13000-APS | Basil, 93 Sweetheart, Shamrock |
| page 160 | unknown | None |
| page 218 | 10456 | Gourmet Picnic |

**KEY:** In blue = Not pictured in the Guide. **S** = Stained, **U** = Unstained, **W** = Whitewash
**HL** = Heartland® Collection, **WT** = Woven Traditions®, **R** = Red, **G** = Green     **311**

| Basket | Collection(Year) | Orig.Price | AVG | HIGH |
|---|---|---|---|---|
| **Pumpkin**<br>9.25$^{RD}$ x 7.25$^H$ | Pumpkin $^{(95)}$ | 47.95 | 103 | 135 |
| **Pumpkin, Large**<br>11.25$^{RD}$ x 9$^H$ | Pumpkin $^{(97)}$ | 117.95 | 142 | 210 C |
| **Pumpkin, Little**<br>5.75$^{RD}$ x 4.25$^H$ | Pumpkin $^{(97)}$ | 34.95 | 65 | 90 |
| **Pumpkin Patch**<br>6.5$^{RD}$ x 6.75$^H$ | Feature $^{(01)}$ | 49.00 | — | — |
| **Pumpkin, Small**<br>7.25$^{RD}$ x 5.25$^H$ | Pumpkin $^{(96)}$ | 40.95 | 77 | 110 |
| **Purse, Kiddie**<br><br><br><br>7$^L$ x 5$^W$ x 3.5$^H$ | Feature (Natrl) $^{(98)}$<br>Regular Line $^{(79-P)}$<br>Retired(Natrl) $^{(94)}$ | 27.95<br>10.95<br>28.95 | 48<br>39<br>40 | 60<br>90<br>60 |
| **Purse, Medium**<br><br>11$^L$ x 8$^W$ x 5.5$^H$ | Retired(1sw/h) $^{(79-97)}$<br>Retired(split lid) $^{(82-86)}$ | 16.95<br>24.95 | 56<br>120 | 119<br>255 |
| **Purse, Shoulder**<br>9.5$^L$ x 5.75$^W$ x 7$^H$ | Retired $^{(96-99)}$ | 84.95 | 90 | 175 |
| **Purse, Small**<br><br>9.5$^L$ x 6$^W$ x 6$^H$ | Heartland $^{(88-98)}$<br>Mother's Day $^{(91)}$<br>Retired $^{(79-99)}$ | 36.95<br>34.95<br>14.95 | 50<br>108<br>54 | 85<br>130<br>110 |
| **Purse, Tall**<br>9.5$^L$ x 5$^W$ x 9.5$^H$ | Retired $^{(79-89)}$ | 27.95 | 62 | 90 |
| **Quilting**<br>12$^{RD}$ x 5.75$^H$ | All-American $^{(89)}$ | 46.95 | 150 | 210 |

**Reach for the Stars(Small)**
   see **Star Bound**
4.75$^L$ x 3.75$^W$ x 2.25$^H$

| Page in Guide | Form No. | Other Baskets Using Same Form |
|---|---|---|
| page 192 | 19402 | None |
| page 192 | 16039 | None |
| page 192 | 16021 | None |
| page 94 | 10621 | None |
| page 192 | 16012 | None |
| page 92<br>checklist<br>page 202 | 10898<br>10731 / 700-EO<br>17019 | Acorn, Basket of Thanks, Tea, Mini Berry, Mini Chore, Mistletoe, Mini Cradle, Baby Easter, Patriot, 91 Hostess Easter, 93 Small Easter, Small Key, 94 Employee Christmas, Star Team, 99 Branch Excellence |
| page 202<br>page 202 | 10901 / 900-E<br>900-QO | 91-P Bee Speaker, Bob and Dolores Hope, Boo Basket, 91 Customer Easter, Red Pottery Thank You, Spring, 96 Statehouse, Sparkler |
| page 202 | 18210 | None |
| page 110<br>page 168<br>page 202 | 10839/800-ECS<br>800-EPS<br>10821/800-EO | Season's Greetings, 94 Regional Sponsored, 99 Branch Sponsoring Excellence |
| page 202 | 1000-EO | 91 Employee Christmas, MBA, Tall Key, Two-Quart, Growing Strong Together, Membership |
| page 18 | 54000-ABRS | Basket of Plenty, High Achiever |
| page 150 | unknown | Business Card |

| Basket | Collection(Year) | Orig.Price | AVG | HIGH |
|--------|------------------|-----------|-----|------|
| **Reach for the Stars(Medium)** see **Shining Star** | | | | |

5.75$^L$ x 3.75$^W$ x 3$^H$

| **Reach for the Stars(Large)** see **Star Team** | | | | |

7$^L$ x 5$^W$ x 3.5$^H$

| **Recipe** | Heartland (98-01) | 39.00 | 40 | 40 |
| | Regular Line (96-P) | 29.95 | 34 | 79 |
| | Regular Line(WWash) (01-P) | 35.00 | 35 | 35 |
| | Retired(Natrl) (99-01) | 25.00 | 34 | 45 |
| | Shades of Autumn (94) | 29.95 | 66 | 75 |
| | Woven Tradition (98-01) | 39.00 | — | — |

8$^L$ x 5.5$^W$ x 4.5$^{FH}$ x 6$^{BH}$

| **Recipe, Small** | Regular Line (01-P) | 34.00 | 34 | 34 |
| | Regular Line(WWash) (01-P) | 34.00 | 34 | 34 |

7$^L$ x 5.25$^W$ x 3.75$^{FH}$ x 4.5$^{BH}$

| **Recruit (1999)** | Incentive (99) | N/A | 133 | 200 |

5.5$^{RD}$ x 4.5$^H$

| **Recruit "All-Star"** | Incentive (93) | N/A | 138 | 200 |

8$^L$ x 4$^W$ x 2$^H$

| **Recruit "Flying High with Longaberger"** | Incentive (92) | N/A | 119 | 125 |

5$^{RD}$ x 4.5$^H$

| **Recruit "Pegged for Success"** | Incentive (96) | N/A | 102 | 135 |

5$^L$ x 5$^W$ x 4.5$^H$

**KEY:**
**314** **Values listed are for BASKET ONLY, unless otherwised noted, (-P)** = to present

# Reach for the Stars (Medium) – Recruit (Pegged)

| Page in Guide | Form No. | Other Baskets Using Same Form |
|---|---|---|
| page 150 | unknown | All-Star Trio, 89 Employee Birthday, Keepsake, Paint the Town, 00 Branch Sales, Rosemary, Sugar and Spice, 90 Sweetheart, Treasure Chest, 95 Horizon of Hope, 98 H.Appreciation, Salt & Pepper |
| page 150 | unknown | Acorn, Basket of Thanks, Tea, Mini Berry, Mini Chore, Mistletoe, Mini Cradle, Baby Easter, Patriot, 91 Hostess Easter, 93 Small Easter, 94 Employee Christmas, Kiddie Purse, Small Key, 99 Branch Excellence |
| page 110<br>checklist, Hostess<br>checklist<br>page 204<br>page 208<br>page 240 | 10596<br>17418<br>10461<br>19542<br>17400<br>10499 | None |
| checklist<br>checklist | 19496<br>10451 | Basket of Plenty, High Achiever |
| page 132 | unknown | 88 Employee Birthday, 89 Inaugural, Forget-Me-Not, 5" Measuring, 92 Employee Christmas, 5" Hanging, Resolution, 92 Sponsor (Small), 5" Canister, Watch Your Business Bloom, 92 Recruit (Flying High) |
| page 130 | 16101 | 94 Hostess Appreciation, Rose Bud 93 Sponsor (Small), Lavender |
| page 130 | 10154 | 88 Employee Birthday, 89 Inaugural Forget-Me-Not, 5" Measuring, 92 Employee Christmas, 5" Hanging, Resolution, 92 Sponsor (Small), 5" Canister, Watch Your Business Bloom, 99 Recruit |
| page 130 | unknown | 93 Inaugural, Candy Cane, Violet, Small Peg, Teaspoon |

| Basket | Collection(Year) | Orig.Price | AVG | HIGH |
|---|---|---|---|---|
| **Recruit** "Rising Star" $12^L$ x $12.25^W$ x $16.25^H$ | Incentive (90-91) | N/A | 185 | 195 |
| **Recruit** "Share the Tradition" $5^L$ x $5^W$ x $2.5^H$ | Incentive (88-89) | N/A | 119 | 175 |
| **Recruit** "Together–We're Growing" $5.75^L$ x $3.75^W$ x $3^H$ | Incentive (90) | N/A | 169 | 180 |
| **Red Pottery** **Thank You** $11^L$ x $8^W$ x $5.5^H$ | Feature (93) | N/A | 123 | 155 |
| **Red, White & You** $5.5^L$ x $6^W$ x $2.25^H$ | Incentive, Recruit (02) | 61.00 | — | — |
| **Regional Basket** $15.75^L$ x $6.5^W$ x $11^H$ | Incentive (88-P) | N/A | 250 | 250 |
| **Regional** **Excellence (98)** $8.5^L$ x $8.5^W$ x $5^H$ | Incentive (98) | N/A | 150 | 170 |
| **Regional Sales (00)** $9.25^L$ x $5^W$ x $6.5^H$ | Incentive (00) | N/A | — | — |
| **Regional Sales (01)** $10^L$ x $9.25^W$ x $4^H$ | Incentive (01) | N/A | — | 125 |
| **Regional Sales (02)** $6.5^L$ x $6.5^W$ x $6.5^H$ | Incentive (02) | N/A | — | — |
| **Regional** **Sales Excellence (99)** $15^L$ x $9.5^W$ x $5.5^H$ | Incentive (99) | N/A | — | 150 |
| **Regional** **Sponsored (91)** $10^L$ x $6^W$ x $4^H$ | Incentive (91) | N/A | 188 | 225 |

**KEY:**
Values listed are for BASKET ONLY, unless otherwised noted, (-P) = to present

| Page in Guide | Form No. | Other Baskets Using Same Form |
|---|---|---|
| page 130 | 1700-DST | Medium Hamper, Small Hamper, 90-91 Sponsor (Superstar) |
| page 130 | 13000-BBRS | 90 Employee Birthday, 93 Regional Sponsored Award, 93 Sweetheart, Potpourri, Shamrock, Sweet Basil, Tee |
| page 130 | 45000-ABRST | All-Star Trio, 89 Employee, Birthday, Keepsake, Paint the Town, Shining Star, Rosemary, Sugar and Spice, 90 Sweetheart, Treasure Chest, 95 Horizon of Hope, 00 Branch Sales, Salt & Pepper |
| page 82 | 190xx | 91- P Bee Speaker, Bob & Dolores Hope, Boo Basket, 91 Customer Easter, Medium Purse, Spring, 96 Statehouse, Sparkler |
| page 132 | unknown | Twinkle Twinkle |
| page 146 | unknown | Branch Basket, Director Basket |
| page 148 | unknown | Large Berry, 91 Bee, 88-89 Sponsor, 96 Bee |
| page 148 | unknown | None |
| page 148 | unknown | 10" Generations |
| page 148 | unknown | None |
| page 148 | unknown | Welcome Home, Small Market, 99 Regional Sponsoring Excellence |
| page 146 | 3400- | Small Chore, 93 Lg Easter, 95 Bee 88 Sm Easter, Gingerbread, $500 Million, Woven Memories |

| Basket | Collection(Year) | Orig.Price | AVG | HIGH |
|---|---|---|---|---|
| **Regional Sponsored (92)** 8.5$^L$ x 5$^W$ x 3.5$^H$ | Incentive (92) | N/A | **195** | **275** |
| **Regional Sponsored (93)** 5$^L$ x 5$^W$ x 2.5$^H$ | Incentive (93) | N/A | **111** | **160** |
| **Regional Sponsored (94)** 9.5$^L$ x 6$^W$ x 6$^H$ | Incentive (94) | N/A | **226** | **250** |
| **Regional Sponsored (95)** 7.5$^L$ x 7.5$^W$ x 3.5$^H$ | Incentive (95) | N/A | **234** | **300** |
| **Regional Sponsored (96)** 10$^{RD}$ x 4$^H$ | Incentive (96) | N/A | **190** | **210** |
| **Regional Sponsoring (00)** 9.25$^L$ x 5$^W$ x 6.5$^H$ | Incentive (00) | N/A | **138** | **175** |
| **Regional Sponsoring Excellence (98)** 4.25$^L$ x 4.25$^W$ x 3$^H$ | Incentive (98) | N/A | — | **127** |
| **Regional Sponsoring Excellence (99)** 15$^L$ x 9.5$^W$ x 5.5$^H$ | Incentive (99) | N/A | — | **150** |
| **Remembrance** 10.5$^L$ x 9$^W$ x 8$^H$ | Feature (96-97) Hostess (90-92) | 99.95 79.95 | **115** **125** | **118** **175** |
| **Renewal (1997)** 9$^L$ x 5$^W$ x 5$^H$ | Collectors Club(97) | 39.95 | **77** | **105** |
| **Renewal (1998)** 8.5$^{RD}$ x 4$^H$ | Collectors Club(98) | 44.95 | **68** | **95** |
| **Renewal (1999)** 6.75$^L$ x 5.75$^W$ x 4.75$^H$ | Collectors Club(99) | 42.00 | **50** | **57** |

**KEY:**

| Page in Guide | Form No. | Other Baskets Using Same Form |
|---|---|---|
| page 146 | 33000- | Be Mine, Small Oval, 93 Sponsor (Large), 97 Small Easter, Rose Petal |
| page 146 | 11321 | Sweet Basil, 90 Employee Birthday, Shamrock, 93 Sweetheart, 88-89 Recruit, Potpourri, Tee |
| page 148 | 800- | Season's Greetings, Small Purse, 99 Branch Sponsoring Excellence |
| page 148 | 1400- | Medium Berry |
| page 148 | 500- | Darning, Crisco Cookie, Daisy 89 Easter, Frosty |
| page 148 | unknown | None |
| page 148 | unknown | Sweet Sentiments, Lots of Luck |
| page 148 | unknown | Welcome Home, Small Market, 99 Regional Sales Excellence |
| page 84 | $16748^R/21^B/30^G$ | Weekender, Top Performer |
| page 124 | 200-YOS | Beachcomber |
| page 44 | 105702 | Candle, 89 Employee Christmas, 90 Sponsor, Medium Key, 96 Perfect Attendance |
| page 46 | 13340 | Basket of Love, Best Supporting Role |
| page 46 | 12998 | None |

| Basket | Collection(Year) | Orig.Price | AVG | HIGH |
|--------|------------------|-----------|-----|------|
| **Renewal (2000)** <br> 6.75$^L$ x 5.25$^W$ x 3.25$^H$ | Collectors Club$^{(00)}$ | 44.00 | **62** | **70** |
| **Renewal (2001)** <br> 5$^{RD}$ x 6$^H$ | Collectors Club$^{(01)}$ | 45.00 | — | — |
| **Renewal (2002)** <br> 6.25$^L$ x 5$^W$ x 1.75$^H$ | Collectors Club$^{(02-03)}$ | 39.00 | — | — |
| **Resolution** <br><br><br> 5$^{RD}$ x 4.5$^H$ | Feature $^{(87)}$ | 16.95 | **118** | **160** |
| **Rings & Things** <br> 7$^{RD}$ x 3$^H$ | Mother's Day $^{(98)}$ | 34.00 | **40** | **65** |
| **Rose** <br> 14.5$^L$ x 7.5$^W$ x 3.75$^H$ | May $^{(91)}$ | 29.95 | **200** | **250** |
| **Rose Bud** <br> 8$^L$ x 4$^W$ x 2$^H$ | Incentive $^{(97)}$ | N/A | **124** | **150** |
| **Rose Garden** <br> 12$^L$ x 7$^W$ x 4.5$^H$ | Incentive $^{(97)}$ | N/A | **65** | **79** |
| **Rose Petal** <br><br> 8.5$^L$ x 5$^W$ x 3.5$^H$ | Incentive $^{(97)}$ | N/A | **66** | **119** |
| **Rosemary** <br><br><br> 5.75$^L$ x 3.75$^W$ x 3$^H$ | Booking$^{(90-92)}$ | N/A | **52** | **65** |
| **Row Your Boat** <br> 13.5$^L$ x 6.5$^W$ x 4$^H$ | Regular Line $^{(02-P)}$ | 54.00 | **54** | **54** |

| Page in Guide | Form No. | Other Baskets Using Same Form |
|---|---|---|
| page 48 | 18783 | None |
| page 50 | 10273 / 10813 | None |
| page 52 | 12081 | None |
| page 82 | 3800-ABS | 88 Employee Birthday, 89 Inaugural, 92 Employee Christmas, Forget-Me-Not, 5" Hanging, 5" Measuring, 92 Recruit, 92 Sponsor (Small), Watch Your Business Bloom, 99 Recruit |
| page 170 | 10383 | Button, Stitching, Cookie, Show Star 93 Employee Christmas, Frosty Jr. |
| page 164 | 4700-CSS | Bakery, Bread (new), Breakfast, Crisco Baking |
| page 152 | unknown | Lavender, 94 Hostess Appreciation 93 Recruit, 93 Sponsor (Small) |
| page 148 | unknown | 97 Large Easter |
| page 152 | unknown | Be Mine, 93 Sponsor (All-Star), 92 Regional Sponsored Award, 97 Small Easter, Small Oval |
| page 32 | 45000-JOS | All-Star Trio, 89 Employee Birthday, Keepsake, Paint the Town, 90 Recruit, Reach for the Stars (Med.), Sugar and Spice, 90 Sweetheart, Treasure Chest, 95 Horizon of Hope, 98 H.Appreciation, 00 Branch Sales, Salt & Pepper |
| checklist | 12494 | None |

| Basket | Collection(Year) | Orig.Price | AVG | HIGH |
|--------|------------------|-----------|-----|------|
| **Saddlebrook Large** $9.5^L$ x $5.5^W$ x $9.25^H$ | Collectors Club$^{(00\text{-}01)}$ <br> Regular Line $^{(00\text{-}P)}$ | 139.00 <br> 139.00 | **140** <br> — | **150** <br> — |
| **Saddlebrook Medium** $7.25^L$ x $4.5^W$ x $6.5^H$ | Feature $^{(01)}$ | 109.00 | **120** | **165** |
| **Saddlebrook Small** $5.5^L$ x $3.5^W$ x $4^H$ | Collectors Club$^{(00\text{-}01)}$ <br> Regular Line $^{(00\text{-}P)}$ | 79.00 <br> 79.00 | **85** <br> — | **95** <br> — |
| **Saffron** $5.5^{RD}$ x $2.75^H$ | Regular Line, Booking$^{(02\text{-}P)}$ | 27.00 | **27** | **27** |
| **Sage** $5.75^L$ x $5.5^W$ x $2.5^H$ | Regular Line, Booking$^{(01\text{-}P)}$ | 27.00 | **27** | **59** |
| **Salt & Pepper** $5.75^L$ x $3.75^W$ x $3^H$ | Regular Line $^{(01\text{-}P)}$ | 34.00 | **34** | **56** |
| **Santa's Little Helper** $5.75^L$ x $3.75^W$ x $3.5^H$ | Feature$^{(99)}$ | 30.00 | **55** | **60** |
| **Seashell** $7.75^L$ x $5.75^W$ x $5^H$ | Good Ol' Summertime $^{(99)}$ | 39.00 | **60** | **85** |
| **Season's Greetings** $9.5^L$ x $6^W$ x $6^H$ | Christmas$^{(92)}$ | 44.95 | **63** | **95** |
| **Senior Employee** $16^L$ x $9^W$ x $6^H$ | Employee $^{(xx\text{-}97)}$ | N/A | **320** | **425** |
| **Senior Employee2** $6.5^{RD}$ x $5^H$ | Employee $^{(97\text{-}P)}$ | N/A | — | **90** |
| **Senior Recognition** $8.75^L$ x $4.75^W$ x $6.5^H$ | Employee $^{(xx\text{-}97)}$ | N/A | **85** | **125** |
| **Serve It Up** $23^L$ x $13.25^W$ x $3.75^H$ | Regular Line, Hostess$^{(02\text{-}P)}$ | 105.00 | **105** | **105** |

**KEY:**

**Values listed are for BASKET ONLY, unless otherwise noted**, **(-P)** = to present

| Page in Guide | Form No. | Other Baskets Using Same Form |
|---|---|---|
| page 50<br>checklist | 15776<br>**19764** | None |
| page 94 | 12306 | None |
| page 48<br>checklist | 15679<br>**17698** | None |
| checklist, Booking | 12524 | Peppermint |
| checklist, Booking | 19585 | None |
| checklist | 12044 | 89 Employee Birthday, Keepsake, Paint the Town, 90 Recruit, Shining Star, Rosemary, Sugar and Spice, 90 Sweetheart, Treasure Chest, 95 Horizon of Hope, 98 Hostess Appreciation, 00 Branch Sales, All-Star Trio |
| page 84 | 19721 | None |
| page 104 | 15296 | None |
| page 38 | 10316$^R$ / 10219$^G$ | Small Purse, 94 Regional Sponsored, 99 Branch Sponsoring Excellence |
| page 70 | unknown | Original Easter, Harvest, 90 Bee Speaker |
| page 70 | unknown | Small Fruit, 94 Perfect Attendance |
| page 70 | unknown | 89 Bee, 92 Employee Birthday, Sophomore & Junior Recognition, Memory, 25th Anniversary (Sm), 20th Century, Tour |
| checklist, Hostess | 60895 | None |

| Basket | Collection(Year) | Orig.Price | AVG | HIGH |
|---|---|---|---|---|
| **Serving Tray** | All-American(00) | 98.00 | **104** | **120** |
| | Collectors Club (99) | 99.00 | **130** | **125** |
| | Hostess (95-02) | 74.95 | **71** | **116** |
| 20$^L$ x 14$^W$ x 3.75$^H$ | Hostess (WWash) (01-02) | 95.00 | — | — |
| **Serving Tray, Small** | Collectors Club (96) | 69.95 | **110** | **125** |
| 11.5$^L$ x 15.5$^W$ x 3.75$^H$ | | | | |
| **Sewing Circle** | Collectors Club (01) | 75.00 | **124** | **132** |
| 8.5$^{RD}$ x 5.5$^H$ | | | | |
| **Sewing Notions** | Regular Line(01-P) | 59.00 | **59** | **59** |
| | Regular Line(WWash) (01-P) | 59.00 | **59** | **59** |
| 11.25$^L$ x 9.25$^W$ x 5.75$^H$ | | | | |
| **Sewing, Rectangular** | Retired (78-83) | 26.95 | **381** | **400** |
| 16$^L$ x 11$^W$ x 9$^H$ | | | | |
| **Sewing, Round** | Feature (no stand) (85, 87) | 37.95 | **207** | **218** |
| | Hostess(95-00) | 89.95 | **96** | **128** |
| | Retired, (no stand) (78-86) | 29.95 | **111** | **187** |
| 13$^{RD}$ x 8.5$^H$ | Retired, (stand) (78-86) | 29.95 | **128** | **250** |
| **Shaker Harmony No.1** | Collectors Club(00) | 95.00 | **126** | **175** |
| 10.75$^L$ x 9.75$^W$ x 4.5$^H$ | | | | |
| **Shaker Harmony No.2** | Collectors Club(01) | 89.00 | **111** | **129** |
| 9.75$^L$ x 7.75$^W$ x 4$^H$ | | | | |
| **Shaker Harmony No.3** | Collectors Club(01) | 79.00 | **88** | **105** |
| 8.75$^L$ x 6.75$^W$ x 3.25$^H$ | | | | |
| **Shaker Harmony No.4** | Collectors Club(02) | 65.00 | — | — |
| 7.5$^L$ x 5.75$^W$ x 2.75$^H$ | | | | |
| **Shaker Harmony No.5** | Collectors Club(01) | 59.00C | **72** | **90** C |
| 6.75$^L$ x 4.75$^W$ x 2$^H$ | | | | |
| **Shaker Taker** | Good Ol' Summertime(00) | 39.00 | **40** | **45** |
| 7.5$^L$ x 3.75$^W$ x 2.75$^H$ | | | | |

| Page in Guide | Form No. | Other Baskets Using Same Form |
|---|---|---|
| page 20 | 15849 | None |
| page 46 | 18091 | |
| page 126 | 60011 | |
| page 126 | 68586 | |
| page 44 | 12629 | None |
| page 52 | 10575 | None |
| checklist | 10424 | Timeless Memory |
| checklist | 10435 | |
| page 204 | 600-F | Large Market, 99 Director Sales & Sponsoring Excellence |
| page 88 | 3200-EO | Planter (Large Fern) |
| page 126 | 13234 | |
| page 204 | 3200-NO | |
| page 204 | 3200-NO | |
| page 50 | 19089 | None |
| page 50 | 18988 | None |
| page 50 | 16870 | None |
| not in this edition | 16861 | None |
| page 50 | 18881 | None |
| page 104 | 17469 | Small Barbeque Buddy |

| Basket | Collection(Year) | Orig.Price | AVG | HIGH |
|---|---|---|---|---|
| **Shamrock** | Feature (90) | 19.95 | **99** | **165** |
| 5$^L$ x 5$^W$ x 2.5$^H$ | | | | |
| **Shining Star** | Incentive (95) | N/A | **113** | **185** |
| 5.75$^L$ x 3.75$^W$ x 3$^H$ | | | | |
| **Shining Star Large** | Holiday Hostess (01) | 109.00 | — | — |
| 13.5$^L$ x 14.5$^W$ x 4.75$^H$ | | | | |
| **Shining Star Small** | Christmas (01) | 59.00 | **75** | **87** |
| 10.25$^L$ x 11$^W$ x 3.75$^H$ | | | | |
| **Show Star** | Incentive (96) | N/A | **118** | **160** |
| 7$^{RD}$ x 3$^H$ | | | | |
| **Sleeve, Sunroom** | Hostess (99-02) | 210.00 | **209** | **231** |
| 24.5$^L$ x 20$^W$ x 14$^H$ | | | | |
| **Sleigh Bell** | Holiday Hostess (94) | 139.95 | **182** | **250** |
| 16.5$^{RD}$ x 11.5$^H$ | | | | |
| **Small Comforts** | Regular Line (01-P) | 42.00 | **42** | **42** |
| 7.75$^L$ x 5.25$^W$ x 4.25$^H$ | | | | |
| **Small Oval** | Mother's Day (90) | 28.95 | **51** | **80** |
| 8.5$^L$ x 5$^W$ x 3.5$^H$ | | | | |
| **Snapdragon** | May (98) | 47.00 | **70** | **90** |
| 7.5$^{RD}$ x 9.25$^H$ | | | | |
| **Snowflake, Large** | Holiday Hostess (97) | 129.95 | **117** | **135** |
| 14$^L$ x 12.75$^W$ x 11.5$^H$ | | | | |
| **Snowflake, Small** | Christmas(97) | 49.95 | **70** | **90** |
| 10$^L$ x 9.25$^W$ x 6.5$^H$ | | | | |

| Page in Guide | Form No. | Other Baskets Using Same Form |
|---|---|---|
| page 82 | 13000-HGS | 90 Employee Birthday, Sweet Basil, 93 Sweetheart, Potpourri, 93 Regional Sponsored Award, 88-89 Recruit, Tee |
| page 150 | unknown | All-Star Trio, 89 Employee Birthday, Keepsake, Paint the Town, 90 Recruit, Sugar & Spice, Treasure Chest, Rosemary, 90 Sweetheart, 95 Horizon of Hope, 98 H.Appreciation, 00 Branch Sales, Salt & Pepper |
| page 116 | $10753^R$ / $10761^G$ | None |
| page 42 | $10734^R$ / $10745^G$ | None |
| page 150 | unknown | Button, Stitching, Rings & Things, Cookie, 93 Employee Christmas, Frosty Jr. |
| page 126 | 15261 | None |
| page 116 | $14427^R$ / $14435^G$ | None |
| checklist | 17558 | None |
| page 168 | 33000-JPS | Be Mine, 93 Sponsor (All-Star), 92 Regional Sponsored Award, 97 Small Easter, Rose Petal |
| page 164 | 10863 | None |
| page 116 | $12661^R$ / $12653^G$ | None |
| page 40 | $12645^R$ / $12637^G$ | None |

| Basket | Collection(Year) | Orig.Price | AVG | HIGH |
|---|---|---|---|---|
| **Sophomore Recognition** 8.75$^L$ x 4.75$^W$ x 6.5$^H$ | Employee $^{(xx-97)}$ | N/A | 67 | 75 |
| **Spare Change** 6.5$^L$ x 6.5$^W$ x 3$^H$ | Father's Day $^{(91)}$ | 21.95 | 58 | 70 |
| **Sparkler** 11$^L$ x 8$^W$ x 5.5$^H$ | All-American$^{(00)}$ | 48.00 | 60 | 75 |
| **Sponsor, Large "All-Star"** 8.5$^L$ x 5$^W$ x 3.5$^H$ | Incentive $^{(93)}$ | N/A | 130 | 175 |
| **Sponsor, Small "All-Star"** 8$^L$ x 4$^W$ x 2$^H$ | Incentive $^{(93)}$ | N/A | 113 | 160 |
| **Sponsor, Large "Flying High with Longaberger"** 7$^{RD}$ x 6.5$^H$ | Incentive $^{(92)}$ | N/A | 125 | 175 |
| **Sponsor, Small "Flying High with Longaberger"** 5$^{RD}$ x 4.5$^H$ | Incentive $^{(92)}$ | N/A | 118 | 175 |
| **Sponsor "Pegged for Success"** 6.5$^L$ x 6.5$^W$ x 8$^H$ | Incentive $^{(96)}$ | N/A | 193 | 225 |
| **Sponsor "Rising Star"** 16.5$^L$ x 16.5$^W$ x 21.5$^H$ | Incentive $^{(90-91)}$ | N/A | 185 | 230 |
| **Sponsor, Superstar "Rising Star"** 12$^L$ x 12.25$^W$ x 16.25$^H$ | Incentive $^{(90-91)}$ | N/A | 155 | 200 |
| **Sponsor "Share the Tradition"** 8.5$^L$ x 8.5$^W$ x 5$^H$ | Incentive $^{(88-89)}$ | N/A | 207 | 325 |

| Page in Guide | Form No. | Other Baskets Using Same Form |
|---|---|---|
| page 70 | unknown | 89 Bee, Dresden Basket, Tour, 92 Employee Birthday, Memory, Junior & Senior Recognition, 25th Anniversary, Hartville, 20th Century |
| page 78 | 1300-JCWS | Small Berry, 98 Branch Excellence |
| page 20 | 18694 | Spring, Bob & Dolores Hope, 91 Customer Easter, 91-P Bee Speaker, Boo, Medium Purse, 98 Perfect Attendance, 96 Ohio Statehouse, Red Pottery Thank You |
| page 130 | 13323 | Be Mine, 92 Regional Sponsored Award, Small Oval, 97 Small Easter, Rose Petal |
| page 130 | unknown | 94 Hostess Appreciation, Lavender, 93 Recruit, Rose Bud |
| page 130 | 10162 | 90 Bee, Poinsettia, 7" Hanging, Barn Raising, 7" Measuring, Maple Leaf, 97 Perfect Attendance, 7" Canister |
| page 130 | unknown | 88 Employee Birthday, 89 Inaugural, 92 Employee Christmas, 99 Recruit, 5" Hanging, Forget-Me-Not, 92 Recruit, Resolution, 5" Measuring, 5" Canister, Watch Your Business Bloom |
| page 130 | unknown | Large Peg, Medium Spoon, 94 Bee, 98 Perfect Attendance |
| page 130 | 1600-DST | Large Hamper |
| page 130 | 1700-DST | Medium Hamper, Small Hamper, 90-91 Recruit |
| page 130 | 1500-BBRS | 91 Bee, Large Berry, 96 Bee 98 Regional Sales Excellence |

| Basket | Collection(Year) | Orig.Price | AVG | HIGH |
|--------|------------------|-----------|-----|------|
| **Sponsor**<br>**"Together–We're Growing"**<br>$9^L \times 5^W \times 5^H$ | Incentive (90) | N/A | 175 | 200 |
| **Spoon, Large**<br>$7.5^L \times 7.5^W \times 10^H$ | Regular Line(82-P)<br>Retired(Natrl) (00-01) | 16.95<br>45.00 | 48<br>— | 65<br>— |
| **Spoon, Medium**<br><br><br><br>$6.5^L \times 6.5^W \times 8^H$ | All-American (90)<br>Feature (96-97)<br>Feature (Natrl) (99)<br>Regular Line (83-P)<br>Retired (Natrl) (00-01) | 27.95<br>36.95<br>28.00<br>14.95<br>34.00 | 74<br>53<br>—<br>36<br>— | 115<br>63<br>43<br>55<br>— |
| **Spoon, Small**<br><br><br><br><br>$5.5^L \times 5.5^W \times 6^H$ | All-American (90)<br>Booking (xx-84)<br>Feature (Natrl) (98, 00)<br>Heartland (88-99)<br>Regular Line (87-P)<br>Retired (Natrl) (00-01) | 23.95<br>N/A<br>19.95<br>23.95<br>19.95<br>26.00 | 93<br>60<br>26<br>34<br>28<br>— | 135<br>65<br>32<br>55<br>45<br>— |
| **Spring**<br><br><br><br><br><br>$11^L \times 8^W \times 5.5^H$ | Easter (87)<br>Feature (Natrl) (98)<br>Heartland (90-97)<br>Mother's Day (88)<br>Regular Line (83-P)<br>Regular Line(WWash) (01-P)<br>Woven Traditions (95-97) | 25.95<br>29.95<br>34.95<br>28.95<br>14.95<br>39.00<br>41.95 | 228<br>35<br>48<br>120<br>39<br>39<br>51 | 300<br>40<br>75<br>155<br>70<br>39<br>65 |
| **Spring Meadow**<br>$16.25^L \times 10.75^W \times 4^H$ | Collectors Club(00) | 95.00 | 111 | 150 |
| **Star Bound**<br>$4.75^L \times 3.75^W \times 2.25^H$ | Incentive (95) | N/A | 215 | 300 |
| **Star Team**<br><br>$7^L \times 5^W \times 3.5^H$ | Incentive (95) | N/A | 219 | 300 |
| **Statehouse**<br><br>$11^L \times 8^W \times 5.5^H$ | Special Event (96) | N/A | — | 80 |

**KEY:**
**330** **Values listed are for BASKET ONLY, unless otherwised noted, (-P) = to present**

| Page in Guide | Form No. | Other Baskets Using Same Form |
|---|---|---|
| page 130 | 1100-ABRST | 89 Employee Christmas, Candle, Medium Key, Collectors Club 97 Renewal, 96 Perfect Attendance |
| checklist<br>page 204 | 11258<br>17680 | Mini Waste / Extra Small Waste |
| page 18<br>page 82<br>page 94<br>checklist<br>page 204 | 11000-OBRS<br>16349$^R$/22$^B$/31$^G$<br>19658<br>11169/11000-OO<br>19658 | 94 Bee, Large Peg, 96 Sponsor, 98 Perfect Attendance |
| page 18<br>page 34<br>page 92<br>page 110<br>checklist<br>page 204 | 10000-OBRS<br>10000-OO<br>10871<br>11096/10000-OCS<br>11088 /10000-OO<br>10871 | Medium Peg, Bittersweet, Carry Along, 97 Bee |
| page 62<br>page 92<br>page 110<br>page 168<br>checklist<br>checklist<br>page 240 | 900-AX<br>10880<br>10936/ 900-AC<br>900-APS<br>10928 / 900-AO<br>11283<br>19038 | 91-P Bee Speaker, Bob and Dolores Hope, Boo Basket, 91 Customer Easter, Medium Purse, Red Pottery Thank You, 96 Statehouse, Sparkler |
| page 48 | 17655 | None |
| page 150 | unknown | Business Card |
| page 150 | unknown | Acorn, Basket of Thanks, Tea, Mini Berry, Mini Chore, Mistletoe, Mini Cradle, Baby Easter, Patriot, 91 Hostess Easter, 93 Small Easter, 94 Employee Christmas, Kiddie Purse, Small Key, 99 Branch Excellence |
| page 214 | 900- | 91-P Bee Speaker, Bob and Dolores Hope, Boo Basket, 91 Customer Easter, Medium Purse, Red Pottery Thank You, Spring, Sparkler |

| Basket | Collection<sup>(Year)</sup> | Orig.Price | AVG | HIGH |
|---|---|---|---|---|
| **Stitching** | All-American $^{(89)}$ | 25.95 | **79** | **130** |
| 7$^{RD}$ x 3$^H$ | | | | |
| **Storage Solutions Large** | Regular Line $^{(01-P)}$ | 139.00 | **139** | **139** |
| 21$^L$ x 16.5$^W$ x 7.5$^H$ | | | | |
| **Storage Solutions Medium** | Regular Line $^{(01-P)}$ | 119.00 | **119** | **119** |
| 17.5$^L$ x 14$^W$ x 6.5$^H$ | | | | |
| **Storage Solutions Small** | Regular Line $^{(01-P)}$ | 69.00 | **69** | **69** |
| 11$^L$ x 9.75$^W$ x 4.75$^H$ | | | | |
| **Strawberry** 6.25$^L$ x 6.25$^W$ x 3.5$^H$ | All-American $^{(01)}$ | 34.00 | **41** | **55** |
| **Stuck On You** 4.75$^L$ x 4.75$^W$ x 2$^H$ | Regular Line $^{(01-P)}$ | 29.00 | **29** | **55** |
| **Sugar and Spice** | Booking $^{(88)}$ | N/A | **32** | **60** |
| 5.75$^L$ x 3.75$^W$ x 3$^H$ | | | | |
| **Summertime** 7.75$^L$ x 4.5$^W$ x 2.25$^{FH}$ x 4.5$^{BH}$ | All-American $^{(96)}$ | 34.95 | **40** | **69** |
| **Sunburst** 22$^{RD}$ | Booking $^{(80)}$ | 3.95 | **181** | **185** |
| **Sweet Basil** | Booking $^{(92-94)}$ | 22.95 | **32** | **60** |
| 5$^L$ x 5$^W$ x 2.5$^H$ | | | | |
| **Sweet Pea** 8.25$^{RD}$ x 7$^H$ | May $^{(96)}$ | 45.95 | **78** | **125** |
| **Sweet Sentiments** 4.25$^L$ x 4.25$^W$ x 3$^H$ | Sweetheart $^{(95)}$ | 28.95 | **46** | **70** |

**KEY:**

| Page in Guide | Form No. | Other Baskets Using Same Form |
|---|---|---|
| page 18 | 5400-ABRS | 93 Employee Christmas, Button, Cookie, Rings & Things, Show Star, Frosty Jr. |
| checklist | 11512 | None |
| checklist | 11520 | None |
| checklist | 11544 | None |
| page 20 | 10141 | None |
| checklist | 11865 | None |
| page 34 | 45000-AO | All-Star Trio, 89 Employee Birthday, Keepsake, Paint the Town, 90 Recruit, Reach for the Stars (Med), Rosemary, 90 Sweetheart, Treasure Chest, 95 Horizon of Hope, 98 H.Appreciation, 00 Branch Sales, Salt & Pepper |
| page 20 | 18911 | Dash Away Sleigh |
| page 34 | 7000-O | None |
| page 34 | 10146 | 90 Employee Birthday, Potpourri, 88-89 Recruit, 93 Regional Sponsored Award, Shamrock, 93 Sweetheart, Tee |
| page 164 | 14915 | None |
| page 218 | 19046 | 98 Regional Sponsoring Excellence, Lots of Luck |

**KEY:** In blue = Not pictured in the Guide. **S** = Stained, **U** = Unstained, **W** = Whitewash
**HL** = Heartland® Collection, **WT** = Woven Traditions®, **R** = Red, **G** = Green    **333**

| Basket | Collection(Year) | Orig.Price | AVG | HIGH |
|--------|------------------|-----------|-----|------|
| **Sweet Treats**<br>8^L x 5^W x 3^H | Sweetheart (97) | 32.95 | **45** | **70** |
| **Sweetheart<br>(1990)**<br><br><br>5.75^L x 3.75^W x 3^H | Employee Birthday(89)<br>Sweetheart (90) | N/A<br>24.95 | **76**<br>**129** | **95**<br>**180** |
| **Sweetheart<br>(1993)**<br>5^L x 5^W x 2.5^H | Sweetheart (93) | 25.95 | **60** | **100** |
| **Tarragon**<br>5.5^L x 5.5^W x 2.5^H | Regular Line, Booking (01-P) | 27.00 | **27** | **40** |
| **Tea**<br><br><br><br><br>7^L x 5^W x 3.5^H | Employee Christmas(94)<br>Feature (Natrl) (98)<br>Regular Line (79-P)<br>Retired (Natrl) (99-01)<br>Woven Traditions (95-99) | N/A<br>19.95<br>7.95<br>25.00<br>28.95 | **102**<br>**29**<br>**27**<br>**33**<br>**36** | **125**<br>**45**<br>**85**<br>**40**<br>**48** |
| **Tea for Two**<br>7.75^L x 5.75^W x 3.25^H | Mother's Day (99) | 39.00 | **55** | **70** |
| **Team Award**<br>9.5^L x 4.5^W x 5^H | Incentive (00) | N/A | **—** | **100** |
| **Team Excellence<br>(1998)**<br>8.25^L x 8.25^W x 3.5^H | Incentive (98) | N/A | **95** | **99** |
| **Team Excellence<br>(1999)**<br><br>15^L x 10^W x 7.5^H | Incentive (99) | N/A | **158** | **165** |
| **Teaspoon**<br><br>5^L x 5^W x 4.5^H | Regular Line (97-P)<br>Retired (Natrl) (00-01) | 24.95<br>25.00 | **26**<br>**—** | **35**<br>**30** |
| **Tee**<br><br>5.25^L x 5^W x 3^H | Father's Day (99) | 29.00 | **38** | **45** |

<u>KEY:</u>
**Values listed are for BASKET ONLY, unless otherwised noted, (-P)** = to present

| Page in Guide | Form No. | Other Baskets Using Same Form |
|---|---|---|
| page 218 | 15938$^R$/62$^G$/54$^B$/71$^P$ | None |
| page 70<br>page 218 | 45000-<br>45000-ARS | All-Star Trio, Keepsake, Paint the Town, 90 Recruit, Shining Star, 95 Horizon of Hope, Rosemary, Sugar and Spice, Treasure Chest, 98 H.Appreciation, 00 Branch Sales, Salt & Pepper |
| page 218 | 11347 | 90 Employee Birthday, Potpourri, Shamrock, Sweet Basil, 93 Regional Sponsored Award, 88-89 Recruit, Tee |
| checklist, Booking | 11830 | 91 Employee Birthday, Ivy, Tarragon 96 Hostess Appreciation, Friendship |
| page 74<br>page 92<br>checklist<br>page 204<br>page 240 | 700-<br>10847<br>10740 / 700-JO<br>10847<br>10710 | Acorn, Basket of Thanks, Mini Berry, Mini Chore, Mistletoe, Mini Cradle, Baby Easter, Patriot, 91 Hostess Easter, 93 Small Easter Kiddie Purse, Star Team, Small Key, 99 Branch Excellence |
| page 170 | 14931 | None |
| page 152 | unknown | None |
| page 152 | unknown | None |
| page 152 | unknown | 88 Bee Speaker, Heirloom, 77-87 Tenth Anniversary, 87 Employee Christmas, 99 Team Excellence, Medium Market, Founder's |
| checklist<br>page 204 | 11665<br>17868 | Small Peg, 93 Inaugural, Candy Cane, Violet, 96 Recruit |
| page 78 | 14940 | 90 Employee Birthday, Sweet Basil, 93 Sweetheart, Potpourri, 93 Regional Sponsored, 88-89 Recruit, Shamrock |

**KEY:** In blue = Not pictured in the Guide. **S** = Stained, **U** = Unstained, **W** = Whitewash
**HL** = Heartland® Collection, **WT** = Woven Traditions®, **R** = Red, **G** = Green

| Basket | Collection(Year) | Orig.Price | AVG | HIGH |
|--------|------------------|------------|-----|------|
| **Tenth Anniversary** (1977-87) 15$^L$ x 10$^W$ x 7.5$^H$ | Incentive (87) | N/A | 175 | 200 |
| **Thanks-A-Million** 5.5$^L$ x 4$^W$ x 4$^H$ | Incentive (99) | N/A | — | — |
| **Thyme** 4.5$^{RD}$ x 3$^H$ | Booking (95-98) Collectors Club (98) | 25.95 N/A | 31 51 | 48 71 |
| **Tic-Tac-Toe** 7.5$^L$ x 7.5$^W$ x 2.75$^H$ | Father's Day (01) | 44.00 | 51 | 58 |
| **Timeless Memory** 11.25$^L$ x 9.25$^W$ x 5.75$^H$ | Mother's Day (97) | 49.95 | 85 | 115 |
| **Tiny Tote** 6$^L$ x 5.5$^W$ x 7$^H$ | Regular Line (02-P) | 59.00 | 59 | 59 |
| **Tissue** 6.5$^L$ x 6.5$^W$ x 6.25$^H$ | Employee Christmas (99) Father's Day (94) Regular Line (97-P) Regular Line(WWash)(01-P) Retired (Natrl) (99-01) | N/A 29.95 31.95 34.00 32.00 | 100 84 32 34 — | 115 100 55 61 — |
| **Tissue, Long** 12$^L$ x 7.25$^W$ x 5.75$^H$ | Regular Line (00-P) | 44.00 | 45 | 45 |
| **Top Performer** 10.5$^L$ x 9$^W$ x 8$^H$ | Incentive (88-94) | N/A | ** | ** |
| **Tour** 8.75$^L$ x 4.75$^W$ x 6.5$^H$ | Employee Birthday(92) Tour (88-99) | N/A ** | 62 ** | 85 ** |
| **Tour II** 7$^L$ x 3.5$^W$ x 4.75$^H$ | Tour (96-99) | 29.95 | 66 | 70 |
| **Tray** 14$^L$ x 9$^W$ x 4.5$^H$ | Holiday Hostess (87) | 32.95 | 76 | 135 |
| **Treasure** 20.25$^L$ x 13.75$^W$ x 7.5$^H$ | Hostess(98-01) | 119.00 | 111 | 140 |

| Page in Guide | Form No. | Other Baskets Using Same Form |
|---|---|---|
| page 140 | 500-A | 88 Bee Speaker, Heirloom, Medium Market, 87 Employee Christmas, 99 Team Excellence, Founder's |
| page 142 | 14940 | Ambrosia, 97 Horizon of Hope, 01 Hostess Appreciation, 01 Inaugural |
| page 34<br>page 46 | 19003<br>19224 | Gold Nugget |
| page 80 | 10346 | None |
| page 168 | 13030 | Sewing Notions |
| checklist | 12512 | None |
| page 74<br>page 78<br>checklist<br>checklist<br>page 204 | unknown<br>18490<br>15831<br>10473<br>14184 | None |
| checklist | 10412 | None |
| page 148-150 | unknown | Weekender, Remembrance, Beachcomber |
| page 70<br>page 224 | 10022<br>5600-BO | 89 Bee, Memory, Sophomore – Senior Recognition, Hartville, Dresden Basket, 20th Century, 25th Anniversay (Sm) |
| page 224 | 15814 | Hartville II, 98 Flag Sponsoring, 99 Bee |
| page 114 | 2300-JGRS | Advisor Recognition, Small Gathering, 92 Bee, 90 Employee Christmas, Pantry |
| page 126 | 18716 | Yuletide Treasures |

| Basket | Collection(Year) | Orig.Price | AVG | HIGH |
|---|---|---|---|---|
| **Treasure Chest** | Incentive (92) | N/A | **192** | **225** |
| 5.75L x 3.75W x 3H | | | | |
| **Tree-Trimming** 12.5RD x 13.5H | Holiday Hostess (91) | 79.95 | **90** | **190** |
| **Tulip** 14.25L x 6.25W x 3.25H | May (95) | 42.95 | **100** | **105** |
| **Twelve Days of Christmas** 13L x 13W x 8.75H | Holiday Hostess(00) | 139.00 | **118** | **166** |
| **20th Century** | Tour (97-99) | 49.95 | **64** | **105** |
| 8.75L x 4.75W x 6.5H | | | | |
| **25th Anniversary** | Special Events (98) | 49.95 | **76** | **130** |
| 8.75L x 4.75W x 6.5H | | | | |
| **25th Anniversary Large** 16L x 8W x 11H | Collectors Club(98) | 115.00 | **157** | **250** |
| **Twinkle Twinkle** 5.5L x 6W x 2.25H | Tree-Trimming (01) | 49.00 | **65** | **80** |
| **Two-Pie** 12L x 12W x 10H | Feature (G.Bonnie) (98) J.W. Collection (86) | 95.00 34.95 | **128** **365** | **175** **575** |
| **Two-Pie Miniature** 4.75L x 5W x 4H | Collectors Club(99) | 130.00 | **136** | **150** |
| **Two-Quart** 9.5L x 5W x 9.5H | All-American (91) Feature (85, 87) | 36.95 28.95 | **93** **74** | **135** **85** |
| **Umbrella** 10RD x 17.5H | J.W. Collection (94) Regular Line, Hostess(98-P) Retired (79-94) | 74.95 100.00 18.95 | **177** **100** **77** | **250** **159** **153** |

**KEY:**
**338** Values listed are for BASKET ONLY, unless otherwised noted, (-P) = to present

| Page in Guide | Form No. | Other Baskets Using Same Form |
|---|---|---|
| page 150 | 45000- | All-Star Trio, 89 Employee Birthday, Keepsake, Paint the Town, 90 Recruit, Shining Star, Rosemary, Sugar and Spice, 90 Sweetheart, 95 Horizon of Hope, 98 Hostess Appreciation, 00 Branch Sales, Salt & Pepper |
| page 114 | 1900-BRGS/BGRS | Banker's Waste, Master Employee, Waste (Inverted, Small Round) |
| page 164 | 14648 | None |
| page 116 | 17833 / 17931 | None |
| page 224 | 17575 | Tour, 89 Bee, Junior, Sophomore & Senior Recognition, Memory, Hartville Basket, Dresden Basket, 25th Anniversary (Sm) |
| page 214 | 17612 | Tour, 89 Bee, Junior, Sophomore & Senior Recognition, Memory, Hartville Basket, Dresden Basket, 20th Century |
| page 46 | 12297 | Magazine, Bread & Milk |
| page 230 | 10664$^R$ / 10672$^G$ | RedWhite & You |
| page 92<br>page 156 | 19241<br>4800-BT | None |
| page 46 | 19356 | None |
| page 18<br>page 88 | 1000-CBRS<br>1000-CO | 91 Employee Christmas, MBA, Tall Key, Tall Purse, Membership, Growing Strong Together |
| page 156<br>checklist, Hostess<br>page 204 | 11215<br>11207<br>11207 /1200-OO | None |

| Basket | Collection<sup>(Year)</sup> | Orig.Price | AVG | HIGH |
|---|---|---|---|---|

| Basket | Collection (Year) | Orig.Price | AVG | HIGH |
|---|---|---|---|---|
| **Vanity** | Mother's Day (96) | 44.95 | **52** | **105** |
| | Regular Line (98-P) | 50.00 | **51** | **65** |
| 14.5$^L$ x 7.5$^W$ x 4.5$^{FH}$ x 6.5$^{BH}$ | | | | |
| **Vegetable, Large** | Feature (96-97) | 61.95 | **79** | **95** |
| | Feature (Natrl) (99) | 48.00 | — | — |
| | Retired (87-00) | 26.95 | **74** | **100** |
| 16$^L$ x 9$^W$ x 3.5$^{FH}$ x 9$^{BH}$ | | | | |
| **Vegetable, Medium** | Feature (Natrl) (00) | 37.00 | **43** | **62** |
| | Heartland (97-99) | 50.95 | **54** | **75** |
| | Retired (83-02) | 14.95 | **47** | **65** |
| | Retired(Natrl) (94) | 38.95 | **60** | **75** |
| 13$^L$ x 7.5$^W$ x 3$^{FH}$ x 8$^{BH}$ | | | | |
| **Vegetable, Small** | Retired (83-02) | 12.95 | **32** | **45** |
| | Shades of Autumn (90) | 35.95 | **145** | **280** |
| | Woven Traditions (95-99) | 35.95 | **40** | **55** |
| 10.5$^L$ x 6.5$^W$ x 3$^{FH}$ x 7$^{BH}$ | | | | |
| **Vintage Blossoms** | Mother's Day (01) | 49.00 | — | — |
| 7.5$^L$ x 5.75$^W$ x 6.5$^H$ | | | | |
| **Violet** | May (90) | 24.95 | **251** | **360** |
| 5$^L$ x 5$^W$ x 4.5$^H$ | | | | |
| **VIP Baskets** | Incentive (86-P) | N/A | ** | ** |
| 12$^L$ x 7$^W$ x 10$^H$ | | | | |
| **Wash Day, Medium** | Regular Line, Hostess(00-P) | 159.00 | **169** | **176** |
| 18.75$^L$ x 18.25$^W$ x 9.5$^H$ | | | | |
| **Wash Day, Small** | Regular Line, Hostess(00-P) | 139.00 | **149** | **150** |
| 16.25$^L$ x 15.75$^W$ x 8.5$^H$ | | | | |
| **Waste, Inverted Large Round** | Feature (87) | 59.95 | **124** | **150** |
| | Retired(no/h) (79-84) | 26.95 | **95** | **130** |
| | Retired(1sw/h) (79-84) | 28.95 | **114** | **120** |
| 14$^{RD}$ x 16$^H$ | | | | |
| **Waste, Inverted Small Round** | Retired(no/h) (79-84) | 21.95 | **90** | **100** |
| | Retired(1sw/h) (79-84) | 23.95 | **75** | **125** |
| 12.5$^{RD}$ x 13.5$^H$ | | | | |
| **Waste, Large Oval** | Regular Line(00-P) | 149.00 | **149** | **149** |
| 16.25$^L$ x 13$^W$ x 16$^H$ | | | | |

<u>KEY:</u>
**Values listed are for BASKET ONLY, unless otherwised noted, (-P)** = to present

| Page in Guide | Form No. | Other Baskets Using Same Form |
|---|---|---|
| page 168<br>checklist | 14753<br>18449 | None |
| page 82<br>page 94<br>page 204 | $16543^R/27^B/35^G$<br>19551<br>15202 /5200-CO | Large Wine |
| page 94<br>page 110<br>page 204<br>page 204 | 18333<br>16713<br>15105/5100-CO<br>15113 | Yuletide Traditions |
| page 204<br>page 208<br>page 240 | 15008 /5000-OO<br>5000-CGUBS<br>15016 | None |
| page 170 | 10222 | None |
| page 164 | 14000-BVS | 93 Inaugural, Candy Cane, Small Peg, Teaspoon |
| page 134-136 | unknown | None |
| checklist, Hostess | 19372 | None |
| checklist, Hostess | 15695 | None |
| page 88<br>page 198<br>page 198 | 2000-BO<br>2000-OO<br>2000-BO | None |
| page 198<br>page 198 | 1900-OO<br>1900-BO | Banker's Waste, Master Employee, Tree Trimming |
| checklist | 19666 | None |

| Basket | Collection(Year) | Orig.Price | AVG | HIGH |
|---|---|---|---|---|
| **Waste, Medium** (or Large Waste) 13.5$^L$ x 13.5$^W$ x 16$^H$ | Feature (Natrl) (98) Retired (79-00) | 71.95 21.95 | — 84 | — 170 |
| **Waste, Medium Oval** 14.25$^L$ x 11.5$^W$ x 12.75$^H$ | Regular Line(00-P) | 104.00 | 104 | 104 |
| **Waste, Mini** 7.5$^L$ x 7.5$^W$ x 10$^H$ | All-American (90) Father's Day (95) Incentive (99-00) Regular Line (82-99) | 35.95 46.95 N/A 16.95 | 111 57 — 48 | 140 81 — 65 |
| **Waste, Small** 9.5$^L$ x 9.5$^W$ x 12$^H$ | All-American (90) J.W. Collection (84) Retired (79-00) | 45.95 34.95 16.95 | 138 1585 66 | 210 2100 90 |
| **Waste, Small Miniature** 3.75$^L$ x 3.75$^W$ x 4.75$^H$ | Collectors Club (97) | 99.95 | 150 | 206 |
| **Waste, Small Oval** 11.5$^L$ x 9.25$^W$ x 10.5$^H$ | Regular Line(00-P) | 79.00 | 79 | 79 |
| **Waste, XLarge Oval** 17.5$^L$ x 15.5$^W$ x 22$^H$ | Regular Line, Hostess(01-P) | 229.00 | 229 | 229 |
| **Watch Your Business Bloom** 5$^{RD}$ x 4.5$^H$ | Incentive (97) | N/A | 90 | 125 |
| **Weekender** 10.5$^L$ x 9$^W$ x 8$^H$ | Feature (87-88) Holiday Hostess (88) Regular Line, Hostess(01-P) | 54.95 65.95 139.00 | 96 154 139 | 150 225 157 |
| **Welcome Home** 15$^L$ x 9.5$^W$ x 5.5$^H$ | Collectors Club (97) | 69.95 | 87 | 125 |
| **Whistle Stop** 10.75$^L$ x 6.25$^W$ x 7.75$^H$ | Collectors Club (01) | 89.00 | 100 | 130 |

**KEY:**
**342** **Values listed are for BASKET ONLY, unless otherwise noted, (-P)** = to present

| Page in Guide | Form No. | Other Baskets Using Same Form |
|---|---|---|
| page 92<br>page 204 | 11789<br>11703/1700-O | None |
| checklist | 19666 | None |
| page 18<br>page 78<br>page 142<br>checklist | 12000-OBRS<br>11266<br>11258<br>11258/12000-OO | Also known as Extra Small Waste and renamed to Large Spoon in 1999 |
| page 18<br>page 156<br>page 204 | 1800-OBRS<br>1800-OT<br>11801 /1800-OO | None |
| page 44 | 17797 | None |
| checklist | 19461 | None |
| checklist, Hostess | 15989 | None |
| page 130 | unknown | 5" Measuring, 89 Inaugural, Forget-Me-Not, 5" Hanging, 92 Recruit, Resolution, 92 Sponsor (Small), 5" Canister, 92 Employee Christmas, 88 Employee Birthday |
| page 90<br>page 114<br>checklist, Hostess | 200-YO<br>200-YRGS<br>10362 | Remembrance, Top Performer, Beachcomber |
| page 44 | 10464 | Small Market, 99 Regional Sales & Sponsoring Excellence |
| page 50 | 10303 | None |

| Basket | Collection(Year) | Orig.Price | AVG | HIGH |
|---|---|---|---|---|
| **Wildflower** 13.5$^{RD}$ x 8.5$^H$ | Hostess $^{(92-98)}$ | 64.95 | 70 | 129 |
| **Window Box** 21.25$^L$ x 9$^W$ x 5$^H$ | Feature $^{(02)}$ | 89.00 | — | — |
| **Wine, Large** 16$^L$ x 9$^W$ x 3.5$^{FH}$ x 9$^{BH}$ | Retired $^{(83-86)}$ | 29.95 | 95 | 135 |
| **Winter Wishes** 12.5$^L$ x 8.25$^W$ x 10.5$^{FH}$ x 12$^{BH}$ | Holiday Hostess $^{(98)}$ | 95.00 | 96 | 130 |
| **Work Load, Large** 24$^L$ x 13.25$^W$ x 8.75$^H$ | Regular Line $^{(01-P)}$ | 179.00 | 179 | 179 |
| **Work Load, Small** 19$^L$ x 10.5$^W$ x 8.25$^H$ | Regular Line $^{(01-P)}$ | 149.00 | 149 | 149 |
| **Woven Memories** 10$^L$ x 6$^W$ x 4$^H$ | Tour $^{(99-P)}$ | 39.95 | ** | ** |
| **Woven Memories (Apple)** 7.5$^{RD}$ x 4.5$^H$ | Tour $^{(02)}$ | 44.95 | — | — |
| **Yuletide Traditions** 13$^L$ x 7.5$^W$ x 3$^{FH}$ x 8$^{BH}$ | Christmas $^{(91)}$ | 38.95 | 50 | 85 |
| **Yuletide Treasures** 20.25$^L$ x 13.75$^W$ x 7.5$^H$ | Holiday Hostess $^{(96)}$ | 129.95 | 149 | 200 |

| Page in Guide | Form No. | Other Baskets Using Same Form |
|---|---|---|
| page 126 | 10111 | None |
| page 96 | 16977 | None |
| page 204 | 5200-CO | Large Vegetable |
| page 116 | 12483$^R$ / 12491$^G$ | None |
| checklist | 11776 | None |
| checklist | 12032 | None |
| page 226 | unknown | Small Chore, 93 Large Easter, 88 Small Easter, Gingerbread, 95 Bee, $500 Million, 91 Regional Sponsored |
| page 226 | unknown | None |
| page 38 | 5100-CRST / CGST | Medium Vegetable |
| page 116 | 18619$^R$ / 18627$^G$ | Treasure |

**Dimensional Search**

# Dimensional search

## How To Use:

Many collectors are not always able to identify their baskets. This reference tool was designed to help you determine which basket you may have by looking at its dimensions. **\*\*Note\*\*** This tool can also be used to identify plastic protectors. Follow the same steps below, except add a 1/2" to an 1" to your protector's dimensions when referring to the basket dimensions.

**STEP 1**

Measure your basket. At the top, measure length and width. If round, measure the diameter across the basket. Next, measure its height. All measurements in this Guide are listed in standard form: **Length$^{(L)}$ x Width$^{(W)}$ x Height$^{(H)}$.** Baskets that are sloped will have both its **Front Height$^{(FH)}$** and its **Back Height$^{(BH)}$** listed.

**STEP 2**

Go to the shape section that your basket most closely resembles. Octagonal baskets are listed as *Round*. The dimensions are in numerical order. Scan down the list to find your dimension. Because these baskets are individually handmade, measurements may vary within a 1/2". Locate the measurement that is *closest* to your basket.

**STEP 3**

Once you have located your basket's dimensions, note the basket name and page number adjacent to it. Refer to that page number in the *"Quick Find"* section. The *"Quick Find"* will tell you:

◎ The different collection in which your basket has been featured. Now is a good time to note distinguishing characteristics of your basket, such as color weaving or commemorative tags that may point you to a specific collection or series.

◎ Other baskets that use the same form.

◎ Its location in the Guide.

If you are still not able to determine which basket you have or have other questions, please feel free to contact us at 1-800-VERIFY IT, ext. 11

## *Square*

| | | |
|---|---|---|
| 15$^L$ x 15$^W$ x 7.5$^H$ | See Medium Picnic | pg. 308 |
| 15.5$^L$ x 15.5$^W$ x 12.25$^H$ | See Evergreen | pg. 272 |
| 16$^L$ x 16$^W$ x 8$^H$ | See Coverlet | pg. 262 |
| 16.5$^L$ x 16.5$^W$ x 21.5$^H$ | See Large Hamper | pg. 282 |
| 17$^L$ x 17$^W$ x 22$^H$ | See Large Hamper, 95 | pg. 282 |

end square

## *Rectangle*

| | | |
|---|---|---|
| 4.75$^L$ x 3.75$^W$ x 2.25$^H$ | See Business Card | pg. 258 |
| 4.75$^L$ x 5$^W$ x 3.25$^H$ | See Let It Snow | pg. 292 |
| 4.75$^L$ x 5$^W$ x 4$^H$ | See Two-Pie, Miniature | pg. 338 |
| 5$^L$ x 3$^W$ x 3.5$^H$ | See Oregano | pg. 302 |
| 5$^L$ x 3.75$^W$ x 4.5$^H$ | See Little Joy | pg. 294 |
| 5.25$^L$ x 5$^W$ x 3$^H$ | See Tee | pg. 334 |
| 5.5$^L$ x 4$^W$ x 4$^H$ | See Ambrosia | pg. 244 |
| 5.75$^L$ x 3.75$^W$ x 3$^H$ | See Rosemary | pg. 320 |
| 5.75$^L$ x 3.75$^W$ x 3.5$^H$ | See Santa's Little Helper | pg. 322 |
| 5.75$^L$ x 3.75$^W$ x 5$^H$ | See Love Notes | pg. 294 |
| 5.75$^L$ x 4$^W$ x 3$^H$ | See Miniature Market | pg. 296 |
| 5.75$^L$ x 5.25$^W$ x 6.25$^H$ | See Branch Sales (02) | pg. 256 |
| 6$^L$ x 3.25$^W$ x 4.5$^H$ | See Miniature Bread & Milk | pg. 258 |
| 6$^L$ x 4.5$^W$ x 2.5$^H$ | See Parsley | pg. 304 |
| 6$^L$ x 5.5$^W$ x 7$^H$ | See Tiny Tote | pg. 336 |
| 6$^L$ x 6$^W$ x 4.25$^{FH}$ x 5.25$^{BH}$ | See Finder's Keeper | pg. 274 |
| 6.25$^L$ x 5$^W$ x 1.75$^H$ | See Renewal (02) | pg. 320 |
| 6.75$^L$ x 4.75$^W$ x 2.25$^H$ | See Horizon of Hope (96) | pg. 286 |
| 6.75$^L$ x 5.25$^W$ x 3.25$^H$ | See Renewal (00) | pg. 320 |
| 6.75$^L$ x 9.25$^W$ x 3.75$^H$ | See Mother's Day (94) | pg. 300 |
| 7$^L$ x 3.5$^W$ x 4.75$^H$ | See Tour II | pg. 336 |
| 7$^L$ x 4.5$^W$ x 2$^H$ | See Miniature Gathering | pg. 278 |
| 7$^L$ x 4.75$^W$ x 7.75$^H$ | See Harvest, Shades of Autumn | pg. 284 |
| 7$^L$ x 5$^W$ x 3.5$^H$ | See Tea | pg. 334 |
| 7$^L$ x 5.25$^W$ x 3.75$^{FH}$ x 4.5$^{BH}$ | See Small Recipe | pg. 314 |
| 7.25$^L$ x 4$^W$ x 4.5$^H$ | See Picture Perfect | pg. 308 |

continued next page

# Rectangle

continued next page

continued next page

# $\mathcal{Rectangle}$

end rectangle

| | | |
|---|---|---|
| 3.75$^{RD}$ x 3.75$^{H}$ | See Gatehouse, Extra Small | pg. 278 |
| 4$^{RD}$ x 4.25$^{H}$ | See Pencil | pg. 306 |
| 4.5$^{RD}$ x 3$^{H}$ | See Thyme | pg. 336 |
| 4.75$^{RD}$ x 3$^{H}$ | See Lucky You | pg. 294 |
| 4.75$^{RD}$ x 7.5$^{H}$ | See Gatehouse, Small | pg. 278 |
| 5$^{RD}$ x 4.5$^{H}$ | See 5" Measuring | pg. 298 |
| 5$^{RD}$ x 6$^{H}$ | See Renewal (00) | pg. 320 |
| 5.25$^{RD}$ x 3.25$^{H}$ | See Miniature Apple | pg. 244 |
| 5.25$^{RD}$ x 4.25$^{H}$ | See Horizon of Hope (01) | pg. 288 |
| 5.25$^{RD}$ x 5.25$^{H}$ | See Miniature Banker's Waste | pg. 246 |
| 5.5$^{RD}$ x 2.5$^{H}$ | See Associate Producer | pg. 244 |
| 5.5$^{RD}$ x 2.75$^{H}$ | See Peppermint | pg. 306 |
| 5.5$^{RD}$ x 3.25$^{H}$ | See Inaugural (97) | pg. 290 |
| 5.5$^{RD}$ x 3.5$^{H}$ | See Discovery | pg. 268 |
| 5.5$^{RD}$ x 3.75$^{H}$ | See Laurel | pg. 292 |
| 5.5$^{RD}$ x 4$^{H}$ | See Bee (00) | pg. 250 |
| 5.5$^{RD}$ x 4.5$^{H}$ | See Recruit 1999 | pg. 314 |
| 5.5$^{RD}$ x 5.5$^{H}$ | See Noel Bell | pg. 302 |
| 5.75$^{RD}$ x 4.25$^{H}$ | See Little Pumpkin | pg. 312 |
| 5.75$^{L}$ x 5.5$^{H}$ x 2.5$^{H}$ | See Sage | pg. 322 |
| 6$^{RD}$ x 2.75$^{H}$ | See Small Easter (01) | pg. 272 |
| 6.5$^{RD}$ x 4.75$^{H}$ | See Gold Rush | pg. 280 |
| 6.5$^{RD}$ x 5$^{H}$ | See Small Fruit | pg. 276 |
| 6.5$^{RD}$ x 6.5$^{H}$ | See Lilac | pg. 292 |
| 6.5$^{RD}$ x 6.75$^{H}$ | See Pumpkin Patch | pg. 312 |
| 6.5$^{RD}$ x 7$^{H}$ | See Bell | pg. 252 |
| 6.5$^{RD}$ x 9$^{H}$ | See October Fields | pg. 302 |
| 6.5$^{RD}$ x 10.5$^{H}$ | See Gatehouse, Large | pg. 278 |
| 6.75$^{RD}$ x 6$^{H}$ | See Daisy | pg. 264 |
| 7$^{RD}$ x 3$^{H}$ | See Button | pg. 258 |
| 7$^{RD}$ x 4.5$^{H}$ | See Pansy | pg. 304 |
| 7$^{RD}$ x 5.5$^{H}$ | See National Sales Level 1 | pg. 300 |
| 7$^{RD}$ x 6.5$^{H}$ | See 7" Measuring | pg. 298 |
| 7$^{L}$ x 6.75$^{W}$ x 3$^{H}$ | See Generations, 7" | pg. 280 |
| 7.25$^{RD}$ x 2.25$^{H}$ | See Catch-All | pg. 260 |
| 7.25$^{RD}$ x 5.25$^{H}$ | See Small Pumpkin | pg. 312 |
| 7.5$^{RD}$ x 4$^{H}$ | See Woven Memories (02) | pg. 344 |
| 7.5$^{RD}$ x 9.25$^{H}$ | See Snapdragon | pg. 326 |
| 7.5$^{L}$ x 7.5$^{W}$ x 4.75$^{H}$ | See Morning Glory | pg. 298 |

continued next page

# Round

includes octagonal & star

continued next page

# *Round*

## includes octagonal & star

| | | |
|---|---|---|
| 14$^L$ x 12.75$^W$ x 5$^H$ | See Generations, 14" | pg. 280 |
| 14$^L$ x 12.75$^W$ x 11.5$^H$ | See Snowflake, Large | pg. 326 |
| 14$^{RD}$ x 16$^H$ | See Waste, Large Inverted | pg. 340 |
| 16.5$^{RD}$ x 11.5$^H$ | See Sleigh Bell | pg. 326 |
| 17$^{RD}$ x 11.5$^H$ | See Corn | pg. 262 |
| 19.75$^{RD}$ x 12.5$^H$ | See Pot of Gold | pg. 310 |
| 24.5$^L$ x 20$^W$ x 14$^H$ | See Sleeve, Sunroom | pg. 326 |
| 25$^{RD}$ x 13$^H$ | See Pottery Ware | pg. 310 |
| 31.5$^{RD}$ x 18$^H$ | See Planter, Sleeve | pg. 310 |

end round

# *Oval*

| | | |
|---|---|---|
| 5.25$^L$ x 4.25$^W$ x 1.75$^{FH}$ x 3$^{BH}$ | See Lucky Charm | pg. 294 |
| 5.5$^L$ x 3.5$^W$ x 4$^H$ | See Small Saddlebrook | pg. 322 |
| 5.5$^L$ x 6$^W$ x 2.25$^H$ | See Twinkle Twinkle | pg. 338 |
| 5.75$^L$ x 5.75$^W$ x 3$^H$ | See Small Easter (99) | pg. 272 |
| 6$^L$ x 5$^W$ x 8.25$^H$ | See 5-Yr Anniversary | pg. 274 |
| 6.25$^L$ x 4.75$^W$ x 2.25$^H$ | See Little Love | pg. 294 |
| 6.25$^L$ x 5.25$^W$ x 3$^H$ | See Horizon of Hope (99) | pg. 288 |
| 6.75$^L$ x 4.75$^W$ x 2$^H$ | See Shaker Harmony No.5 | pg. 324 |
| 6.75$^L$ x 5.75$^W$ x 4.75$^H$ | See Renewal (99) | pg. 318 |
| 7.25$^L$ x 4.5$^W$ x 6.5$^H$ | See Medium Saddlebrook | pg. 322 |
| 7.5$^L$ x 3.75$^W$ x 2.75$^H$ | See Shaker Taker | pg. 324 |
| 7.5$^L$ x 4.5$^W$ x 3.5$^H$ | See Century Celebration | pg. 260 |
| 7.5$^L$ x 5$^W$ x 6$^H$ | See Easter (96) | pg. 268 |
| 7.5$^L$ x 5.75$^W$ x 2.75$^H$ | See Shaker Harmony No.4 | pg. 324 |
| 7.5$^L$ x 5.75$^W$ x 6.5$^H$ | See Vintage Blossoms | pg. 340 |
| 7.5$^L$ x 7.5$^W$ x 3.75$^H$ | See Large Easter (99) | pg. 270 |
| 7.5$^L$ x 8$^W$ x 3$^H$ | See Little Star | pg. 294 |
| 7.75$^L$ x 5.75$^W$ x 3.25$^H$ | See Tea for Two | pg. 334 |
| 7.75$^L$ x 6.25$^W$ x 2.75$^H$ | See Small Easter (02) | pg. 272 |
| 8$^L$ x 4$^W$ x 2$^H$ | See Lavender | pg. 292 |
| 8.5$^L$ x 5$^W$ x 3.5$^H$ | See Small Oval | pg. 326 |

continued next page

# *Oval*

end oval

# Additional
## notes

# *Additional* notes

notes

# Additional notes

# Additional
## notes